Please remember that this is a library book,
and that it belongs only temporarily to each
person who uses it. Be considerate. Do
not write in this, or any, library book.

EARLY CHILDHOOD EDUCATION

Special Environmental, Policy, and Legal Considerations

Editors

Elizabeth M. Goetz

K. Eileen Allen

University of Kansas
Lawrence, Kansas

AN ASPEN PUBLICATION®
Aspen Systems Corporation
Rockville, Maryland
London
1983

Library of Congress Cataloging in Publication Data
Main entry under title:

Early childhood education.

Includes index.
1. Child rearing.   2. Education, Preschool.
3. Day care centers.   4. Infants—Care and hygiene.
5. Day care aides.   6. Educational law and legislation—
United States.
I. Goetz, Elizabeth M.   II. Allen, K. Eileen, 1918-
    HQ769.E28   1983   372'.21   83-9950
ISBN: 0-89443-879-4

Publisher: John Marozsan
Editorial Director: R. Curtis Whitesel
Executive Managing Editor: Margot Raphael
Editorial Services: Ruth Judy
Printing and Manufacturing: Debbie Collins

Library of Congress Catalog Card Number: 83-9950
ISBN: 0-89443-879-4

Printed in the United States of America

1   2   3   4   5

To Ray Goetz and Roy Allen
whose unfailing support
and abundant good cheer
have been the mainstay as well as the spur
to our endeavors over the years.

Contributors

Jennifer Ashton-Lilo
Lynne H. Embry
Rebecca R. Fewell
Deirdre Hickey
Judy A. Mantle
Lynn R. Marotz
Marion O'Brien
Nancy L. Peterson

Joan L. Reiber
Todd R. Risley
Ann K. Rogers-Warren
Neil J. Salkind
Susan R. Sandall
Jan B. Sheldon
Jean Ann Summers
Carolyn L. Thomson

Steven F. Warren

Table of Contents

Preface

This text presents the results of continuing behavior analysis studies developed by researchers in the Edna A. Hill Child Development Laboratory Preschools at the University of Kansas. Two contributors, Rebecca D. Fewell and Susan Sandall, are not affiliated with the University of Kansas but have been closely associated with the kind of work that characterizes the relationship between the Washington group and the Kansas group as described in our previous volume, *Early Childhood Education: Special Problems, Special Solutions.*

Like that text, the present one is the work of experienced early childhood educators who are also skilled in research methodology. In addition, this second text addresses such important issues in early childhood education as public policy, efficacy, interagency cooperation, and legal concerns. The emphasis in both books is on helping young handicapped and nonhandicapped children fulfill their potential.

Elizabeth M. Goetz
K. Eileen Allen
August, 1983

Introduction

Journey with us backward in time, not far, just ten years. Picture in your mind's eye a four-year-old retarded boy named Jay. He is unable to walk, indeed, barely able to stand; and cannot speak intelligibly. "Regular" preschools will not accept him, because he is disabled. His days are spent in undirected play with a puppy dog, his parents, and occasionally the nonhandicapped children of his parents' friends. In Chapel Hill, North Carolina—a town dominated by a university with a national reputation for research in child development—there is nothing, absolutely nothing, for this young child once he has been thoroughly evaluated. There is no transition from evaluation to referral, from referral to service. He is too young and too exceptional. The plight of Jay and his parents would be the same almost anywhere in the country at this time.

Desperate to find a "placement" for him, his parents learn of a program in the next town, ten miles away. The preschool is sponsored by a women's club and is located in three tiny rooms in the far end of a wing of a church. There, disabled preschoolers of many kinds—mentally retarded, autistic, cerebral palsied—are gathered into several small groups to be trained and cared for. Some of the staff are teachers or speech or physical therapists. Many are uncertified, but nonetheless skillful; some serve as aides, indispensable foot soldiers in this small army. The children's parents bring them to Sarah Barker School not only from Durham and Chapel Hill, but also from Roxboro, Hillsborough, and Carboro. From typical American towns come atypical parents to an atypical school in an atypical setting. Picture, then, parents whose lives are disrupted because of their children's disabilities, and a school that is unusual in its very existence, in a setting that was not designed for the instruction or accommodation of handicapped children. Fix that image into your mind, and remember, if you can, how representative it is of what was true ten years ago.

Now journey ten years forward to 1982, to another town. Imagine another preschool handicapped child. Call her Chrissy. Her expression is intelligent, but her speech is impaired. She is wheelchair bound; her deeply-padded chair with velcro straps and headrests encompasses her throughout much of her days. Unlike Jay, however, she is not dependent on her parents for learning experiences, and she is not barred from going to school with nonhandicapped preschoolers. Instead, she attends a "demonstration" preschool, and quite a school it is. Housed in the university building that contains the offices, classrooms, research facilities, and students of the internationally distinguished faculty, this school integrates disabled and nonhandicapped children in the same program. Staff members have degrees in child development, education, speech, audiology, physical therapy, occupational therapy, or nursing. Supervisors are masters' and doctoral-level students in early childhood special education. They provide small-group and individualized instruction to Chrissy and her classmates in preacademic, social, self-help, speech, gross and fine motor, and other necessary skills. When she gradutes from the preschool, she may attend the primary-grades class associated with and identical in quality to the preschool at the university, or a mainstreamed special education program in the local schools. Those schools cooperate with the university in cosponsoring Chrissy's preschool program.

Just around the corner special education and child development specialists work with young emotionally disturbed children; others are involved in a language project preschool; still others in a preschool reading project; yet others in preacademic day-care programs. The halls of this building teem with young children, their parents, their teachers, and university faculty, students, and staff. At the University of Kansas in Lawrence, things are different from the way they were ten years before at Chapel Hill.

It is not that Lawrence and Chapel Hill are qualitatively so different; they are now very much alike in direct service to preschool children and their families. Rather, it is that ten years have passed—years that represented wasted opportunities for Jay and grand chances for Chrissy, years that have seen remarkable progress made in the establishment of early childhood education programs for handicapped and nonhandicapped children.

Finally, travel into the future with us. Try to imagine another handicapped child, too young for kindergarten. It is 1992, and this child—call her Suzanne—attends a preschool for disabled and nondisabled children in another town, one not blessed with a university capable of contributing directly to her education. On the library shelves of this school is a dog-eared copy of Goetz and Allen's *Early Childhood Education: Special Environmental, Policy, and Legal Considerations.* It is this very book. Teachers, parents, and advocates of the children in Suzanne's school have used it to create a program for Suzanne like the one in Haworth Hall, Kansas University. They have also relied heavily on its companion text, Allen and Goetz's *Early Childhood Education: Special Problems, Special Solutions.*

And what have they learned? The same things that you are about to learn from this unusual book. First, you will become well grounded in the current research into early childhood education and its theoretical bases. Rebecca Fewell and Susan Sandall address the complexities of screening and assessment, discussing the differences between the two, and offer a critique of the many evaluation instruments and methods. They present a convincing argument that early intervention with knowledgeable screening, assessment, and school- and home-based intervention will result in reduced costs for special education.

O'Brien and Risley's description of the Infant and Toddler Centers at Kansas University stresses the applicability of this model for other dependent people, especially institutionalized retarded adults and the aged. We know the efficacy of individualization, but we need to know more about the relationships between care and learning, effective communication with parents and other caregivers, the practical limitations on individualized programs, and cost effectiveness in quality care. O'Brien and Risley show us those relationships. Rogers-Warren and Warren describe the role of parents or care-givers in language development and provide practical advice on developing language. Thomson and Ashton-Lilo give more "good housekeeping" suggestions for designing an environment and organization that is conducive to effective education of preschoolers. Marotz shows how health, safety, and nutrition factors affect the child's ability to learn. Reiber and Embry stress the importance of parent participation in early childhood education and the basic principles of effective staff-parent communications. Their sensitivity to the fact that there are many different types of parents, and their candor in identifying problem areas and offering solutions, make this chapter very valuable.

Hickey's chapter on mainstreaming offers valuable suggestions for integrating handicapped and nonhandicapped children.

Peterson and Mantle offer an insightful analysis of the ways that systems can be shaped to help children, explaining how to achieve effective interagency collaboration. The emphasis is on more effective service, cost containment, and client accountability. Summers examines the problem of day care and early childhood programs. Drawing on political science research, she demonstrates the inequities that have resulted from poor policy decisions, and the potential for further harm.

Summers and Salkind take the reader from the realities of classrooms, government, and law to the harsher realities of fiscal and political considerations. Salkind emphasizes the critical question of efficacy: do our programs accomplish what they set out to do? By applying a model of policy analysis to early childhood education, he offers persuasive arguments on behalf of these programs. Finally, Sheldon provides a comprehensive review of legal issues, reminding us that the ethical and legal duties of staff run first to children and parents, and only second to themselves.

You see, reader, it was a policy of passivity, of nonintervention, that affected Jay in 1972. But it is a course of action based on research, practicality, understanding of legal and ethical concepts, and policy analysis that affects Chrissy ten years later. And the same course of action, we fervently hope, will affect Suzanne in 1992. That is the purpose of this fine book: it is a compelling call to parents, educators, and policy makers not to allow Suzanne's preschool years to be wasted as Jay's were. We regret that our son Jay was born ten years too soon, but we are confident that this book and its companion text will benefit Suzanne, just as it now does Chrissy.

H. Rutherford Turnbull, III
Ann P. Turnbull
August, 1983

Foreword: A Tradition of Excellence

This text and the comparison text that precedes it present an integrated account of applied behavioral research conducted in a university preschool setting—the Edna A. Hill Child Development Laboratory Preschools at the University of Kansas. For more than fifteen years the preschools have provided a place for students and faculty to work together. Two of the goals are to better understand how to educate handicapped and nonhandicapped children, and to help children acquire the social, motor, language and preacademic skills that will best facilitate their developmental journey. A third goal, and perhaps the most important, is to systematically develop a program in which succeeding generations of students can build on what has been previously accomplished and make their own contributions to a knowledge base that can be used to ensure that all the children who come to the preschool have the maximum opportunity to develop their potential.

In the early 1960s at the University of Kansas a laboratory preschool was flourishing under the leadership of Edna A. Hill. Also, there existed at the University of Kansas a state mandated Bureau of Child Research, under the direction of Richard Schiefelbusch, a speech pathologist with a special interest in retarded and handicapped children. Upon Edna Hill's retirement from the Department of Home Economics, her successor, Frances Degen Horowitz, and Schiefelbusch began, together, to plan a strategy to recruit a cadre of talented and energetic individuals in the area of child development. The department was renamed Human Development and Family Life (HDFL). The first faculty person to be recruited was Donald M. Baer of the Developmental Psychology Laboratory at the University of Washington, which provided a model for the approach that would become the hallmark of the work at Kansas. Once Baer decided to join the faculty recruitment proceeded apace: Montrose Wolf, Barbara Etzel, Todd Risley, Jim Sherman, and Vance Hall. All had been trained at the University of Washington; all had a commitment to a style of education and research that involved a dynamic partnership between students and faculty and a dedication to the importance of the systematic collection of data as a basis for building a technology of education.

When the first University of Wisconsin contingent came to Kansas during 1965-1967, an active preschool program was already established. The two preschool classrooms and a toddler center were in separate locations, however, and it soon became obvious that if the preschool program was to become an integral part of a research program, additional staff and better facilities were needed. Carolyn Thomson of the University of Iowa and Margaret Cooper of Iowa State University joined the faculty at this time. Barbara Etzel was named director of the laboratory preschools and Alita Cooper, director of the toddler center, joined her. These four women began to fashion a new kind of program. With Nancy Mann, also from the University of Iowa, they became an effective team that slowly transformed the preschool from an eclectically oriented program for training traditional preschool teachers into an active and unique research and training center. The new center exemplified the use of behavioral techniques, deriving its vitality from the belief that improving the effectiveness of education depended upon empirical verification of the functionality of principles and practices in the classroom.

Barbara Etzel, along with Don Baer and Montrose Wolf, assumed responsibility for supervising the work in the preschool and helped shape the philosophy that resulted in a program designed to train students as experimentalists as well as preschool teachers. The University's commitment to the program was reflected in an agreement to accommodate the Department of Human Development and Family Life and the Bureau of Child Research in the plans to construct Haworth Hall and what would become the John T. Stewart Children's Center. The building and Center were completed in 1969, bringing the new facilities together under one roof. The laboratory preschools were renamed in honor of Edna A. Hill.

The new facility was the site of training and research programs that were highly productive—the productivity is reflected in this and the previous volume. The teaching and training activities were soon enhanced by training grants from NICHD and NIMH to both the Department and to the Bureau of Child Research. These resources enabled the development of a programmatic approach to research and training and permitted continuity in the work in progress.

The leadership and dedication of the staff was a central element in guiding the developments that occurred. Judi LeBlanc came as a graduate student, subsequently became Director of the Laboratory, and is now co-chairman of the department. Elizabeth Goetz (currently the Director of the Laboratory), Wilma Holt, and Trudylee Rowbury, laboratory supervisors, were added shortly thereafter. A later addition was K. Eileen Allen, a teacher-researcher in the original Developmental Psychology Laboratory at the University of Washington. She joined the Kansas program as a supervisor in 1975.

Although it is important to note that the preschool laboratory model was developed from the behavioral analysis preschool at Washington, it should also be mentioned that Barbara Etzel, Frances Degen Horowitz, and Carolyn Thomson had taken degrees from the University of Iowa, where behaviorism of the Spence-Hull tradition held sway. Hayne Reese, of the same background, also joined the HDFL faculty. This group of individuals ensured a strong commitment to research and along with John Wright, Howard Rosenfeld, Aletha Huston, and Eli Michaelis have helped the department and program maintain contact with diverse views and research strategies.

The faculty was rounded out by the addition of Don Bushell and Keith Miller, sociologists by training but oriented to behavior analysis. Muriel Johnson, an anthropologist, and Marie Cross, a nutritional biochemist who had been previously associated with the Department of Home Economics, remained. A particularly important addition occurred when John Wright joined the Department. Trained at Harvard and Stanford, he was for a number of years a faculty member at the Institute of Child Development at the University of Minnesota. When he joined the University of Kansas faculty, Wright brought his broad cognitive-Piagetian perspective along with a tolerance for behaviorism and an incomparable talent for integrating diverse points of view. Howard Rosenfeld, trained at Stanford and then Michigan, was originally a member of the Bureau of Child Research at the University of Kansas. He is also a member of the Department of Psychology and is affiliated with the Department of Human Development and Family Life, thus contributing a developmental social psychology perspective and exceptional expertise in analysis of social interaction.

At Parsons, Kansas, the site of an institution for retarded children, Joe Spradlin and Fred Girardeau, who had taken their work at Peabody, were eager collaborators in child research. Soon Vance Hall, Betty Hart, Bill Hopkins, George Semb, David Born, Aletha Huston, Ed Morris and Eli Michaelis joined the program. This amazingly nurturant group of individuals provided support for each other and created a highly reinforcing and collegial atmosphere. The outcome was a productive outpouring of empirical work, stimulating ideas, and the birth of a junior colleague model for the training of graduate students—a hallmark of the Kansas program.

When the original faculty came to the new Department of Human Development and Family Life, their intention was to begin a training program in which they would teach preschool teachers to manage behavior through social reinforcement. They knew that it was possible to do this, but, aside from the early work at the University of Washington, little research had been done on the training procedures. The goals of the group were to provide a laboratory in which to investigate in greater detail the use of social contingencies to manage behavior. Subsequently the notion was expanded to include not only the management of social behavior but the promotion of academic and conceptual skills as well.

Graduate students were included in a manner that allowed their theses studies to be a part of the ongoing programmatic investigation. The preschool itself became a topic of investigation. The preschool teachers and the investigative scientists thus became true colleagues, a state of affairs important to keep in mind in considering the studies reported in this book.

As the problems to be investigated became more complex, additional research techniques were developed and new educational methods investigated. As a result, a new type of professional early childhood educator came into being—one who had a thorough knowledge of developmental principles and understood the power of social reinforcement, the use of stimulus control procedures, and the arrangement of major variables that needed to be included in instructional program techniques. Their work provided exemplars of ways that behavioral sciences can be applied to every aspect of preschool education.

The behavioral and experimental training for students and teachers was augmented in meetings that involved researchers, teaching staff, and graduate students. A half-day each week was devoted to these research meetings in which intensive work went into consultation, teaching, and advising.

It was out of this combination of events and concentrated efforts that a remarkable positive arrangement evolved, where work was enthusiastically fast paced and highly rewarding to all who were involved. With the intellectual leadership of a small nucleus of experts, research, training, and service became the central force of the program. The laboratory preschools were soon extended into other areas of the John T. Stewart Children's Center* to include not only normal and precocious children from middle-class environments but also developmentally delayed and handicapped children and children from lower income families. The positive social climate that was arranged for preschool children and their teachers also permeated the entire departmental group.

The activities of the early childhood laboratory are probably best understood in the context of the overall philosophy of the department's education approach. Degree requirements were derived not from course listings but from the ideal set of competencies students were expected to acquire—research, analysis, writing, oral presentation, and teaching competencies—while at the same time gaining substantive knowledge.

Research has been conceived as an activity system in which the student is enrolled. An essential part of the program is that each student is involved immediately upon arrival in a program of research. In this scheme it is mandatory that faculty members accepting graduate students have an active, ongoing research program. Sometimes these research programs involve more than one faculty member. Typically, each program also has a nucleus of graduate students associated with the research. Thus, the new graduate student is socialized into the department by fellow graduate students who are involved in that particular

---

*The Children's Center was one of the units of the Kansas Center for Mental Retardation and Human Development.

program of research. The high morale of graduate students may be more a function of the essential role each graduate student plays in a research program than of the nature of the research problems. Undoubtedly, however, the content of the research and the potential or relatively immediate contribution of the data being collected to the solution of problems concerned with children, education, and society have been important factors contributing to the remarkably high morale among students and faculty alike.

The Edna A. Hill Preschools have developed and evolved in a unique university setting characterized by a particular group of dedicated people who were enabled to carry out the development of a philosophically consistent program of research and training. In many ways the chapters in this book are testimony to the productivity that has been a significant identifying feature of the program at the University of Kansas. Though sometimes parochial, and perhaps even occasionally on the wrong track, the work has been carried along by a singular dedication: the fostering of good research and training conducted in a humane fashion, benefiting children, and advancing an understanding of behavioral development. The content of this book reflects the research that has been developed and maintained in a system of student-faculty collaboration where each participant has contributed an essential component to the research outcome. In turn each participant has occupied a role that may be thought of as one that is satisfyingly and productively enhanced in a functional environment where research, training, and service are interrelated.

Frances Degen Horowitz
Richard L. Schiefelbusch
August, 1983

Part I

Early Identification and Follow Up Procedures with Atypical Children

Chapter 1

Assessment of High-Risk Infants

Rebecca R. Fewell and Susan R. Sandall

The numerous prenatal and postnatal factors that are associated with developmental delay can nowadays be identified by means of a variety of assessment procedures. Once it has been determined that one or more of these factors is present and an infant is at risk for developmental delay, appropriate interventions during the early years, in addition to a nurturant home environment, can improve the child's ability to cope with the later demands of both school and home, and in the long run reduce the costs of education that might have been incurred if the problems had not been discovered early. Thus, the assessment of high-risk infants is extremely important. Assessment does not consist of merely a single action or product, but rather is a multifaceted and ongoing process that encompasses the child, the members of the family, and the environment.

SCREENING

Screening can be defined as a process of confirming the atypical development of a child by means of quickly and easily administered procedures. This process does not identify the nature of the problem, nor the reasons for it; screening merely indicates the existence of a condition that is not normally seen in the child's chronological age mates.

Screening Instruments

Screening measures are typically based on observations of the child and interviews with the child's parents rather than direct testing. These measures (Table

The authors are indebted to Dr. James Pruess for his assistance in the preparation and review of this manuscript.

3

1-1) may focus on a single manifestation of development, such as vision, or may be applicable to a number of domains, such as language, ambulation, fine motor skills, or personal-social behaviors. Professionals in any discipline relevant to the development of children can administer the appropriate screening instrument, and the process can take place in a variety of settings; nevertheless, a parent or other person who is familiar with the child must nearly always be present.

Apgar Scoring System

The purpose of the Apgar Scoring System (Apgar, 1953) is to measure a newborn child's physical responsiveness, development, and overall state of health. It is usually administered by medical personnel at the place of delivery, within minutes after birth (60 seconds, then repeated at 3, 5, and 10 minutes following birth).

Pulse (heart rate), respiration (respiratory effort), grimace (reflex to stimulation), activity (muscle tone), and appearance (color) are scored as 0 (not present), 2 (in the best possible condition), or 1 (given for all conditions between 0 and 2). The optimal Apgar score is 10. A low Apgar score seems to indicate the presence of a severely handicapping or stressful condition that may be hazardous to the life of the newborn.

The relationship between Apgar scores and later development, especially intelligence, is not clear. For example, Serunian and Broman (1975) compared the Bayley mental and motor scores of 8-month-old infants with the Apgar scores obtained at their birth and found that infants whose Apgar scores had been between 0 and 3 had significantly lower mental and motor scores than infants whose scores had been between 7 and 10. On the other hand, Shipe, Vandenberg, and Williams (1968) compared children whose Apgar scores had been 5 or below to a matched sample of controls at 3 years of age and found no differences between the groups. Thus, the Apgar instrument is valuable chiefly because it focuses on a newborn's current status and identifies that status quickly and easily. The instrument should not be used for predicting long-term outcomes, since low scores have virtually no validity with regard to future levels of functioning.

Brazelton Neonatal Behavioral Assessment Scale

Like the Apgar, the Brazelton Neonatal Behavioral Assessment Scale (BNBAS) measures the physical maturation and responsiveness of the infant. Similarly, it is usually administered by medical personnel, or by professionals who have been trained in the administration and scoring of this measure. It is appropriate for examining infants through the first month of life. The examination (20 to 30 minutes in length) should occur in a "quiet, somewhat darkened room" (Als, Tronick, Lester, & Brazelton, 1979, p. 191) in order to minimize the external environmental stimuli that might interfere with the infant's performance.

Table 1-1 Screening Tools

Name	Age Range	Copyright Date	Content	Format	Comments
Apgar Scoring System	Birth	1960	Pulse, respiration, grimace, activity, appearance	Administered by medical personnel; requires just minutes to administer	Each item scored as 0, 1, 2; optimal total score is 10; assesses current status, not predictive
Brazelton Neonatal Behavioral Assessment Scale (BNBAS)	Birth to 1 month	1973	Reflexes and movements; habituation, orientation, motor maturity, variation, self-quieting abilities and social behaviors	Administered by medical personnel or trained professional; requires 20-30 minutes	Neurological items scored on 4-point scale; behavioral items on 9-point scale. Infant rated on best performance. Final score classified as abnormal, suspect, or normal. Assesses current status, not predictive
Denver Developmental Screening Test (DDST)	Birth to 6 years	1975	Gross motor, language, fine motor, adaptive, personal-social skills	Administered by professional or paraprofessional	Yields a score that is classified as normal, abnormal, or questionable; further assessment suggested if score is abnormal or questionable
Developmental Profile II	Birth to 9 years	1980	Physical, self-help, social, academic, communication skills	Parent interview conducted by professional or paraprofessional; requires 20-40 minutes	In each of the 5 areas yields a developmental age that can then be graphically displayed on a profile sheet; also used for placement and programming purposes
Milani-Comparetti Motor Development Test	Birth to 2 years	1977	Motor development	Administered by trained medical personnel in 4-8 minutes	Developmental profile from scoring chart; used to determine if child's motor development corresponds to norms; if used over time, may yield developmental trends
Prescreening Developmental Questionnaire (PDQ)	3 months to 6 years	1975	Gross motor, language, fine motor, adaptive, personal-social skills	Parent-answered questionnaire; can be completed in 5 minutes	Shortened version of the DDST; designed as a prescreen to DDST
Developmental Screening Inventory (DSI)	1 to 18 months	1974	Gross motor, fine motor, adaptive, language, personal-social skills	Administered by medical personnel or others experienced in infant assessment; requires 20-30 minutes	

The scale is divided into 20 elicited items and 26 behavioral items. These items need not be observed in any fixed order, since the purpose of the test is to elicit the infant's best possible performance without excessive manipulation. The elicited neurological items consist of reflexes, such as plantar grasp, hand grasp, automatic walking, placing, Moro, rooting, sucking, and passive movements of the arms and legs. The behavioral items include state measures (i.e., states ranging from deep sleep to crying), general measures (e.g., degree of alertness, cuddliness, irritability, lability of skin color, self-quieting activity, smiling). The neurological items are rated on a 4-point scale; the behavioral items on a 9-point scale with the midpoint denoting the behavior expected of a 3-day-old infant.

The results of the BNBAS indicate whether an infant falls into the category of abnormal (having more than one major or two minor neurological abnormalities), suspect (having two minor neurological abnormalities), or normal (lacking the signs of any abnormalities). Like the Apgar instrument, the BNBAS measures an infant's status at the time the instrument was administered and merely calls attention to any distressing condition present at that time. As the child matures, the instrument becomes less reliable as a predictor of the child's developmental future.

A revised version of this instrument, the Neonatal Behavioral Assessment Scale with Kansas Supplements (NBAS-K), includes new scales that rate the quality of the infant's overall responsiveness during the examination (Horowitz, Sullivan, & Linn, 1978). For example, the reinforcement value scale provides the examiner with an opportunity to evaluate how reinforcing the child is to the examiner while being tested. The NBAS-K also allows the examiner to record both the child's best responses and modal (or more typical) responses during the examination so that a score for the difference between the best behavior and the modal behavior can be calculated.

Denver Developmental Screening Test

A well-known instrument, the Denver Developmental Screening Test (DDST) (Frankenburg, Dodds, & Fandal, 1975) was developed for the purpose of quickly determining developmental deviations in children between birth and 6 years of age. It can be administered by either professionals or nonprofessionals (once they have read and comprehended the accompanying manual) in almost any kind of environment in which the child feels at ease. The DDST covers the areas of gross motor, language, fine motor, adaptive, and personal-social skills. The test is administered by giving the child approximately 20 age-appropriate items (i.e., items that have been passed by 90 percent of the children in a normative sample). The child's score is then classified as normal, abnormal, or questionable (borderline).

Frankenburg (1981), one of the authors of this instrument, has stated that an initial abnormal or questionable score may be due to the child's ill health, fatigue, or feelings of anxiety at the time of testing; hence, the child should be retested one week later in order to rule out these factors. A second score in the questionable category indicates that further testing is needed, while a score of abnormal signals that diagnostic evaluation is needed.

DDST scores should not be used as a basis for programming or evaluation. Nevertheless, the reliability and predictive validity of this instrument are considered relatively high as compared with those of other measures. For example, in a study comparing children's DDST scores with their scores on the Bayley Scales of Infant Development (Bayley, 1977) or Stanford-Binet Intelligence Scale (Terman & Merrill, 1973), the DDST identified 92 percent of children with development quotients (DQs) below 70 and 97 percent of those with DQs or intelligence quotients (IQs) of 70 or above (Frankenburg, 1981). Thus, for the teacher, the value of the DDST lies in its ability to identify in a quick, reliable, and accurate manner children whose performances are abnormal and who are likely to be moderately or even severely handicapped.

Even quicker and more economical is the Prescreening Developmental Questionnaire (PDQ), a shortened version of the DDST. This prescreening device consists of 97 DDST items that have been rewritten as questions to be answered by parents. Children who receive suspect scores are rescreened with the PDQ a week or two later; if the results again indicate a possible problem, the children are given the complete DDST. Researchers have found that the PDQ was accurate and cost-efficient in identifying middle-class children with deficits, but was less successful in regard to screening the children of low-income families (Frankenburg, 1981).

Developmental Profile II

A revision of the original Developmental Profile, Developmental Profile II (Alpern, Boll, & Shearer, 1980) is intended to screen the development of children between birth and 9 years of age with regard to skills in five areas: physical, self-help, social, academic, and communication. The screening takes the form of an interview (20 to 40 minutes in length) with parents that can be conducted by either professionals or nonprofessionals. The scale that profiles child behavior is divided into 13 age levels, most of which contain three items per area. The results of the screening are expressed in terms of a developmental age or DQ. On the basis of this indicator, teachers or other professionals can refer the child for assessment and additional services, if required.

Vision Screening Instruments

The vision of infants cannot easily be screened simply because infants cannot describe what they see. Researchers have developed a number of sophisticated procedures to study infant perception, however. The electroretinogram, for example, is a record of slow changes of electrical potential produced by the retina when it is exposed to light. With this technique, an active electrode embedded in a contact lens is placed against the anterior surface of the eye, and a reference electrode is placed on the forehead. The retina's response to a diffuse light is recorded. The more light that reaches the retina, the stronger the response. Because many other variables affect the response (e.g., intensity, duration, size of stimulus), the entire procedure must be carefully monitored. It is usually done when infants are asleep. The information is useful in assessing how well the receptors are functioning, but the procedure has not been widely used with infants (Maurer, 1975).

The visually evoked potential is a change in the electrical potential produced by the brain in response to a visual stimulus. The electrodes are placed on the scalp. As with the electroretinogram, numerous variables affect the response, and these measurements are even more difficult to interpret. Although the data can reveal much about the infant's visual development, this sophisticated type of measurement is more likely to be used when very specific problems with the child's vision have already been identified.

More frequently, an infant is shown a moving, repetitive pattern and the responses are directly observed or recorded by electro-oculography. The usual response to such a stimulus is an optokinetic nystagmus, and its absence is felt to be related to neurological pathology. Optokinetic nystagmus has been used to measure a number of characteristics of infant vision, including acuity.

The procedures that have been discussed are for the most part performed in the laboratory and are not normally used to screen infant vision. Even when they are used, the results do not indicate how to develop further a child's use of vision.

Several vision screening measures have been developed to screen functional use of vision in the developmentally young. Stangler, Huber, and Routh (1980) provide a practical yet comprehensive overview of such vision screening tests (Table 1-2).

The Denver Eye Screening Test (Barker, Goldstein, & Frankenberg, 1972) is actually a battery of vision screening tests. In the Pupillary Light Reflex Test (also called the Hirschberg Corneal Reflex Test) a pen flashlight is used to detect strabismus in children who are either too young or too restless to respond to more precise testing procedures. A simplified adaptation of the Snellen Illiterate E Test measures the central visual acuity of older preschool children, who (from a distance of 15 feet) are supposed to observe the letter E on a card and signify in which direction its "legs" are pointing. In addition, the battery includes several "cover tests" (in which the ability of each eye to attain or retain object fixation for both near and distant vision is evaluated), a fixation test, and a picture card test, all of which are appropriate for use with very young children.

Table 1-2 Appropriate Techniques for Screening Vision of Young Children

Age	Screening Test or Technique	Primary Goals for Screening
Newborn period	1. Identification of factors that place children at risk for visual problems (may include written questionnaire, parental interviews, visual observation of the child, review of the medical record) 2. Pupillary response to light 3. Blink reflex 4. Fixation response, possible following (tracking) 5. Optokinetic fixation response	Determine the possibility of ocular or cortical blindness and/or the presence of factors that may inhibit visual development

1 month to 3 years	1. Observation
	2. Optokinetic fixation response
	3. Fixation and following
	4. Subjective response tests for distance visual acuity for some children
	  a. Letter matching—HOTV
	  b. Picture matching—Preschool Vision Test
	5. Hirschberg Corneal Reflex Test
	6. Cover test
	7. Alternate cover test
		Determine the presence of cortical vision
		Identify impaired visual acuity
		Identify presence of strabismus

3 to 6 years	1. Observation
	2. Subjective response tests for distance visual acuity
	  a. Letter matching—HOTV
	  b. Picture matching—Preschool Vision Test
	  c. Direction matching—Snellen Illiterate E Test
	5. Hirschberg Corneal Reflex Test
	6. Cover test
	7. Alternate cover test
		Identify impaired visual acuity
		Identify presence of strabismus

The Parsons Visual Acuity Test (Spellman, DeBriere, & Cress, 1979) was designed to determine the functional use of vision in children who have already been labeled severely handicapped. The test requires the child to discriminate (by means of pointing or eye blinking, for example) among pictures of a bird, a hand, or a cake that are presented together at various distances in mixed order.

The Functional Vision Inventory for the Multiply and Severely Handicapped (Langley, 1980) focuses on the relationship between visual impairments and the learning process of the visually impaired child. Using a variety of stimuli, one examiner interacts with the child to elicit a variety of responses that are recorded by a second examiner. The resulting profile provides data on structural defects, behavioral abnormalities, reflexive reactions, eye movements, near vision, distant vision, visual field preference, and visual perception. These data are useful for educators who must devise instructional programs that take into account any remaining visual capability in the young handicapped pupil.

Hearing Screening Instruments

The techniques for screening hearing in young children vary with the child's age. Stangler et al. (1980) provide a list of techniques that are appropriate for various age levels (Table 1-3).

For screening the hearing of very young infants, behavior observation audiometry has been the simplest procedure. The administrator, usually a specialist, merely presents a sound and observes the infant's response. However, professionals have felt that, even in combination with a physical examination and case history inquiry, behavior observation audiometry is too gross a measure to be effective in screening large numbers of infants. Thus, several more sensitive procedures have been developed for more precisely identifying hearing-impaired children between 3 and 13 months of age.

Watrous, McConnell, Sitton, and Fleet (1975) isolated the different ways in which infants respond to sound during the first year of life: reflexive and early attending responses (e.g., eye widening, body startle, brow movement), attending responses (e.g., cessation of activity, increase in activity, prolonged facial grimace, searching), and localizing responses (e.g., fixed listening behavior). Children 18 months of age or over can be tested by the following screening measures:

1. pure tone audiometric screening, in which a pure tone audiometer is used to measure the child's reception of pure tones over a range of frequencies.
2. impedance audiometry, during which the child need not respond at all, but is a passive subject for a typanometry test (eardrum compliance or resistance) and a test of stapedial reflex muscle to pure tone signals.
3. speech audiometry (Green, 1981), in which the child's hearing ability is determined by means of the speech reception threshold, i.e., the lowest

Table 1-3 Appropriate Techniques for Screening the Hearing of Young Children

Age	Appropriate Screening Techniques	Primary Goals for Screening
Newborn period	1. Identification of high-risk factors (e.g., written questionnaire, parental interview, visual observation of child, review of medical record) 2. Behavioral observation 3. Otoscopy	Detect severe to profound hearing loss due to congenital problems and perinatal events Detect middle ear pathology
4 to 24 months	1. Follow-up of high-risk factors 2. Structured parent questionnaires 3. Orienting tests 4. Communication and developmental scales 5. Otoscopy 6. Immittance* audiometry	Further identification of severe to profound hearing loss Detection of mild to moderate hearing loss due to middle ear pathology that may impair language acquisition during a critical age for speech and language development
2 to 3 years	1. Parental report 2. Otoscopy 3. Communication and developmental scales 4. Immittance* audiometry	Detection of hearing loss that is primarily due to middle ear pathology
3 to 5 years	1. Parental report 2. Otoscopy 3. Pure tone sweep audiometry (play conditioned) 4. Immittance* audiometry	Detection of hearing loss that is primarily due to middle ear pathology
5+ years	1. Parental or teacher's report 2. Otoscopy 3. Pure tone sweep audiometry 4. Immittance* audiometry	Detection of any hearing loss that will keep a child from functioning to capacity in the classroom

*The term adopted by the American Speech and Hearing Association to denote either acoustic impedance or acoustic admittance.

Source: From *Screening Growth and Development of Preschool Children: A Guide for Test Selection* by S.R. Stangler, C.J. Huber, and D.K. Routh. Copyright © 1980, McGraw-Hill Book Company. Used with the permission of McGraw-Hill Book Company.

frequency at which the child is able to hear words through earphones. Speech comprehension or discrimination is tested by presenting a list of one-syllable words for the child to repeat aloud. The child's number of correct responses is converted to a percentage score (speech discrimination score).

These screening measures should be administered only by audiologists and other professionals who have been trained to use them and to interpret the results. Once again, less than adequate responses indicate that something is wrong with the child's hearing, but they do not identify the problem or clearly prescribe remediation; for this, in-depth assessment is necessary.

Home Observation for Measurement of the Environment

In order (a) to demonstrate that the home environment has a major influence on the conditions of a young handicapped child from birth to age 3, and (b) to isolate the precise factors within the environment that have the greatest impact—with a view to modifying them—The Home Observation for Measurement of the Environment (HOME) was developed (Caldwell & Bradley, 1982). The measure consists of a home interview and observation scale that measures behavioral items in six areas:

1. the emotional and verbal responsiveness of the parent
2. acceptance of the child's behavior (i.e., the degree to which the parent refrains from restricting the child's movements or expressing hostility toward the child)
3. organization of the physical and temporal environment
4. provision of adequate play materials
5. parent involvement with the child
6. opportunities for variety in daily stimulation

The HOME should be administered by professionals who work with young children in their homes. The results of the screening can be used by teachers and other child care personnel to reduce those factors in the home environment that hinder the successful development of the at-risk child. Unlike the other screening instruments mentioned, the HOME is not restricted to an evaluation of the physical condition and behavior of the child, but encompasses those environmental factors that impinge on the child's state and activity. Thus, the instrument represents an adaptive perspective that is important for understanding what must be done to serve at-risk infants.

Problems in Screening

Several problems have arisen with regard to the use of many of these screening instruments. First, there is the question of predictive validity. In other words, how effective are these instruments in identifying young children who will experience significant developmental or learning problems later in life? Furthermore, to what extent does an identified developmental deficit in a young child predict whether that child will, in fact, behave ''normally'' or ''abnormally'' later?

There is evidence to indicate that, except in the case of the most obvious handicapping conditions, screening measures that focus exclusively on the child, or on a single aspect of the child, are of limited use in detecting a child who will experience developmental delays (Goodwin & Driscoll, 1980). As Eaves and McLaughlin (1977) stated, the evidence from screening devices is too "mushy" to make reliable predictions about children.

In a discussion about the inaccuracy of infant tests for predicting later IQs, McCall (1981) argued that the low scores of at-risk infants should be regarded as an indication of problems that exist at the time of the test, difficulties that can be addressed through treatment and intervention. This observation is appropriate for the results of screening as well. After all, screening measures indicate that there is something wrong with the status of a child at the time of the measurement and that additional examinations of the child are needed in order to ascertain the extent of the problem and to prescribe remedies.

McCall (1981) also noted that the parents' education or socioeconomic status are more important predictors of developmental delays in at-risk infants. Professionals who want to identify children more effectively as targets for early intervention are supplementing the measurement of the child's specific behaviors or physical states with measurements of the home environment (Caldwell & Bradley, 1978), the socioeconomic status of the family (Tyler, 1965; White & Watts, 1973), the style of interaction between parents and infant (Barnard, 1981; Bromwich, 1981; Kearsley, 1979; Marshall, Hegrenes, & Goldstein, 1973). This shift accompanies a realization that purely biological or psychological phenomena are by themselves insufficient to indicate the true nature of a child's behavior, which is shaped by "the [child's] active engagement in an adaptive transaction with [the] environment" (Sameroff & Cavanagh, 1979, p. 368). In other words, this adaptive perspective, and the relevant perceptions of the infant (Affleck, Allen, McGrade, & McQueeney, 1982), are based on an understanding of the relationship of social, economic, and ecological factors to high-risk conditions. Attention to these factors during the screening process can increase the number of at-risk infants identified and lead to provision of services that will lessen the need for special care in the later lives of these children.

A related problem is the all too frequent tendency for errors to occur in the identification and labeling of children who are screened. Screening procedures may result in the classification of some infants as handicapped when they are normal (false-positives) or as normal when they are handicapped (false-negatives). In either instance, the consequences of such an error in judgment can be serious for both the child and the parents. With regard to the false-positives, parents may become unduly alarmed at the news of their child's alleged handicap; when this anxiety is communicated to the child during the course of parent-child interactions, the result may be iatrogenic retardation, a form of developmental delay in the child that more or less conforms to the lowered expectations of the parents (Kearsley, 1979). With regard to the false-negatives, parents will eventually be faced with the costs of a later evaluation and treatment, often without knowing whether the child's problems could have been successfully remediated through an early intervention program if the initial screening had been accurate.

Scott and Hogan (1982) noted that screening tests are frequently evaluated in terms of their reliability and validity coefficients. They suggested, however, that these instruments are more appropriately judged in terms of their sensitivity to human and monetary costs. Human cost is a measure of the number of correct judgments versus errors in identification. Monetary cost refers to the actual cost per administration (i.e., tester's time and materials) considered in conjunction with the number of cases that are likely to be positively identified in a given population (Stangler et al., 1980).

Finally, screening instruments are sometimes used for purposes that were not intended by their designers. For example, the DDST has been used as a basis for programming and evaluation. In other words, the results of screening are sometimes thought to be appropriate for developing an instructional program for a child and evaluating the child's responses to it. This activity, however, properly belongs to the realm of assessment. Because of their brevity and singleness of purpose, screening measures cannot produce the information that is required for the development of intervention programs.

ASSESSMENT FOR IDENTIFICATION/PLACEMENT

Once screening has determined that an infant's behavior or development is questionable or differs significantly from the norm, the infant undergoes an additional, more detailed professional scrutiny. Morrow and Coulter (1977) have described two purposes of this in-depth assessment that are important for infants who have been screened and are in need of further attention: identification/placement and intervention/programming. The former precedes the latter in both logical and temporal sequence. "Identification" pinpoints the problem sufficiently so that the infant can be "placed" to receive the attention and treatment most appropriate for remediating the problem.

Many nonmedical professionals have wondered whether the term *diagnosis* is really appropriate for the assessment that occurs at this stage. Do teachers need to know the cause of a handicapping condition before drawing up a plan of educational intervention? Such a precise knowledge is not always possible or even feasible, given the commitment of professionals to intervention as soon as a problem has been satisfactorily identified. In addition, the causes may be beyond control, while the condition or state can be mitigated with the proper action. Thus, most assessment measures can provide professionals with sufficient information about a child's condition to design appropriate intervention strategies, even if the professionals do not know the exact factors that are responsible for the condition.

Identification/placement has become especially important with the advent of P.L. 94-142, the Education for All Handicapped Children Act. The mandate of a free appropriate public education for all handicapped children means that children with a variety of handicaps must be correctly identified and appropriately placed. Rules and regulations for the implementation of the law serve as guidelines for administrative decisions on the placement of handicapped children in suitable programs. These decisions, including those on planning programs and allocating funds for them, must be based on reliable data about the conditions and needs of young children, data that are elicited by means of assessment.

The persons who are responsible for identification/placement assessment are almost always professionals who are certified in the particular discipline in which they make assessments. They use the terminology of this discipline in isolating and describing atypical conditions. The content of the assessment tool itself is frequently specific to a particular domain and discipline. Nevertheless, there are basically two kinds of assessment measures for identification/placement, each of which has its own uses and strengths.

Norm-referenced measures are tests that determine the extent of deviations in behavior or performance from a norm. For example, the score of the infant being assessed is compared with scores obtained by assessment of normal infants of the same age and, in some cases, same sex. Thus, the performance of the infant being tested is compared with the mean performance of a normal reference group. The score is usually expressed in the form of a standard score (for example, z), or with a mean for the appropriate reference group and a standard deviation to permit its interpretation relative to the score of others. Norm-referenced measures must be standardized, as the teacher or other would-be service provider must know with what kind of "normal" group of age mates the assessed child is being compared. With the exception of certain norm-referenced achievement tests, these measures are not necessarily directly relevant for instructional purposes; they were not designed as aids to instruction and often contain material not intended to be taught in schools.

With criterion-referenced measures, an infant's performance is compared with a specified level or standard of achievement in order to discover in what way and to what degree it deviates from a display of skills that are necessary for independent functioning. While norm-referenced measures permit the determination of normal or nonnormal states with regard to a group of normal children, criterion-referenced measures permit the determination of mastery or nonmastery with regard to an absolute standard of performance. This standard is usually based on a synopsis of the skills that are needed for survival in the classroom; hence, criterion-referenced measures, more than norm-referenced ones, are useful (and more frequently used) for purposes of classroom assessment. Their results can be easily translated into intervention and programming decisions. These necessary classroom skills are broken down into their component responses, which then become the content of the criterion-referenced measure. The score is a number that is expressed in percentage form or some fraction of the score representing the absolute standard of performance (e.g., 75 percent of mastery, 30 of 40 steps) against which the assessed child is being compared.

Since the content of criterion-referenced measures is so often keyed to the mastery of skills in the classroom, it may be asked whether early childhood assessment instruments can be accurately called criterion-referenced. What criterion is being referenced for these instruments? In many early childhood assessment areas, such as psychomotor skills, the criterion is simply a standard of performance that is the norm for children in a particular age group. With the DDST, for example, a child's developmental status is determined to be normal, questionable, or abnormal for his or her age by comparing the child's performance with empirically derived standards of functioning. According to Goodwin and Driscoll (1980), however, the developers of the test established these standards after administering the instrument to large numbers of children with developmental delays. Hence, the criterion in this instance is not a predetermined level of mastery for required skills in the classroom, but a level of performance abstracted from the "normal" capabilities of a nonnormal category of children.

The problem of determining standards of mastery contributes to a major weakness of criterion-referenced measures: the arbitrary nature of the criterion. Goodwin and Driscoll (1980) noted that this is especially troublesome when the cutoff score for mastery of some content domain must be determined (e.g., 80 percent correct). In addition, two sets of items, both concerned with the same content, may have different levels of difficulty so that a score of 80 percent correct on one test does not indicate the same type of "mastery" as a score of 80 percent on the other.

In sum, the selection of norm-referenced or criterion-referenced measures by a teacher depends on the nature of the task to be accomplished. Norm-referenced measures are most useful for identifying a child who is eligible for a particular program because program eligibility criteria have traditionally been specified in terms of deviation from normal or typical behavior. On the other hand, criterion-referenced measures are most useful for determining a child's skill in a particular area, which may facilitate appropriate placement of the child.

ASSESSMENT FOR INTERVENTION/PROGRAMMING

Once screening and assessment for identification/placement are complete, assessment information is gathered specifically for planning instruction. This is the prescriptive level of assessment.

The purpose of assessment for intervention/programming is to determine an individual's current status and functioning level. This assessment results in a description of the individual's functioning in specific skill areas that is more detailed than those made available in the earlier phases. The information collected is used to develop relevant and appropriate goals and objectives. This phase ends with the design of the individualized instructional package.

During this phase of assessment, the interventionist seeks to answer as accurately as possible a series of questions. What can the infant do? Does the infant smile, crawl, bang toys together, or play peek-a-boo? The interventionist is also interested in how the baby performs these activities. For example, a baby may bang toys together by holding them neatly in each hand and bringing them together at midline or may brace one against the table or floor and bang the other against it. The child may bang the toys together purposefully, apparently taking pleasure in it, or may knock the toys together with seeming disinterest. The interventionist is interested not only in the simple performance of a behavior, but also in the quality of the performance.

In addition to determining what the infant does and in what fashion, the interventionist must ask what the infant needs to learn next. Is the baby demonstrating solid patterns of development and learning? Does the baby demonstrate clusters of similar skills? Or, is the baby displaying isolated or scattered skills? For example, a child may be able to build a tower of blocks but be unable to demonstrate other tasks requiring eye-hand coordination, such as stacking other objects, placing chips through a slot, or dropping clothespins into a bottle.

The interventionist also investigates what the baby cannot do and the reasons for it. For example, a young child with cerebral palsy may not be able to lift cloths, cups, or boxes to find hidden toys. Is the child failing to perform these tasks because of a lack of cognitive requisites or because of an inability to perform the required physical movement? Task failure may signal not only the need for instruction and practice on that task, but also the need for alternative testing and/or teaching strategies. Physical, sensory, and/or neurological disabilities may limit performance. These disabilities may also account for uneven performance across developmental domains. Medication may also affect the performance of the handicapped infant (Simeonsson & Simeonsson, 1981).

When an infant is being assessed for purposes of instruction, it is also important to ask how this infant learns best. A sensory, neurological, or motor impairment affects the child's learning style. Some infants may not yet demonstrate coordinated use of sensory channels, such as looking and hearing or looking and reaching. Learning style considerations are also important contextual factors. The baby may perform and learn best when interacting with a particular person (often the mother), in a particular position or setting, or with favorite toys and materials. These are additional factors to consider when planning the infant's intervention package. When assessment for intervention/programming is performed skillfully and thoughtfully, the direct outcomes are long-range goals and short-term objectives that are individualized for that infant.

Infant assessment information is available from and can be collected by multiple agents, e.g., the diagnostician, the interventionist (teacher or therapist), and the parent. Some assessment instruments require special training and thus are the province of professionals. However, valuable insights and perspectives can be offered by others who have contact with the infant. Simeonsson, Huntington, and Parse (1980) proposed that clinical judgment be recognized as an important component of assessment. They define clinical judgment as "reasoned evaluation based on intuition and/or personal experience" (p. 66). Thus, the assessment process can be enhanced by the inclusion of parents and other caregivers who have the opportunity to make multiple and frequent assessments of their infants.

Gradel, Thompson, and Sheehan (1981) noted that, in practice, the actual use of the information from these multiple sources is related to their assumed credibility. Parental information is often minimized, while the diagnostician's data may be overemphasized in program planning. The information obtained by the interventionists falls in the middle range of assumed credibility. These researchers compared mothers' estimations of their infants' and preschoolers' performance level with professional assessments of these children. They found that the mothers' estimates were highly correlated with professional judgments, although mothers tended to rate their children's performance more highly than the professionals did. This difference could be viewed as any mother's overestimation of her child or, conversely, as a professional underestimation of functioning level. Fewell, Langley, and Roll (1982), in a comparison of several screening measures that had been administered to the same group of children, discovered that the ratings of teachers were higher than the ratings of diagnosticians, thereby suggesting a similar tendency toward overestimation on the part of the teachers.

Disagreements tended to occur on emergent items. Emerging skills that had been demonstrated at home were less likely to be seen in the classroom or clinic. These results suggest that mothers (and ostensibly fathers and other caregivers), who have frequent opportunities to observe and evaluate their child's behavior across multiple contexts, can add important information to the assessment process. This, in turn, should lead to a more appropriate intervention plan for the child.

Comprehensive Developmental Assessment Tools

To expedite the movement from assessment to instruction, the interventionist often seeks a comprehensive assessment tool that can be given easily and quickly. These comprehensive instruments typically assess an infant's behavior in the developmental areas—motor, cognitive, language, social, and self-help— although the actual number and names of developmental areas vary from instrument to instrument. A growing number of these assessment tools are becoming available for assessment of high-risk infants (Table 1-4).

Table 1-4 Comprehensive Assessment Tools

Name	Age Range	Copyright Date	Developmental Areas						Format	Curriculum-Linked	Comments
			Gross Motor	Fine Motor	Cogni- tive	Lan- guage	Social	Self- help			
Portage Project Checklist	0 to 6 years	1976	X	X	X	X	X	X	May be filled out by observation, report, or other testing data; criterion-referenced	Yes; cross-referenced to Portage Guide to Early Education Curriculum	Also includes an infant stimulation section; designed for use in home-based special education programs by professionals and paraprofessionals
Early Learning Accomplishment Profile (Early-LAP)	0 to 36 months	1975	X	X	X	X	X	X	Completed by direct testing of infant; criterion-referenced	Yes; instructions for teaching these developmental skills in the Learning Accomplishment Profile for Infants; other supplementary materials	Yields developmental profile. Failed items become the infant's instructional objectives
Memphis Comprehensive Developmental Scale	3 to 60 months	1974	X	X	X	X	X	X	May be completed by information from observation, report, and direct testing; criterion-referenced	Yes; Lesson Plans for Enhancing Preschool Developmental Progress	Yields rough developmental age. About 3 skills for each 3 month interval area are sampled. May be insufficient sample for multihandicapped
Early Intervention Developmental Profile (EIDP)	0 to 36 months	1981	X	X	X	X	X	X	Completed by direct testing of infant by multidisciplinary team or individual; criterion-referenced	Yes; accompanied by Stimulation Activities (Volume 3 of *Developmental Programming for Infants and Young Children*)	Yields a profile of developmental functioning. Provides instructions for programming

Table 1-4 continued

Name	Age Range	Copyright Date	Gross Motor	Fine Motor	Cogni-tive	Lan-guage	Social	Self-help	Format	Curriculum-Linked	Comments
			Developmental Areas								
Callier-Azuza Scale	0 to 9 years	1978	X	X			X	X	Completed by parents or teachers based on observation in structured or unstructured settings; criterion-referenced	No, but test items considered appropriate objectives	Yields a rough developmental age. Profile is also a result. Designed for deaf-blind children
Adaptive Performance Instrument (API)	0 to 2 years	1980	X	X	X	X	X	X	Completed by direct testing, observation, and interview; criterion-referenced	No, but test items designed to be appropriate instructional objectives	Consists of three domains: physical intactness, self-care and sensorimotor. Designed for severely handicapped, provides adaptations for physically and sensorily impaired
Uniform Performance Assessment System	0 to 6 years	1981	X	X	X	X	X	X	Direct testing by interventionist; some items through observation; criterion-referenced	No additional curriculum; test items considered appropriate instructional objectives	Items failed may become child's objectives. Can be used for initial and ongoing assessment and program evaluation
Brigance Diagnostic Inventory of Early Development	0 to 6 years	1978	X	X	X	X	X	X	Information collected through parent judgment, and observation of child performance; criterion-referenced	Not yet	Yields a rough age estimate and profile of functioning

Instrument	Age range	Year								Administration/Scoring	Standardized	Comments
Carolina Curriculum for Handicapped Infants	0 to 12 months	1979	X	X	X	X	X	X	X	Direct testing assessment by interventionist; criterion-referenced	Yes; component of the Carolina Curriculum	Includes 19 developmental sequences which correspond to the traditional areas. Assessment data are transferred to a chart which serves as visual display of progress
Bayley Scales of Infant Development	2 to 30 months	1979	X	X	X	X	X	X		Mental and motor subscales completed by direct testing; infant behavior record based on observation; norm-referenced measure	No; may provide base for setting goals but needs additional assessment for pinpointing objectives	Most technically adequate of the developmental scales. Yields developmental index, may also yield an age equivalent. Training necessary for accurate administration
Gesell Developmental Schedules	1 to 72 months	1974, 1979	X	X	X	X	X	X		Complete by direct testing and parent report; norm-referenced measure	No	Model for most other developmental measures. Yields a developmental age for each domain, and thus a profile of skills. Training is required for proper administration

Most instruments designed for young children are based on normal sequences of development, because it is believed that such a tool will tell the user which skills will emerge next. There are other advantages: the items are usually observable skills, many items are important achievements, and professionals in other disciplines are familiar with normal development. There are also major disadvantages to this approach, however. First, high-risk infants, especially those who are severely handicapped, may not develop normally or evenly across all developmental areas. Second, while the items on developmental scales tend to be similar, different criteria have been used for age placement (e.g., 50 percent of the standardization sample, median performance) so that similar items may be placed at different age levels on different scales. Third, some scales include not only major milestones, but also incidental or nonfunctional skills.

Some developmental scales are promoted (or misused) as criterion-based or curriculum-based measures. That is, users teach to the test items. A logical developmental sequence is often assumed, i.e., that x comes before y and must be taught in such an order. The result may be the teaching of educationally irrelevant items (Garwood, 1982) or the teaching of isolated, limited skills (Orlando, 1981). This is perhaps the major disadvantage of developmental scales.

An alternative to this approach is presented by Johnson, Jens, and Altermeier (1979). While based on normal development, their curriculum and assessment procedure presents teaching/testing sequences based on how the skills should be taught. Furthermore, these authors recognize that some severely damaged infants will never be "normal" and that highly adaptive, yet nonnormal skills must be taught to some children.

A slightly different alternative is offered by Schafer and Moersch (1981). Again, this is an assessment and curriculum based on normal development, but these authors and their co-workers emphasize developmental *processes* rather than developmental *skills*. Rather than teaching directly to a test item, interventionists who follow such an approach are encouraged to provide instruction in the underlying concept, movement, or process.

Comprehensive assessment-for-instruction tools also differ in format. Child performance data may be gathered in a variety of ways. Some instruments rely on parent interview, which requires the interventionist to possess those interviewing skills needed to obtain accurate information. Other instruments specify a self-administrative procedure in which the interventionist completes the form by recalling specific examples of an item. Still other instruments involve the direct testing of the infant's skills, in either structured or unstructured situations. Often, a combination of these formats can be used.

Many assessment-for-instruction instruments are behavior checklists that clearly define behavior performed to given standards under given conditions (Walls, Werner, Bacon, & Zane, 1977). When Walls et al. reviewed and rated over 200 behavior checklists, they found many to be lacking in objectivity, i.e., clarity of items, definitions, and instructions. Unfortunately, many checklists are not based on reliable and valid information. The review of Walls et al. points to the limitations of many commonly used checklists, but such limitations do not necessarily refute their usefulness.

Following administration of any of the comprehensive tools, a raw score is generally calculated. Some instruments produce a developmental age (Callier-Azuza Scale). Others provide a visual display of the results. Hawaii Early Learning Profile (HELP), for example, provides large wall charts on which each achieved item is marked; a different colored marker is used at each successive assessment (Furuno, O'Reilly, Hosaka, Inatsuka, Allman, & Zeisloft, 1979). Another visual display is provided by the Early Intervention Development Profile (EIDP), in which the highest item or raw score within each area is circled; the circles are connected, resulting in a profile across developmental areas.

The EIDP is one component of the publication *Developmental Programming for Infants and Young Children* (Schafer & Moersch, 1981), a set of volumes that includes an assessment and application manual and stimulation activities. The profile was designed to assess the developmental status of children in the 0 to 36 month age range. It consists of six scales in the areas of perceptual/fine motor, cognitive, language, social/emotional, self-care, and gross motor development. Items are grouped in three-month spans for year 1, and four-month spans for years 2 and 3. The EIDP is designed to yield a comprehensive profile of the young child's functioning at the time of assessment, and it leads directly to the writing of individualized objectives. The items that comprise the profile reflect not only the usual developmental milestones, but also current developmental theory. Thus, the gross motor and feeding sections emphasize neurodevelopmental theory. The cognitive section is Piagetian in orientation, and the social/emotional section is based on current knowledge of attachment and bonding.

The profile was designed to be administered by a multidisciplinary team, although a single team member can learn to give the entire profile. With familiarity, it can be administered in roughly one hour, either at a center or in the home. Most of the items are scored by direct testing of the child, but some information may be obtained by parent interview. Users must obtain their own materials, but these materials are common to most infant programs. Procedures for administration and scoring are carefully outlined in the manual. Complete test item descriptions are also provided, as are adaptations for infants with visual, hearing, or motor impairments. The manual also provides step-by-step guidelines for moving into the intervention phase.

The profile has not been standardized on either an exceptional or normal population. Items were assigned to age ranges by determining averages of item placement from traditional scales or child development literature. Unlike many other curriculum-linked assessments, the EIDP has been subjected to validation studies (although limited). In a sample of 14 exceptional infants, correlations between developmental levels on the EIDP and those on the Bayley Scales (Bayley, 1977), Vineland, and Bzoch-League Receptive-Expressive Emergent Language Scale for the Measurement of Language Skills in Infancy (REEL) (Bzoch & League, 1972), as well as a motor evaluation, ranged from 0.75 to 0.96. Mean inter-rater reliability is reported at 89 percent agreement for 100 items and nine raters. Test-retest reliability is also reported for 15 subjects. Correlations were significant.

The EIDP represents one of the best assessment-for-instruction tools available for this age range, as it was designed specifically to bridge the gap between assessment and instruction. It provides a comprehensive profile of functioning, leads directly to programming objectives, and is based on current developmental research.

Assessment of Infant-Caregiver Interaction

Historically, infants have been seen as relatively passive beings who develop through environmental or genetic effects. Consequently, in infant programs, assessment for intervention/programming often consisted solely of determining an infant's functioning level at the time of assessment. Following this, a plan was put into effect to change the infant's status by changing environmental events. In contrast, infants are now viewed as agents who act on their environments (e.g., reach for spectacles, pick up bits of paper, crawl to seek contact with objects) and on their caregivers (e.g., signals to be picked up, to be fed, to be hugged). Of great current interest to infant workers are the ways in which infants affect their caregivers and vice versa.

Assessment (as well as intervention) that involves only the baby's strengths and weaknesses misses a vital component of development—the interactional system that develops between the baby and the caregiver. The baby emits signals that the caregiver reads and to which the caregiver responds. The caregiver also emits signals that the baby gradually learns to read and to which the baby learns to respond. This reciprocal interpreting and reacting is dynamic and cyclic; it should result in positive change for all participants.

Today, one emphasis in intervention programs for high-risk infants is this infant-caregiver interactional system. The supposition that the nature and quality of interactions between the baby and the caregiver exert a major influence on the baby's development (Bromwich, 1981) raises a number of issues for the interventionist. First, the interventionist must consider the numerous factors at work in the infant-caregiver system and ask which factors are amenable to change. Then the interventionist must determine how to assess a given infant-caregiver system adequately, determine if changes are needed, and propose a change plan. Programs that focus on the infant-caregiver interactional system must assess the current status of this system, plan the intervention based on the assessment data, and also evaluate the effects of the intervention.

A growing number of instruments that can be used to assess this system are becoming available to interventionists. Some of these are outgrowths of laboratory-based research projects and involve sophisticated (and expensive) machinery and analytical procedures. Others are more accessible and practical for the typical infant program.

Interviews

Ramey (1979) described what he termed the generic methods by which information is gathered on infant-caregiver social interactions. For example, information may be gathered in a structured or unstructured interview with parents. Generally, a rating form is completed during or after the interview. The Parent Behavior Progression (PBP) developed by Bromwich, Khokha, Fust, Baxter, and Burge (1978) is an example of this method.

The PBP is a product of the UCLA Infant Studies Project. The aim of this project was to enhance the development of high-risk infants by supporting and facilitating desirable parenting behaviors. The PBP was designed as a tool for assessing levels of parenting behaviors, as well as to assist infant specialists in focusing on the parent in child-parent interactions.

There are two forms of the PBP. Form 1 is designed for parents of children from birth to 9 months; form 2 is for parents of children between 9 and 36 months. On each form, six levels of parenting behaviors are defined and described. The first three levels are labeled "the affective base," and they include such items as "pleasure in watching infant" and "mutuality of enjoyment" in interaction. The next three levels emphasize behaviors that actively provide the infant with "growth-promoting experiences," such as "interacting with infant to enhance his play" and "anticipating next steps in development." A manual accompanies the PBP and gives full descriptions and examples of behaviors at each level. A rationale for the content of the PBP is also provided in the manual as well as in the project description (Bromwich, 1981).

The PBP is designed to be used by those infant specialists who work directly with the family. The information on the form is derived from conversation with and observation of the family. The form is not filled out in the presence of the family, nor is formal interviewing indicated. (These issues are discussed in the manual and in Bromwich, 1979.) Familiarity with the instrument and recall of specific observed behaviors seem crucial to the accurate use of this instrument. Scoring procedures are provided in the manual.

A major advantage of the PBP is that it provides interventionists with information about parent behavior. Changing or facilitating parenting behavior has become a stated goal of many infant programs. In addition, the progression is relatively easy to use. It does not require extra contact time or expensive equipment.

As a relatively new assessment tool, limited validity information is available. An earlier version of the PBP was used in the UCLA project both for assessment and evaluation purposes. Data from this project gave initial support for both construct validity and predictive validity (Bromwich & Parmelee, 1979). Its use with parents of handicapped infants needs additional demonstration, however. The major drawback to the use of the PBP appears to be both inter- and intrascorer reliability. There are no guidelines specifying amount, frequency, or quality of behaviors; these judgments are left to the users. This problem could be solved in part by individual users developing their own scoring guidelines.

The Infant Temperament Questionnaire (Carey & McDevitt, 1977) focuses on infant behavior. This is a 70-item multiple choice questionnaire to be answered by the primary caregiver. It takes approximately 20 minutes to administer and 10 minutes to score. The questions concern feeding, sleeping, soiling and wetting, bathing, diapering and dressing, visits to the physician, responses to illness, reactions to new places and situations, and play behavior. The questionnaire was designed for 4- to 8-month-old infants with adaptations for older children available. Items are grouped into nine summary categories:

1. activity level
2. rhythmicity or regularity
3. adaptability to change
4. approach
5. threshold to stimulation
6. intensity
7. mood
8. distractibility from interesting stimuli and crying
9. persistence

Each category receives a high, medium, or low score. In addition, the difficulty or ease of temperament can be scored. The questionnaire is used mainly as a basis for discussion and as a source of information for dealing with clinical problems of which temperament can be a part. Information gathered in the interview context is relatively quick and inexpensive to obtain. These data are subject to inaccuracy, however, because of poor recall and parents' desire to respond in socially acceptable ways. Interviewer skill is also a critical variable.

Naturalistic Observation

Infant-caregiver interactions can also be assessed by naturalistic observation. Using this method, an observer records the ongoing behavior of the infant, the caregivers, and any others present, ideally without altering the patterns of behavior in any way. The observer selects the behaviors of interest and makes observations either with or without predetermined codes. The accuracy of data collected in this manner is influenced not only by the reliability of the observer and the coding instrument, but also by the effect the observation has on the caregivers. The HOME, which was discussed earlier, is an example of naturalistic observation.

Simeonsson (1979) has developed the Carolina Record of Individual Behavior (CRIB) to assess basic behavioral characteristics of children with handicapping conditions. It is an observational measure that is both an adaptation and extension of the Infant Behavior Record, a part of the Bayley Scales (Bayley, 1977). The CRIB is completed in conjunction with or directly following an extensive period of observation. Part I was designed to document the child's level of activity/arousal according to nine state levels derived from the literature. Part II consists of Sections A, B, and C. The eight behaviors assessed in Section A are

1. social orientation
2. participation
3. motivation
4. endurance
5. communication (expressive)
6. communication (receptive)
7. object orientation
8. consolability

These behaviors are assumed to be ordinal in nature, and each is rated on a scale of 1 to 9 points. Section B of the CRIB also includes eight behaviors, each rated on a 9-point scale. Because these items are not developmental, 1 and 9 reflect polar extremes, and 5 is the optimal value. The behaviors included are

1. activity
2. reactivity
3. goal directedness
4. response to frustration
5. attention span
6. responsiveness to caregiver
7. tone or tension of body
8. responsiveness to examiner

Section C includes 23 specific behaviors, such as a number of items that reflect rhythmic habit patterns, exploratory patterns, and communicative style. A 5-point scale is used to indicate the frequency with which the child exhibits the behavior.

Simeonsson, Huntington, Short, and Ware (1982) reported on a study involving 360 children; mean chronological age was 35.6 months (SD = 16.0) with a range of 3 to 89 months. The developmental age of a subset of 155 children ranged from 1 to 60 months, with a mean of 14.9 months (SD = 12.0). The handicaps of the group included mental retardation and hearing, speech, vision, emotional, and orthopedic problems, singly or in combination. The mean number of handicaps was 1.88 per child.

The CRIB can be completed by observers after only minimal training. Mean reliabilities between the results obtained by observers who were familiar with the instrument and those obtained by less experienced observers were found to be consistently in the 0.80s. Results of Section A indicate lower mean scores for children who were mentally retarded or who had more than one handicapping condition than for children who had auditory problems, orthopedic impairments, or Down's syndrome. Variability in scores was greater for mentally retarded and multihandicapped groups than for other subgroups.

Of the items examined by Simeonsson et al. (1982) in Section C, the most frequent rhythmic habit patterns observed were hand/finger sucking, foot kicking, arching body, throwing body back, and body rocking. The habit patterns differed substantially across subgroups.

The authors reported that developmental indexes of chronological and developmental age were correlated more frequently with higher values for Section A subscales than for Section B subscales, as expected. The strongest correlations were between developmental age indexes and object orientation ($r = 0.53$) and expressive and receptive communication ($r = 0.72$).

Other investigations enabled the authors to conclude that the CRIB is appropriate for use in documenting behavioral characteristics of children with various handicapping conditions. Of the three subscales examined by the authors in some detail, each offers information that is not covered in the other scales. The instrument permits a profiling of the child's relative strengths and deficits as documentation for intervention and measurement of progress over time.

Standardized Observation

With the standardized observation method described by Ramey (1979), the physical context and the available materials are typically held constant. No constraints are placed upon the behaviors that may take place, nor are specific behaviors requested. The Communication Intention Inventory (Coggins & Carpenter, 1981), an observational system for describing children's early gestural, vocal, and verbal communicative behaviors, is an example of this assessment method. It consists of eight intentional categories:

1. requesting action
2. requesting object
3. commenting on action
4. commenting on object

5. requesting information
6. answering
7. acknowledging
8. protesting

Operational definitions are given for each category.

Administration of the inventory involves observing and videotaping the infant and the caregiver in a free play situation. A variety of toys, such as puppets, blocks, cars, and wind-up toys, are available. Before the assessment session begins, a set of instructions is read to the caregiver; these serve as the guidelines for the caregiver's role in the session. Basically, the caregiver is encouraged to play and talk with the infant as if they were at home. Scoring the inventory involves coding the observed behavioral sequences. The inventory can be used as a criterion-referenced tool, and the behaviors assessed on the inventory can become the target objectives for an intervention program.

In standardized observation, the context of the situation is created and defined for the observer. This method is useful for examining differences in individual behaviors. Nevertheless, the constraints that are inherent in the method may limit the ability of the observer to generalize the resulting data to real life strategies.

Constrained Observation

Infant-caregiver assessment data can also be obtained by constrained observation, in which attention is paid to only a few preselected behaviors. Task behaviors to be coded and observation setting are all manipulated and controlled by the observer or investigator.

The "strange situation" developed as a research measure by Ainsworth and Bell (1969) is an example of constrained observation. In this procedure, infants are introduced in a standard sequence to a variety of events that are apt to elicit stress and thus evoke a display of attachment behavior. The events include being in a strange room, being introduced to unfamiliar adults, and being separated briefly from parents. The way in which the infant responds to these events, especially to the parental reunion, has been the focus of much research.

The advantages and disadvantages of constrained observation are similar to those of standardized observation. Both are often used for determining individual differences. In addition, it is sometimes possible to infer causality through such observations.

Techniques of Observation

There are basically three techniques for gathering observational data. In live observation, the observer records behavior as it occurs. While this technique may be practical, behavioral events that the observer fails to notice or record can never be recovered. The other two techniques, film and videotape, allow observers to look at the assessment situation again and again. Expense and availability of equipment may be issues in the use of these techniques, however.

Observational methods for assessing infant-caregiver interactions involve several issues, including categorization of behavior, data-recording methods, reliability, and statistical analysis procedures. (For a discussion of these factors, the reader is referred to Sackett, 1977.) In the selection of measures of infant-caregiver interaction, the interventionist faces the dilemma of obtaining an accurate and representative data sample in a relatively quick and inexpensive manner. While there are no simple solutions to this dilemma, the interventionist is encouraged to strike a reasonable balance between personal skills and resources in conjunction with the goals and objectives of the program.

Assessment of Cognitive Development

In order to provide appropriate educational interventions for high-risk infants, it is important to assess their cognitive capacities. Assessment of cognition in infancy is problematical, because cognition as an inner mental process cannot be directly measured or observed. Cognitive capacity must be inferred from the observation of individual behavior within a specific context; cognitive development, from the observation of changes in behavior in similar contexts over time. For example, the infant who accidentally bumps the crib and activates a mobile is likely to repeat this random activity. Later, the child will deliberately hit the mobile with a hand or foot to activate it or may "tell" the primary caregiver to activate the music box in the mobile by pointing to it and vocalizing. From these behavioral changes, cognitive development can be inferred.

The Bayley Scales of Infant Development (Bayley, 1977) provide standards for infant mental development. The scales were developed in the psychometric tradition; items were empirically selected because of their usefulness in discriminating between infants at different ages, not because of any intrinsic importance. For this and other reasons, the use of the Bayley as a criterion-referenced assessment tool is inappropriate (Garwood, 1982). Furthermore, the Bayley and other early infant mental tests rely heavily on motor behaviors to provide information on which to base inferences about cognitive functioning, which places severe restrictions on the performance of many high-risk infants.

Unlike the Bayley and other lists in the psychometric tradition, Piagetian scales are based on a theory of development. They can be modified for impaired infants and can lead to instructional objectives. Piaget "described development as a series of hierarchical qualitatively different stages, containing horizontal and vertical movement, and inextricably bound to environmental exchange" (Yang, 1979, p. 178). This view of development has resulted in several scales that assess sensorimotor development, such as the Albert Einstein Scales of Sensorimotor

Development (Escalona & Corman, 1969), Casati-Lezine Scale (1968), Ordinal Scales of Psychological Development (Uzgiris & Hunt, 1975), Decarie Objectal Scale (1965), and Mehrabian-Williams Piagetian Tests (1971). These scales present an ordinal progression of six stages of a child's development in the sensorimotor period.

The Uzgiris-Hunt Ordinal Scales of Psychological Development are perhaps the most widely used assessment instrument of this type. The infant's performance is measured on a continuum that delineates the progression of the underlying developmental processes. There are six branches or major domains assessed:

1. object concept (visual pursuit and object permanence)
2. means-ends relationships
3. imitation (vocal and gestural)
4. operational causality
5. construction of object relations in space
6. development of schemes for relating to objects

Each scale is ordinal in character. The examiner identifies the sensorimotor levels of performance that an infant has achieved by noting the highest item passed in each branch of development. The number of sequential landmarks included on each scale varies from 7 (operational causality) to 14 (visual pursuit and object permanence). While these scales are based on Piagetian theory and parallel his descriptions of attainment, they are not designed to assign an infant to a specific sensorimotor stage, but rather to describe the level of organization demonstrated by the infant in each of the branches of psychological development.

Administration of the Uzgiris-Hunt requires direct testing of the infant, as described by the developers (1975). Dunst (1980) offers a guide for the use of these scales in clinic or school programs. In addition, the examiner can modify test items in order to ascertain whether an impaired infant has the underlying concept or process even though the infant may demonstrate it in an atypical fashion. Fetters (1981) suggested an excellent modification for the assessment of object permanence concepts in infants with motor handicaps, for example. The nontraditional procedure entailed the placement of the child and parent in front of a puppet stage. A toy lion was moved on a conveyor belt to various points on the stage. A screen was located at midpoint on the stage, and objects could be hidden from view behind the screen and then made to reappear. A videotape camera recorded the child's visual and postural responses, as well as the movement of the object on stage. This adapted procedure enabled Fetters to detect a severely impaired subject's understanding of object permanence without direct manipulation of objects.

Infant performance on these scales provides data for an assessment of cognitive functioning. This makes such scales highly relevant for instruction and programming. Because of their ordinal nature, it is appropriate to identify failed items as instructional objectives. *Infant Learning* (Dunst, 1981a) is an example of a curriculum guide for handicapped infants based on the Uzgiris-Hunt Scales.

Alternative Measures of Cognitive Development

Because of dissatisfaction with the information derived from the more traditional measures of cognitive development, several authors have proposed alternative measures. These alternative procedures include observation of state of arousal, rhythmic habit patterns, and temperament (Keogh, 1982; Simeonsson et al., 1982); evaluation of affective behaviors (Jens & Johnson, 1982; Dunst, 1981a); expectancy to perceptual-cognitive events (Kearsley, 1981; Zelazo, 1979); sustained attention (Krakow & Kopp, 1982); and play behavior (Belsky & Most, 1981; Largo & Howard, 1979; Westby, 1980).

The assessment of affective expression may be a useful alternative to the traditional measures of cognitive capacity that rely heavily on motor skills (Johnson, Jens, Gallagher, & Anderson, 1980; McCall, 1972). The two types of affective responses that have been measured are the pleasure response (smiling and laughter) and fear (crying, withdrawal, and other distress signs).

The developmental course of these affective responses and those stimuli that are apt to evoke the responses at different ages have been described (Campos, Hiatt, Ramsay, Henderson, & Svejda, 1978; Scarr & Salapatek, 1970; Sroufe & Wunsch, 1972). Researchers have begun to study the course of the development of these responses in handicapped youngsters. Cicchetti and Sroufe (1976), for example, studied the development of smiling and laughter in Down's syndrome children. They found a similar but delayed sequence of development; the delays were correlated with traditional measures of cognition. These researchers also studied fear responses of Down's syndrome children, using the "visual cliff" (Cicchetti & Sroufe, 1978). The visual cliff is an elevated glass platform of two sections. On the "shallow" side a checkerboard patterned surface rests just below the platform and on the "deep" side the patterned surface rests several feet below, giving the impression of a steep drop. The child is placed on the surface and enticed to crawl to the parent across what appears to be a dropped surface. Other researchers have incorporated the "strange situation" and measured the infant's response (Berry, Gunn, & Andrews, 1981). Again, affective responses of Down's syndrome children appeared to be positively correlated with measures of cognition (usually Bayley scores). Jens and Johnson (1982), in a review of these studies, noted that affective reactions do indeed appear to be related to cognitive abilities. They suggested that the assessment of positive affect may be especially promising for high-risk infants.

At present, there is little information as to the usefulness of these measures for intervention and programming. Assessment of the infant's response to such stimuli as tickling, blowing in the face, or a mask would not seem to lead directly to the definition of instructional objectives. The information gained from such assessment may provide useful data for intervention in infant-caregiver interactions, however.

Affective measures may be used to assess cognitive mastery. Infants and older children have been found to smile very little in response to cognitive tasks that are solved easily, smile most often in response to tasks that are solvable but difficult, and not to smile in response to tasks that are too difficult to be solved. Dunst (1981b) studied this index of cognitive mastery in seven Down's syndrome infants. He found that these babies, studied over a four-month period, smiled more frequently as they successfully solved Uzgiris-Hunt items than when they dealt incorrectly with other items. He identified a pattern, i.e., an onset of smiling during successful problem solving followed by a decrease in smiling as the same tasks are repeated successfully because they have become too easy; he suggested that this pattern could be used as an observable measure to evaluate the infant's adequate mastery of tasks being practiced.

Zelazo (1979) presented an assessment technique that takes advantage of cognitive expectancy. With this technique, sequential visual and auditory stimuli are presented and the infant's responses (such as smiling, vocalizing, and heart rate) observed. The same series of stimuli are presented until a clear expectation is established; then a discrepant event is introduced. In this manner, the infant's response to thwarted expectation can be assessed. Findings show certain predictable patterns of response, as well as age-related changes in these patterns that suggest an association with memory and information processing. Since correct responses are not predetermined, the technique does not appear to discriminate against physically handicapped and other high-risk infants.

Kearsley (1981) used the expectancy procedure to assess the cognitive capacities of children with varying handicaps, including severe physical impairments. Some children who display significant delays on traditional measures perform at age-appropriate levels when assessed by this procedure. Both Zelazo and Kearsley have suggested that this technique may be an appropriate measure of cognitive functioning in difficult-to-test children.

Brinker and Lewis (1982) investigated the ability of handicapped infants to detect and utilize co-occurrences, particularly those involving actions of their own that co-occur with events in the environment. These researchers believed that detection and response to co-occurrences indicate an infant's motivational, attentional, and cognitive development. They described a process approach to assessment and intervention by which the assessor/teacher identifies and then elaborates the infant's contingency awareness from the level of primary circular reactions to simple means-ends behaviors. The infant's behavior is analyzed, and subsequent interventions are programmed through use of a microcomputer.

Sustained attention, the ability to remain engaged in a play situation or task, is yet another technique being considered as an alternative to traditional cognitive assessment. Krakow and Kopp (1982) studied sustained attention in infants by observing their play behavior in a setting that included both the mother and a small set of standard toys. Preliminary findings suggest that Down's syndrome infants/toddlers show more restricted play behaviors than do normal children. A critical variable appeared to be not just simple duration of sustained attention but the qualitative aspect of the children's play. The Down's syndrome children showed stereotypic and repetitive activities. The authors suggested that these aspects of their play may have an inhibitory effect on development. Information from the assessment of sustained attention in play settings would seem to be relevant to intervention. Objectives that are designed to increase exploratory play behaviors could be developed for children with such deficits.

Many other researchers are interested in the development and assessment of exploration and play during infancy (Belsky & Most, 1981; Largo & Howard, 1979; McCune-Nicolich & Carroll, 1981; Westby, 1980). Belsky and Most hypothesized that there is a 12-level sequence of exploratory play and that the sequence begins with mouthing of objects and culminates with double substitution in which two materials are transformed in a single act to represent something else. Their investigation involved observing mothers and their babies at home. The infants were presented with two sets of preselected toys and were observed playing with each set for 15 minutes. The observer described the infant's ongoing play behavior in a "play narrative" that was transcribed and coded at a later time. Findings from this study showed developmental changes in exploratory play. The authors suggested that measures such as these may offer an alternative to traditional cognitive measures in that the infant defines the problem or task, attends to the task, and persists with it. Furthermore, assessment of play behaviors may direct the teacher to the development of instructional objectives.

GUIDELINES FOR ASSESSING HIGH-RISK INFANTS

The validity and usefulness of assessment results can be improved through careful planning and consideration of several factors. Brooks-Gunn and Lewis (1981) proposed the following solutions to some of the current pressing problems of infant assessment:

1. Present results as profiles rather than single scores.
2. Do not stress developmental milestones to the exclusion of other measures.
3. Emphasize several developmental domains.
4. Examine the interactions between and among several developmental domains.

5. Use assessment techniques developed in research settings.
6. Develop an assessment profile for each infant to be used for educational planning.

Fewell (1982) has offered additional guidelines for planning and conducting assessment with high-risk infants. For example, the assessment should occur on more than one occasion, should take place in more than one environment, and should involve various members of the child's family and various members of the assessment team. During the actual assessment, the examiner should be sensitive to the correct positioning and handling of the child, avoid timing test items (an inappropriate concern at this point), and create an environment in which the infant can demonstrate adaptive and exploratory behaviors.

REFERENCES

Affleck, G., Allen, D., McGrade, B., & McQueeney, M. Home environments of developmentally disabled infants as a function of parent and infant characteristics. *American Journal of Mental Deficiency,* 1982, *86*(5), 445-452.

Ainsworth, M.D., & Bell, S.M. Some contemporary patterns of mother-infant interaction in the feeding situation. In A. Ambrose (Ed.), *Stimulation in early infancy.* London: Academic Press, 1969.

Alpern, G.D., Boll, T.J., & Shearer, M.S. *Developmental profile II manual* (Rev. ed.). Aspen, CO: Psychological Development Publications, 1980.

Als, H., Tronick, E., Lester, B., & Brazelton, T. Specific neonatal measures: The Brazelton Neonatal Behavior Assessment Scale. In J. Osofsky (Ed.), *Handbook of infant development.* New York: John Wiley & Sons, 1979.

Apgar, V. A proposal for a new method of evaluation of the newborn infant. *Current Researchers in Anesthesia and Analgesia,* 1953, *32,* 260-267.

Barker, J., Goldstein, A., & Frankenburg, W.K. *Denver eye screening test.* Denver: LADOCA Project and Publishing Foundation, 1972.

Barnard, K. An ecological approach to parent-child relations. In C. Brown (Ed.), *Infants at risk: Assessment and intervention.* Palm Beach, FL: Johnson & Johnson Baby Products Company, 1981. (Pediatric Roundtable Series)

Bayley, N. *Bayley scales of infant development.* New York: Psychological Corp., 1977.

Belsky, J., & Most, R.K. From exploration to play: A cross-sectional study of infant free-play behavior. *Developmental Psychology,* 1981, *17,* 630-639.

Berry, P., Gunn, P., & Andrews, R. Behavior of Down syndrome infants on a strange situation. *American Journal of Mental Deficiency,* 1981, *85,* 213-218.

Brinker, R.P., & Lewis, M. Discovering the competent infant: A process approach to assessment and intervention. *Topics in Early Childhood Special Education,* 1982, *2*(2), 1-16.

Bromwich, R. *Parent behavior progression: Issues concerning its use.* WESTAR Series Paper No. 2. Monmouth, OR: Western States Technical Assistance Resource, 1979.

Bromwich, R. *Working with parents and infants: An interactional approach.* Baltimore: University Park Press, 1981.

Bromwich, R., Khokha, E., Fust, L.S., Baxter, E., & Burge, D. *Manual for the parent behavior progression.* Northridge, CA: California State University, 1979.

Bromwich, R., & Parmelee, A. An intervention program for preterm infants. In T.M. Field, A.M. Sostek, S. Goldberg, & H.H. Shuman (Eds.), *Infants born at risk.* New York: Spectrum, 1979.

Brooks-Gunn, J., & Lewis, M. Assessing young handicapped infants: Issues and solutions. *Journal of the Division of Early Childhood,* 1981, *2,* 84-95.

Bzoch, K.L., & League, R. *Assessing language skills in infancy: A handbook for the multidimensional analysis of emergent language.* Gainesville, FL: The Tree of Life Press, 1972.

Caldwell, B.M., & Bradley, R.H. *Home observation for measurement of the environment.* Little Rock, AR: Center for Child Development and Education, University of Arkansas, 1978.

Caldwell, B.M., & Bradley, R.H. Screening for handicapping environments. In E. Edgar, N. Haring, J. Jenkins, & C. Pious (Eds.), *Mentally handicapped children: Education and training.* Baltimore: University Park Press, 1982.

Campos, J., Hiatt, S., Ramsay, D., Henderson, C., & Svejda, M. The emergence of fear in the visual cliff. In M. Lewis & L.A. Rosenblum (Eds.), *The development of affect.* New York: Plenum Press, 1978.

Carey, W.B., & McDevitt, S.C. *Infant temperament questionnaire.* Unpublished manuscript, 1977. (Available from W.B. Carey, 319 West Front St., Media, PA 19063)

Casati, I., & Lezine, I. *Les etapes de l'intelligence sensori-motrice.* Paris: Les Editions de Centre de Psychologie Appliquée, 1968.

Cicchetti, D., & Sroufe, A. The relationship between affective and cognitive development in Down's syndrome infants. *Child Development,* 1976, *46,* 920-929.

Cicchetti, D., & Sroufe, A. An organizational view of affect: Illustration from the study of Down's syndrome infants. In N. Lewis & L. Rosenblum (Eds.), *The development of affect.* New York: Plenum Press, 1978.

Coggins, T., & Carpenter, R. The communication intention inventory. *Applied Psycholinguistics,* 1981, *2*(3), 235-251.

Decarie, T. *Intelligence and affectivity in early childhood.* New York: International Universities Press, 1965.

Dunst, C.J. *A clinical and educational manual for use with the Uzgiris and Hunt scales of infant psychological development.* Baltimore: University Park Press, 1980.

Dunst, C.J. *Infant learning: A cognitive-linguistic intervention strategy.* Hingham, MA: Teaching Resources, 1981. (a)

Dunst, C.J. Social concomitants of cognitive mastery in Down syndrome infants. *Infant Mental Health Journal,* 1981, *2,* 144-153. (b)

Eaves, R.C., & McLaughlin, P. A systems approach for the assessment of the child and his environment: Getting back to basics. *Journal of Special Education,* 1977, *11*(1), 99-111.

Escalona, S.K., & Corman, H.H. *Albert Einstein scales of sensorimotor development.* Unpublished manuscript, Albert Einstein College of Medicine, 1969.

Fetters, L. Object permanence development in infants with motor handicaps. *Physical Therapy,* 1981, *61*(2), 327-333.

Fewell, R.R. Assessing handicapped infants. In S.G. Garwood & R.R. Fewell (Eds.), *Educating handicapped infants: Issues in development and intervention.* Rockville, MD: Aspen Systems Corporation, 1983.

Fewell, R.R., Langley, M.B., & Roll, A. Informant versus direct screening: A preliminary comparative study. *Diagnostique,* 1982, *7*(3), 163-167.

Frankenburg, W.K. Early screening for developmental delays and potential school problems. In C. Brown (Ed.), *Infants at risk: Assessment and intervention.* Palm Beach, FL: Johnson & Johnson Baby Products Company, 1981. (Pediatric Roundtable Series)

Frankenburg, W.K., Dodds, J., & Fandal, A. *Denver developmental screening test: Reference manual.* Rev. ed. Denver: LADOCA Project and Publishing Foundation, 1975.

Furuno, S., O'Reilly, K.A., Hosaka, C.M., Inatsuka, T.T., Allman, T.L., & Zeisloft, G. Hawaii early learning profile. Palo Alto: Vort Corporation, 1979.

Garwood, S.G. (Mis)use of developmental scales in program evaluation. *Topics in Early Childhood Special Education,* 1982, *1,* 61-69.

Goodwin, W.L., & Driscoll, L.A. *Handbook for measurement and evaluation in early childhood education.* San Francisco: Jossey-Bass, 1980.

Gradel, K., Thompson, M.S., & Sheehan, R. Parental and professional agreement in early childhood assessment. *Topics in Early Childhood Special Education,* 1981, *1,* 31-39.

Green, W.W. Hearing disorders. In A.E. Blackhurst & W.H. Berdine (Eds.), *An introduction to special education.* Boston: Little, Brown & Co., 1981.

Horowitz, F.D., Sullivan, J.W., & Linn, P. Stability and instability in the newborn infant: The quest for elusive threads. In A. Sameroff (Ed.), *Organization and stability of newborn behavior: A commentary on the Brazelton Neonatal Behavioral Assessment Scale. Monographs of the Society for Research in Child Development,* 1978.

Jens, K., & Johnson, N. Affective development: A window to cognition in young, handicapped children. *Topics in Early Childhood Special Education,* 1982, *2*(2), 17-24.

Johnson, N., Jens, K., & Altermeier, S. Carolina curricula for handicapped infants. Chapel Hill, NC: University of North Carolina, Frank Porter Graham Child Development Center, 1979.

Johnson, N., Jens, K., Gallagher, R., & Anderson, J. Cognition and affect in infancy: Implications for the handicapped. In J. Gallagher (Ed.), *New directions for special education: The young handicapped child.* San Francisco: Jossey-Bass, 1980.

Kearsley, R.B. Iatrogenic retardation: A syndrome of learned incompetence. In R.B. Kearsley & I.E. Sigel (Eds.), *Infants at risk: Assessment of cognitive functioning.* Hillsdale, NJ: Lawrence Erlbaum Associates, 1979.

Kearsley, R.B. Cognitive assessment of the handicapped infant: The need for an alternative approach. *American Journal of Orthopsychiatry,* 1981, *51,* 43-54.

Keogh, B.K. Temperament: An individual difference of importance in intervention programs. *Topics in Early Childhood Special Education,* 1982, *2*(2), 25-31.

Krakow, J.B., & Kopp, C.B. Sustained attention in young Down syndrome children. *Topics in Early Childhood Special Education,* 1982, *2*(2), 32-42.

Langley, M.B. *Functional vision inventory for the multiply and severely handicapped.* Chicago: Stoelting Co., 1980.

Largo, R.H., & Howard, J.A. Developmental progression in play behavior of children between nine and thirty months: I. Spontaneous play and imitation. *Developmental Medicine and Child Neurology,* 1979, *21,* 299-310.

Marshall, N., Hegrenes, J., & Goldstein, S. Verbal interactions: Mothers and their retarded children versus mothers and their non-retarded children. *American Journal of Mental Deficiency,* 1973, *77,* 415-419.

Maurer, D. Infant visual perception: Methods of study. In L.B. Cohen & P. Salapatek (Eds.), *Infant perception: From sensation to cognition.* New York: Academic Press, 1975.

McCall, R. Smiling and vocalization in infants as indices of perceptual-cognitive processes. *Merrill-Palmer Quarterly,* 1972, *18,* 341-348.

McCall, R. Predicting developmental outcome: Resume and redirection. In C. Brown (Ed.), *Infants at risk: Assessment and intervention*. Palm Beach, FL: Johnson & Johnson Baby Products Company, 1981. (Pediatric Roundtable Series)

McCune-Nicholich, L., & Carroll, S. Development of symbolic play: Implications for the language specialist. *Topics in Language Disorders*, 1981, *2*, 1-15.

Mehrabian, A., & Williams, M. Piagetian measures of cognitive development for children up to two. *Journal of Psycholinguistic Research*, 1971, *1*, 113-126.

Morrow, H., & Coulter, A. A collection of adaptive behavior measures. In A. Coulter & H. Morrow (Eds.), *The concept and measurement of adaptive behavior within the scope of psychological assessment* (Technical Report No. 4). Austin, TX: Texas Regional Resource Center, 1977.

Orlando, C. Multidisciplinary team approaches in the assessment of handicapped preschool children. *Topics in Early Childhood Special Education*, 1981, *1*, 23-30.

Ramey, C. Methods of assessing mother-infant interactions. In B.L. Darby & M. May (Eds.), *Infant assessment: Issues and applications*. Monmouth, OR: Western States Technical Assistance Resource, 1979.

Sackett, G.P. (Ed.). *Observing behavior: Data collection and analysis methods* (Vol. 2). Baltimore: University Park Press, 1977.

Sameroff, A.J., & Cavanagh, P.J. Learning in infancy: A developmental perspective. In J.D. Osofsky (Ed.), *Handbook of infant development*. New York: John Wiley & Sons, 1979.

Scarr, S., & Salapatek, P. Patterns of fear development during infancy. *Merrill-Palmer Quarterly*, 1970, *16*, 53-87.

Schafer, D.S., & Moersch, M.S. *Developmental programming for infants and young children*. Ann Arbor, MI: University of Michigan Press, 1981.

Scott, K.G., & Hogan, A.E. Methods for the identification of high-risk and handicapped infants. In C.T. Ramey & P.L. Trohanis (Eds.), *Finding and educating high-risk and handicapped infants*. Baltimore: University Park Press, 1982.

Serunian, S.A., & Broman, S.H. Relationship of Apgar scores and Bayley mental and motor scores. *Child Development*, 1975, *46*, 696-700.

Shipe, D., Vandenberg, S., & Williams, R.D. Neonatal Apgar ratings as related to intelligence and behavior in preschool children. *Child Development*, 1968, *39*, 861-866.

Simeonsson, R.J. *Carolina record of individual behavior*. Unpublished manuscript, Carolina Institute for Research on Early Education of the Handicapped, University of North Carolina, 1979.

Simeonsson, R.J., Huntington, G.S., & Parse, S.A. Expanding the developmental assessment of young handicapped children. *New Directions for Exceptional Children*, 1980, *3*, 51-74.

Simeonsson, R.J., Huntington, G.S., Short, R.J., & Ware, W.B. The Carolina record of individual behavior: Characteristics of handicapped infants and children. *Topics in Early Childhood Special Education*, 1982, *2*(2), 43-45.

Simeonsson, R.J., & Simeonsson, N.E. Medication effects in handicapped preschool children. *Topics in Early Childhood Special Education*, 1981, *1*, 61-75.

Spellman, C., DeBriere, T., & Cress, P. *Parsons visual acuity test*. Final Report. Parsons, KS: Parsons Research Center, 1979.

Sroufe, L.A., & Wunsch, J. The development of laughter in the first year of life. *Child Development*, 1972, *43*, 1326-1344.

Stangler, S.R., Huber, C.J., & Routh, D.K. *Screening growth and development of preschool children: A guide for test selection*. New York: McGraw-Hill, 1980.

Terman, L.M., & Merrill, M.A. *Stanford-Binet intelligence scale*. New York: Houghton Mifflin, 1973.

Tyler, L.E. *The psychology of human differences*. New York: Appleton-Century-Crofts, 1965.

Uzgiris, I., & Hunt, J. McV. *Assessment in infancy: Ordinal scales of psychological development*. Urbana, IL: University of Illinois Press, 1975.

Walls, R.T., Werner, T.J., Bacon, A., & Zane, T. Behavior checklists. In J.D. Cone & R.P. Hawkins (Eds.), *Behavioral assessment: New directions in clinical psychology*. New York: Brunner/Mazel, 1977.

Watrous, B.S., McConnell, F., Sitton, A., & Fleet, W. Auditory responses of infants. *Journal of Speech and Hearing Disorders*, 1975, *40*(3), 357-366.

Westby, C. Assessment of cognitive and language abilities through play. *Language, Speech and Hearing Services in the Schools*, 1980, *11*, 154-168.

White, B.L., & Watts, J.C. *Experience and environment: Major influences on the development of the young child*. Englewood Cliffs, NJ: Prentice-Hall, 1973.

Yang, R.K. Early infant assessment: An overview. In J.D. Osofsky (Ed.), *Handbook of infant development*. New York: John Wiley & Sons, 1979.

Zelazo, P. Reactivity to perceptual-cognitive events: Application for infant assessment. In R. Kearsley & I. Sigel (Eds.), *Infants at risk: Assessment of cognitive functioning*. Hillsdale, NJ: Lawrence Erlbaum Associates, 1979.

Chapter 2

Infant-Toddler Day Care: Practical Considerations and Applications to Children with Special Needs

Marion O'Brien and Todd R. Risley

In 1970, the Living Environments Group at the University of Kansas established a group day care center in which what was known about ways to structure physical surroundings and human interactions was used to fashion a total living and learning environment for infants. A few years later, a second program, one for toddlers up to the age of 3, was added. Both the Infant Center and the Toddler Center have essentially the same goals: to foster competence and independence by encouraging active involvement with materials and people, and to incorporate learning into all the day's activities.

These goals are particularly appropriate for groups who are dependent on others for all their care and stimulation. There is a real risk that very young children and the mentally and physically handicapped, because they lack the skills to alter their environment and to initiate and prolong social contact, may be neglected in group care settings. The programs at the University of Kansas were organized to address the issues of quality care for children of limited skills.

The Infant and Toddler Centers were not based on any preconceived model of group care facilities, nor were they intended to duplicate the typical home. Instead, known principles of child development and learning were applied to establish quality group care for dependent people. Many of the problems faced are common to other group care settings, particularly those for the handicapped. Like the care of the mentally and physically handicapped, the care of very young children must be individualized. Feedings, diaperings, and naps must be timed to suit the children's needs, not the program schedule. Similarly, learning opportunities cannot be organized by groups, but must be incorporated into all aspects of the day so that those served can select the experiences they are ready to assimilate. Thus, institutions for the mentally retarded, programs for physically handicapped children and adults, and nursing homes for the elderly could all make use of some aspects of these infant-toddler programs.

BACKGROUND

In the United States, infants and toddlers have traditionally been cared for at home. Within the nuclear family, babies have only occasional contact with peers other than siblings and infrequent experiences of being cared for by adults other than parents. Only after the age of 3, when many parents enroll their children in preschools or nursery schools, do children have regular contact with playmates and adults outside their families.

With the dramatic increase in the number of working mothers, however, this societal model is changing. Many women—out of choice or necessity—are returning to work within weeks or months of a baby's birth. When a neighbor or nearby relative is willing to care for the child, the baby may experience little change from the traditional pattern. However, many infants whose mothers work are being exposed to an environment and set of experiences that are considerably different from those our society has considered typical and desirable. Whether in home-based or center-based day care, these infants and toddlers are routinely in contact with other children of a similar age and spend many hours each day in the care of unrelated adults. Despite this reality and the magnitude of the social change that has brought it about, the basic model for infant care that is set forth in the child care literature is that of intensive mothering of one child (HEW, 1972; White, 1975). This is seen as the "ideal" toward which group care should strive (Prescott, 1978; Willis & Ricciuti, 1975).

Following the mother-infant dyad model, infant day care programs are typically organized so that each staff member has total responsibility for several babies—to feed them, diaper them, entertain them, comfort them, and generally see to all their needs, just as a good mother would. When one person must assume total care for a group of babies of similar age, however, problems arise. It is impossible, for example, for one person to diaper one baby, get food ready for a second, and greet an arriving parent at the same time. Thus, even though two babies may need attention simultaneously, only one can be cared for; while one is being cared for, the other must be left unattended. Centers that have used this model, provided they employ enough staff to give individual care, have often provided excellent care for their babies, and the infants have thrived. The mother-infant dyad model is inappropriate for group care, however. No mother of quadruplets would attempt to care for her children alone, yet these are the demands placed on an infant caregiver or home day care provider who assumes total responsibility for a group of babies.

If the mother-infant model is not workable, where *do* we turn for guidance in developing group care programs for babies and other dependent persons? The most well established group model is the preschool. The long tradition of early childhood education has produced an efficient, effective model for the care and education of children in groups. Again, however, when this approach is applied to children younger than 3 or those who are handicapped, the model is found wanting. The preschool demands a certain developmental level in its participants that is not always present in very young or handicapped children.

A new model, based on the reality of babies' needs, caregiver limitations, and society's demands, is required for group care of infants and toddlers. This new model is based on an arrangement of the physical and human environment that promotes all aspects of development throughout the day, rather than concentrating learning experiences into short, intensive periods. It is appropriate not only for infants and toddlers, but also for older handicapped and retarded children whose developmental or functional levels are equivalent to those of infants and toddlers. Overall, the model provides for individualized, responsive care that is workable, can be afforded by parents, and provides quality care and learning experiences for people who are almost entirely dependent on their caregivers for social interaction and learning opportunities.

DEVELOPMENTAL CONSIDERATIONS

The developmental considerations of infant-toddler day care require an environment and pattern of care that is considerably different from those of the typical preschool. Some have major implications for the design of day care programs.

Rate of Developmental Change

Children change more rapidly during infancy than at any other time in their lives (Kagan, Kearsley, & Zelazo, 1978; White, 1975). They not only grow and change physically, but also they change from totally dependent beings into individuals who have considerable social, cognitive, and motor skills. From week to week, infants' feeding and sleeping patterns change, their motor development advances noticeably, and they interact with the world in new and different ways. Doting grandparents may take special note of such developmental milestones as first words and first steps, but infant caregivers must be alert to each small achievement that may signal new developmental needs.

With handicapped children, developmental change is often so slow as to appear almost nonexistent. In this case, it is even more vital that caregivers be alert to small indications of change and be responsive to new opportunities for skill development.

Closely related to this issue is the wide variation in development between individuals. Within any group of normal infants, there are likely to be variations of many months from accepted norms of motor skill acquisition. Even greater variability is common in social, language, and emotional development. Furthermore, there is great individual day-to-day variation in eating, sleeping, and fussing. Handicapped children may be grouped in any number of ways, but the same wide variation in developmental level will exist within any grouping.

Clearly, then, a group care model must be based on individualization. Infant day care cannot enroll a group of babies in September, teach them according to programmed lesson plans during the school year, and "graduate" them to toddler-hood in June. Neither can a caregiver set up a daily schedule for four babies with lunch at noon and naps at 12:45. Similarly, no two retarded children are likely to be ready for the same set of activities at the same time. Thus, play and learning activities must be individualized, social interaction must be responsive to and centered on one person at a time, and individual attention must be maximized all day long.

Dependence

Group care for infants and toddlers also differs markedly from the preschool model in terms of the amount of physical care provided. Preschoolers take care of their own toilet needs (most of the time), feed themselves, follow directions, and tell the caregiver if they are sick or hurt. Babies do none of these things. Infants and physically handicapped children often cannot even get from one place to another without an adult to carry or help them.

The impact of this difference on group care organization is substantial. People working with infants and toddlers, as well as those working with severely handicapped or retarded children, must be willing to assume a demanding burden of physical care—lifting, stooping, diaper changing, feeding. Because the children's social skills are not well developed, caregivers often receive little intrinsic satisfaction from their hard work. Thus, the environment must be organized to make the physical care routines both efficient and humane. The focus of the program must be shifted from teaching, which is the goal of most preschools, to care. However, caregivers must be trained not to foster dependence but instead to encourage independence and self-help. Thus, babies who can sit in a high chair and chew soft foods should be given finger foods so that they can feed themselves. Toddlers learning bowel and bladder control also need to learn to dress and undress themselves as much as possible. Even severely retarded children can learn to help themselves, provided that they are given the opportunity.

Language

The differences in language development between children younger than 3 years of age and those older than 3 years of age also set infant and toddler care apart from preschools. Most models of formal teaching are verbal, making them ineffective with infants and toddlers. Similarly, most methods for managing children's behavior rely on language. When children are nonverbal, routines that do not demand language competence must be established. At the same time, as soon as children begin to understand and then to use words, caregivers must give them maximum opportunities to develop communication skills. If some attractive toys are placed on out-of-reach shelves, for example, children quickly learn to request them. When a 13-month-old child finds a wind-up toy frustrating, that child must be taught to ask an adult for help. A deaf child needs to learn sign language and to practice using it.

Social Skills and Persistence

Preschool programs often rely on reinforcement from play activities and peers to keep children busy and groups functioning. Infants and toddlers have so limited a social repertoire that it is difficult for two children to maintain an interaction for more than a few seconds. Even older toddlers' interactions often end in conflict. As Robinson, Robinson, Darling, and Holm (1979) said, "Toddlers do not provide very effective language models for one another, nor are they expert listeners. It takes attentive and clever adults to assure that every-day interactions of toddlers are positive growth experiences" (p. 229).

Unlike the preschool, where the teacher often serves as a catalyst to peer interaction that then maintains itself, the adult in an infant-toddler day care setting must be constantly attuned to children's contacts with one another. Despite the evidence that children imitate each other, centers for handicapped children have commonly ignored the potential learning opportunities inherent in interactions between children. Caregivers in these settings need training in effective techniques both to extend positive interactions and to end negative ones.

The social skills and attention spans of babies and toddlers affect the type of play and learning activities that can be offered. It is not possible to regiment infants and toddlers. They will not line up, they can follow only the simplest of verbal directions, and they have no interest whatsoever in the end product of an activity. Their attention is maintained only as long as the process is varied and the materials are responsive to their actions. Unless they have chosen the activity for themselves, very few children at this developmental level remain attentive as long as five minutes; with infants and severely retarded children, the time is more likely to be counted in seconds. Efforts to coordinate such fleeting attention spans into group activities are futile, making completely individualized activity programs necessary.

A NEW MODEL FOR INFANT-TODDLER CARE

If group care for dependent children—infants, toddlers, and the handicapped—is to be successful for the children and accepted by parents and professionals, it must solve many problems. The program must take into account a wide range of individual differences, adapt to rapid developmental changes within each child, assume responsibility for total physical care of the children, individualize every aspect of the daily routine and curriculum, and reassure parents and other observers of the children's psychological, physical, and emotional well-being. Furthermore, it must provide care within the economic range of the typical parent. To accomplish this juggling act, the physical and human environment must be organized to make it maximally efficient yet maximally responsive to children as individuals.

This approach, represented in the Infant Center and Toddler Center operated by the Living Environments Group over the past 12 years, is described completely in Cataldo and Risley (1974); Herbert-Jackson, O'Brien, Porterfield, and Risley (1977); and O'Brien, Porterfield, Herbert-Jackson, and Risley (1979). The same program components have been incorporated into the Roadrunner model at Western Carolina Center (Risley & Favell, 1979). These models base caregiving on task analysis and divide responsibilities by function. For children, the programs are completely individualized, and the environment provides maximum opportunities for learning and practice of language, self-help, social, and motor skills.

The Environment

The floor space in the Infant and Toddler Centers is divided into functional areas, e.g., for receiving children and for playing, eating, and sleeping. All areas are visually open to one another to ensure that children and staff can always be supervised (Twardosz, Cataldo, & Risley, 1974). Low barriers keep babies in child-designated areas but let adults move quickly from area to area. Each of the areas is organized to make the caregiver's job as efficient as possible while encouraging adult-child interaction, exploration of the environment, and children's involvement with toys and other people. Those areas of the environment that contain dangerous equipment or materials, such as kitchens and bathrooms, are off-limits to children unless a staff member is there with them.

One environmental component found to be especially useful is a large schedule board displayed on the wall where it can be seen easily throughout the center (LeLaurin, 1974). On such a schedule board, parents' recommended feeding times for infants, planned play activities for toddlers, and motor and self-help skill development activities for handicapped children can be posted as a reminder to staff (Figure 2-1). On activity display boards, children's names can be flagged to be sure everyone is aware of a need for special treatment or medicine (Figure 2-2). These schedule boards are important components in the effort to individualize the programs.

Child areas of the Infant and Toddler Centers are arranged to promote exploration and play while ensuring safety. Active exploration of a varied physical environment not only allows the child maximum opportunity to gain cognitive skills and practice motor skills, but also adds substantially to any planned curricu-

Figure 2-1 Schedule Board

ACTIVITIES		FEEDING & SLEEP SCHEDULE	ACTIVITIES		FEEDING & SLEEP SCHEDULE
SURPRISE BOX	7^{30}		SOCIAL	12^{30}	JOE TONY ROSA JOHN TRUDE SHAY HOLLY BEN
LARGE MOTOR	8	CARRIE SAM	INDIVIDUAL	1	ANDY RACHEL ANNA
INDIVIDUAL	8^{30}	JOE SALLY TONY JOHN MED.	VISUAL-SMALL MOTOR	1^{30}	CARRIE SALLY TONY JOAN
BUBBLES	9	JOHN ROSA ANDY CARRIE	SURPRISE BOX	2	SIMON ALEX SHAY MED. JOE ANDY JOHN
VISUAL-SMALL MOTOR	9^{30}	JOHN RACHEL TRUDE ANNA SALLY	LARGE MOTOR	2^{30}	CARRIE ZOE SHAY HOLLY ROSA
SOCIAL	10	ALEX SAM MED. JOE TONY	SOCIAL	3	SAM SALLY JOE TRUDE BEN ZOE MED. ALEX
BOOKS	10^{30}	ZOE SIMON SHAY	INDIVIDUAL	3^{30}	TONY JOAN ROSA ANDY SIMON
VISUAL-SMALL MOTOR	11	HOLLY BEN JOAN ANDY JOHN	BUBBLES	4	JOHN RACHEL ANNA
LARGE MOTOR	11^{30}	CARRIE ROSA RACHEL JOHN	LARGE MOTOR	4^{30}	
BALLOONS	12	SAM SALLY JOAN TRUDE ANNA ZOE SIMON	MUSIC	5	

Figure 2-2 Activity Board

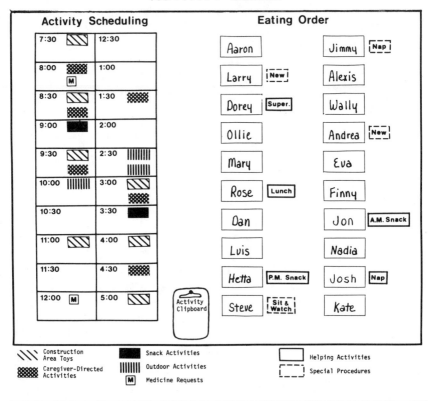

ACTIVITY BOARD

Activity Scheduling	Eating Order

Activity Scheduling table:

7:30	12:30
8:00 (M)	1:00
8:30	1:30
9:00	2:00
9:30	2:30
10:00	3:00
10:30	3:30
11:00	4:00
11:30	4:30
12:00 (M)	5:00

Eating Order:

Aaron — Jimmy [Nap]
Larry [New] — Alexis
Dorey [Super.] — Wally
Ollie — Andrea [New]
Mary — Eva
Rose [Lunch] — Finny
Dan — Jon [A.M. Snack]
Luis — Nadia
Hetta [P.M. Snack] — Josh [Nap]
Steve [Sit & Watch] — Kate

Activity Clipboard

Legend:
- Construction Area Toys
- Caregiver-Directed Activities
- Snack Activities
- Outdoor Activities
- Medicine Requests (M)
- Helping Activities
- Special Procedures

lum. The play areas, for example, contain a wide variety of age-appropriate toys placed within easy reach of the babies. Children are encouraged to select their own toys and are helped to use the toys and to develop and practice new skills by elaborating their play. Toys are collected and washed frequently during the day, and any toys with broken pieces or sharp edges are removed. Those toys that require adult help—such as art materials—are stored on shelves out of the children's reach and brought down only when an adult is available to help the children use them. Some large toys in the Toddler Center are also stored on high shelves, but they are kept where children can see them, giving children an opportunity to use their growing language abilities to request help from a caregiver to get the toy they want.

The toddler playground contains equipment scaled to the children's small size. A sandbox, a small grass-covered hill, and a cement track for bikes and push-pull toys enable children to explore at will without the need for an adult to hover over them for protection. A few pieces of outdoor equipment sized for toddler legs—a dome climber, an extra wide slide, and a set of stairs—are available when a caregiver can be there to teach the children safe ways to use them.

Even within a residential institution, a ward can be rearranged during the day shift to provide a day treatment program focused on a play area. Children can then be provided with stimulating materials and opportunities for interaction during most of their waking hours, not only during brief interaction or training sessions.

In the Infant Center, where many of the babies are not yet crawling, a special part of the larger play area is set aside for tiny babies. Surrounded by a low, soft barrier (which also serves as a support for older babies learning to stand) or raised above floor level and fenced with mesh, the noncrawler area is equipped with mobiles, toys that respond to slight arm or leg movements, and other materials that provide stimulation and enhance perception.

Play materials for infants are attractive and provide opportunities for manipulation and exploration of their properties. In the Toddler Center, the play area is subdivided into toy areas where materials of a similar type are grouped for ease of use (Junker, 1976). A doll-housekeeping area sets the scene for early sociodramatic play, a construction toy area contains materials for building and experimenting with relations between objects, and a "bike" and push-pull toy area offers a chance for large motor activity. Children become confused when too many items are presented at one time, but other materials, such as books, music boxes and instruments, stuffed animals, a water table, paper and crayons, trucks and cars, and dress up clothes, can be brought out regularly to provide diversity and keep children's—and caregivers'—interest level high.

At Roadrunner, toys are fastened to clear Plexiglas toy holders that attach to wheelchairs (Jones, 1980). These toy holders keep materials readily available and can increase toy use by as much as 80 to 90 percent.

Small group developmental or preacademic type play activities are also scheduled to introduce new skills to infants and toddlers. For handicapped children, more specialized developmental programming can be implemented within the day's activities. Records of children's development enable caregivers to keep track of the acquisition of motor, language, and social skills and to identify potential developmental problems as well as achievements.

Division of Caregiving Responsibilities

In this model, caregiving responsibilities are assigned by function; at least one caregiver assumes responsibility for each area in which children need care (LeLaurin & Risley, 1972). These areas include diapering, meal serving, and nap, as well as play. To provide diversity of duties for caregivers, staff members change responsibilities frequently throughout the day, usually on the half-hour. As children move from area to area according to their needs and interests, a caregiver is always available to greet and care for them. The care of each child is thus shared by all caregivers, and a center supervisor is responsible for overseeing everyone.

Functional, or "zone," staff assignments mean that no child is ever left unattended while, for example, a caregiver changes a diaper for another baby. This organization of duties also allows caregivers to center their attention on the children who are in their area and to respond to them individually according to their needs and requests. Because the children who are in an area are there because they *want* to be, they are more likely to be responsive to teaching sorts of interactions.

Finally, this model of staff organization allows the children maximum freedom to move from one area to another as their interests change and their needs require. For example, during the Toddler Center's lunchtime, children can move individually from the play area, where one caregiver is overseeing them; to the lunch table, where a second caregiver and several other children are eating; to the bathroom area, where a third caregiver is ready to help them use the potty or to change their diaper; back to the play area for a few minutes; and then to the sleeping area, where a fourth caregiver is waiting to put them down for a nap. No two children have to follow exactly the same schedule. The younger toddlers, who may need early naps or who like to push and poke at food for a while before eating it, can begin lunch while the older ones are still busy putting puzzles together. No child has to wait at the table while the others finish eating; no child's time is wasted waiting for the group to be ready to move.

Similarly, babies at the Infant Center can eat and sleep as they are accustomed to doing at home or as their needs of the moment require. There are always caregivers assigned to the feeding area, to the diapering area, and to the play area, and there is always a supervisor to be sure parents are met at the door and babies are put down to nap when they are sleepy. When babies awaken, they can be taken immediately from their cribs, changed, and put on the floor to play under the watchful eye of the caregiver who is responsible for the play area.

Routines for Quality Care

Each specific aspect of routine care—changing a diaper, feeding a baby, serving lunch to a small group of retarded children—is explicitly described for caregivers in a written step-by-step format. The combination of efficient arrangement of space and specification of tasks allows the caregivers to concentrate time and thought on individual interaction with the children, rather than on the mechanics of the job. Examples of some Infant and Toddler Center routines, in slightly abbreviated form, appear in Table 2-1. Caregivers learn and perform these routines to 100 percent accuracy as part of their formal job training, and their supervisor makes routine monthly post-training checks of job performance. These spot checks,

Table 2-1 Caregiving Routines at the Infant and Toddler Centers

Infant Center	*Toddler Center*

Feeding

1. Wash hands.
2. Prepare food according to parent instructions and record amounts prepared.
3. Return unused food to refrigerator.
4. Take all food and supplies to feeding area and place within easy reach.
5. Record time of feeding on chart and schedule board.
6. Bring child to area and get him ready to eat.
7. Feed the child, making the mealtime pleasant.
8. Burp child gently after bottle.
9. Stay within arm's reach of the child at all times.
10. When feeding is completed and child is in another area, clean up.
11. Record amounts eaten for center and parents.

Serving lunch

1. Get ready to work with food and children.
2. Get eating area ready with everything close at hand.
3. Have your toddler helper do something with you.
4. Call children individually to lunch, let them find their own places and sit, giving help only as needed.
5. Ask each child to name a food and/or utensil.
6. Have each child taste all foods before giving seconds.
7. As a child finishes, have her clear cup and plate from table and wipe table clean.
8. Encourage requests for seconds before inviting a new child to lunch.
9. Record seconds before serving.
10. Talk up to each child during the meal.
11. Handle disruptions with sit and watch; dawdling with a timer.
12. Maintain high standards of cleanliness throughout the meal.

Diapering

1. Get all materials ready before bringing child to area.
2. Diaper correctly—wash, dry, apply ointment, change clothes if wet.
3. Interact with child beyond contact involved in diapering.
4. Protect child at all times.
5. Dispose of diaper properly.
6. Keep wet clothes separate from clean in diaper bin.
7. Clean area after each child.
8. Scrub hands with soap and water.
9. Record diapering on center chart and parent slip.

Managing Potty

1. Ask if child's pants are wet or dry and wait a few seconds for reply before checking.
2. Praise every child who is dry.
3. Handle each child appropriately to his stage of training.
4. Use ask-say-do to encourage independence.
5. Do not leave child sitting on potty longer than two or three minutes.
6. Keep two or three children moving through the area at a time.
7. Praise every child who goes on the potty.
8. Wash every child's hands.
9. Do not let any child leave the area with dirty hands or face.
10. Clean up after each child and wash hands thoroughly.
11. Record all potty trips for center and parents.

Table 2-1 continued

Infant Center	*Toddler Center*
Sleep	Nap
1. Check child's diaper and have him changed if needed.	1. Set up cots for each child.
2. Follow parents' sleep instructions and record crib number.	2. Have a toddler helper help set up cots.
3. Get crib ready before bringing child.	3. Call children to bed only when they are sitting quietly.
4. Raise and latch crib sides.	4. Spend only a few seconds getting each child settled unless special instructions are needed.
5. When child awakens, check diaper and have her changed if necessary.	5. Praise awake children quietly for resting calmly each time a new child enters the area.
6. Take child to play and give her a toy.	6. Use sit and watch for disruptions.
7. Clean crib thoroughly.	7. Never leave the nap area.
8. Do not leave an awake child in crib more than 15 minutes.	8. Record nap times.
9. Record sleep times.	

along with verbal and written feedback on specific strengths and weaknesses, keep caregiver performance at the 100 percent level (Sheppard, 1974).

All the caregiving routines were developed over years of observing experienced caregivers, consulting with health professionals, and testing components with people inexperienced in child care. All the caregiving routines have in common components that promote efficiency, quality health care, and individual child-adult interactions.

Focus on Engagement

To maximize children's opportunities to learn and to minimize occasions of inappropriate behavior, it is important that children be as involved as possible with the materials, people, and activities around them. Thus, staff routines are designed to focus on children's engagement with the environment. Caregivers prepare an area and/or materials ahead of time so that the children do not have to wait idly while the caregiver readies something for them to do. Similarly, children generally leave when they are finished with an activity (whether it is making an art project, eating a snack, getting their shoes on, or practicing hand-eye coordination) rather than waiting for a group to complete the task. Transitions are individual; waiting is minimized.

High Standards of Health and Safety

Each routine at the centers was developed with an eye toward the children's overall health and safety. Thus, cleanliness plays a major role in many of the routines: all cribs are washed after each use, the diapering tables are disinfected between each change, toys are washed and air-dried several times each day, and the entire center is cleaned daily as part of regular staff routines. In the morning, each child is given a head-to-toe health check, and caregivers receive routine training and regular practice in emergency procedures.

Record Keeping

Because communication with parents and between caregivers is so important in caring for babies and toddlers, the performance of every caregiving routine is recorded on forms that are kept on clipboards in the appropriate area. By looking at the records, a parent, the center supervisor, another caregiver, or any visitor to the program can learn what children ate, how often their diapers were changed, and the special play activities in which they participated. These records are also used by the supervisor and the program director in quality checks of the center. Complete records are vital when care of a dependent child is being shared among several people.

Focus on Interactions

Each caregiving routine clearly specifies interaction components, and caregiver training emphasizes that these interactions are an important part of quality care. A diaper change is not just an occasion to get rid of wet pants, but to cuddle and sing, to tickle and play, and to encourage language and self-help skills. Getting ready to go outside on a cold, windy day provides both opportunities for conversation and a chance for a toddler to practice buttoning. Bath time in the Roadrunner ward is not just getting clean but exercising and water play. It is within these necessary daily routines that the difference between quality care and merely adequate care may lie: making the most of *every* opportunity for interaction helps to keep routine care from becoming burdensome and custodial.

The interaction components that are incorporated into each of the caregiving routines not only augment each caregiver's individual skills in talking with the children, but also provide consistency in adult responses to the children's actions and initiations. By making the human environment responsive and predictable, caregivers help the children make sense of their surroundings and gain confidence in their own abilities to affect their world.

Each interaction routine has a different purpose, and all are incorporated into regular caregiving routines.

Talking Up. It is easy for adults to fall into the habit of talking down to small children: constantly giving directions, correcting their behavior, or interpreting what they want without waiting for them to ask. Thus, a routine called talking up was devised to give caregivers an alternative way to interact with children.

In play, for example, caregivers are expected to give their attention to busy toddlers in a way that encourages active involvement with materials and people, and to talk to the children about their play in a way that allows the children to respond at their own level. Thus, to a 15-month-old playing with Lego blocks, a caregiver might say, "Carrie, you can put your tower on wheels and make a bus. Show me the wheels." The child's expected response would be to pick up the wheeled platform. To a 30-month-old in the same situation, the caregiver might work toward greater elaboration and a verbal response: "Jason, that's a very tall tower. What color blocks did you use? You could make a different tower for each color, and you'd have a whole city." In this case, the child would normally point to the colors and possibly begin sorting the blocks into different colors in order to build more buildings. Meanwhile, the caregiver would move on to talk up to other children who are busy with other toys.

Talking up, which is part of every caregiving routine at the Toddler Center, simply encourages positive comments focused on what the child is interested in at the moment. It replaces nagging and correcting ("Find something to do " or "Go build a tower ") and requires more than just general praise ("Great building!"). Talking up always provides an opportunity for a toddler to respond, either with words or by eye contact or elaboration of play.

Ask-Say-Do. Because one goal is to promote children's independence and competence, caregivers are encouraged to let children do as much as possible for themselves. It is important, then, that children be given the time and the opportunity to help themselves. Specifying this idea in the form of an ask-say-do routine helps adults, who are normally in a hurry to get a job done, to understand that the process—e.g., putting the shoe on the foot—is more important than the product— e.g., a toddler ready to go outside. Thus, a child standing with socks in hand is first asked, "What do you want to do with those socks?" If the child does not reply after a few seconds, the next step is for the caregiver to say what is to be done: "You want them on your feet, don't you? Why don't you sit down and put your socks on?" Finally, if the child is unable to do the task alone, the caregiver sits down and together they put on the socks. This same routine is particularly appropriate in institutional settings where staff have a tendency to do too much for children.

Sit and Watch. Toddler misbehavior is usually very mild, but continued toy snatching, hitting, or biting can seriously interfere with other children's play and happiness. Many people involved with group care of young children recommend a redirection procedure, i.e., distracting the child before he or she has a chance to attack, to handle toddler behavior problems (e.g., Fowler, 1980). Redirection tends to give the disruptive child a greater share of adult attention than that accorded the peaceful child, however, and it is not really a learning procedure.

Furthermore, the goal is not to eliminate disruptive behavior, but rather, as children's social and motor skills increase, to teach them the limitations on their behavior and the rules for getting along with others. Redirection tends to prevent or obstruct conflict and therefore interferes with learning.

The Toddler Center has adopted a contingent observation procedure that has become known as sit and watch. It involves a short (20 to 30 seconds) interruption of play and includes brief verbal descriptions of the child's transgression and what would have been acceptable behavior in the situation. During the brief timeout, the caregiver talks up to other children, who are behaving appropriately. Children who are in sit and watch must respond positively to a caregiver's invitation to return to play. A typical sit-and-watch episode might go like this:

Tess grabs three puzzle pieces from Charlie, pushing them behind her and making it impossible for Charlie to finish the puzzle he has been doing. The caregiver gently picks Tess up and carries her to a nearby spot at the edge of the play area where no toys are within easy reach.

"Tess, we don't take others' toys. We find our own toys to play with. Sit and watch how the other children are playing with their own toys."

While Tess sits, the caregiver continues to comment on other children's play. "Rosa, what a good cook you are. Did you make chocolate soup again?" and "Steve, you found the right place for that circle. Say 'circle.' "

In a few seconds, the caregiver returns to Tess. "What toys do we play with?"

Tess responds, "Own toys," and the caregiver gently helps her stand.

"That's right. We find our *own* toys. Why don't you see if you can put the Big Bird puzzle together?"

A few seconds later, the caregiver returns to the area where Tess is playing and talks up to her once again. "Tess, you have Big Bird's feet and head put together. Here are his wings. Where do they go?"

For a child who refuses to sit (a rare occurrence when sit and watch is used consistently and correctly), there is a backup quiet place in the Toddler Center, a playpen wrapped with a colorful sheet.

Naturally, the children must want to be involved in play for the sit-and-watch routine to be effective. If the play situation is unpleasant or uninteresting to children, the timeout has no impact.

A study in the Toddler Center to compare the effectiveness of sit and watch with that of redirection showed sit and watch to be far more effective. It was also found to be acceptable to parents and caregivers as a mild correction procedure suitable to the children's age (Porterfield, Herbert-Jackson, & Risley, 1976). In addition, it was shown that sit and watch, when used consistently, completely eliminates nagging of children by staff, thus creating a more pleasant environment for everyone. Older physically or mentally handicapped children also respond to a slightly modified form of sit and watch in which the timeout period is lengthened to one or two minutes and the quiet place is a safe but isolated area.

Incidental Teaching. Although developed as a technique for use in teaching language to preschoolers (Hart & Risley, 1974, 1975), incidental teaching is useful with toddlers as well. The times that children initiate an interaction with an adult— whether to ask for a toy, to share a picture, or to complain of wet or dirty pants— are ideal for encouraging elaboration of language.

Curriculum

Many demonstration programs for infants have concentrated heavily on structured or individual learning programs, often in an effort to combat potential retardation arising from sociocultural factors (Caldwell & Richmond, 1968; Garber & Heber, 1977; Kagan, Kearsley, & Zelazo, 1978). In these programs, large blocks of time are often devoted to one-on-one skill training sessions. Several of these programs have been notably effective, as measured by the intelligence quotients (IQs) of the children compared with those of siblings and/or comparison groups from similar backgrounds. It is obvious, however, that the dollar cost of such intensive training of infants is higher than society is willing to pay routinely.

Many programs for handicapped children provide only short bursts of intensive training, followed by long periods of social isolation and inactivity. Those who use this approach claim the cost of providing individualized training by specialists makes more than brief interventions impossible.

Other programs, including those of the Infant and Toddler Centers, have taken an alternative approach, one that recognizes the importance of routine care as well as teaching (Cataldo & Risley, 1974; Willis & Ricciuti, 1975). A broad range of play and learning activities is specified for caregivers to conduct with children, and caregiving routines have built-in strategies for teaching self-help and for encouraging functional language use. Rather than focusing specifically on curriculum and skill training, these programs facilitate learning and practice of skills throughout the child's waking hours by maximizing engagement with the physical environment and positive interaction with caregivers and other children. Because self-selection of activities and individual transitions between areas are emphasized, the children in these programs are actively involved and interested in what they are doing. This makes them eager to listen and do, the best situation for teaching and learning.

Problem Areas and Solutions

Maintaining Quality

The structure of the Infant and Toddler Centers contains all the components required for quality care of babies. It is essential that all these components be continuously used by staff. The environment must be kept clean and safe, caregivers must work to interact with children at high rate and high quality, and health routines must be scrupulously followed.

Because caring for babies, toddlers, and handicapped persons is hard work that is both physically and emotionally demanding, it is easy for staff members to feel ineffective and unappreciated. It is not always obvious to caregivers that filling out the diapering record form and letting Sam zip up his own coat are as important as ensuring that all the babies have been fed by 1:30. Furthermore, the intrinsic rewards—not to mention the pay—are low. No matter how nice and attentive a caregiver may be, babies will cry. No matter how good the food, children will refuse or spill it. No matter how many times they are asked to sit and watch, toddlers will take toys from one another. Because direct care staff must handle these day-to-day and minute-to-minute problems, it is often difficult for them to see the overall needs of the children and the influence small lapses in caregiving can have on the quality of care. Thus, programs must have a system of checks of job performance, feedback to staff on how well they are doing, and regular review of overall quality.

These models therefore include an administrative structure and system of quality checks to ensure a high level of care over years of operation and continual changes in personnel. A supervisor in each center is responsible for managing the day-to-day operation of the center, hiring and training staff, keeping records, giving attention to individual children's needs, making contacts with parents, and scheduling the day's activities. The supervisor also conducts regular checks of each caregiver's job performance in each of the caregiving routines. These checks are done formally by the use of checklists, on which each step of a routine is listed. The supervisor gives caregivers both written feedback and informal comments. Because this is done frequently, most feedback is positive; however, regular checks also let the supervisor know if retraining is needed.

A program consultant is also part of the model. The consultant is ultimately the child advocate for the program, overseeing the quality of the program from the child's point of view and reviewing the performance of the supervisor. The consultant reviews each week's records and prepares a weekly report to the supervisor describing his or her view of its daily operation, helping to define and solve problems, and keeping track of individual children's needs. The consultant also visits the program on a regular basis, observing the children and the staff. Each month the consultant prepares a monthly review of program operation to help the supervisor identify areas of strength and to point out areas in which improvement is needed. The consultant is not an everyday, full-time presence at the center, but the consultant's objectivity is vital to the operation of a quality program.

Communicating with Parents

Day care for children who are under 3 and for those who are handicapped is still uncommon enough that many parents are unsure about their decision to enroll their child in a group day care center. Often their own parents may disapprove, friends may show surprise or ask troublesome questions, and husbands and wives may even disagree as to the wisdom of group care. In addition, no matter how committed to a career outside the home or how in need of relief, many new mothers feel guilty about leaving their children in the care of others. Thus, caregivers of infants, toddlers, and handicapped children must be particularly sensitive to parents' fears and worries, and must attempt to provide reassurance without giving unwanted advice or seeming to be possessive of the children.

Communication with parents is particularly important in the care of totally dependent children. Continuity of care in terms of feeding, naps, toilet training, and health requires parents and caregivers to be in close touch so that each knows about the child's daily activities and special needs. Yet most parents of children in day care are very busy people with little time to attend parent meetings, confer at length with teachers, or visit the center.

At the Infant and Toddler Centers, it was found that parent communications are best made on a daily, routine basis. Each time parents come to the center to bring or pick up their child, they have an opportunity to talk with a caregiver who knows them. There is also a formal method of transferring information about the child, i.e., the daily parent report (Figure 2-3). The top portion is filled out by parents when they bring their child in the morning; it supplies information about how the child ate or slept and what special needs the child might have that day. It also represents a formal transfer of responsibility from parent to center. At the end of the day, the report is returned to the parents with the bottom portion completed. This gives the parents information about the child's day at the center: when and how much the child ate, diaper changes, naps, play activities, health problems, special events. Again, the responsibility for the child is transferred.

Because parents must stop at the door long enough to sign in their child in the morning and to pick up their child's belongings at the end of the day, the parents and the supervisor, who is generally responsible for greeting parents, have an opportunity to get to know each other. This leads to greater openness when a problem or concern arises on either side. The supervisor also has an opportunity to reassure a worried parent and to relate anecdotes about the child's day, making parents feel a part of all aspects of their child's life.

Figure 2-3 Parent Report

PARENT REPORT

Day _____ Departure time _____ Child's name _____

Did your child sleep well last night? _____ Has your child had breakfast? _____

Any special instructions for today?   *Phone number if different for today:* _____

Today's play activities	Meals

Individual

Art or Science

Large group

Helping

Outdoor

Other

Meals:
✓ = type of snack food served
+ = ate lots
1 = ate one serving
0 = ate little

	a.m. Snack	Lunch	p.m. Snack
Protein source			
Fruit/Juice			
Vegetable			
Bread/Cereal			
Milk product			

General disposition

Nap: *Slept from* _____ *to* _____

Potty: *Number of accidents* _____

Comments:

Medicine given at:

_____

_____

_____

Substitute foods for:

a.m. Snack: Serve _____ *instead of* _____

Lunch: Serve _____ *instead of* _____

p.m. Snack: Serve _____ *instead of* _____

Medicine for:

Medicine	Dosage	Time	Given by

Signature: _____
Date: _____

In the Infant Center, where parental anxiety is apt to be highest and where the need for information is greatest, parents are asked to fill out a feeding schedule, sleep schedule, and diapering instruction form on a monthly basis. This tells the center staff how parents handle their baby's needs and gives parents the security that the center staff will not depart radically from the parents' standards. These records also give the center staff a better understanding of the baby's daily life at home.

Naturally, parents who have the time are invited to visit the center. An observation window makes it possible for parents to watch their child in the typical play situation. In general, however, parents receive most of their information through the daily parent reports and through their everyday conversations with caregivers at the door.

Economic Concerns

The economics of day care is a problem with no ready solution. It is becoming more and more difficult each year to provide quality care for a group of children at any age at a price working parents can afford. It becomes harder and harder to find caregivers and teachers who have the training, experience, competence, and emotional stability to work well with children and who are also willing to work for the low wages necessary to keep day care prices at a level most parents can afford. Yet there are no signs that quality child care is becoming a high national priority.

The Infant and Toddler Center programs were developed on the premise that group day care should be an option for parents of all children, and the centers were intended to be financially self-supporting. The program can be operated by nonprofessional staff, even with the high staff turnover rate inevitably associated with low paying jobs, because efficient, effective caregiving routines have been developed and a training procedure that allows people to learn these routines quickly and to a high degree of proficiency has been established. In both centers, parent fees cover month-to-month operating expenses, including rent and utilities. It has been found that many more parents are willing and able to pay these fees than there are places for children.

In order to operate these programs, each center must enroll at least 20 children. Enrollment of fewer children so reduces the income that it is impossible to employ enough staff members to cover all the activity areas of the center. This thereby forces a reduction in overall quality, even though the staff/child ratio remains the same. Many states, as well as the most recent federal guidelines for day care licensing (HEW, undated; NAEYC, 1979), consider a group size of 20 too high for children under 3 years of age, however. These regulations do not take into account the needs and desires of parents to have quality group care available for their babies. Instead, the limits on group size effectively stifle efforts to provide quality care that deviates from the widely accepted but inappropriate "good home" model for infant care. This dilemma must be faced.

CONCLUSION

The need for quality day care is real. The evidence shows that day care has no ill effects on children or families. The challenge is to make day care for all children possible, available, and affordable.

The programs that have been described are appropriate for use not only with normal infants and toddlers but also with severely handicapped and mentally retarded children who are totally dependent on others for care and stimulation. The infant-toddler model has been successfully adapted for daily use in a residential ward for severely and profoundly retarded children (Risley & Favell, 1979; Jones, Favell, & Risley, in press). Other groups of largely dependent people could also benefit from care environments established according to the principles of these infant-toddler programs.

A child's first three years are the foundation for future learning and development. As society changes, social models must be reevaluated and the special needs of infants and toddlers—and their parents—considered in planning day care programs.

REFERENCES

Caldwell, B.M., & Richmond, J.B. The children's center in Syracuse, New York. In C.A. Chandler, R.S. Lourie, & A.D. Peters (Eds.), *Early child care—The new perspective*. New York: Atherton Press, 1968.

Cataldo, M.F., & Risley, T.R. Infant day care. In Ulrich, Stachnik, & Mabry (Eds.), *Control of human behavior* (Vol. III). Glenview, IL: Scott Foresman, 1974.

Fowler, W. *Infant and child care: A guide to education in group settings.* Boston: Allyn & Bacon, 1980.

Garber, H., & Heber, R. The Milwaukee project: Early intervention as a technique to prevent mental retardation. In E.M. Hetherington & R.D. Parke (Eds.), *Contemporary readings in child psychology.* New York: McGraw-Hill, 1977.

Hart, B.M., & Risley, T.R. Using preschool materials to modify the language of disadvantaged children. *Journal of Applied Behavior Analysis, 1974, 7,* 243-256.

Hart, B.M., & Risley, T.R. Incidental teaching of language in the preschool. *Journal of Applied Behavior Analysis,* 1975, *8,* 411-420.

Herbert-Jackson, E., O'Brien, M., Porterfield, J., & Risley, T.R. *The infant center: A complete guide to organizing and managing infant day care.* Baltimore: University Park Press, 1977.

Jones, M.L. *The analysis of play materials for the profoundly retarded, multi-handicapped.* Master's thesis, University of Kansas, Department of Human Development, 1980.

Jones, M.L., Favell, J.E., & Risley, T.R. Socio-ecological programming. In J.L. Matson & F. Andrasik (Eds.), *Treatment issues and innovations in mental retardation.* New York: Plenum Press, in press.

Junker, D. *Structuring toddlers' toy use: Areas versus no areas.* Master's thesis, University of Kansas, Department of Human Development, 1976.

Kagan, J., Kearsley, R.B., & Zelazo, P.R. *Infancy: Its place in human development.* Cambridge, MA: Harvard University Press, 1978.

LeLaurin, K. *The organization of day care environments: An examination of the duties of supervisor in a day care center for children under walking age.* Doctoral dissertation, University of Kansas, Department of Human Development, 1974.

LeLaurin, K., & Risley, T.R. The organization of day care environments: "Zone" versus "man-to-man" staff assignments. *Journal of Applied Behavior Analysis,* 1972, *5,* 225-232.

National Association for the Education of Young Children (NAEYC). Proposed federal interagency day care requirements. *Young Children,* July, 1979, 67-69.

O'Brien, M., Porterfield, J., Herbert-Jackson, E., & Risley, T.R. *The toddler center: A practical guide to day care for one- and two-year-olds.* Baltimore: University Park Press, 1979.

Porterfield, J., Herbert-Jackson, E., & Risley, T.R. Contingent observation: An effective and acceptable procedure for reducing disruptive behaviors in young children in group settings. *Journal of Applied Behavior Analysis,* 1976, *9,* 55-65.

Prescott, E. Is day care as good as a good home? *Young Children,* January, 1978, 13-19.

Risley, T.R., & Favell, J.E. Constructing a living environment in an institution. In L.A. Hamerlynck (Ed.), *Behavioral systems for the developmentally disabled: II. Institutional, clinic and community environments.* New York: Brunner/Mazel, 1979.

Robinson, N.M., Robinson, H.B., Darling, M.A., & Holm, G. *A world of children: Daycare and preschool institutions.* Monterey, CA: Brooks/Cole, 1979.

Sheppard, J. *The evaluation of the adequacy of training procedures for transmitting job skills from one staff member to another across successive generations of day care workers.* Honors thesis, University of Kansas, Department of Human Development, 1974.

Twardosz, S., Cataldo, M.F., & Risley, T.R. Open environment design for infant and toddler day care. *Journal of Applied Behavior Analysis,* 1974, *7,* 529-546.

U.S. Department of Health, Education and Welfare. *Infant care* (Publication No. OHD 75-15). Washington, D.C.: DHEW, 1972.

U.S. Department of Health, Education and Welfare. *Model for day care licensing.* Undated manuscript.

White, B.L. *The first three years of life.* Englewood Cliffs, NJ: Prentice-Hall, 1975.

Willis, A., & Ricciuti, H. *A good beginning for babies: Guidelines for group care.* Washington, DC: National Association for the Education of Young Children, 1975.

Chapter 3

Facilitating Early Language and Social Development: Parents as Teachers

Ann K. Rogers-Warren and Steven F. Warren

The anxiety and trauma experienced by parents who discover their young child is unresponsive and possibly developmentally delayed have been well documented (Turnbull & Turnbull, 1978). Often these parents feel helpless in the face of their child's condition and assume that their only option is simply to wait; they hope that either their child will outgrow the problem or will be eligible to receive direct educational services in center-based programs. However, there is another option. Through understanding the ways in which communication and language develop and the ways in which this development can be stimulated, parents can help their child overcome the handicap, at least to some extent.

During the first years of life, children acquire a wide range of skills. The development of social communication and the emergence of a comprehensive language repertoire are particularly important aspects of children's early development. Children, starting in early infancy, bring to language learning a considerable array of skills and abilities; however, a responsive and well-tuned environment greatly facilitates their development and mastery of language in social communication. Typically, great attention is given to ensuring that the physical environment meets children's basic health and nutritional needs and provides a stimulating and secure background for development. Although the quality of the physical setting is important, the environmental characteristics that are most essential to language learning are the behaviors of caregivers.[1] Care-

---

[1]Throughout this chapter, caregiver, parent, mother, and father are used interchangeably. Most research on early social-linguistic interaction has been done with mothers as subjects; however, a small body of literature describing the behavior of fathers indicates that the sex of the caregiver is not a critical variable in the patterns of interaction. A still smaller body of literature examining the behavior of nonparents during interaction with young children indicates patterns that are sufficiently similar to those of parents to be considered together.

Preparation of this manuscript was supported in part by two grants from the Office of Special Education (USOE G0079-05112 and USOE 300-77-0308).

givers arrange the physical and social environment in ways that enhance the development of language and social skills.

The process of language development and the mechanisms that permit the mastery of a rich and varied social communication repertoire have been the subjects of much study and controversy in the last 15 years. Recently, however, there has been a modest coalescence of views; some general agreement about the role of the environment in early language development has emerged (Rogers-Warren & Warren, in press). This consensus has paralleled the experimental study of young children's social and communicative behaviors in the first two years of life. Increasing attention has been directed to the study of prelinguistic (before formal language) communicative behavior (Bates, 1976; Bruner, 1975) and of child language in the context of children's interactions with their caregivers (Ferguson & Snow, 1977; Moerk, 1977).

The role of the environment in general and the behaviors of caregivers in particular have become specific concerns of those interested in child language. Two broad classes of environmental variables have been examined: (1) characteristics of the language displayed by children who are in the process of learning language and (2) patterns of interaction among children and their caregivers. Studies of the first type show that, when they speak to a young child, adults (both parents and nonparents) systematically adjust their language to accommodate the skill level of the child (Ferguson & Snow, 1977). Other studies (Moerk, 1976; Schachter, 1979) describe the interactional strategies that parents use to support their children's early communication attempts. Together, experimental and descriptive studies suggest a model of social language development in which early caregiver-child interactions are integral components.

THE SOCIAL INTERACTIONAL BASIS OF LANGUAGE

Language is too often thought of as only a system of words and rules for combining them. Although language does encompass vocabulary and syntax, it is primarily a *social* system, a system for conveying social meanings. It is a part of a class of behaviors that mediates the behavior of others (Skinner, 1957). Language is a means to an end. That end is controlling the environment, particularly the behavior of persons in the environment.

Language usually occurs during a social interaction between a speaker and a listener. In these transactions, language performs specific functions:

- to greet (e.g., ''Hello.'' ''Goodbye.'' ''It's good to see you.'')
- to protest (e.g., ''No, not me.'')
- to seek information (e.g., ''Is this yours?'')
- to provide information (e.g., ''No, it's not mine.'')

- to solicit the listener's attention (e.g., "Hey, look at this!")
- to make requests (e.g., "Please give it to me.")

Among adults, language often serves a commenting or requesting function. Speakers describe the environment and events (e.g., "It's raining." "This conference is boring." "I'm going to Hawaii tomorrow."). The behavior change accomplished in these transactions may be very small (a second comment from the listener) or dramatic (compliance with a serious request, such as "Please marry me!").

The basic functions of language are not strictly dependent on the spoken word for expression. Thus, it is possible to answer with a head nod, request by pointing to the desired object, and question with raised eyebrows. The linguistic form of language makes communication more efficient and usually more effective, however. Formal language allows speakers to specify the particulars of their intentions (e.g., "I want a cheeseburger with pickles, onions, and catsup.").

Since functional communication does not depend on use of a linguistic system, it can and does begin well before children speak their first words. Social communication requires (1) a speaker (although not necessarily one who speaks in the literal sense), (2) a listener, (3) a common code (which may be verbal or nonverbal, simple or elaborate), and (4) a resulting behavior change by the listener. All four components are part of each caregiver-child interaction and have been observed in very early parent-child encounters.

Early caregiver-child interaction has all the critical components for successful communication, largely because adults systematically adapt their behavior to permit the communication of children's intent (Schachter, 1979). The typical parent-listener is intensely interested in what the young "speaker" has to say, focusing on the child and providing a rich communication-oriented interpretation of the child's behavior. In essence, parents assign meaning to the child's earliest cries and movements. By consistently responding to certain child behaviors in the same way and by modeling the forms that express the child's intention in common words or gestures, parents encourage the child to develop the standard linguistic means for communicating with listeners.

Bruner (1975) described a sequence by which mothers shape vocal requesting from their children. The sequence begins with the child's reaching or pointing gesture, a cross-culturally recognized communicative gesture to indicate a desired object or to draw attention to an object. When a child first gains sufficient motor control to direct gestures outward, the child may intentionally or accidentally point toward objects that the mother assumes the child wants. The child points, the caregiver responds with an interpretive comment (e.g., "Oh, you want the bottle.") and provides the object for the child. With many repetitions, the child's pointing comes to have a social meaning both for caregiver and for child. The child has successfully communicated what is wanted without words because the care-giver (most likely without any intention of doing so) has generously interpreted the child's behavior as communicative.

Throughout the first years of the child's life there are many similar episodes. The parent, with a continuing interest in the child's wants, needs, and interests, gently but regularly translates the child's idiosyncratic vocal and nonverbal communication forms into linguistic forms that are generally recognized by people in the environment. From these exchanges, the child learns the functional relationship between communication and control of the environment, and the child has many opportunities to hear the forms that explicitly request objects, describe settings, and answer queries.

Although parents' interpretation and shaping of children's language are generally consistent, they are also extremely subtle and unobtrusive. Parental guidance occurs in the context of social and caregiving interactions between child and parent. Parents do not usually intend to teach their child (although later they may actively teach their child names of colors, shapes, and counting skills). Rather, in responding to their child's physical and social needs, parents promote communication skills that will permit their child more direct control of the environment. Much of the "teaching" is playful, occurring as games involving sounds and mouth movement (Moerk, 1977) when caregiver and child are engaged in shared activities, such as feeding, diapering, bathing, or playing with objects.

As parents introduce linguistic forms to help their child gain control of the environment, they are also introducing the child to some of the specific social functions of language. For example, parents teach children about greetings and farewells (e.g., "bye-bye," which is one of the first words with a specific function that young children acquire) and about polite request forms (e.g., "please" and "thank you"). Not only are parents providing an important lesson in the standard forms of language when they practice such language forms, but also they are drawing the child's attention to the situations in which these forms are used. In this way, the child's social repertoire is expanded and shaped toward the cultural standard. Some underlying social rules are exemplified, gently but frequently: say hello to people you know, ask before you take things, and acknowledge people when they give things to you.

BEFORE FIRST WORDS

As discussed earlier, children communicate long before they say their first words, partly because parents make their children's behavior function as social communication. Although there is evidence to suggest that some infant behavior is independently social, even without parent interpretation (Bower, 1982), parents assist children in controlling the environment by interpreting their babies' behavior as if it were communicative from the first days of life. Parents arrange the relationship between young children's behavior and the environment in ways that permit the children to learn about the contingent relationships between communication and changes in the world about them. This relationship is arranged in several ways.

Children begin "conversations" with their parents in the first weeks of life. Holding a child in a face-to-face position (i.e., nestled in the arms of the parent, who looks down toward the baby) while feeding establishes mutual gaze between the parent and the child. At first, the baby's gaze is brief and undirected. Any mutual gazing is controlled almost entirely by the parent. Within a few weeks, the infant sustains the gaze and directs it toward objects and people. Mutual gazing emerges as a truly cooperative effort of parent and child at this point and is often accompanied by parent verbalizations (Stern, 1974). A simple game of turn taking comes into play: I look, then you look. This purposeful exchange of glances resembles the beginnings of conversational turn taking (I talk, you talk).

As the infant's gazing becomes fully directed and more obviously controlled, the parents begin to solicit the child's attention by calling the child's name or by moving a toy or other object near the child. As the child systematically gazes toward objects in the environment, the parents begin using the child's gaze as a cue for language. For example, when the baby looks at the bright mobile above the crib, the caregiver may notice what the baby is looking at and comment, "Oh, look at the pretty birdie." Parent comment serves several purposes. First, it may reinforce the child's looking and, thus, may increase the likelihood that the baby will again gaze toward the attractive object. Second, the caregiver models the role of language in the turn-taking scheme, while allowing the child to take a turn that is well within the child's developmental repertoire (just looking). Finally, the caregiver models words that describe the event being noticed by the child. The immediate association between labeling and child attention to the event being labeled is critical to the child's learning of first words (Whitehurst, 1979). The child will understand words, i.e., associate them with an event, long before the child utters a word.

This general pattern for early "conversations" has many variations. The critical characteristics are spontaneous and responsive child behaviors (visual, motor, or vocal), caregiver notice of these behaviors, timing of the caregiver's response to the child's behavior, interpretation of behavior as social communication, and repeated turns by both child and caregiver. The interaction is bidirectional; child and caregiver each control the behavior of the other (Lewis & Rosenblum, 1977). The child not only cues the caregiver, but also encourages the caregiver by smiling, moving in synchrony with the caregiver's words, imitating sounds and gestures, and by noticing the caregiver's presence. The caregiver provides a structure for turns and interprets the child's behavior, allowing the child to function communicatively. Verbal interpretations include models of context-appropriate language; however, the caregiver's nonverbal responses (coming when the child cries, handing a toy when the child gestures, looking at the same objects the child is viewing) are also part of the communicative interaction. The timing of caregiver responses and caregiver elicitation of child responses also maintains the flow of the interaction (Stern, 1974).

Caregiver-child interactions are often social. Many interactions occur during caregiving routines; these interactions and other noncaregiving episodes are often enjoyable both for the child and for the adult. This pleasant social context makes learning and teaching unobtrusive and perhaps generally reinforces both participants for their involvement in the interactions.

Three classes of child behavior that develop in the first year of life allow children to participate in and learn from their "conversations" with caregivers: vocalization, imitation, and visual and auditory perception skills.

Child Vocalizations

Healthy babies vocalize from birth, usually letting out lusty yells to announce their entry into the world. Child vocalizations are especially important precursors to communicative competence. Differentiation of several distinctive vocalizations occurs early, and caregivers quickly learn to discriminate among sounds made by children. Mothers typically report that they can distinguish as many as six different meanings for their children's cries during the first months (Moerk, 1977). Most mothers, for example, say that they can distinguish the cries announcing hunger from those proclaiming pain or tiredness. Other vocalizations (coos, laughs, babbling, sound play) also emerge in the first months and are gradually differentiated into distinguishable sound patterns. At approximately 3 months, infants begin engaging in vocal dialogue with their parents (Stern, Beebe, Jaffe, & Bennett, 1977). Children vocalize a range of sounds to fulfill their turns in these conversation-like exchanges. The basic turn-taking structure observed in the exchange of gaze and mutual attention to the immediate setting characterizes these exchanges.

Children's vocalizations are communicative even in the first months of life. Children vocalize to solicit attention from caregivers; to respond to movements, sounds, and changes in the environment; to participate in social turn taking; and sometimes, apparently, simply to entertain themselves. A child of 8 months produces a range of specific sounds and expresses a number of social intentions consistently, i.e., uses specific intonational patterns to mark particular events (Lewis & Rosenblum, 1977). Using a combination of sounds and gestures, the infant is able to take turns in simple sound games and to direct listeners' attention toward desired objects. Such a child is socially oriented and an active explorer of the visual, tactile, and auditory world. This kind of interest in the environment provides many opportunities for caregivers to draw the child's attention to the forms and functions of language.

At first, parents respond to almost all child vocalizations, just as they respond to nearly all cries, smiles, and grimaces (Bruner, 1975). Such intensive caregiver responding encourages the child to continue these behaviors and teaches the child that attention and assistance can be obtained in this way. Perhaps because parental delight in first vocalizations seems to wane slightly with repetition, because the child learns that certain vocalizations convey particular meanings more effectively than others, or because parents have consistently responded to their child's attempts to communicate with models of standard forms, there is a systematic increase in the range of vocalizations that the child produces and a differentiation of intonations into patterns that convey particular meanings. At about 8 months of age, sometimes much earlier, the child has a vocal pattern for requesting that is clearly different from the vocalizations made in sound play or in attempts to imitate caregiver models.

Imitation

Infants appear to begin synchronizing their movements with the vocalizations of adults during the first few hours of life. Evidence of interactional synchrony (small movements of the infant in rhythm with an adult's words) has been offered (Condon & Sander, 1974), but the significance of this behavior is still controversial (Bower, 1982). Interactional synchrony may be a form of general communication that, although it does not transmit a message, indicates some degree of rapport between baby and adult (Bower, 1982). Possibly, early synchronous movements are the immediate precursors of imitation. In any case, such movements suggest an early sensitivity to language and the social presence of the caregiver.

Imitation as a social behavior appears in the first weeks of life (Maratos, 1973; Dunkeld, Note 1). Turn taking, a skill that is essential in communication, is seen in these imitative interchanges between adult and child: father opens his mouth, the baby opens the mouth; mother protrudes her tongue, baby protrudes the tongue. Babies as young as 1 week old imitate movements of particular body parts. This complex skill requires the integration of visual discriminations and complex motor actions. Furthermore, such imitations seem to indicate a child's early orientation toward social interactions (Bower, 1982).

During the first 18 to 24 months, a child frequently relies on imitation as a means of participating in interactions and practicing new behaviors. Early imitative interactions may promote the child's mastery of general communication patterns. The target of imitation changes with the child's increasing skill. At first, the child imitates motor movements; later, individual sounds and sound combinations. When the child has achieved relative mastery of a particular movement or component of the linguistic system, imitation of that class of events decreases rapidly. Older children and even adults, however, continue to use imitation as a strategy for learning new or especially complex nonverbal or linguistic behavior.

The caregiver is essential to the development of motor and verbal skills through imitation. Caregivers not only provide models of movements and sounds, but also they reinforce the child's imitative responses with attention, imitate the child's behavior with their own, and expand the child's behavior into culturally recognized communication forms. Child imitations are embedded in a bidirectional interaction pattern in which caregiver and child respond to each other's behavior; this dynamic interaction is basic to more elaborate social-communicative interchanges.

Visual and Auditory Skills

During the first years of life, children develop an impressive array of visual and auditory skills that form the basis for receptive language (Horowitz, Note 2). Newborns detect small variations in sounds in their environment (e.g., the difference between /p/ and /b/) that are critical to mastering spoken language. Babies only a few weeks old can distinguish their mothers' voice from those of other speakers (Mills & Melhuish, 1974). By 4 months of age, infants differentiate many sights and sounds and perceive relationships between events in the visual and auditory modalities (Spelke, 1976).

Studies of caregiver verbalizations to infants suggest that adults alter their speech in ways that maximize these emerging perceptual skills. Caregivers use a higher than usual pitch when speaking to infants, in this way possibly bringing their vocalizations into a frequency range that is preferred by infants (Sachs, Brown, & Salerno, 1976). The special style of caregiver speech (sometimes called baby talk or motherese) includes rhythmic and temporal patterns that attract children's attention and make the sounds of language more obvious to them. Adults typically include in their vocal interactions with infants babbling or sound play that incorporates simple consonant vowel combinations (e.g., baba, mama). The inclusion of these simplified sounds and sound patterns provides both models for children to imitate that are within the range of their abilities and, not incidentally, an opportunity for parents and children to take turns in a social interaction.

The frequency of parental vocalizations to their children may also affect children's language development. Lewis and Freedle (1973) have reported strong correlations between the frequency of mother vocalizations and the frequency of child vocalizations during the first 2 to 3 months of life. Clarke-Stewart (1973) has reported a positive relationship between the quantity of child-directed vocalizations and a child's linguistic competency during the period between 9 and 18 months.

As children begin to shape their first words, parents make systematic changes in the ways that they respond (Moerk, 1977). Typically, when children are very young, parents alter the tone, pitch, and rhythm of their speech, but they talk in sentences similar in length to those used with adult listeners; when the children are 8 to 9 months old, however, parents begin simplifying their language. Now parents speak in shorter sentences (typically around three or four words in length) emphasizing words that describe the immediate environment. They use questioning intonations more often, even though they may still be answering most questions themselves. These changes draw attention to the names of objects and assist children in acquiring vocabulary and simple syntactic forms.

FIRST WORDS AND BEYOND

A child's first words are a major developmental milestone for both the child and the caregivers. They mark the child's formal entry into the social-linguistic community in which the spoken word is a main mode of interaction. Surprisingly, it is often difficult to determine *exactly* when a child's first words were uttered. A child usually begins using words about 12 to 14 months of age, although there is considerable variability. Long before the first word is intelligible to an unfamiliar listener, however, the child is using consistent sound patterns to mark objects or events (Bates, 1976). These sound patterns may not be conventional words, but their consistent use suggests that the child has mastered a general premise of conventional language: specific utterances mark specific things.

Mastery of the articulation patterns that characterize standardized speech is gradual and not fully complete until the child is about 5 years old. The child's words are at first difficult to recognize and may continue to differ from standard forms for some time. Also, because the child is ascertaining the parameters of meaning for these forms at the same time, the child uses words in atypical contexts (Bowerman, 1978). For example, at first all four-legged, furry animals may be called doggie (or some phonetic derivative such as /oggie/ or /goggie/). When the form is used in an unusual context, the adult listener may not immediately recognize the child's attempt to label an event with words.

Parents and caregivers who are familiar with the child's emerging communication skills recognize and anticipate first words long before unfamiliar listeners are able to do so. Because of their many opportunities to observe the child's emerging receptive language skills, caregivers know what words or phrases the child understands, and their estimation of the child's language skills is quite likely to be different from that of a naive listener. Probably as a result of their familiarity with the child's idiosyncratic communication and their awareness of the child's receptive skills, parents begin making adjustments in their speech well before the child's first words are easily recognized. Parents continue to reflect what children say, however. They repeat and clarify utterances, as well as expanding them into more complete, formal sentences.

The tasks for the parent during the period when the child's language is developing rapidly are to continue to make the child's communication attempts function to control the environment, to offer further models of standard forms, and to encourage and support the child's use of language. Parents facilitate the child's learning of standard forms and of the conceptual information that underlies those forms. They use strategies that fit (by slightly exceeding) the current receptive and productive skills of the child. They alter their strategies to coincide with the child's mastery of simpler skills and to fit the context and purposes of particular interaction episodes (Moerk, 1976). The child's perceptual, vocal, and imitative skills and the early patterns of interaction established in the first year of life form the bases for the elaboration of the child's social and language skills. Emerging interaction patterns are consistent with those first seen in nonverbal turn-taking and game-playing interchanges, but the forms more closely resemble adult language. Almost always, parental teaching is low key, unobtrusive, and embedded in the context of positive, natural interactions (Schachter, 1979).

Parents and caregivers for the most part are extremely skillful in their structuring of the social-linguistic environment to facilitate language learning. They use a variety of strategies, including modeling, receptive testing, questions, sequences that ensure child participation and success in conversational interactions, feedback, and routines.[2] By employing a range of techniques, parents are able to adjust to the child's skills and the situation while maintaining a smooth, conversational interchange.

Modeling

All language potentially serves a modeling function. When caregivers talk while they diaper or feed young children, they typically describe the ongoing events, using words that refer to immediate events. Such parallel talk or incidental modeling of language is an important part of caregiver-child interactions. Using short sentences, varying the intonation to emphasize key words, and speaking slowly are ways parents may model their speech for their young child.

Parents also model language in specific ways that prompt the child to imitate. Parents encode, pairing names with objects and events. They often pause for a child repetition during the period when child imitations are most frequent (usually around 18 to 22 months). Models are embedded in questions ("Is this a ball?"), and imitations are occasionally requested directly ("Say ball."). Specific modeling and prompted imitations occur frequently during the time the child is acquiring first words. Although informal modeling continues for some time, active prompt-

---

[2]These categories are derived from Moerk (1976) and have been shown to be reliable in a longitudinal study of mothers and their normal and handicapped children (Rogers-Warren, Note 3).

ing of child imitations decreases soon after the child is able to imitate single words consistently (Nielsen, Note 4). Apparently, modeling and eliciting imitation are strategies parents use during the transitional period when the child is initially acquiring a productive vocabulary and is refining the articulation of sounds. Parents continue modeling as a form of corrective feedback, however.

Effective modeling follows the same conversational format observed in parent-infant interaction. When the child has shown an interest in a particular object or event, the caregiver follows the child's lead and presents models while the child's attention is focused. The model-pause sequence provides an opportunity for the child to participate in the conversation by using a standard linguistic form.

Receptive Testing

Parents often ask a child to demonstrate knowledge. Particularly during the time the child is mastering first words, many parent queries are presented in a form that allows the child to indicate understanding by responding nonverbally (e.g., "Where's your tummy?" "Give me the ball." "Show me the doggie."). Gradually, caregivers alter their questions to require a verbal response (Nielsen, Note 4). Receptive testing type questions do occur in parent-child conversation after the child has a considerable verbal repertoire, but they are used primarily when the child is mastering new skills (such as color names) and as a backup when the child is unable to answer a question (e.g., "Where did the boy go?" "Can you show me where he went?").

Receptive testing fulfills a variety of important functions. First, it helps the parents ascertain what their child currently knows so that they can adjust their own language to the child's skill level. Second, it introduces the child to the functions of questions, but allows the child to make nonverbal responses that are within the child's level of competency (Rogers-Warren, Warren, & Baer, 1983). Third, receptive testing provides the parents with opportunities to model specific forms (such as color names) contingent on the child's nonverbal responses or to offer elaborations if the child imitates. In addition, receptive testing may prompt the child to answer questions verbally, since such questions often include a model for a child response (e.g., "Where's the blue one?").

Receptive testing ensures at least a three-unit conversation: (1) caregiver question, (2) child response, and (3) caregiver feedback or comment. As the child becomes verbally imitative, a four- or five-unit conversation is possible. Sometimes, parents request nonverbal answers in series, and a long interchange occurs. They may also embed receptive testing questions in stories to maintain the child's attention. Because child responsiveness to receptive testing is typically high, it is an especially useful strategy for maintaining child participation in conversations, even before the child has an extensive verbal repertoire.

Questions

In general, questions are used to determine what the child knows and to maintain child participation in interactions. Caregivers ask questions that vary in both form and function (Shatz, 1978; Nielsen, Note 4). Although the forms of questions change as the parents' child-directed language becomes more complex, the critical variable in the use of questions is the complexity of child response required. At first, parents ask for simple responses,[3] such as labels for objects and actions. Later, they ask about attributes and relationships. As the child's language increases in complexity, parents begin to ask questions that have more open-ended answers (e.g., "Why do you wear boots when it is raining?") or questions that depend on the child's understanding of temporal relationships (e.g., "What would you like to do after you have your lunch?"). Gradually, parents stop asking questions for which they probably know the answer (e.g., "What is this?") and begin to ask questions that solicit the child's opinion or information not already available to the parents (e.g., "What did you have for lunch at preschool?").

Questioning is one of the primary conversational structures in which parents teach interactions, because it allows the child to be a full participant in such interchanges. The shifts in the complexity of form, the response required of the child, and the cueing value of the question are adjusted to fit the child's changing linguistic and conceptual skills (Shatz, 1978). By following the child's comments with questions that seek elaboration, the parent facilitates the child's acquisition of typically relevant, sequenced statements to describe a particular event or object. By linking the child's statements together, they may be helping the child to develop some of the more complex conversational skills that are used by adults and older children. As in most other instances of parents' efforts to facilitate language, the parents follow the child's lead, using questions either to gain needed information or to support the child's portion of the conversation.

Sequences or Chains of Parent Behavior

Parent comments, models, receptive testing, and questions sometimes occur in sequences that appear to support the child's learning or allow the child to respond correctly. Parental efforts to reduce the complexity of the required child response and thus to ensure a successful conversational episode have been described as "breakdowns" by Moerk (1972, 1977) and as "scaffolding" by Schachter (1979). An example of such a sequence is:

---

[3]This hierarchy of questions is based on Lee (1974). It has been verified and used to categorize mothers' questions and child answers by Nielsen (Note 4).

Speaker	Question or Response	Type of Response Expected
Mother:	What happened?	Open-ended
Mother:	Where did the doggie go?	Specific response
Child:	(No response)	
Mother:	Did he go in his house or did he follow the boy?	Choice of specific responses required
Child:	(No response)	
Mother:	He followed the boy, didn't he?	Yes/no response to affirm mother's description required by tag question
Child:	Yeah.	
Mother:	Yeah, he followed the boy to the store.	None; mother expands child response

Typically, mothers use only two or three questions in sequence, but long chains are occasionally observed (Nielsen, Note 4). Moerk (1977) reported that mothers sometimes use sequences of questions to increase the complexity of the child's responses. Such sequences begin with a simple question and, following an appropriate child response, proceed to a more complex question; they are called buildups.

Series of questions, particularly those ordered from complex to simple, may shape more complex child responses by modeling possible alternative answers (as in the example, when the mother gave a choice of responses following her open-ended and specific questions). They may also help familiarize children with the various types of questions and answers, and the relationship among them. Such series reflect parents' attention to children's abilities and may be one of the ways in which form and function of language are taught.

Feedback

The importance of caregiver feedback has been one of the most controversial issues in the study of child language. Since the early 1960s, linguists have consistently argued that there was no evidence of parental reinforcement for correct use of forms in parent-child interactions (Brown & Hanlon, 1976); at the same time, behaviorists have posited a critical role for reinforcement. Subsequent studies have confirmed that there is little parental praise per se for correctness, but other types of feedback occur with considerable regularity (Schachter, 1979; Rogers-Warren, Note 5) and may have a reinforcing function for child language. Adult feedback takes both verbal and nonverbal forms.

The caregiver's compliance with a child's requests is an important type of nonverbal feedback for communicative behavior. The caregiver functionally reinforces the child's attempts to communicate by allowing the child's "communications" to control the caregiver's behavior. Caregivers provide verbal feedback in a variety of ways: they imitate what the child says; they expand the child's brief utterances into longer, more semantically or syntactically complete forms; they attempt to interpret what the child says; and they provide general confirmation of the child's utterances, even when they do not precisely agree with the form of the utterance. Caregivers also provide corrective feedback, usually in a subtle and positive form, that is another form of potential reinforcement. Parents rarely correct the form of child utterances, although they do occasionally correct the information aspect of an utterance. The following are examples of several types of parent feedback:

Child Utterance	Parent Feedback	Type of Feedback
Cookie?	Do you want a cookie?	Interpretation and expansion
Me going.	Yes, you're going, too.	Acknowledgment (and acceptance of grammatically immature form)
It's a doggie.	No, it's a *lamb*. It just looks like a doggie.	Correct for content
Jamie coming.	Uh-huh, Jamie's coming up the walk.	Acknowledgment and expansion of child's form.
I rided my trike.	Yeah, you rode your trike.	Acknowledgment and correction for form

Almost all feedback is given in a positive, confirming tone of voice, suggesting that caregivers are more interested in generally supporting the child's use of language to communicate than in correcting form or content. When corrections are made, they are framed in the same types of positive statements used to confirm child utterances. Many researchers have reported examples of parents confirming the child's utterance and continuing to offer a correct model (as in the last statement of the example).

Expansion of a child utterance into a form that more nearly resembles a correct adult form is one of the most frequent and effective means of providing models for appropriate language (Schumaker & Sherman, 1978). The effectiveness of expansions as teaching devices may be related to the fact that they are contingent on the child's utterance and immediate interest. Parental expansions following child utterances exemplify two basic rules of parental language teaching: (1) follow the child's lead, and (2) talk about the here and now. The immediacy of expansions also creates an opportunity for the child to contrast his or her utterances with those of the parent, which may facilitate discriminating the differences between the two utterances.

Routines

Almost immediately, routines are established in the shared day-to-day existence of parent and child. Shared activities, such as feeding, bathing, and dressing, establish contexts in which specific types of communication are repeated. Other routines, such as saying goodbye, playing favorite games (e.g., peek-a-boo, where's your tummy?), reading familiar stories, or saying nursery rhymes also provide contexts that support language use. Because the contexts are relatively consistent and because the verbal responses that occur in those contexts are usually limited, the child masters a set of verbal skills appropriate to these contexts rather quickly. When routines are familiar, the child can anticipate what comes next and add an appropriate verbalization to the sequence. Parents sometimes facilitate the child's participation in the verbal portion of routines by prompting with incomplete sentences (e.g., "and this little piggy went . . .").

SPECIAL PROBLEMS OF HANDICAPPED CHILDREN AND THEIR CAREGIVERS

In principle, the task facing caregivers of handicapped children is identical to the one encountered by caregivers of normal children. Caregivers must structure a child's immediate social communication environment to facilitate the development of increasingly sophisticated and conventional communication skills. They must establish patterns of positive social interaction with the child in order to provide a framework for shaping communication skills, and they must match their strategies to the child's abilities. Behaviors of both child and caregiver change over time, but the critical match that facilitates communication development must be maintained. The social communication repertoire of the normal child changes over time; most caregivers adapt to the child's range of behaviors and rate of change with apparent ease. The adaptations made by caregivers to support the normal child's communication are an extension of the skills required in normal adult conversation, and the direction of change for both child and adult is toward the format of adult social communication (Figure 3-1).

Figure 3-1 Communicative Match between Caregiver and Child

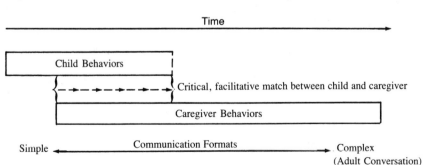

It is more difficult for caregivers to establish and maintain the facilitative match when the child is handicapped. Caregivers must make greater adaptations in their behavior to create a match that supports the handicapped child's participation in interactions and promotes the development of more sophisticated communication. Because the handicapped child's ability to communicate is impaired, adaptations may be required of the caregiver that are beyond the usual range of conversational skills of competent adult speakers. Even if the caregiver has the specific skills required to facilitate language development in the handicapped child, the need for intense, long-term application of those skills may make it difficult for the caregiver to create and sustain the critical match between child and caregiver. Furthermore, behavioral characteristics of the handicapped child may be less reinforcing than are those of a normally responsive child so that the caregiver may be required to continue with relatively less support from the child. As a result, the pairing of caregiver strategies and child responses necessary for language learning may not occur frequently enough to foster the rapid development of communication skills.

Characteristics of Handicapped Children

Several characteristics of developmentally delayed children may impede care-giver-child interactions: problems of vision and learning; a general lack of respon-siveness and social initiative; difficulties in determining subtle differences among objects (e.g., shades of color or differences in shape); problems in determining cause-and-effect relationships (e.g., flipping a light switch and a light coming on); generally low levels of motivation. These impairments share a common basis in the lack of discrimination and generalization skills, which are integral to all learning; the language learning that occurs in the context of caregiver-child interactions is no exception. Generalization is the tendency to respond to a new stimulus (e.g., a new object, word, action, person, or place) in a way that was already learned as a response to another, similar stimulus. Conversely, discrimi-nation is the tendency to respond to a new stimulus only when it is identical or very similar to the stimulus with which the response was originally acquired (Hill, 1981). Deficits in these basic processes are manifested in several ways that affect caregiver-child interactions.

The normal infant brings a wide range of skills to the task of language learning. These skills include the ability to detect small differences in sounds, particularly those of human speech. For a variety of physiological and environmental reasons, the developmentally delayed child may have fewer auditory processing skills. Not only does this make the task of learning the sounds of spoken language more difficult, but also it may hinder the child's recognition of sounds in the environ-ment that typically signal caregiver-child interaction. For example, if the child does not readily distinguish the caregiver's voice from other voices or differentiate child-directed utterances from adult-adult conversation, it is unlikely that the child will attend when the caregiver initially speaks. The recognition of a familiar caregiver is important to both the child and the caregiver, however. The direction of the child's attention offers an opportunity to observe (and to learn) something specific about the environment. The caregiver cooperates by noticing the child's attention and responding to it, e.g., by talking, by smiling, or by touching the child. The child's attention also reinforces the caregiver, maintaining the caregiver's attention.

The more severely handicapped the child, the fewer basic motor and perceptual abilities are intact and available for use in interactions during the first few weeks or months of life. Although these abilities may eventually emerge, they are likely to develop at a slower rate than those of a normal child. For example, the period of time in which the child is unable to control reaching or systematically direct gazing is relatively longer for the handicapped child. During this longer development period, the caregiver must make more adaptations to the child's behavior than are typically required during a normal child's development. Encouraging a severely delayed child to shape a communicative pointing gesture and to vocalize concurrently to indicate wants may take months, whereas a similar response might be mastered by a normal infant in a few days.

In general, the handicapped child is less responsive to the physical and social environment. Combined with the handicapped child's delayed or deficient perceptual and motor abilities, this lowered responsiveness impedes the establishment of the turn-taking types of interactions that characterize early social communication between caregiver and child. As noted earlier, in caregiver-normal child dyads, turn taking in a conversation-like format is well established in the visual, vocal, and motor modes by the time the child reaches 12 months of age. Vietze, Abernathy, Ashe, and Faulstich (1978) reported that developmentally delayed children and their parents are much slower to develop turn-taking interchanges. At 12 months of age, developmentally delayed children have not usually mastered the vocal turn-taking structure of conversations. Instead, they continue to vocalize concurrently with their mothers, frequently do not take their turns, and are not fully imitative in these exchanges. Because caregiver teaching occurs in conversational formats that depend largely on the child's responsiveness to the adult, the delay in establishing such patterns of interaction further slows the handicapped child's development.

Most handicapped children are less responsive to adult feedback than are normal children. Behaviors that support or serve a reinforcing function in interactions with normal children (e.g., continued conversation, eye contact, adult proximity) may not do so with developmentally delayed children. No evidence suggests directly that adult attention is less reinforcing for developmentally delayed children; however, the responsiveness of retarded children is known to improve when tangible or more intense social reinforcers are provided contingent on target behaviors. At least a part of the difficulties that developmentally delayed children have in learning language in natural interactions may be due to a lack of functional reinforcers available in those interactions.

Developmentally delayed children may present certain behavior problems that alter the content and focus of parent-child interactions. Children who do not follow instructions readily require more specific directions, typically in the form of repeated instructions or physical assistance. The relative difficulty of everyday tasks for developmentally delayed children and their typically short attention spans also contribute to the need for additional instruction from the caregiver. Marshall, Hegrenes, and Goldstein (1973) reported that mothers of developmentally delayed children differ significantly from mothers of young normal children in the proportion of instructions in their child-directed speech. This distribution of the content of mothers' speech is a logical adaptation to the behavioral characteristics of developmentally delayed children. However, as was emphasized earlier, language teaching occurs most frequently and most effectively at the lead of the child and without an adult agenda for direct instruction (Schachter, 1979). Caregivers' adaptations to the behavioral characteristics of developmentally delayed children may result in fewer opportunities for teaching language-related skills.

Finally, as the child grows older, the same deficiencies that define developmental delay (e.g., difficulty in acquiring and generalizing new information, short-term memory constraints, difficulty in making fine discriminations between similar stimuli) continue to make language learning through interaction more difficult for the developmentally delayed child. The child who does not easily discriminate fine cues for behavior must rely on the more obvious ones. In learning grammatical conversational speech, the older developmentally delayed child may rely only on direct cues, such as questions or instructions, and may not respond to the more subtle cues, such as pauses in the caregiver's speech, content of language other than instruction, facial expressions, and gestures that indicate an opportunity to speak. The child's attention to discrete cues in caregiver behavior seems especially necessary in view of the descriptions of caregiver feedback and support for verbal behavior. Caregivers seldom praise or punish for verbalizations, but they typically provide corrective feedback in the form of models or expansions of the child's utterance. If the child cannot discriminate the content of the feedback, the reinforcing function of the feedback is lost. As a result, handicapped children may have considerable difficulty mastering the subtleties of complex language.

Although handicapped children show a range of impairments and some are more serious than others, any developmental deficit in a child is likely to make the caregiver's job more difficult. The caregiver must directly elicit more responses from the handicapped child, must make the auditory and visual aspects of the environment more distinguishable, and must provide events that are more specifically reinforcing for the child. When the developmental delay is relatively mild, such adaptations may be accomplished much as they are for normal children.

When the child is severely impaired, however, special strategies may be needed to support child language learning.

It is important to recognize that the handicapped child's behaviors may change the social environment in specific, important ways. The amount of time required for caregiving activities is likely to be greater when the child is developmentally delayed. When the child begins to talk, or if the child is learning an alternative communication mode (e.g., sign language), the caregiver may need to direct more effort toward eliciting clarifications (e.g., when the child's articulation of sounds is impaired) or interpreting the child's response and elaborating it into a complete, standard communication form. The combination of the child's special needs and the lengthened developmental period may significantly reduce the proportion of caregiver-child interaction time that has a language teaching function. Overall, the environment of the handicapped child may be significantly different from that of the normal child. Only a few studies have examined the characteristics of mothers' speech to their handicapped children (see Rogers-Warren, Warren, & Baer, 1983 for a review of these studies). The most scientifically sound of these (Rondal, 1978) did not show significant differences in the semantic content or syntax of mothers' speech to normal and handicapped children; however, no study has examined patterns of mother-child interaction across more than a few weeks.

Environments for Language Learning by Handicapped Children

The everyday interactions of caregivers and children are apparently adequate for most normal children to acquire language. When a child is not acquiring language normally, adjustments in the environment and specific intervention with the child may be necessary to make the normal child-rearing environment function as a language learning setting. Large-scale changes in parent support for language (e.g., increased questions, increased prompts, use of material reinforcement) are effective in increasing a child's level of verbalization (Harris, 1975). In addition, incidental or environmentally based interventions to teach social communication behaviors or learning strategies may be a useful, long-term means of improving communication skills.

One-to-one structured teaching effectively increases vocabulary and syntax, but generalization of new learning across persons, settings, and events is sometimes difficult to ensure and is not a certain outcome of intervention efforts (Stokes & Baer, 1977; Warren, Rogers-Warren, Baer, & Guess, 1980). Such training, therefore, does not guarantee productive language use. Although increased rates of child-directed language may increase child responses, there is no evidence to suggest that parents effectively maintain their increased prompting across settings and events or that increases in child-initiated interaction result from these procedures. Thus, the procedures may work while they are being actively employed, but the generality of their employment and, consequently, of their effect is unknown.

More importantly, intervention strategies that rely on major, artificial changes in the environment do not prepare the child to respond in other, more typical settings where the intervention is not in effect. In addition, parent-based or therapist-based techniques often place the child only in the role of the respondent and do not teach social interaction skills that ensure further participation in interactions.

The ideal environment for the language-deficient child is one in which learning to learn is stressed, rather than learning answers. To this end, the environment should be arranged to support the handicapped child's active exploration and description of the setting in much the same way that caregivers support and accommodate the normal child's attempts to learn about the environment. The single difference in the environment for a developmentally delayed child is the amount of effort required from the caregiver to support continuously approximations of communication that allow the child to be both initiator and responder. Thus, the ideal teaching environment contains persons who do not feed into the child's lowered responsiveness, but seek to increase responsiveness without becoming unusually directive of the child's behavior.

Like the language learning environment for a normal child, an ideal environment for the developmentally delayed child should include appropriate language models presented when the child's attention is focused on relevant aspects of the setting or interaction; frequent opportunities to respond and appropriate cues for responding; and a supportive, responsive caregiver who follows the child's lead and consistently provides feedback about the child's attempts to communicate. It may be necessary, however, to compensate for the characteristics of developmentally delayed children that typically disrupt the normal teaching processes. Because the child is typically less responsive, the environment should evoke and support verbalizations in more obvious ways. For example, the environment must contain things the child wants so there will be a need to request (Hart & Rogers-Warren, 1978). The same objects or events that are of interest to the normal child may not attract a developmentally delayed child, so a range of possible play materials should be provided and the child's interests observed. The caregiver must notice what the child finds attractive and use instances of focused attention to support language. Because the child is less active (or at least less directed), the natural teaching opportunities may be fewer; because the child's attention may be of short duration, teaching opportunities may be brief.

It is important for caregivers to be aware of the child's precise skills. While caregivers typically adjust the structural aspects of their input to the child's level, there is no information to indicate how exactly they tailor their requests for information and feedback. Caregivers of a less responsive child may have a more difficult time matching their behavior to the child's skill level. Furthermore, because the developmentally delayed child progresses more slowly, changes in child skill may not be noted immediately. Cheseldine and McConkey (1979) reported that parents alter their language to include more appropriate models for specific forms once they have been instructed about their child's linguistic skills and goals for needed skills have been set.

It is critical that caregivers not only offer consistent information about the structure of the child's language, but also assist the child in learning about the ways in which language can be used to control the environment. Bates (1976) and others have pointed out that one of the most important aspects of parent-child communication is the assumption of intentionality by the parents. Parents typically treat a young child's utterances as having meaning, discriminate different meanings among utterances marked by constant sounds but different intonation, and assist the child in communicating his or her intentions. Consistent parental responses to different types of early nonverbal communication attempts seem gradually to shape those attempts into recognized gestures, words, and sentences. Bruner's analyses of normal mother-child interactions (Bruner, 1975; Bruner, Roy, & Ratner, 1980) and their impact on the development of language suggest such a process.

Finally, it is important that at least some settings be arranged specifically for language learning. Settings that are pleasant and playful for both the child and the caregiver allow them to focus their attention on language and social interaction. While a great deal of language may be learned incidentally by the normal child, the developmentally delayed child may require relatively less complex contexts to notice and acquire new linguistic information. A context and purpose for communication and interaction should be established and maintained, however, through games and activities that engage the child's attention. Teaching and learning must be integrated in the context of social interaction prompted by the stimuli available in the setting.

Caregiver Behaviors for Language Learning by Handicapped Children

Arranging the social communication environment involves several specific caregiver behaviors (Hart, in press; MacDonald, in press).

Recognize the Child's Communication Attempts and Make Them Functional

The primary motivation for communication is control of the environment. By making the child's attempts to communicate control some aspect of the setting (e.g., access to toys, food, continued physical contact), it is possible to increase the child's communication attempts and to demonstrate repeatedly the functional contingencies for language. When the child regularly communicates with the caregiver, modeling and requests for elaborated utterances can be incorporated into the interaction without decreasing child participation.

The handicapped child may have a variety of atypical communication strategies. It is important to recognize these communication attempts, to make them functional for the child, and to build on them as a means of teaching more standard communication forms. Until the child is regularly communicating, however, function is more important than form; that is, using any form of communication is more important than using the correct form (i.e., gesture, word, or sentence). Thus, attention should be focused on making the communication attempt function to control the environment before feedback for form is given.

Arrange the Environment To Encourage Child Attention and Engagement

The setting should contain objects and events that are known to be interesting and motivating for the child, although it may take careful observation to determine what objects and events are attractive to a severely handicapped child. Whatever they are, the environment must offer opportunities for the child to control them. This includes opportunities for the child to control the behavior of the caregiver and implies that the caregiver is first and foremost responsive to the child's attention and interests. The more limited the child's abilities, the more specific the arrangements needed to stimulate engagement with the environment. For example, toys on a high shelf may elicit requests from a typical 3-year-old, but it may be necessary to place toys at eye level in order to attract the attention of a nonambulatory child.

Follow the Child's Lead

Establishing joint attention, providing immediate feedback, and giving direct language models all depend on the caregiver's timing and attention to the child's behavior. Because the handicapped child is less likely to solicit attention, the caregiver must follow the child's lead and direct the teaching at those times when there is a close relationship between language and event *for the child*. Modeling is effective only when it coincides with the child's attention; following the child's lead is likely to result in more frequent opportunities for effective modeling. The caregiver should teach when the child indicates an interest; the caregiver should talk with, never at, the child.

Increase the Saliency of Modeling and Feedback, while Maintaining the Flow of Conversational Interactions

Children with hearing impairments may need more visual support for the language that they are hearing. Talking about the here and now, using gestures, and pointing to the object being talked about may increase the child's comprehension of caregiver speech. The strategies of normal children's caregivers, e.g., using a higher pitched voice, speaking more slowly, and using more varied pitch in child-directed utterances, may be useful.

Allow Time for the Child To Respond

When a child is slow to respond, caregivers tend to keep talking. The inclusion of an obvious delay or waiting period after a question to prompt an answer or an initiation has been shown to be a useful means of increasing a child's verbal responses (Halle, Marshall, & Spradlin, 1979). Including pauses allows the child to take a turn and may help the child learn about the natural cues for verbalizations.

If the Child Does Not Respond or Responds Inappropriately, Request a Simpler Response

Breaking the required response down into components, offering choices, or allowing the child to answer nonverbally are all strategies for maintaining the child's participation in the conversation.

As the Child's Skills Increase, Ask for More

Systematic shaping of child responses (i.e., first asking for one word, then requiring two words when the child has mastered a one-word response) can be used within conversational interactions to expand the child's productive repertoire. Simple prompts (e.g., "Tell me more." or "Give me a whole sentence.") that require the child to finish a sentence may be used to encourage more complex responses. Shaping, based on natural contingencies (e.g., requiring the child to request a desired object) may be highly functional when the child has reached that level of linguistic competence.

Limit Instructions and Directives

There are few appropriate child verbal responses to a directive, and the proportion of speech given to instructing the child directly affects the proportion of speech that can be given to language teaching. Sometimes, increasing child compliance may be a necessary first step in altering the social interactions of the caregiver and the child. In other instances, simply giving clearer, more appropriate instructions and helping the child comply may be sufficient to shift the distribution of caregiver speech away from intense instruction giving.

Make Use of Routines and Games To Teach Language

Language can be learned during dressing and feeding routines as well as in play. The systematic nature of routines can help a child who has difficulty with rapidly changing verbal and social settings. The inclusion of verbalizations in established routines provides opportunities for a child to "fill in" the verbal components and to anticipate the next step. When paired with specific teaching techniques, routines can provide many regular language teaching opportunities throughout the day.

Prompt and Reinforce the Child's Communication

The environment is arranged and caregivers' behavior altered to promote language use and to facilitate its occurrence. Because language is a social behavior, prompting and reinforcing should occur in the contexts of social interchanges, not simply as a training strategy. Stereotypic questioning and routine praise are not functional social behaviors for the child or the adult.

The quality of prompting and of reinforcing may be as important as the quantity (Hart & Rogers-Warren, 1978). The difference between a parent who is delighted at the child's first words and the parent who is providing a token and praise for a correct answer is considerable. It is not always possible to be delighted, but it is possible to focus intensely on the child's attempts and respond to them with pleasure and interest. Both prompts and reinforcement are tremendously important, but they must be built into the overall social, turn-taking interaction, not imposed on it artificially.

Do Not Punish the Child for Mistakes

It is critically important that parents do not punish a young child for mistakes, stammering, or articulation errors. This could cause the child to talk less, not more. When the child makes errors, one of the corrective techniques previously specified should be used, or the error should be ignored. In any case, since the primary goal is to keep the child talking, punishment must be avoided in all cases.

MEASURE OF ENVIRONMENTAL EFFECTIVENESS

One measure of the extent to which an environment enhances language learning is through an assessment of child initiative and rate of spontaneous talking. If the child is frequently engaged in interactions with the caregiver and play materials available in the setting, the environment is probably functioning well for the child. If the rate of spontaneous verbalization (i.e., verbalization that does not result from direct questions or demands) is moderate and if there are regular interchanges between caregiver and child, opportunities to learn language are occurring and the child is probably responding to these opportunities. Over time, the rate at which a child is acquiring or displaying new forms and new functions for language in a particular setting should indicate the effectiveness of that setting as a language learning environment.

CONCLUSION

The acquisition of language is the most significant developmental accomplishment of young children. This is no less true for handicapped children. Historically, no special efforts were made to facilitate the language development of handicapped children until they reached elementary school age. By then, however, the children had lost crucial years during which development might have been accelerated. Furthermore, when treatment did begin, parents were typically excluded from major roles in the remediation effort. Recent increases in knowledge about the ways in which children learn language suggest a completely different strategy. Intervention efforts should begin as soon as possible, and parents should play a major role in arranging an optimally facilitative learning environment. Parents, teachers, and therapists must be educated in the basic process of language acquisition and its facilitation and must actively program the environment of these children. Such efforts could greatly enhance the development of handicapped children and ensure them of the brightest future possible.

NOTES

1. Dunkeld, J. *The function of imitation in infancy.* Unpublished doctoral dissertation, University of Edinburgh, 1978.
2. Horowitz, F.D. *Receptive language development in the first year of life: A selective review of literature.* Kansas Early Childhood Research Institute, University of Kansas, Lawrence, KS, 1978.
3. Rogers-Warren, A.K. *Kansas Early Childhood Institute: Final Report.* June 1982. Available upon request from the Early Childhood Institute, Working Paper Series, 130 Haworth Hall, University of Kansas, Lawrence, KS 66045.
4. Nielsen, L.M. *Mothers' questions to their language-learning children.* Unpublished thesis, University of Kansas, Department of Human Development, Lawrence, KS, 1982.
5. Rogers-Warren, A.K. *It takes two: Toward a behavioral analysis of mother-child interactions.* Paper presented at the annual meeting of the Association for Behavior Analysis, Milwaukee, Wisconsin, May 29, 1981.

REFERENCES

Bates, E. *Language and context.* New York: Academic Press, 1976.

Bower, T.G.R. *Development in infancy.* San Francisco: W.H. Freeman, 1982.

Bowerman, M. Semantic and syntactic development: A review of what, when and how in language acquisition. In R.L. Schiefelbusch (Ed.), *Bases of language intervention.* Baltimore: University Park Press, 1978.

Brown, R., & Hanlon, C. Derivational complexity and order of acquisition in child speech. In J.R. Hayes (Ed.), *Cognition and the development of language.* New York: John Wiley & Sons, 1976.

Bruner, J.S. The ontogenesis of speech acts. *Journal of Child Language*, 1975, *2*, 1-19.

Bruner, J., Roy, C., & Ratner, N. The beginnings of request. In K.E. Nelson (Ed.), *Children's language* (Vol. 3). New York: Gardner Press, 1980.

Cheseldine, S., & McConkey, R. Parental speech to young Down's syndrome children: An intervention study. *American Journal of Mental Deficiency,* 1979, *83,* 612-620.

Clarke-Stewart, K.A. Interactions between mothers and their young children: Characteristics and consequences. *Monographs of the Society for Research in Child Development,* 1973, *38*(6-7, No. 153).

Condon, W.S., & Sander, L. Neonate movement is synchronized with adult speech: Interactional participation and language acquisition. *Science,* 1974, *183,* 99-101.

Ferguson, C., & Snow, C. (Eds.). *Talking to children: Language input and acquisition.* Cambridge: Cambridge University Press, 1977.

Halle, J.W., Marshall, A.M., & Spradlin, J.E. Time delay: A technique to increase language use and facilitate generalization in retarded children. *Journal of Applied Behavior Analysis,* 1979, *12,* 431-439.

Harris, S.L. Teaching language to nonverbal children—With emphasis on problems of generalization. *Psychological Record,* 1975, *82,* 565-580.

Hart, B. Environmental techniques that may facilitate generalization and acquisition. In S.F. Warren & A. Rogers-Warren (Eds.), *Teaching functional language.* Baltimore: University Park Press, in press.

Hart, B., & Rogers-Warren, A. Milieu language training. In R.L. Schiefelbusch (Ed.), *Language intervention strategies.* Baltimore: University Park Press, 1978.

Hill, W.F. *Principles of learning.* Sherman Oaks, CA: Alfred Publishing, 1981.

Lee, L.L. *Developmental sentence analysis.* Evanston, IL: Northwestern University Press, 1974.

Lewis, M., & Freedle, R. Mother-infant dyad: The cradle of meaning. In P. Pliner, L. Kramer, & T. Alloway (Eds.), *Communication and effect: Language and thought.* New York: Academic Press, 1973.

Lewis, M., & Rosenblum, L.A. *Interaction, conversation, and the development of language.* New York: John Wiley & Sons, 1977.

MacDonald, J.M. Language through conversation: A model for intervention with the severely language delayed. In S.F. Warren & A. Rogers-Warren (Eds.), *Teaching functional language.* Baltimore: University Park Press, in press.

Maratos, M.P. Nonegocentric communication abilities in preschool children. *Child Development,* 1973, *44,* 697-700.

Marshall, N.R., Hegrenes, J.R., & Goldstein, S. Verbal interactions: Mothers and their retarded children vs. mothers and their nonretarded children. *American Journal of Mental Deficiency,* 1973, *77,* 415-419.

Mills, M., & Melhuish, E. Recognition of mother's voice in early infancy. *Nature,* 1974, *252,* 123-124.

Moerk, E.L. Principles of dyadic interaction in language learning. *Merrill Palmer Quarterly,* 1972, *18,* 229-257.

Moerk, E.L. Processes of language teaching and training in the interactions of mother-child dyads. *Child Development,* 1976, *47,* 1064-1078.

Moerk, E. *Pragmatic and semantic aspects of early language development.* Baltimore, MD: University Park Press, 1977.

Rogers-Warren, A., & Warren, S.F. Pragmatics and generalization. In R.L. Schiefelbusch (Ed.), *Communicative competence.* Baltimore: University Park Press, in press.

Rogers-Warren, A., Warren, S.F., & Baer, D.M. Interactional bases of language learning. In K. Kernan, M. Begab, & R. Edgerton (Eds.), *Environments and behavior: The adaptation of mentally retarded persons*. Baltimore: University Park Press, 1983.

Rondal, J.A. Maternal speech to normal and Down's syndrome children matched for mean length of utterance. In C.E. Meyers (Ed.), *Monograph No. 50 of the American Association on Mental Deficiency,* 1978.

Sachs, J., Brown, R., & Salerno, R. Adults speech to children. In W. von Raffler-Engle & Y. Lebrun (Eds.), *Baby talk and infant speech*. Lisse, Netherlands, Swets & Zeitlinger, 1976.

Schachter, F.F. *Everyday mother talk to toddlers*. New York: Academic Press, 1979.

Schumaker, J.B., & Sherman, J.A. Parent as intervention agent. In R.L. Schiefelbusch (Ed.), *Language intervention strategies*. Baltimore: University Park Press, 1978.

Shatz, M. Children's comprehension of their mothers' question-directives. *Journal of Child Language,* 1978, *5,* 39-46.

Skinner, B. *Verbal behavior*. New York: Appleton-Century-Crofts, 1957.

Spelke, E. Infants' intermodal perception of events. *Cognitive Psychology,* 1976, *8,* 553-560.

Stern, D. Mother and infant at play: The dyadic interaction involving facial, vocal, and gaze behaviors. In M. Lewis & L. Rosenblum (Eds.), *The effect of the infant on its caregiver*. New York: John C. Wiley & Sons, 1974.

Stern, D.N., Beebe, B., Jaffe, J., & Bennett, S.L. The infant's stimulus world during social interaction: A study of caregiver behaviors with particular reference to repetition and timing. In H.R. Schaffer (Ed.), *Studies in mother-infant interaction*. London: Academic Press, 1977.

Stokes, T.F., & Baer, D.M. An implicit technology of generalization. *Journal of Applied Behavior Analysis,* 1977, *10,* 349-367.

Turnbull, A.P., & Turnbull, H.R. *Parents speak out*. Columbus, OH: Charles E. Merrill, 1978.

Vietze, P.M., Abernathy, S.R., Ashe, M.L., & Faulstich, G. Contingent interaction between mothers and their developmentally delayed infants. In G.P. Sackett (Ed.), *Observing behavior: Theory and applications in mental retardation* (Vol. 1). Baltimore: University Park Press, 1978.

Warren, S.F., Rogers-Warren, A., Baer, D.M., & Guess, D. The assessment and facilitation of language generalization. In W. Sailor, B. Wilcox, & L. Brown (Eds.), *Methods of instruction for severely handicapped students*. Baltimore: Brooks Publishers, 1980.

Whitehurst, G.J. The acquisition of meaning. In G.J. Whitehurst & B. Zimmerman (Eds.), *The functions of language and cognition*. New York: Academic Press, 1979.

Part II

Environmental Considerations for the Practitioner

Chapter 4

A Developmental Environment for Child Care Programs

Carolyn L. Thomson and *Jennifer Ashton-Lilo*

The environment is often overlooked when educational goals and objectives are established for preschool children, even though ecological psychologists have demonstrated that it has a marked influence on the behavior of both typical and atypical children (Barker & Gump, 1964; Gump, 1975; Kounin & Gump, 1974; Schoggen, 1975; Smith & Connolly, 1980). Curriculum planning should involve not only an outlined program for the child, however, but also an analysis of environmental adaptations that may be necessary if the child is to function competently and comfortably during the school day (Ashton-Lilo, 1981). In this chapter, the term *environment* is used broadly to refer to the physical and human factors with which the child comes into daily contact: preschool activities and materials, the daily schedule, the arrangement of space and equipment, the aesthetics of the classroom, and all types of contacts with other children and adults. Centers vary a great deal in their environments because of the limitations of the physical space, the type of program, the quantity and quality of materials and equipment, and the interaction patterns between children and caregivers. As a result, the impact of the environment on children varies from program to program.

The majority of buildings used for early education in the United States were not originally designed with young children or handicapped children in mind. Many programs are conducted in remodeled houses, in buildings designed for business or office operations, or in church rooms intended to house young children for an hour or two during church services or Sunday school at the most. Adults who work in such redesigned spaces know the value of child-oriented bathrooms (i.e., with adapted stalls for wheelchairs, low basins, and diaper-changing areas) attached to the classroom. A play yard adjacent to the children's room is also invaluable. Ready access to a play yard can facilitate positive social interaction among children and can add to the teachers' enjoyment of the day, too, since teachers are not forced to regiment the children as they travel to and from the play yard. Convenient storage areas are also important, because materials that are not readily accessible tend to remain on the storage shelf instead of being used to provide a more varied and interesting program for the children served. Stairs, wherever they are, only serve to complicate and inconvenience the operation of a program for handicapped children.

Thought must be given also to the comfort and support of adults, who frequently experience fatigue and tension in working with children daily. Too often, there is no pleasant space for staff to relax and plan (Cohen, 1974). Such inconveniences contribute to teacher "burnout" and can result in a high rate of teacher turnover. Environmental factors must be examined in terms of the teachers' well-being in order to ensure adult continuity in programs for young children. Even though young children are cared for by dedicated adults day after day, that care can be improved when appropriate changes or environmental adaptations are made to assist teachers in preventing behavior problems, promoting appropriate behaviors, and maximizing development (Ashton-Lilo, Thomson, & Baer, 1981).

Regardless of a center's location, the program's overall philosophical goals and a variety of practical considerations (e.g., amount of space, number of staff) are the basis for many decisions concerning the classroom environment. Individual differences and developmental variations required by growth and changes in children should also have a major influence on determining appropriate environmental modifications.

Arrangement, organization, size, density, noise level, even the color of the classroom directly and indirectly invite a range of behaviors from children and teachers. Generally, the more pleasant classrooms have good lighting, are attractively painted, and are clean and uncluttered (Greenberg, 1975; Hess & Croft, 1972). Since direct manipulation of materials and a variety of sensory experiences are extremely important to the development of many types of skills, the room should offer many interesting activities to motivate children to explore and experiment throughout their social day.

Space and equipment must be arranged to support selected goals for the center and for individual children. Reducing the probability of the occurrence of unwanted behaviors is important. Crowding, for example, inhibits social interaction, although it also inhibits aggression (Loo, 1972; McGrew, 1970). Too few materials for children's use may lead to excessive competition for those materials, resulting in aggression (Rohe & Patterson, 1974). Such responses from children are obviously in direct opposition to the developmental goals of increasing positive peer interaction. A classroom with no extra space makes it difficult for children to leave a project that is being worked on until it can be finished, which might inhibit the development of long-range attending skills, as well as pride in the completion of tasks. Too much space can also be a problem, however, since it tends to invite children to run around aimlessly (Smith & Connolly, 1980). Spaces that are unnecessarily large or facilities that consist of several separate rooms make supervision difficult and may reduce children's awareness of available activities.

Lack of awareness in turn may limit the development of specific skills or practice in the self-selection of activities, which is often a major program goal. Furthermore, if teachers must move children in groups to use the bathroom, play yard, or napping area, it is difficult to support the developmental goals of independence and self-management for the children in the group.

Materials should be stored in readily accessible areas so that children have maximum opportunities for choosing and selecting materials according to their own tastes and wishes. The access to materials by nonverbal children may be especially important in a teacher-dependent organizational system because these children may be unable to request desired materials. Good organization and child accessibility can help all children by reducing unnecessary waiting (Thomson, Ashton-Lilo, & Baer, 1981). Good organization is particularly important in terms of preventive discipline, too, for behavior problems often develop when there is no particular activity focus. Placement of activities is another important factor; because of children's distractibility, books and preacademic activities should not be placed adjacent to noisy areas.

Thus, knowingly or unknowingly, goals for children are supported or discouraged by the physical organization, arrangement of equipment and furnishings, and the architectural layout of the facility.

PROGRAM CONCERNS

The effects of the physical environment on the quality of life for a young child must be of primary concern to teachers. Consideration must be given to functional arrangements of materials and equipment, organization, beauty and craftsmanship, and the proper care of the facility, the equipment, and the materials used in daily living. Children placed in makeshift surroundings receive a subtle message that they are not important enough to be given primary consideration and that surroundings in which many adults would be reluctant to spend an entire day are good enough for children.

Health and safety regulations define minimum standards for the children's physical well-being, but the effect of the environment goes far beyond physical safety. Teachers may unwittingly foster sterile learning experiences because of undue concern about messiness or dirt. For example, they may present fingerpaints, woodworking materials, or waterplay only infrequently and thus may limit children's opportunity to use a wide range of materials. Such reluctance on the part of a teacher can deprive children of many types of desirable learning experiences. In such ways, priorities of this nature can influence a program to the detriment of children, for a child is more likely to profit from the experience of working with real tools and making something with wood than to profit from not making the mess that the experience would have created.

The organizational structure of a center directly affects the quality of the children's program in a variety of ways. One such organizational factor is group size. Ruopp (1978) reported that, in smaller sized groups (15 or fewer children), there were more positive and more frequent teacher-child interactions, both individually and in subgroups. In other words, teachers were more responsive to children when the class size was smaller. In addition, the children were engaged in more reflective and innovative thinking, were generally more cooperative and compliant, and demonstrated less aimless wandering and noninvolvement. Finally, the children were less distracted by other children and could give more attention to adults when class size was smaller.

The ratio of staff to children in a group has also been shown to influence the program. When there is a generous ratio of adults to children, teachers command and correct children less, interact more with other caregivers, and participate more in center-related activities, such as planning, arranging and cleaning up materials, and keeping records (Ruopp, 1978). As the number of children per adult increases, so do aggressive, destructive, and aimless behaviors. If materials and activity accessories are added to crowded settings, however, cooperation and constructive participation can be increased (Rohe & Patterson, 1974).

Staff organization affects the quality of everyday life for children and their teachers. Assigning staff the responsibility for children in areas (zones) has been demonstrated to have a number of positive results (LeLaurin & Risley, 1972). With a zone arrangement, teachers supervise a specific area, rather than a specific group of children. It has been shown that children can move through routines much more quickly and efficiently under this arrangement, thus having greater amounts of time to spend on play and other important learning experiences.

The physical space and choice of equipment and materials in a center should provide a wide range of sensory experiences. Many centers lack variety in the hard and soft aspects of materials and equipment that have been selected for them (Jones & Prescott, 1978). Environmental softness (e.g., upholstered chairs, pillows, carpet, laps, clay, sand, water, mud, Play-Doh) facilitates sensory responsiveness. Materials characterized by softness more closely resemble those things found in a child's home and are more responsive to certain kinds of child manipulation. Such a softness dimension is particularly important for children in all day programs, because these children need greater variety in sensory stimulation and more inviting opportunities to curl up and relax. For this purpose, an excess of space is an advantage because it provides room for large, upholstered chairs and sofas, as well as variety in other furniture.

A center's provision of interesting play spaces and a variety of choices encourages children's participation and use of play materials (Kritchevsky, Prescott, & Walling, 1969). These researchers reported that (1) the more activities that are offered, (2) the more variable the play spaces, and (3) the more complex the play spaces (addition of accessories and additional play mediums, e.g., water in the housekeeping area and flour for Play-Doh), the less likely it is that teachers will be required to guide children in finding activities or be called upon to settle disputes between children. These considerations are important when teachers' goals are to help children acquire self-direction through self-selection of activities and concentrated participation in those activities.

Another influential environmental factor in children's learning is the sequence of events throughout the day. For example, children are less attentive to a teacher who is reading stories aloud if storytime is preceded by a physically active period than they are if reading time is preceded by a physically inactive period. In addition, the amount of transition time from one activity to another and the number of disruptive behaviors during transitions increase when transitions follow physically active periods. Rearranging the schedule so that a physically inactive period precedes transition decreases both the time required and the number of disruptive episodes during transition (Krantz & Risley, 1977).

Clearly, the physical facility, equipment and materials, staff assignments, and daily schedules all have an impact on the quality of children's programs. While some of these factors may not be conveniently adapted, others could be easily restructured to improve the program and to make it a more comfortable and pleasurable daily experience for both children and adults.

DEVELOPMENTAL CONCERNS

Environmental arrangements and adaptations must be sensitive to individual differences if the developmental goals for each child are to be met. Teachers must understand sequences of development and the impact of one skill area on another. For example, teachers must be aware of the ways in which fine motor skills affect the acquisition of cognitive skills and, in turn, the ways in which cognitive skills affect the development of social skills. If a child is having difficulty, is not making developmental progress, or is demonstrating behavior problems, the first step toward more effectively meeting that child's individual needs is to examine the environment carefully and make adjustments as needed. Adjustments may be made in several ways: by rearranging the physical environment, by modifying a particular material or activity, or by encouraging participation in specific areas. Such modifications may facilitate the development of particular skills, which may then stimulate other areas of development.

The acquisition of motor, cognitive, language, self-help, and social skills are underlying developmental goals in most programs. Often overlooked, however, are ''survival'' skills, which encompass not only the skills mentioned, but also those needed in all other settings—group care, the child's home, the neighborhood.

Functioning Independently

Learning to function independently, to take charge of one's own needs, and to make decisions is a most important aspect of sound development. Overdependence in children (and adults) is burdensome for others and makes the dependent person feel even more helpless. If children are willing to try to care for their personal needs, teachers may be more willing to help with other important tasks. Fortunately, most children demonstrate a strong desire to do things on their own very early. Toddlers, for example, try very hard to feed and dress themselves (Bee, 1978); all such efforts at self-help must be respected.

In the preschool and day care environment, the teacher can foster children's independence by

- making materials accessible to children. Low, open shelves that make it easy for children to remove and return materials give children a sense of control. If a teacher occasionally notices and comments that the material was correctly placed by saying ''You put the _____ on the right shelf all by yourself!'', the child will probably be encouraged to remove and return materials appropriately the next time, too.
- providing child-sized furniture and individual containers for materials. This allows the children to move about and adapt the environment to personal needs.
- inviting children to participate in decision making. Letting children make choices, discuss options, and have some control over their own lives increases children's awareness of their own ability to make decisions.

Developing Responsibility

Learning to take responsibility often evolves from a sense of independence and confidence in one's own ability to do something without assistance. The teacher can arrange the environment to help children take responsibility by

- expecting children to help in set-up and clean-up of activities. Such participation encourages a sense of belonging, as well as concern for the room, material, and other children's rights.
- asking older children to help younger ones. Putting an older child in charge of getting the snacks, a ball, or a tricycle with a younger child helps the older child take responsibility in completing an instruction as well as in helping another child.
- planning child-directed activities. If a teacher is too directive and if the environment is not arranged with the development of responsibility in mind, children are denied opportunities to develop responsibility.

**Responding, Initiating, and Maintaining Appropriate Interactions
with Adults and Peers**

There are many different ways in which normal young children, as well as those
who are developmentally delayed or impaired, respond to others and initiate
interactions. They may use not only language, but also a variety of nonverbal and
less traditional ways of communicating. As children develop and become more
skilled, however, language plays an increasingly important role in communication
and in social interactions with others. Communication and social interaction are
composed of three basic components: responding to others, initiating (for compan-
ionship or help), and continuing an interaction. The teacher can arrange the
environment to facilitate communication and social interaction by

- setting up activities so that two or more children can participate at one time.
  For example, placing easels next to each other, dividing puzzle pieces into
  two bowls, having one paint container for every two or three children, putting
  two chairs at a small table on which science materials have been placed,
  providing equipment (e.g., a rocking boat) that requires two or more children
  to activate it are ways of promoting interaction, and a child need not have
  fully developed communication skills to benefit from these techniques. In
  fact, as in these examples, the teacher can arrange the environment so that the
  environment interests the children and gets them next to each other, which is a
  most important start for any social interaction.
- presenting accessories to games (e.g., fire hats and hoses) that need more than
  one person to play. In fact, games of all kinds can be excellent vehicles for
  interaction if they are developmentally appropriate and not too structured.
- suggesting that one child choose another child to help in an activity. If, for
  example, one child is helping the teacher move a table, the teacher may
  suggest that the child find a friend to help. Such redirection provides opportunities for interaction with peers that is often avoided by a child who is
  always seeking to be "teacher's helper."

Engaging in Activities Alone

Just as appropriate peer and adult interaction is important, so is it important for
children to be able to occupy and entertain themselves independently through
work or play. Most day care and preschool settings allow little time or space for
children to do things alone; children are in groups most of the time. There are
times, however, when a child may not wish to be with peers or adults. Children
should be encouraged to develop the skills to engage in appropriate individual
activities, since such activity helps to promote independence. Teachers must

watch for the occasional child who withdraws excessively and plan specifically for such a child to ensure that time alone does not become an avoidance or escape time. The teacher can arrange the environment to provide a variety of opportunities for the child to be alone by

- providing each child with a private space. This space may also be used to hang coats, store special mementos, or keep treasures from home. If there is enough space, a corner for unfinished "products" is also desirable. Such a private space conveys that a child is special and unique, which may be particularly important in large child care centers.
- arranging a cozy corner where a child can go to be alone with a friend or book. The corner may have pillows, a large carton (in which to hide), big chairs, a small couch, or a card table covered with a sheet.
- making various materials available to the child for self-selection and providing a mat or space designated for that child's own work materials. Such an arrangement allows a child to get some Lego, parquetry, or a puzzle and to work on the individual mat for some period of time without interference. Self-selection allows children to make choices and decisions and to come to the realization that they do have some control over their lives.

Engaging in Self-Expression

Most children seem to enjoy exploring materials of all kinds. Self-expression and exploration require the freedom to try old materials in new ways and to discover new materials. The ways in which the environment is arranged can either encourage or discourage exploration. The teacher can arrange the environment to prompt self-expression by

- providing various materials and experiences, both familiar and unfamiliar, for children to explore. Commonly, self-expression is related to the arts. Giving children paints, clay, and collage materials of different textures, consistencies, and colors allows them to create and experiment. The same principle holds true in the areas of language and dramatic play. Imitating sounds, rhyming words and sounds, and making up new words with children tend to stimulate new ideas and thoughts. Changing the location of furniture and equipment or setting the table in a new way are other ways to encourage self-expression. Letting the children move furniture to help in the rearrangement may also have interesting results.
- asking questions rather than continuously instructing or giving directions. Teachers should let children explore to find out for themselves. Covering a table with a sheet and then speculating as to what might be under it may

provoke interesting ideas and investigation. Teachers' comments concerning the process itself rather than products will often maintain or encourage further interest and exploration. For example, "How are you getting that beautiful color of pink?" is much more likely to prompt self-expression than is "You made a beautiful pink color."

- spending private time with each child to become better acquainted. By spending time alone with the child (weekly, if possible), a teacher will become aware of the child's special interests and can use this knowledge to extend the child's exposure to materials and activities, thus encouraging exploration of special interests. Such understanding often enhances the teacher-child relationship, which, in turn, facilitates the resolution of problems that may arise with that child.

- suggesting exploration instead of making models for children. Some children may be unwilling to explore because they "know" that they do not have the skills to reproduce a model even remotely as "good" as the teacher's. With materials and opportunities to create freely without models that dictate an ideal product, however, children at all developmental levels are usually willing to participate in exploration and experimentation, assuming the teacher values the process itself as a prime learning experience.

- appreciating and noting good ideas and trys. A wink, a smile, a nod, or an approving comment by the teacher is important, especially for children lacking in self-confidence. Acknowledgment encourages children to try to generate more good ideas and more diverse ways of using a material.

Learning New Skills by Building on Established Ones and Integrating Them

The goals and philosophy of individual centers, in large part, determine the general direction of the center and its programs. As the population of the center changes, perhaps because of the integration of younger children or delayed or handicapped children, the philosophical direction of the center may also need to change. For example, it may become necessary to involve more parents or to add a home-based component.

Regardless of the philosophy of the center, activities should be provided that not only allow children to perfect previously acquired skills, but also stimulate the emergence of new skills. To ensure that such learning occurs, the activities that are offered should be chosen according to the answers to questions such as the following:

- Is there a match of activities to children's skill levels?
- Is the activity presented attractively in order to increase children's interest?

- Is the activity checked for children's safety?
- Is it accessible to children?
- Is the activity versatile in teaching various skills?
- Is there a sufficient quantity of materials for encouraging exploration?
- Can the materials be adequately supervised with the existing staff/child ratio?

How can teachers assess interactions between a child and the environment? A formal assessment is often a beginning point, but formal assessments often fail to provide information about which activities a particular child might enjoy or how that child might function within a larger group situation. Thus, teachers must translate specific assessment information into real life classroom situations; this is not an easy task. A better approach is the use of observations, checklists, and one-to-one special times, when a child and teacher are together but not necessarily "working." Such informal assessments provide teachers with additional information about the child's development level and special interests, as well as about the impact of the environment on the child.

In classrooms that are arranged in interest areas, a teacher can use checklists for recording skills as they are demonstrated by a child. By means of a simple scoring system, a teacher can easily determine, within the art area, for example, which children can match, point to, or label colors without assistance or prompting. Based on this information, the teacher can present materials and activities in an individualized manner, ensuring that children are kept on their own learning edge, i.e., the point at which they use already acquired skills to learn new ones. Such a "match" (Hunt, 1961) assumes a point of maximum interest that is most likely to encourage learning.

Another way for teachers to facilitate a good match is by presenting materials that can be adapted for children who are hesitant to participate. For those children who tend not to participate in a variety of activities, color cards might be given for children to "spend"; each time they enter an area, they spend a card. When all cards are spent, they may go back to a preferred area. Such a system is one way for teachers to ensure that children sample different areas. Sometimes, the room itself can be rearranged to give certain activity areas prominence, thereby increasing the likelihood that children will take notice of certain materials.

Always, the room should "speak for itself"; that is, activities should be set up in such a way that children can tell what is available and how many children can participate. The placement of dividers, shelves, or tables can indicate the type of activities appropriate for a given area. For example, one chair or mat with a material on it indicates to a child that the activity is to be done independently; two chairs signal that a friend can participate. Both types of activities (alone and in groups) should be set up within the classroom in order to foster the acquisition of social skills.

ECOLOGICAL COMPONENTS

Space, grouping of children, scheduling, and activity set-up have a direct influence on the children. These factors cannot easily be separated from other factors, such as the quality of teacher attention, peer interaction and the curriculum content. Each component embodies a particular philosophy and a resultant influence; all components intertwine in the daily stimulation of children through planned and unplanned experiences.

Space

Finding adequate and appropriate space for an early education program is oftentimes a challenge. Because state and local regulations determine the type of space in which licensed programs for young children can be operated, there are variations from state to state and from city to city. Most states require 35 square feet per child, exclusive of halls, bathrooms, and storage space; frequently, 50 square feet of play space per child is suggested as desirable. Most educators would welcome 50 square feet per child, but it is nearly impossible to find that much space on ground level unless a center is built specifically for children. Where that amount of space is available, it often has intervening walls that limit supervision, thus increasing the staff needed. In addition, there are financial considerations. While it may be possible to find large quarters for one class of children, it is not always financially feasible to operate a center with fewer than three preschool classes. Infant and toddler classes must charge high fees to pay the required personnel. When administrative and rental costs are added to this expense, the cost of care often becomes prohibitively high.

Most early childhood programs suffer from a lack of money, understaffing, and limitations of equipment and materials. The added element of daily inconvenience for the adults only adds to the frustrations. Everyone benefits—children, staff, and parents—when necessary routine activities can be carried out with a minimal investment of time and effort.

Several areas and their basic functions must be considered in rearranging an existing facility or planning a prospective physical layout. For example, the entrance should be of sufficient width to accommodate the parent, child, and accompanying siblings, or a family with a child on crutches or in a wheelchair. The lobby space should be large enough to accommodate several parents and sets of children in the process of coming and going. Because the lobby is probably the most traveled portion of the building and the source of many first impressions, it should be as spacious and attractive as possible.

Teachers, parents, and visitors need a place for private conferences, orientations, and group meetings. Depending on the importance that the center attaches to parent involvement and education, it may be necessary to designate specific space for this function. In any event, confidential teacher-parent interactions should not take place in the classroom, where there are many distractions, or in the offices of the administrative staff, who have their own responsibilities. Space must be provided in which such confidential conversations can be scheduled. Separate office(s) near the entry way can enable staff to be conveniently available to parents. Glass windows can make it possible for staff to keep aware of events going on in the immediate area and still provide privacy and confidentiality.

If at all possible, bathroom facilities should be built within the classroom to facilitate teachers' supervision and children's learning of self-help skills. Sinks and toilets should be child-high and wheelchair-accessible. Rooms for infants and toddlers should be large enough to allow for diapering tables and several potty chairs for children who are in toilet training. Children's toilet rooms should have one doorway for entering and one for exiting in order to reduce confusion and accidents generated by children coming and going through a single door simultaneously.

Food should be prepared in an area sufficiently distant from classrooms to provide protection to children who might wander into the kitchen or be drawn to it by the smell of cooking. A kitchen that can accommodate young children participating in cooking experiences makes a valuable contribution to the learning experiences offered in the program, however.

A separate all-purpose room that can be used for eating, rainy day activities, and napping frees teachers from having to perform the daily ''miracle'' of transforming a single room from a play activities area to a lunch room to a nap room to a snack area to a play activities area once again—all within the space of a few hours. The extra room is a great convenience in other ways, too; if children are in one room all day long, teachers may not be able to reorganize or set up new activities easily; too, a dining area spares the classroom floor from dropped or spilled food, thus keeping the classroom cleaner.

Napping frequently takes place in the classroom. This is inconvenient for the teachers, however, because they are unable to arrange and prepare the next set of activities while the children are napping. Storage of cots is another inconvenience; their storage may use space that could be much better used for other purposes. Furthermore, if children nap in the same room as the playroom, children who awaken early must remain on their cots until it is time for everyone to get up; such a situation makes individualizing nap schedules difficult.

The problem of sick children is one that confronts every center. Children who are not feeling well, who are coming down with a communicable disease, or who are convalescing might remain at school if an appropriate isolation room is available. An isolation room with a glass wall makes it possible for sick children to be supervised by an administrative staff member or a teacher. With such services available, parents would not be forced to leave work and possibly forfeit salary because their child became mildly ill during the school day.

Small quiet rooms are desirable and serve several functions. They can be used for tutoring individual children and for talking privately with a child. They can be used, too, as a place for a few children to hear a story, to play a game without interference, or to experiment with noisy materials, such as musical instruments. Some facilities have found ways to provide for such special activities within the classroom itself by using large panels of plywood that hinge and lock into each other.

Planning and preparation space for teachers is essential for ongoing assessment of children and review of the program. These activities might be carried out within the classroom if children eat, play, or nap in another room; record keeping, use of curriculum resources, and teacher discussions simply cannot occur in the classroom when children are there. The allotment of time and space for these activities is vital to maintaining quality of program and of individual progress, however. Too frequently, it is assumed that planning and training will occur even though teacher space is not made available. The truth is that the less convenient the facilities are for staff planning and preparation, the less likely it is that such planning and preparation will occur, resulting in negative consequences for the program.

Adults need a place for personal belongings and relaxation, however brief, to minimize the tensions of teaching. Going to the bathroom occasionally is no relief from the unending strain of day long interactions with children. Such space need not be large, and it can be combined with space for teacher planning and training. In any event, the adults' space should be cheerfully painted and decorated, provide a reasonable measure of comfort (chairs, tables, and sofas), and some degree of privacy. It is desirable to have cold drinks and coffee available, too.

Playgrounds are most convenient when adjacent to classrooms. Doorways that open directly into the yard make it possible for indoor and outdoor play to take place concurrently in agreeable weather. Such an arrangement also allows children self-management of toileting and independent comings and goings. Sliding doors or doors that have Plexiglas windows in the lower half decrease the risk of opening a door into a child standing on the other side. Playgrounds that vary in contour, ground texture, play media, and equipment invite young children to try different types of activities and so acquire a variety of skills. Covered outdoor space adjacent to the classroom makes the outdoor space usable over longer portions of the year in that play can be confined to the sheltered area and thus children can be protected from rain and the hot summer sun. Opportunities for interesting play experiences are increased if water is available (when the weather is warm enough) for sand and water play and for mud and garden experiences. Space for both active and sedentary play should be arranged with concern for safety and continuity in activities. Movable equipment, such as certain climbing apparatuses and various walking board arrangements, present opportunities for frequent rearrangement of portions of the playground. Shrubs and trees, placed strategically, help to provide protection, boundaries, and privacy.

Spatial Considerations in Classrooms

Classrooms should be arranged to accommodate both group and individual activities: open-ended activities, such as blocks and art, and more closed or structured activities, such as puzzles and parquetry. Traffic patterns should be arranged so as to avoid interference with the children's activities. The arrangement of rooms that must be reorganized each day for meals and naps should be carefully thought out so that this reprogramming can be done in minimal time, with minimal adult effort, and with minimal disruption of the children's program.

Accidents that occur frequently in a certain area of the classroom are a signal to the adults to look for underlying causes in equipment arrangement, architectural design, or daily scheduling. There may be dead-end passageways or bathrooms with only one doorway that leads to collisions and bumps; furthermore, these areas may be difficult for children on crutches or in wheelchairs to navigate. If the existing space layout presents such problems, teachers may need to schedule children at different times for different activities. For example, it may be necessary to have some children go to the bathroom and then to help put toys away, while another group does the reverse. Another cause of accidents may be that some activities have been set up under unsafe conditions. The protection afforded by nonslip, absorbent rugs under the water containers is a must in water play activities, for example. In addition, teachers must check to see that there are clearly defined traffic patterns to direct the movements of children around activities and that toys and materials are not allowed to clutter passageways. Such precautions are particularly important for children with impaired vision or unstable mobility skills.

Learning activities or interest centers can be set up on a permanent basis if space allows. If the room must be reorganized several times daily, however, some learning centers may have to be created daily. Folding tables and chairs that stack greatly facilitate multiusage of the classroom. Locating learning centers around the periphery of the classroom not only leaves the center area open for general traffic or for assembly of a group of children, but also facilitates transition times. Open space can be used for blocks, play, music, and movement. In addition, special learning center activities can be set out on carpet squares or a flat surface made of hollow block, thus using the open space more flexibly than when it is dominated by tables and chairs.

Crowding

The number of children playing in a space may facilitate or impede positive social interaction. Research indicates that a higher density of children for a given space results in less social interaction and physical contact (Loo, 1972; McGrew, 1970; Shapiro, 1975). Rohe and Patterson (1974) did find some increase in aggressive, destructive, and unoccupied behaviors in high density situations. However, those behaviors were greatly increased when there were few materials for children to play with rather than many materials to use. High density increases cooperative behavior if many materials are available for children to use, but decreases cooperative behavior if few resources are available. Thus, it appears that crowding of children obstructs one of the most common goals of parents and teachers of young children—the development of social interaction skills. If, for some reason, a high number of children must be in a given space, Rohe and Patterson suggested that materials be added to increase the number of activity options, thereby facilitating constructive cooperative participation.

Kritchevsky and associates (1969) suggested that the integration of two or more materials into a single activity increases the holding power of that activity in terms of the child time invested and relevance of child participation. Examples of such combinations might be Play-Doh, flour, rolling pins, and cookie cutters; blocks, wooden people, and small cars; movable packing boxes, hollow blocks, and a blanket; or sand, water, and digging tools. As opposed to clay, blocks, boxes, or sand alone, these "super units" prove to be more interesting to most children and tend to require less teacher effort, both in helping children to find new things to do and in dealing with play disruptions. Thus, while adding additional resources may decrease the open space in a room and increase the complexity of activity, it also may be a strategy for increasing positive behavior in a difficult situation.

Staff Resources and Grouping of Children

Children may be variously grouped at different times for different reasons. A group may be designed for formal learning, for various types of social experiences, or for small "family" groupings. Family grouping is designed to strengthen relationships between a teacher and a small group of children. The teacher has a special responsibility for each child in the group: monitoring each child's progress, seeing that individual tutorial needs are met, and "living" with each child through daily care experiences. Greenberg (1975) calls these "minigroups" and plans such experiences on a daily basis. Such a grouping strategy is especially useful in all day programs; it can reduce discipline problems, ensure that a child is not neglected (a possibility if all teachers are responsible for all children), add a good measure of pleasure to teaching young children in an all day setting, and relieve social density in the playroom in that minigroups can be taken out of the room on a staggered basis. If the number of children in a room at one time is reduced from 18 to 12, the feeling of an entire session is changed; it provides a sense of space that is relaxing to both children and teachers.

Groups are frequently composed of children who are at a similar level of skill development, which makes it easier to plan and implement activities. However, older children may be skilled at subgrouping, while a group of young children may need help simultaneously. This may create havoc for the teacher. In such instances, the only alternative may be to create more and smaller groups or to create groups that are more heterogeneous. Such a grouping strategy makes it possible to split up subgroups of children whose interaction with each other has become more important than teacher instruction and provides opportunities for more skilled children to assist less skilled children. If the age range of the children is a spread of two to three years, such a group could be seen as more closely resembling siblings in a family—an important consideration for some people. Selection of activities in a heterogeneous group may be more complicated, but the socially disruptive behaviors may decrease. When staff is minimal, developing such alternative ways to provide group experiences becomes important. Whenever possible, volunteers can be utilized to help supervise children in self-selected activity periods.

One staff person for every 5 or 6 children is a desirable ratio. Obviously, when the ratio is one adult for every 9 or 10 children, it is much more difficult to respond personally to each child. Yet, the financial structures of many child care settings can support only two adults in a classroom of 14 to 20 children. Small group experiences are still possible, however; one way to maintain the small group component in such a program is to have one teacher manage a subgroup while the other teacher monitors the remaining children.

Scheduling

In determining a sequence of activities, teachers must be sensitive to the overall needs and preferences of the children. All day programs have quite different constraints on their schedule and organization than do other programs. Overall, there are six basic issues to be considered when planning a schedule:

1. What does each child need to learn?
2. At what level is each child developmentally?
3. What materials or activities can be used to teach needed skills?
4. How can an individual child's goals be integrated into the daily schedule?
5. How can the environment be set up to invite maximum child participation?
6. Which staff members work best with which children?

Teachers must have a global outlook of the day, of the room, and of what the room and setup can teach. This global view will and should vary during the year as the teachers and children get to know each other better and as children acquire a greater array of skills. The length and type of activities may vary greatly from fall to spring and from spring to summer. In the fall, children may need longer active periods to help them adapt to the new group situation. In the spring, the time spent in small groups or alone may be increased as children are able to tolerate longer quiet periods and longer self-management periods. The summer schedule in most climates should include more outdoor time to give both the teachers and the children a welcome change of pace. Regardless of the time of year, teachers should attempt to plan a schedule that is comprehensive in its scope of activities and includes time for the practice of a variety of skills during the day. The basis for such scheduling is individualized assessment of children and their interactions with the environment. Adaptations can then be planned as needed.

Whatever daily events are included in a schedule, periods of high physical activity should be alternated with periods of rest or quiet activity. As noted earlier, learning experiences that follow physically active periods are more likely to be marked with inattention, slow compliance in carrying out group instructions, and disruptions than are activities that follow a quiet or restful period. Therefore, a teacher may be wise to avoid scheduling activities such as large group experiences, which require a high level of attention from children, immediately after a physically active period (Krantz & Risley, 1977).

Traditionally, classroom schedules contain several basic components and routines: child-selected activities; small group periods for preacademics and planned learning experiences; large group activities, such as songs, rhythms, and games; bathroom routines; and mealtimes. All day programs also include nap or rest time, lunch, and even breakfast.

Child-Selected Activities

Self-selected participation involves activities in which children are allowed to make choices within certain specified and subtly arranged situations. The teacher plans for the activity in advance and gives instructions only to guide and encourage participation; the teacher does not tell the children how to use the material or carry out the activity. In these periods of the day, children have options—they can choose to participate in the activity and decide for themselves how to use the materials if they do become involved. The type of activity, the number of children and staff involved, and the physical layout dictate the type of play that ensues. Many children become more involved and exhibit fewer problem behaviors in child-directed activities when an adult is on hand to serve subtly as facilitator.

In most centers, there is little teacher observation of children and their abilities or deficits during these free activity periods. This omission is unfortunate, for child-initiated play periods are prime opportunities for teachers to determine which activities children prefer, which they participate in, and what their level of participation may be. Seldom is information gathered about how the participation changes as children become more skilled or as the location is changed (e.g., if painting is moved outside), even though such information is critical to individualized programming and should be incorporated in teachers' planning for individual children and for the group.

Small Group Time

Generally, small group time occurs at a scheduled time each day. Typically, children work at tables on given activities for a specified amount of time. Although the children all begin together, they finish at different times because of individual variations in skill levels. Behavior problems often emerge if children have to wait for the next activity, however, and scheduling changes may be needed. For example, small group experiences could be integrated into free choice time. Since preacademic skills are generally emphasized during the small group portion of the day, the classroom could include as one choice a special "work" table or interest center. With this kind of arrangement, children with limited attention spans could alternate "work" and "play" time. They could spend time at the work table, go to the blocks for a short period when finished, and then return to the work table (Rowbury, Baer, & Baer, 1976).

If all children work in small groups simultaneously, the amount of time that a teacher can spend with a child who needs extra attention may be limited. Rotation of children, therefore, may not only decrease the disruptiveness or boredom that can result from unnecessary waiting, but also may allow the teacher to spend more time with each child. It must be remembered that an occasional child may need additional one-to-one tutorial sessions for learning certain skills.

Large Group Activities

There are several basic reasons for large group activities: (1) to teach basic group participation skills, such as listening to others, taking turns, and paying attention to the teacher; (2) to extend the teaching of concepts, such as farm animal names, counting, and rhyming through songs, games, and chants; and (3) to have a "holding" activity for children while waiting for various other activities to be set up (this holding time may also serve as the transition time in which children meet as a group to plan for the day). In addition, a large group time has been a traditionally popular part of most preschool programs.

The preparation, setup, and content of large group activities are important. The setup can be almost anywhere in the room, or it can be outdoors. Regardless of where it takes place, the content should be lively, varied, and well planned in order to maintain children's interest and participation. Group experiences, because they demand a great deal of attention, should occur in a setting where there are minimal distractors.

When skill acquisition is the emphasis, careful consideration should be given to the individual needs of the children in the group. A first consideration is the length of time that each child would be expected to participate. Fifteen minutes is perhaps too long for some children, especially for those who are very young, have impaired hearing or vision, or have short attention spans. During large group time, another activity may be necessary for them. These children could be included briefly at the beginning or end of the group time with the length of their participation increased as they become more skilled or oriented to the expectations that are held for the group as a whole.

The activities for this type of group learning should also be geared so that each child is allowed to participate at his or her own level. If the activity has to do with farm animals, for example, and John is working on developing vocabulary and Mary on the awareness of sounds, then John could be asked to label the cow and Mary to make the sound of a cow. Other children can be served in still other ways: to develop concept extension, "Sue, can you think of a different animal?" or to develop memory, "Bobby, can you tell us what animal you asked us to sing about yesterday?"

If group participation skills are emphasized, then the teacher should minimize distractors that might compete for the child's attention and interfere with the learning of the skills that the teacher has in mind. For example, holding a group time next to the shelf where the trucks are stored can be too tempting for some children. In this situation, it might be necessary to move the location of the group activity or to use dividers or curtains to cover the trucks. Another way to minimize distractions is to have children sit on mats, a rug, or on chairs; having their own "space" clearly indicated helps some children to be more attentive. Such an arrangement clearly defines each child's place and also makes teachers' corrections clear: "Jody, please sit on your mat."

Bathroom Routines

The bathroom or toileting sequence is made up of child learnings important at two levels. At one level is the acquisition of a set of necessary self-help skills— toileting, hand-washing, getting a drink of water, and self-management of clothing. At another level is the learning of consideration for others who must use the same facility. Common courtesy dictates that children learn to leave the facility clean and ready for someone else to use. The two basic learnings are accomplished by teaching all children a standard routine procedure. The children learn to accomplish quickly and automatically this important self-help routine with minimum effort and time away from more important activities; at the same time, because teachers have made sure that all children learn and carry out the same basic routine, no one child creates a time-consuming bottleneck during toileting routine, and the facility is always ready for the next user.

In order to make the routine simple for children, the facilities must be of a size appropriate for children, with toilet and faucet handles and knobs that turn or push easily so children can operate them. In addition, paper towel and cup dispensers must be close at hand and in good working order. Trash baskets should have openings wide and deep so that children have no trouble in disposing of used towels and cups in them. Picture sequences for toileting and hand-washing can be mounted on the bathroom wall as teaching aids at first, then as reminders. Some creative teachers have made up rhymes or chants to accompany the pictures. When children have learned bathroom procedures that allow them to care for themselves and leave the bathroom clean for others, the frequency of a teacher-scheduled routine can be decreased, assuming the bathroom is adjacent to the classroom; children, on their own, can take care of their toileting needs.

In many facilities, children must be taken for toileting because the bathroom is some distance from the classroom. The management of children in this routine depends on the distance, the size of the bathroom, the skill level of the teachers, and the ability of the children to accomplish this routine independently. Where bathrooms are within view of the classroom door, one teacher may both supervise the bathroom and monitor the coming and going of children down the hallway while another monitors activities in the room, releasing children to go to the bathroom one or two at a time or in small groups. Where bathrooms are further away from the classroom, children must be taken in groups. It is unsafe to let children wander in halls without teacher supervision. Whether the children and teachers go together or in small groups may depend on the skill of the children and the teachers.

When children are learning the skills of toileting, there should be close teacher supervision. A teacher who is to teach children these skills should take only a few children at a time. When children know the routine and can carry it out rather skillfully, a teacher can manage a large number of children in a group. A teacher who is skillful at teaching bathroom routines must also be skillful in managing children who are waiting.

Large groups of children can be managed by all going to the bathroom together, by splitting the group in half (especially useful if there is more than one bathroom), or withdrawing even smaller groups of children in sequence. The time needed for toileting in any one of these formats is about the same. Taking all children in one group with two or more teachers is useful when one of the teachers is learning group management. In this situation, the skillful teacher models ways to teach toileting procedures and to manage a group of children in waiting. The other teacher gradually takes one and then the other of the responsibilities. When both teachers can manage both responsibilities, the format is open for review.

One advantage of all children and teachers going together is the sharing of responsibility. The teacher who is managing the waiting children can reduce their disruptive behaviors by turning this time into an educational experience, e.g., by reading stories, discussing topics of interest, chanting, singing songs, and teaching concepts (Maul, 1978). In her study of bathroom procedures, Maul found that the format in which a teacher monitored both toileting procedures and waiting by having a planned educational experience was the least disruptive. This may be affected by the size of the bathroom, i.e., whether there is room for children to sit and wait, whether the teacher can sit near the door and manage both groups of children, or whether children can be trusted to care for themselves and thus need very little monitoring.

Transporting children for toileting can be one of the most difficult problems in child care operations. In addition, it is one routine that must be repeated several times during the day. Time spent in studying an appropriate format for teachers and children might reduce frustration for teachers and increase positive experiences for children, and it would cost little in terms of dollars. (For children with special toileting problems or those in the process of being toilet trained, refer to Chapter 6.)

Mealtimes

Another prime opportunity to help young children acquire a variety of necessary social skills arises at mealtimes. First of all, snack and mealtimes should be pleasant and relaxed. Children should not be nagged about eating or sitting up straight. Conversations can be fun and instructive. Small group snack time and lunchtimes can be used to facilitate the acquisition of various eating skills, such as pouring; using a fork, knife, and napkin; and keeping food on the plate. Pitchers should be child-sized, and the drinking glasses should be broad and squat enough to fill easily yet resist spilling. Built-up tables, plates with high edges, and spoons with special adapters can help children with feeding problems to become more independent. Mealtimes should be set up in such a way that children can help serve, clean up, and feed themselves as much as possible. Time should be scheduled so that all children have plenty of time to eat, but also so that children may leave the table when they finish.

Napping

Naptime can be an easy time for some children and a difficult time for others. Some children are not comfortable resting quietly away from home, and some do not want to sleep at all. Some children, although tired, resist sleep and create their own diversion. Others investigate the possibilities of enticing adults into a power struggle over napping. Naptime is rarely easy for teachers. It is frequently required by state regulation, and its goal is rest and relaxation for the children, even if they do not actually sleep. There are three primary considerations in developing a napping strategy: an environment conducive to rest, clear expectations for child behavior, and consistent teacher behaviors conducive to child relaxation.

The room environment should suggest a quiet relaxing period. The room can be darkened. Distracting materials should be made inaccessible and chairs stacked to suggest nonuse. Soft and rather slow-paced music is relaxing and requires that children be quiet if they wish to hear the music. Any necessary conversation should be quietly whispered to emphasize quietness. Movable dividers can be used to block distractions and to semiisolate disruptive children or nonresters. Sleep mats (whether foam pads, cots, or plastic forms) should be arranged by teachers in strategic positioning, which includes:

- positioning disruptive resters beside quiet resters
- placing all disruptive children together so that other resters are subject to less distraction
- asking children to lie on their cots so that all heads are not at the same end of the cots, but rather in an alternating pattern of feet and heads across cots in order to reduce interaction with peers
- positioning for maximum space between cots

All of these aspects of the physical environment should be explored by teachers in developing a rest strategy for a particular group of children.

Some situations may need a clear cue that naptime is now beginning. Useful cues may consist of:

- meeting children at the door, telling them that it is naptime, and insisting that they walk quietly into the naproom
- turning off lights
- stating that it is now rest time, and that there will be no talking
- telling a short story or playing a record or tape

Teachers need to experiment with such cues to see what fits their situation. Naps are often easier if there is a specific room, but good naps are possible in the classroom. In any event, children must be taught what any particular cue means before it will elicit an automatic appropriate response.

Naps will be facilitated if teachers are consistently clear about what behavior is expected from children. Resting and napping are incompatible with vocalization or verbalization. Resting is better accomplished when the child is lying down and when his entire body is on the cot. In addition, arms and legs should be generally quiet. Many children amuse themselves by twiddling fingers, tapping the cot, wiggling toes, etc. While such body movements may help the child to stay awake, such movements do not generally prevent other children from resting or sleeping and are therefore acceptable to many teachers. Appropriate nap behavior can often be encouraged if teachers briefly "tuck" each child in and ask if they need anything before they rest. A great many children will respond (in which case a teacher complies if possible), thus voluntarily giving tacit agreement to resting behavior.

Consistent behavior from all teachers in implementing napping strategies will greatly facilitate resting by the children. Verbal statements should be kept to a minimum and should be whispered. If adults use a speaking voice, children can be expected to imitate that behavior.

While it is helpful to check with each child initially to make certain each is ready to nap, it is very important that the teachers move slowly about the room to facilitate the feeling of relaxation. Backrubs relax some children, but stimulate other children and keep them awake. Any motion used in backrubs or bodyrubs should be light, gentle, and slow. Many children tell a teacher where they wish to be stroked, e.g., feet bottoms, legs, ears, back, or tummy. Gentle stroking at the preferred area frequently facilitates resting or napping. Stroking a child who is active or disruptive frequently reinforces that behavior and increases the likelihood of more nonresting behavior, however. Such children should be told that a teacher will come and rub a back when they are quiet on their cots.

The child who has difficulty in relaxing may respond to bodyrubbing, the company of a favored stuffed toy that (the teacher might suggest) needs to be "put to sleep" by the child, competing with the teacher (or a peer) to see who can get to sleep first, or even counting items of quantity, such as blocks on a shelf or tiles in the ceiling. Such a child needs teacher support and freedom from demands in order to relax. In this situation, requests for concentrated attending are usually counterproductive to resting.

Naptime can be a convenient occasion for a child to engage in a power struggle with a teacher. Several strategies to overcome this problem are available to the teacher; the mildest should be tried first. For example, the child can be isolated in an area of the room away from peers or other distracting materials. If this is not possible, a portable divider placed between the child and peers or other distractors may decrease the likelihood that this child's outbursts will produce any response and thus decrease the frequency of outbursts.

The child can be removed from the room if isolation within the room does not work. This separates the child from the audience of peers, but it requires the attendance of a teacher who may be needed in the room and thus is not always a feasible alternative. If removal from the room is used, the teacher must be very matter of fact about finding a place for this child so others can continue their rest. After giving a very brief reason for going to another room, the teacher refuses to be engaged in discussion by the child at this time. It is important that the child *not* be left alone. The teacher must remain near the child should anything serious occur, but should avoid pleasant interaction with the child. Although this procedure is not meant to be a punishment, neither is it intended to be a particularly happy occasion for the child. It should be an emotionally neutral experience that separates the child from all sources of reinforcement for inappropriate behavior.

Finally, the teacher can insist that the child who refuses to rest remain on the cot until he or she rests and can plan to outlast the child in this demand. The child is told privately that he or she must rest quietly before getting up. Each time the child is disruptive, the teacher places a mark or chip where the child can see but not handle it to indicate a minute of rest time that must be made up after rest time is over and other children are doing something pleasant. When rest time is over and the other children are getting up, the disruptive child stays on the cot, perhaps repositioned to an out-of-the-way area, and begins to work off marks or chips by resting appropriately for a minute per chip. The awareness that disruptive behavior at naptime costs a child valuable play time is usually quite effective in discouraging disruptive behavior. In children 3 years of age and older, a few days is usually time enough for them to learn to avoid "learning to rest" while other children are playing (Lathrop, 1981). Although this procedure can be effective, it costs the staff a teacher to deal only with this problem for a few days. A week of teacher time directed squarely to this problem can save many future hours of naptime frustration for teacher and children, however, and can prove to be an economical use of teacher time.

Daily Activity Setup

Attractive Presentation

The attractiveness of materials and activities usually motivates children to explore and experiment. Even an old, familiar puzzle can become more interesting when placed on colored paper or on a mat. Lego pieces, divided and sorted into several sized boxes or baskets, look more interesting and different than they do when jumbled together in one box. Colored tape used to divide work areas on a table may have the same effect as colored shelves in calling attention to materials. Color coding of materials and labeling of shelves with pictures of the material to be stored there can help teach children to return materials to proper storage places.

Flowers, plants, and pictures borrowed from the library can stimulate discussion and add a homelike touch. The display of children's art projects hung at the child's eye level and framed in various inexpensive ways often prompts children to be more interested in art without interfering with their unique efforts to create it.

Organization is another critical element of an attractive environment. If books, for example, are disorganized, chances are they will be looked at seldom or that they will be misused (Pisani, 1980).

Safety

All materials and classroom areas should be safe and clean. A wet floor, whether as a result of spills from water play or from mud tracked in from outdoors, is neither safe nor clean. Large bath towels, old throw rugs, or an old shower curtain can help facilitate clean-up in water play; teaching children to scrape their shoes thoroughly before coming indoors can solve the mud problem. All climbing equipment should be checked daily and removed if unsafe. Certain equipment, such as teeter-totters or high climbing frames, may be off-limits unless an adult is available to supervise. Electrical outlets should be covered and special areas blocked off for cooking. Such equipment as scissors should be used only under supervision and then with clear rules that teachers consistently enforce, e.g., children use scissors only while sitting at a table.

Accessibility

Heavy items, such as large trucks, hollow blocks, and doll houses, should be stored on low, open shelves so that they are easy for children to manage. Other items, such as block accessories, should be available as needed; otherwise, children with limited attention spans may become disruptive or disinterested if they must wait for a teacher to get the required items. Clean-up materials should also be readily accessible, not only because children should not be left unsupervised while the teacher gets the materials, but also because ready accessibility of needed materials encourages children's involvement in the clean-up process. For children with limited speech or mobility, accessibility of materials also encourages independence. With a little effort, these children can make their wants known through gestures and with minimal adult assistance. With a little help from other children, they can obtain or replace materials.

In planning activities, teachers must decide which area in the room is most appropriate for each activity. "Messy" activities should be offered close to a water supply; block play, close to shelves where the accessories are stored. If storage is a problem or if there is little storage space in the classroom, decisions regarding the rotation of materials must be included in the monthly and weekly planning. It is important always to keep materials fresh, interesting, and varied. Thus, there should be a plan for removing old books from the classroom and rotating them with new books from a hall closet, a plan for exchanging puzzles, and a plan for putting fresh table toys and manipulative materials on the shelves on a regularly scheduled basis.

Versatility

In purchasing materials and equipment, especially if funds are limited, teachers should consider the number of different ways in which a material can be used and the variety of skills that children may learn from the material. Skills are best learned when taught with various materials and in various situations. For example, if colors can be integrated into both the block activities and lunchtime, children find color naming and color discrimination skills functional and so learn these desirable skills more quickly. In addition, materials are usually more interesting if they teach a variety of skills. Blocks, water, clay, and manipulative materials, such as Lego and parquetry, or kitchen items for pretend cooking can provide occasions for spontaneous learnings in self-expression, language concepts, social skills, and motor and cognitive development.

Many commercial materials are highly versatile for teaching such basic concepts as color, shape, quantity, and texture. In using materials with multiple attributes, however, teachers must make sure that children are not confused and perhaps making errors based on ambiguous information. For example, a child may be sorting a material on the basis of its color rather than on the basis of its shape, and the teacher may assume that the child can discriminate shapes when actually the child is only matching colors.

Quantity

The number of materials available is another factor that affects children's responses to the learning environment. Children learn from materials by interacting with them; it follows then that there must be enough materials provided for children to have time and opportunity to work with them (Smith & Connolly, 1980). Kritchevsky and associates (1969) suggested that there should be multiple play materials to allow children to engage in adequate self-selection. Very young children or children with limited exposure to materials require more opportunities to learn what a material's or activity's potential might be. Thus, for very young children, it may be necessary to provide larger quantities of fewer materials.

Supervision

In planning the schedule, teachers should include time for child-directed and child-selected activities, as well as time for teacher-directed and teacher-selected activities. Such options allow children to select and explore as they wish during certain times of the day and to learn to make decisions as to what they want to do with a material. At the same time, teachers can provide experiences and activities that they deem important to a well-rounded learning environment by organizing group and individualized activities according to their program plans. The environment and schedule should be set up also, so that children are cued as to whether they have a choice of activities. For example, if children are supposed to be in one and only one activity, the rule should be indicated and consistently enforced: "It is time to work at the table now. You can play with the blocks *after* music."

PRACTICAL CONCERNS OF A SPECIAL NATURE

A first step in solving special problems is an analysis of the learning environment. Often, it is a worrisome or an inappropriate response on the part of a child that prompts a teacher to review possible environmental cues to which that child may be responding.

Nonparticipation

Susan moves from activity to activity. She watches the other children, but seldom participates in any activity. Rarely does she approach crowded or noisy areas of the room.

- Are there a variety of activities appropriate to Susan's developmental level? Teachers may need to observe what Susan appears to be attracted to, even if only briefly.
- Are there activities individualized to Susan's interests? Teachers can ask her parents what materials and activities Susan is especially interested in at home and make these available to her at school.
- Might Susan be looking for the security of a protected area? Teachers might try putting dividers around an activity they think would interest Susan and invite only one or two children with whom she might be comfortable to participate with her. If this is not successful, teachers might bring an activity known to be attractive to Susan to an area she often frequents and then protect the area with dividers. Once Susan can participate fully, dividers can be gradually removed and the activity moved to its usual area.

Attending to Materials

Brad rarely completes any activity. He fingers puzzle pieces for an excessive period of time before attempting to place them. When playing with open-ended materials, i.e., those for which there are no "correct" uses, he often dawdles and looks around. He may watch a peer who is using material and help from time to time, leaving his own materials undone.

- Is Brad using materials that have a "correct" procedure (zipping his coat) or a final correct answer (matching identical cards)? If so, is the activity placed near high artificial lighting or windows to ensure good vision? Is the activity located away from noisy areas to encourage a high level of concentration? Is the environment free of clutter? An area that has only the materials to be attended to reduces the competition for a child's interest, thus aiding the development of attending skills.
- Is Brad using open-ended materials, such as blocks, play in the house, or art materials, with which play is dictated by the demands the child makes on the materials? If so, perhaps a teacher should model very simply the delight of creating and prompt Brad to try for himself.
- Is the activity free of distractions that compete for Brad's attention? Perhaps the activity could be moved farther away from other activities and turned around to cut down on visual distractions.

- Are there too many children in the activity? Crowding of children into small spaces, even voluntarily, may be overwhelming to some children. Teachers can limit the number of children in an area by posting a sign with the number of children permitted in the area designated by "stick" figures; a child who wishes to enter the area could count to see if there is enough room for one more person to play there. If there is a planning period before free play activities, teachers can help children consider certain activity areas, thus handling the crowded problem in advance.

- Are there too many children for the amount of materials available? Teachers must help limit the number of participants to the number of children the available materials can serve. Teachers might use play extenders, such as a set of animals incorporated with the blocks.

- Does Brad have an idea of what to do with the materials? Teachers might ask Brad which unit blocks he plans to use next or where he is going to add more blocks to help him explore the possibilities of the material. Teachers might also provide encouragement by commenting approvingly on any beginning efforts and praising his "good ideas." Such reinforcement procedures increase the probability of extending Brad's appropriate use of materials.

Aggression

James, although a likeable child in many ways, is impatient with peers and wants a chosen play material immediately, regardless of who may be in possession of it. As a result, he takes toys from peers without asking and, if necessary (from his point of view), hits children who resist. He also hits any child who bumps or jostles him or his materials. An additional problem is that James frequently calls peers insulting names and threatens to bring in his father for assistance, a threat that seems to intimidate his peers effectively.

- Does James play in areas where there are too many children and too few materials? Since aggression has been found to increase with a higher density of children and fewer resources, perhaps James should frequent an area with fewer children and more resources. Many activities can be enriched and extended by adding items to the play, e.g., airplanes for the blocks, water for dishes in the kitchen, and more textures and shapes for collage prints in the art area.

- Is there one toy that is particularly attractive? Frequently, attractive or intricate single toys elicit competition and quarreling over their use. Teachers might purchase multiples of such toys to reduce aggression, particularly if the children are younger and have difficulty taking turns.

- Is James developmentally ahead of children in his classroom? Children who are physically larger than their peers often use their size to get their own way. If, in addition, James is verbally more skilled than his peers, he may find that the other children are unable to defend themselves against his wishes or fearful of doing so. Teachers should consider assigning James to a group of children who function at his skill level or higher. If, on the other hand, James is less skilled verbally and smaller physically than his peers, teachers may need to observe carefully to note whether his aggression is an initiating action or a response to peer initiations. In either event, James needs specially planned teacher intervention to assist in decreasing his aggression.

Low Social Interaction

Diane is a pleasant child who likes to talk to teachers. She is also an active child who participates in most of the available activities on a regular basis. She rarely initiates interactions with peers, however, although she does occasionally respond to a peer's invitation to participate in an activity.

- Are there numerous children around Diane most of the time? Is it possible that there are too many children in the space available? Teachers might increase the amount of space for play by moving out some of the furniture and equipment. They might decrease the number of children—permanently, if finances allow, by decreasing overall class size or temporarily, on a daily basis, by one adult taking a group of children on a walk or to another room for a special activity during the morning or afternoon. This leaves the same amount of space and number of activities for a fewer number of children and increases the likelihood of peer interaction.
- Do the activities and materials encourage social interaction with peers? A rocking boat, which requires two children to rock well, or a tricycle with a trailer allows two children an experience in cooperative play. A sheet over a card table is likely to attract more than one child. Special dramatic play assignments, such as putting Diane in the role of airline hostess on an airplane, increases the likelihood that she may become more assertive with her peers; such an inviting arrangement also increases the probability that peers will accept her initiations and respond to her.
- Is Diane clearly less skilled socially than her peers? If so, it might be beneficial to group Diane for a time with children who are younger and perhaps closer to her level of social development. In this kind of regrouping, her small, first steps in social initiations may be recognized and responded to by peers; her unsophisticated social response would be functional with peers. Another strategy might be to have teachers develop a plan for prompting and reinforcing peer interactions for Diane.

Failure To Take Turns

Eric is a child who becomes totally engrossed in certain toys and materials. He plays with these favored toys for long periods of time and does not want to give them up. He puts them away at the end of play time only reluctantly.

- How old and at what developmental level is Eric? Taking turns with materials is a learned behavior and comes about only as children develop an awareness of peers and become interested in interacting with them. For younger children and toddlers, who have not yet reached this stage, multiples of attractive materials make it possible for them to play without having to share before they are developmentally ready or able to wait for long periods of time to use a favored toy. When teachers wish to teach shared use of an item, it is well to select single materials judiciously. For example, one flour shaker at the Play-Doh table, needed only briefly at a time by each child, is more easily used in turn by several children than a toy cash register or a single new doll. In addition, there must be clear rules about leaving an activity to be completed or to reuse later. Such rules help to reduce the number of disagreements regarding the shared use of materials.
- What words and expectations do teachers use when talking about more than one child using a particular toy? Teachers often use the word *share* interchangeably with the words *taking turns*. Many children are willing to share on request of a teacher, but not so likely to share voluntarily. Too often, sharing or taking turns appears to mean giving up and being left with nothing. It might clarify things to use *taking turns* in the sense of a rule or teacher expectation and *sharing* as the child's voluntary cooperation in giving up an item. Consideration should be given to the child who is using the favored toy. It may not always be reasonable to expect a child to give it up, especially immediately. If the toy in question is needed to complete a project or is essential to a social experience the child is having, it is probably in that child's best interests to allow a continuation of the play with that toy. Children should be taught that asking for a turn sometimes results in a "No" response; as necessary, they should receive adult help in accepting such a response. The teacher then can arrange matters so that the child requesting the toy gets an opportunity to use that particular toy in the very near future.

Unwillingness To Clean Up

Matthew participates in most activity centers during a morning. When he has finished using the materials, however, he leaves them strewn about on the table and goes on to the next activity. At the end of the play period, when the other children are busily putting away materials, Matthew invariably finds something else to do. Teachers, of course, have discovered that Matthew rarely puts materials away by using well-timed avoidance strategies.

- Are materials organized so that children can easily return them? Children are more likely to replace small containers that they can easily grasp, for example. Storage containers and contents should be light enough for children to lift easily. Visual cues, such as a matching code of color/letters/numerals or a picture of the item in the place where it is stored, also encourage children to return materials.
- Is enough time allowed for children to participate in clean-up? Teachers can emphasize the importance of clean-up by allowing sufficient time for every child to participate and checking to ensure that materials are, in fact, returned to the correct places. If children are in a hurry to get to the next scheduled activity, the return of materials may be haphazard and the likelihood of accidents and aggression often increases.
- Does the teacher demonstrate how materials are to be handled, stored, and returned? Modeling the entire process, with the teacher taking the majority of the responsibility, is the first step in teaching children correct procedures to care for materials. Thereafter, the teacher can model the entire process but gradually let children complete greater portions of the chain. As the teacher models, praise is given to children who are handling the materials appropriately: "You are putting the cylinder blocks in the right place, John." Such descriptive praise increases the probability that children will help as well as learn from and enjoy the clean-up activities.
- Are the teachers' expectations clear? Using well-stated contingencies, such as "*After* you have put the puzzle on the shelf, Matthew, then you may play in the block area," helps the child to know exactly what he is to do. It is important, of course, that the teacher hold firmly to the after-then contingency, making sure that a child like Matthew does not move into block play (or anywhere else) until he has, in fact, returned the puzzle to the shelf.

CONCLUSION

The environment affects children's behavior to a much larger extent than may be recognized. Teachers are probably the greatest influence on child behavior, yet physical space, licensing regulations, available staff, and physical accessibility for handicapped children limit program possibilities. However, time spent in designing the use of space, arranging and selecting activities, grouping children, and planning schedule alternatives for both children and adults may result in better educational programs, more extensive individualizing for children, and less burnout for teachers. These factors are all-important factors in the quality of life that is provided for young children in preschool and day care settings.

REFERENCES

Ashton-Lilo, L. Pinpointing teacher goals to assist in a successful preschool classroom. *Topics in Early Childhood Special Education*, 1981, *1*(1), 37-44.

Ashton-Lilo, J., Thomson, C., & Baer, D. *Trouble shooting common behavior problems for teachers of young children*. Lawrence, KS: University of Kansas, Bureau of Child Research, 1981.

Barker, R., & Gump, P. *Big school, small school*. Stanford, CA: Stanford Press, 1964.

Bee, H. *The developing child*. New York: Harper & Row, 1978.

Cohen, D.J. *Serving preschool children* (Day Care Series, No. 3, U.S. Department of Health, Education and Welfare Publication No. 7401057). Washington, DC: U.S. Government Printing Office, 1974.

Greenberg, P. *Day care do-it-yourself staff growth program*. Winston-Salem, NC: Kaplan Press, 1961.

Gump, P. Ecological psychology and children. In M. Hetherington (Ed.), *Review of research in child development* (Vol. 5). Chicago: University of Chicago Press, 1975.

Hess, R.D., & Croft, D.J. *Teachers of young children*. Boston: Houghton Mifflin, 1972.

Hunt, J. McV. *Intelligence and experience*. New York: Ronald Press, 1961.

Jones, E., & Prescott, E. *Dimensions of teaching—Learning environments: II. Focus on day care*. Pasadena, CA: Pacific Oaks College, 1978.

Kounin, J., & Gump, P. Signal systems of lesson settings and the task related behavior of pre-school children. *Journal of Educational Psychology*, 1974, *66*(4), 554-562.

Krantz, P., & Risley, T. Behavior ecology in the classroom. In K.D. O'Leary & S.O. O'Leary (Eds.), *Classroom management: The successful use of behavior modification* (2nd ed.). New York: Pergamon Press, 1977.

Kritchevsky, S., Prescott, E., & Walling, L. *Planning environments for young children: Physical space*. Washington, DC: National Association for the Education of Young Children, 1969.

Lathrop, P. *Setting and contingency variables in naptime behavior of daycare children*. Unpublished thesis, University of Kansas, 1982.

LeLaurin, K., & Risley, T. The organization of day care environments: "Zone" versus "man-to-man" staff assignments. *Journal of Applied Behavior Analysis*, 1972, *5*, 225-232.

Loo, C. The effects of spatial density on the social behavior of children. *Journal of Applied Social Psychology*, 1972, *2*, 372-381.

Maul, N. *The effect of group size and teacher directed activities on child disruptions and time required during a bathroom transition*. Unpublished thesis, University of Kansas, 1978.

McGrew, P. Social and spatial density effects on spacing behavior in preschool children. *Journal of Child Psychology and Psychiatry*, 1970, *11*, 197-205.

Pisani, P. *Ecological and reinforcement variables in the picture-book usage of preschool children in two daycare classrooms: The effects of vicarious and personal attention, prompts and book location in the classroom*. Unpublished thesis, University of Kansas, 1980.

Rohe, W., & Patterson, A.H. The effects of varied levels of resources and density on behavior in a day care center. In D.H. Carson (Ed.), *Man-Environment Interactions, EDRA*. Skoudsberg, PA: Dowdery, Hutchinson, and Ross, 1974.

Rowbury, T., Baer, A., & Baer, D. Interactions between teacher guidance and contingent access to play in developing preacademic skills of deviant preschool children. *Journal of Applied Behavior Analysis*, 1976, *9*, 85-104.

Ruopp, R.R. *National Day Care Study, Preliminary Findings and Their Implications*. Cambridge, MA: ABT Associates, 1978.

Schoggen, P. An ecological study of children with physical disabilities in school and at home. In R. Weinberg & F. Woods (Eds.), *Observation of pupils and teachers in mainstream and special education: Alternative strategies*. Minneapolis: University of Minnesota, Leadership Training Institute/Special Education, 1975.

Shapiro, S. Preschool ecology: A study of three environmental variables. *Reading Improvement*, 1975, *12*, 236-241.

Smith, P.K., & Connolly, K.J. *The ecology of preschool behavior*. Cambridge, England: Cambridge University Press, 1980.

Thomson, C., Ashton-Lilo, J., & Baer, D. *You can individualize in small groups* (Videotape and trainers guide). Lawrence, KS: University of Kansas, Bureau of Child Research, 1981.

Chapter 5

The Influence of Health, Nutrition, and Safety

Lynn R. Marotz

Good health and physical well-being are necessary for optimum growth and development of all young children, both nonhandicapped and handicapped. Thus, children's health must be a major concern of preschool and day care personnel who spend their days teaching and caring for young children whose developmental levels and individual needs may be quite different.

Fortunately, Americans are becoming more health conscious. The evidence is everywhere. Television commercials stress the "natural" properties of foods, the need for dental care, good nutrition, and opportunities for families to exercise together. Magazine and newspaper articles elaborate on the effects of stress, the benefits of exercise, the hazards of smoking, and the prevention of illnesses.

Health awareness has grown in response to several recent developments. First, research has demonstrated possible links between many chronic illnesses and personal life styles (Bedworth & Bedworth, 1978), suggesting that many chronic problems stem from lifelong poor health habits. For example, excessive salt intake may contribute to hypertension (high blood pressure); unfortunately, parents often teach children to like salt by adding it to their food. Questions have been raised concerning the relationship between childhood obesity and subsequent coronary heart disease and diabetes. Also, dietary deficiencies and malnutrition in early childhood are thought to have long-term effects on behavior and brain development (Ricciuti, 1981; Winick, 1980). For years, chronic illnesses have been accepted as a part of the process of living for many individuals. Today, with new knowledge, many factors that affect the quality of health in both normal and atypical individuals can be controlled.

Because we, as a nation, are beginning to realize that some alternative must be found for total dependence on the medical profession, preventive health care is a growing trend. Many families simply cannot afford medical treatment, especially families with handicapped children, whose medical needs are usually complex, frequent, and extremely expensive. Delays in necessary treatment because of financial constraints often complicate the situation and increase long-run costs. Adults and children must become better informed about preventive health care and assume a more active role in avoiding, to the maximum extent possible, illness and injury. At the same time, however, they must also learn when it is appropriate to seek medical attention.

CHOICE VS. CHANCE

Health is a relative quality. It begins with specific inherited biological materials and is continually affected by environment and daily experiences. Health encompasses all facets of life: physical, social, mental, spiritual, and emotional. Control is exercised by making choices and decisions that will promote good health. Clearly, health education is essential to the success of the preventive health care approach; the attitudes and habits of the informed individual are more likely to lead to good health.

Current interest in preventive health care has also had important implications for children. Great strides have been made in implementing preventive health care concepts in programs that serve handicapped and nonhandicapped children. However, specific programs and their administration are always vulnerable to executive and legislative constraints.

One of the first major attempts to provide comprehensive preventive health care for young children was initiated in 1964. It made available a variety of medical services and screening procedures to children enrolled in Head Start programs. This project clearly demonstrated the values of early identification of children with handicapping and potentially handicapping conditions.

Children from low-income families are known to be at greater risk for handicapping and potentially handicapping conditions (Allen, 1980). Through the years, programs have been targeted at this group of children with hopes of improving their overall health. Financial assistance, made available through the Medicaid Amendment to the Social Security Act (Title XX), has made it possible for low-income families to secure medical care for their children. An extension of the Medicaid program (the Early and Periodic Screening, Diagnosis and Treatment Act), which was passed several years later, allowed for comprehensive screening of all children from low-income families. Under the current administration, funding for these programs has been shifted to the social service block grants allocated to each state. Well child clinics and immunization programs, available through most public health departments, offer free or low-cost medical care to all children under 6 years of age. Preventive health care programs for children depend on strong public support for their continuing survival, however.

The federal government has begun to recognize the important contributions of a good diet to health through funding of a variety of child nutrition programs intended to combat hunger, malnutrition, and chronic degenerative diseases. The Child Care Food Program, Summer Food Service Program for Children, School Lunch Program, Special Milk Program and WIC (Supplemental Food Program for Women, Infants and Children) provide nutritious meals or foods, as well as nutrition education for parents, in an attempt to improve the general health and well-being of young children. However, in spite of their proven value, these programs are only reaching approximately 25 to 30 percent of the families in need (Children's Defense Fund, 1983). At the same time, many of these same programs are undergoing sharp budget cuts, reorganization and confusing shifts in responsibility for their administration.

Concern for the safety, welfare, and protection of children is reflected in the growing awareness of child abuse and neglect. The Child Abuse Prevention and Treatment Act (P.L. 93-247), signed into law in 1974, requires all states to establish a means for reporting suspected cases of abuse and neglect. This important piece of legislation goes beyond society's genuine concern for children's safety in their own environments to recognize the potentially handicapping effects that physical and emotional abuse and neglect can have on children's growth and development. Greater public awareness of the problems of child abuse and neglect is a most encouraging development, especially when it is realized that about half the abused children are under 6 years of age and a relatively high proportion of these are handicapped (O'Brien, 1980).

Attempts are also being made to incorporate preventive health care concepts into other areas of child concern. The introduction of child restraint and seat belt legislation, consumer protection for infants' and children's toys and equipment, research, and public education programs reflect a growing interest in improving the quality of life for children.

THE TRIO

The preventive health care approach recognizes the close interrelationships of health, nutrition, and safety. A child's health status cannot be evaluated without also taking into account the child's nutritional state and safety of the child's environment, because each factor has a direct influence on the quality of the others (Marotz, Rush, & Cross, in press).

A diet complete in the essential nutrients is not only necessary for life, but also contributes to the fulfillment of growth and development potentials, behavior, resistance to illness, and repair and maintenance of body tissues. Young children require a daily intake of all the essential nutrients for normal growth and development, as well as sufficient calories from the food they eat. These needs may be even greater for some handicapped children, because their bodies often require so much more energy for locomotion, maintenance, and resistance to illness. Obesity must be carefully guarded against in atypical children, however. Parents often force food consumption on their handicapped child as a way to compensate for their feelings of guilt or anxiety about their child's problems.

Well-nourished children are generally more energetic, more alert, and more curious about the world around them. They are less susceptible to infections and illness and recover more quickly when they are ill. Poorly nourished children may be quiet, withdrawn, or apathetic. They often lack the energy to engage in vigorous play. Their ability to resist illness is lower, and their recovery rate is longer than that of well-nourished children. An obese child may be slower, less coordinated, and more accident prone, as well as subject to the ridicule of other children. In each of these instances, the child's physical, emotional, and social well-being may be affected.

Not all poorly fed children come from low-income families, although a lack of money may be one of the more common reasons for a poor diet. A problem of growing concern, however, is that of poor dietary habits among all children: skipping meals, consuming junk or snack foods in place of nutritious foods, and relying on fast food meals to satisfy hunger.

Good nutrition is also important for safety and accident prevention. The child who does not eat before coming to school, for example, may be less alert and slower to react because of low blood sugar. A child's chances of being involved in an accident or receiving an injury, as a result, are much greater. Appetite may be lessened as a result of pain or injury, in spite of the fact that additional nutrients are required for the healing process.

A safe environment that encourages good dietary habits, physical exercise, rest, leisure time, love, and preventive medical and dental care also encourages optimal health. Accident prevention must be given special consideration in planning safe environments for both typical and atypical children. Injuries disrupt a child's participation in classroom activities and learning.

Off to a Good Start

It is well-known that good health contributes to a child's ability to learn effectively and enjoy life (Oberteuffer, Harrelson, & Pollock, 1972), but a survey of early childhood texts reveals a lack of material on the health, nutritional needs, and safety of young children. Why has a topic that has such tremendous impact on the quality of children's learning been so neglected? Perhaps it is because pre-school children are presumed to be healthy. Their bright eyes, rosy cheeks, clear skin, endless energy, sunny dispositions, and apparent ability to eat and sleep at a moment's notice certainly suggest that this is the case. Parents and teachers, however, must be able to look beyond the healthy glow and recognize the subtle clues and signs of possible health impairments, be they physical, neurological, or psychological.

Both the nonhandicapped and handicapped preschool child must be in the best possible state of health to meet the challenges of growing up and learning. Defective vision, painful dental caries, hunger, chronic infection, or a hearing loss can interfere not only with a child's ability to receive and interpret information properly, but also with the child's ability to devote full attention to the tasks at hand. It is often difficult, however, for the young child to realize that something is wrong. For example, a child who suffers frequent ear infections may experience a gradual or temporary hearing loss. Because the loss occurs slowly, the child may be unaware of it. Over a period of time, however, the inability to hear properly can affect the child's acquisition of speech, as well as the child's ability to respond to cues in the environment (Friedman, 1975). It is easy to see that the health needs of young children require constant surveillance in both the home and school settings.

The importance of nutrition education must not be overlooked. It should focus on the needs of typical and atypical children and encompass the attitudes and knowledge necessary to establish good dietary habits. Not to be overlooked, either, are the feeding problems that often accompany handicapping conditions. (See Chapter 6 for discussion on this issue.)

Safety is also a prime consideration. Teachers have an obligation and an opportunity to provide an environment that is both physically and psychologically safe. Educational experiences should expand the children's knowledge of ways to work and play safely, and the preschool is the ideal place to begin such teaching. It is also the place (and time) to begin to teach normally developing children to be concerned for the safety and well-being of handicapped children in the group. Young children can learn, for example, to keep toys picked up so that children who are blind or who walk with crutches do not encounter unnecessary hazardous obstacles.

The Role of the Teacher

As more mothers return to work and the family structure continues to change, demands for child care services are growing more rapidly than ever before. As a result, teachers and day care providers are finding themselves more involved and more responsible for children's health care. Although teachers play an important role in fostering the growth and developmental potential of each child, they do not have to be experts on children's health care. They have many opportunities to promote the well-being of young children through the use of observational skills, knowledge of typical and atypical children, and their unique position as liaison between parents and health care specialists.

Perhaps one of the most valuable contributions that teachers can make is the early identification of children with handicapping or potentially handicapping health impairments. A teacher is in a unique position to observe and record changes in a child's health or behavior. Daily, the teacher sees the child interacting with adults and other children, coping with success and failure, and functioning on "good" or "bad" days. The following checklist can be used by the teacher to assess the child's health status:

1. general appearance: weight change (gain or loss), fatigue, excitability, skin color, size for age group
2. scalp: itching, sores, cleanliness
3. face: general appearance, expression (e.g., fearful, anxious, happy), color
4. eyes: redness, tearing, puffiness, coordinated eye movements, sensitivity to light, squinting, frequent rubbing, styes or other sores
5. ears: drainage, frequent earaches, bewildered looks or inappropriate responses
6. nose: runny discharge, sneezing, deformity, frequent rubbing, congestion
7. mouth: cavities or malformations of teeth; redness, spots or sores, malformations on inside of mouth; mouth breathing
8. throat: enlarged, red or infected tonsils or red throat with or without white spots
9. neck: enlarged glands
10. chest: wheezing, rattles, labored breathing (shortness of breath), frequent coughing with or without other symptoms
11. skin: color, rashes, scratches, bumps, bruises, unusual scars
12. speech: clarity, substitution of letter sounds, stuttering, monotone voice, nasality, appropriate for age
13. extremities: equal length, straightness, posture, coordination, pigeon toes, bowed legs
14. behavior: level of activity, alertness, degree of cooperativeness appropriate for age, appetite, sleep habits, irritability or excitability, motor skills

This checklist is by no means exhaustive or the only method available. It does, however, give the teacher an idea of the types of observations that should be made, and it alerts the teacher to areas of concern.

Sometimes parents recognize problems, but either find them too difficult to accept or do not know where to go for help. The teacher is in an excellent position to coordinate arrangements for various screening procedures, help interpret test results to the child's parents, and plan corrective programs. Teachers can call on pediatricians, nurses, dentists, psychologists, speech therapists, and other clinicians for their own information when they are concerned about a child's health problems. Teachers are not qualified, however, to diagnose a child's particular problem; this must be left to health professionals.

A classroom atmosphere that encourages independence, curiosity, self-esteem, cooperation, and feelings of security and acceptance of typical and atypical children also encourages their healthy growth and development. The teacher's attitude and genuine interest in children as individuals create a classroom atmosphere that is also conducive to good mental health. Measures taken by teachers to make the classroom a safe and healthy environment for both nonhandicapped and handicapped children not only protect the safety of children, but also convey concepts of safety education.

BASIC POLICIES

A policy could be defined as a definite course of action that is adopted as expedient. In preschool or day care settings, policies serve as points of reference that standardize or regulate actions.

Policy Making

Health and safety policies are especially important in child care settings. They help parents and staff to understand the philosophy and goals of a program, and they describe the behaviors deemed necessary for achieving these goals. Early childhood programs bring together parents and children from a variety of backgrounds, each with different needs and expectations. Policies provide a consistent, standardized set of guidelines to be followed by everyone.

Primary consideration should be given to those policies that concern the welfare of the children. More specifically, these policies should relate to children's health, nutrition, and safety. Questions related to such policy decisions include

- Who is responsible for administering first aid?
- When are parents to be notified in case of illness?
- What types of meals and snacks should be served?
- Who is responsible for supervising food preparation?

Additional policies may be formulated to meet state requirements governing child care facilities, such as

- How often must a child have a physical examination?
- What immunizations are required before entrance into the program?
- What types of activities, e.g., field trips, research, photographs, will require special parental permission?

Still other policies may be developed to afford legal protection to a center and its staff members:

- What ratio of teachers to children should be maintained?
- Should children be transported in privately owned vehicles driven by parents for field trips?
- Can teachers give medication to children?

Many of these policies must be determined before a program begins to accept children; others can be dealt with as circumstances require them.

The methods used to formulate basic policies vary with the size and organization of each program. In large centers, many persons may be involved in the decision-making process. A board of directors may make policy decisions jointly with the director and staff members in small programs. In other centers, an advisory committee comprised of parents, health professionals, lawyers, dietitians, and educators from the community may decide policies. In the case of a privately owned preschool or day care program, policy decisions may be made by one person.

To avoid misunderstanding and confusion, policies should be written in clear, concise terms that are intelligible to everyone. Some policies can be expressed in a single brief statement, while others require more lengthy descriptions and explicit details. Policies should not be unnecessarily restrictive or threatening. Rather, they should serve to inform and reassure both teachers and parents of the school's expectations. Copies of all policies should be made available and explained to parents and staff members.

A policy is useful only if it is enforced, and it can be enforced only if all staff members and teachers understand the purpose of the policy and are familiar with its requirements. Each policy should include a plan of action for dealing with those who do not comply. Caution should be exercised, however, before any action is taken against a parent or a teacher for failure to comply; every effort should first be made to find out why the person in question did not comply.

Records

Record keeping is often viewed as a time-consuming, unnecessary task. Yet, most early childhood practitioners recognize the value of records. The records maintained by schools range from those that contain general information about a child to those that are very specific, such as a teacher's anecdotal records. In many states, preschool and day care programs are required by law to maintain certain types of records, although the exact requirements vary from state to state. For handicapped children in federally funded mainstream settings, written records related to programming are also required.

Permanent health records should be kept on file for every child enrolled in an early childhood program. They should include a complete child and family history, a copy of a recent medical health assessment or physical examination, immunization records, emergency information, dental visits, and attendance records. Whenever parents request that medicine be given to their child, a special form with the name of the medicine, directions for administration, and the parent's signature should be completed and placed in the child's permanent file (Figure 5-1). A record of all doses administered by the teacher should later be attached to this form.

Parent contacts or conferences related to a child's health, nutritional status, safety, or special needs should also be placed in the child's file. The date, topic of discussion, and decisions that were reached should be included. When special testing, such as vision, hearing, or speech testing, is appropriate, a special permission form should be obtained from the parents and kept in the child's permanent file.

Records of all accidents and injuries, regardless of their seriousness, should be kept on file for a period of at least five years. Information concerning the nature of the accident, type of injury sustained, first aid treatment administered, condition of the child after treatment, date, time, and teacher's name should appear on the record. It is especially crucial to keep notes such as these in the case of handicapped children, because legal issues often surround accidents involving these children.

Information in a child's health records can be useful not only for assessing health status, but also for following the child's progress in school and for initiating and coordinating intervention programs. Teachers and medical personnel may also utilize such information to evaluate the success of treatments, as when an overly active child is placed on various daily dosages of a depressant type medication. Occasionally, the information is used for research purposes. Health records, however, contain privileged information that should be made available only to staff members who are directly involved with the child. This information should not be shared with any other group of individuals or programs without first obtaining written permission from the child's parents. A release form should be dated and should clearly designate the nature of information that is to be released and to whom it is to be sent (Figure 5-2).

For the sake of expediency, one person should be responsible for the maintenance of all health records. Staff members, however, should contribute their observations, concerns, findings, and communications with parents regarding a child's health in order to make these records complete. Records must be kept current, with all entries dated and expressed in clear, concise terms. Because health records can serve as legal documents, they should remain on file at the center or school for a period of approximately five years.

Figure 5-1 Sample Administration of Medicine Form

Child's name _____
Prescription # _____ Date of prescription _____
Physician prescribing medicine _____
Medication being given for _____
Time medication is to be given by staff _____
Time medication last given by parent _____
Amount to be given each time (dosage) _____

I, _____, give my permission for the staff to administer the
above prescription medication (according to the above guidelines) to _____
_____. I understand that the staff cannot be held responsible for allergic
reactions or other complications resulting from administration of the above prescription drug
according to the directions as stated in the prescription.

_____
Parent or Guardian

_____
Date

STAFF RECORD

Staff accepting medication and form _____
Is drug in original bottle or other container? _____
Is original label intact? _____
Is written permission from the physician attached (or the original prescription)? _____

_____
Signature of Accepting Staff Member

ADMINISTRATION RECORD

Date	Time	Amount Given	Staff Administering	Initial

Figure 5-2 Sample Medical Release Form

Permission is hereby granted for _____
                                            Name of person, agency, or school

_____ to release medical information

to the University of Kansas, Department of Human Development and Family Life, regarding

_____

Child's name

Birthdate _____

Sex _____   Date _____

_____

Signature of Parent or Guardian

_____

Type or Print Name of Parent or Guardian

SCREENING SERVICES

Recent interest in the early identification of children with handicaps and special problems makes it imperative that early childhood programs utilize available screening services. The main objective of any screening program is to identify those children with conditions that require more extensive evaluation. Teachers can administer some types of screening tests, but the services of specially trained personnel are required for the administration of others.

Vision Screening

All children should have their vision tested before the age of 6 in order to identify and treat amblyopia, or "lazy eye." A child with amblyopia uses only the stronger eye to see, while the lazy eye is not forced to work; vision gradually deteriorates in the weaker eye. Treatment is less effective after the age of 6. Preschool children should also be observed for strabismus, or crossed eyes, and referred for any needed corrective treatment.

Several vision screening tests are available for use with young children, e.g., the Snellen E Chart, the Children's Early Recognition Test, the Michigan Junior

Vision Screening Tests, and the Sjogren Hand Test. Teachers and parent volunteers can be trained by health professionals to administer these tests. Information about specific tests, methods, symptoms, and supplies can be obtained by writing to the National Society for the Prevention of Blindness, Inc., 79 Madison Avenue, New York, NY 10016. A search of community resources, such as the local health department, school district, medical organizations, or service groups, can sometimes provide an alternative to teacher-administered testing.

Hearing Screening

A child's ability to hear affects the development of language, speech, and learning skills, as well as the quality of social interactions. For this reason, early diagnosis of hearing impairments is vital. The possibility of a hearing loss should be considered if a child suffers from repeated colds, ear infections, or allergies. Clues to a possible hearing loss include difficulty in understanding directions, inappropriate answers, mispronunciations, frequent use of gestures rather than words, use of loud voice tones, or quiet and withdrawn behaviors. Additional information regarding signs and symptoms of hearing loss and testing procedures can be obtained from the National Association of Speech and Hearing, 919 18th Street, N.W., Washington, DC 20006 or the American Speech and Hearing Association, 9030 Old Georgetown Road, Washington, DC 20014. Preschools and day care centers can contact the local health department, school district, or speech and hearing clinics for assistance in locating qualified persons to conduct auditory screenings. Similar sources of aid can be found for other specialized types of testing, such as speech, dental, perceptual-motor, or other developmental discrepancies.

Reliability of Screening Tests

No screening procedure is completely reliable. There are always some children who fail the test, but have no real problem. Conversely, children with a disorder may pass the test. For example, a child with intermittent serous otitis media (fluid in the middle ear) may experience periods of temporary hearing loss. If auditory testing is conducted while the child is relatively free of symptoms, the child may pass the screening at acceptable levels; however, the same child may fail the identical screening several weeks later. Similar false-positives can occur in other types of testing. A child may pass a vision screening, for example, as a result of coaching from the examiner or by peeking around the occluder during testing. Test results should be regarded with caution, especially when a teacher or parent has reason to believe that a child's behaviors indicate a potential problem.

Convincing parents that testing should be repeated to validate the original findings may prove, in some instances, to be more difficult than convincing them that the child who has actually failed a particular screening procedure should undergo additional testing. In either situation, it is important to initiate follow-up contacts with parents to ensure that they have sought additional diagnostic testing or treatments.

CONTROL OF COMMUNICABLE ILLNESS

Episodes of communicable illness among young children are commonly encountered by early childhood practitioners. Several factors are responsible for this phenomenon. First, the fact that the preschool child often has had only limited contacts with groups of other children is an important consideration, because it means that the child has had only limited exposure to illness. When exposed to a communicable illness, a child's immune system is stimulated to produce antibodies. These antibodies provide protection against recurrences of the same illness. Immunity for some communicable diseases, such as measles, mumps, chickenpox, and smallpox, is lifelong. For other infectious illnesses, such as colds, flu, strep throat, and tonsillitis, however, immunity is only short-term. Because antibodies do not develop until the child has been exposed to illness, a child's first experiences in group situations are often marked by frequent illness.

Many communicable illnesses are transmitted via the respiratory tract; the relatively short distances between a child's mouth and lungs or nose and ears facilitate the development of such illnesses. As the child grows older and the respiratory tract matures, the child also has had time to build up antibodies against some communicable illnesses. This combination of events enables the child to develop at least some resistance.

Many children with multiple or severely handicapping conditions or chronic illnesses, such as leukemia, cystic fibrosis, or sickle cell anemia, are extremely susceptible to communicable illness, especially upper respiratory tract infections. Children with Down's syndrome frequently exhibit signs of a continuous cold with runny nose, congestion, watery eyes, and a cough (Smith & Berg, 1976). It has been suggested that a defect in antibody production and hormonal deficiencies may be responsible.

The most important measure that teachers have available to control the transmission of communicable illnesses is health observation. Through daily contacts with the children, teachers and day care workers have an excellent opportunity to know each child as an individual, and they become familiar with each child's normal appearance and behavior. An awareness, for example, that Jacob is usually reluctant to join in group activities first thing in the morning, that Linda's allergies cause frequent skin rashes, and that Sammy's lack of vitality is most likely related to grandmother's visit can be useful in explaining changes. Day-to-day observations make it easy for a teacher to recognize departures from the child's usual health status, since young children do not conceal illnesses very well. Changes in their actions, appearance, or things they say are often sufficient to warn an adult of an approaching illness. As children grow older, however, they ignore many early signs and symptoms, making early diagnosis more difficult.

Early recognition of symptoms and the exclusion of sick children from the group can help prevent the rapid spread of many communicable diseases, since many are contagious in the early stages. Some of the early symptoms to watch for include

- red, watery eyes
- rash, spots, or lesions
- frequent sneezing or coughing
- red or sore throat
- lethargy
- chills or fever
- flushed or pale appearance

A child with these early signs of illness can be kept out of the classroom, thereby exposing fewer children to the infection. A special room or quiet area screened off with dividers should be available for a sick child to rest and wait for parents to arrive. An adult should remain near the child at all times; a child should never be left unattended. School policies should state explicitly the grounds for exclusion and readmission. Teachers should become familiar with the guidelines and help to enforce them in the classroom, not only among the children, but also among the staff.

The quality of the environment should be considered carefully as a control measure. Particular attention should be paid to adequate ventilation of rooms occupied by children; doors and windows should be opened for fresh air whenever the weather permits. Rooms are often kept much too warm for children. Temperatures around 68°F in the winter and 80°F in the summer are most comfortable for young children. Humidity can be added to the air, thus increasing the comfort of the room, by using a warm or cool steam vaporizer. Close contacts can be limited during class by controlling the number of children seated at tables or playing in each area. During nap times, children can be placed on their cots or rugs in alternating directions, head to foot, to discourage talking and breathing in each other's faces.

The values of health education as an instrument of disease control cannot be overemphasized. The teacher can take advantage of many spontaneous events to teach and reinforce good personal health practices, e.g., hand-washing, covering coughs and sneezes, disposing properly of tissues. Local public health departments, physicians, and school nurses can be called on to answer questions and supply information about various communicable illnesses. Assistance can also be obtained from state health departments or state offices of education. Many good reference books are also available in bookstores. Two of these are *Child Health Encyclopedia* by Richard I. Feinbloom, M.D., and *The Parent's Guide to Baby and Child Medical Care,* edited by Terril H. Hart, M.D.

HEALTH EDUCATION: STAFF, CHILDREN, AND PARENTS

The success of a program to help typical and nontypical young children achieve their maximum health and productivity depends greatly on effective education of the staff, children, and parents. Such a health education program requires careful planning and sharing of information. Teachers, children, and parents must work together to develop a health education program that contributes to the well-being of each child.

Teachers must first recognize and accept the value of health education in early childhood programs. They should be trained in the art of observation and have a base of knowledge related to normal growth and development. They should be able to work closely with parents, gaining the trust and cooperation necessary for a successful health program. Teachers must also learn to be resourceful, locating and directing parents to health services available in the community and to funding sources when families need extra assistance.

Teachers and staff should be familiar with the illnesses and special health problems commonly associated with early childhood. It is not enough, for example, to know "a little something" about nutrition; instead, teachers must learn specifically how to plan inviting menus for young children, which nutrients are essential for optimum growth, and how illness or injury alters dietary needs. Completion of a basic first aid training course will enable a teacher or staff member to act with confidence in the event of emergency.

The subjects of children's health, nutrition, and safety make excellent topics for in-service education programs for teachers. Speakers from many disciplines, such as social work, dietetics, nursing, medicine, speech and hearing clinics, dance and movement, and dentistry can be invited to share their knowledge with teachers. Hospitals, public health departments, Red Cross associations, county extension offices, local school systems, and numerous private organizations offer continuing education programs and workshops related to childhood health, nutrition, and safety.

The majority of health education at the preschool level is accomplished through incidental learning. The behaviors, actions, and examples of teachers are the most influential and effective methods for teaching both nonhandicapped and handicapped children desirable health behaviors. Seeing teachers wash their own hands before serving meals or eating snacks, for example, reinforces the importance of such practices. Teachers should not only model the health behaviors they expect young children to learn, but also explain the reasons for their actions.

The preschool or day care setting is an ideal environment for involving young children in their own health care. Recently established links between poor health practices and the subsequent development of health problems emphasize the need for health education programs for young children, since health habits and attitudes learned early in life are usually long-lasting. It is important, therefore, to help young children establish good health practices and attitudes while they are eager to learn, receptive to new ideas, and forming lifelong health attitudes and habits.

Topics selected for health education should be closely related to the developmental needs, interests, and abilities of the young child. A health education program for preschool children should include instruction in the following areas:

- personal cleanliness
- dental hygiene
- dressing appropriately for the weather
- nutrition
- good posture
- good manners
- play and exercise
- sleep and rest
- feelings and emotions
- body awareness

Health information should be presented in simple terms and limited in scope so that children can grasp the meanings. Incorporating health concepts and skills into the curriculum helps both typical and atypical children to relate these experiences to their daily lives. The value of sleep and rest, for example, can be discussed when children first arrive in the morning, after a vigorous game outdoors, and during creative play when dolls must "go to bed."

A good health education program also actively involves the parents. When parents are included in planning and policy making, serve as volunteers to assist with health screening procedures, and participate in various aspects of health education, they are more likely to support the center's efforts. The teacher who shares health information with parents through conferences, letters, informal visits, or planned programs is more likely to gain their cooperation, thus establishing continuity between school and home. Teachers should also attempt to learn something abut the uniqueness of children and their families—the cultural, social, and ethnic differences that influence their views of health and health practices. These insights enable teachers to develop a health education program that is tailored to the individual needs of children.

ENVIRONMENTAL SAFETY

Accidents are one of the greatest threats to the lives of young children. The major causes of accidental deaths include motor vehicle accidents, fires, drownings, falls, and poisonings. More than one-third of all deaths among children under 4 years of age are the result of accident-related injuries, and accidents are responsible for nearly one-half of all deaths in children between the ages of 5 and 15 years (Feinbloom, 1975). These figures do not reflect the thousands of additional children who are injured seriously enough to require medical attention, but they demonstrate the importance of including safety awareness and accident prevention in school programs, day care settings, and the home.

Many of the characteristics that make young children interesting and exciting to work with also make them more likely victims of accidents. Their adventurous and inquisitive nature encourages investigation into the yet unexplored boundaries of their world. Curiosity entices them to taste, crawl into, and poke at everything in sight. Their penchant for jumping from the top of a playhouse or jungle gym, climbing a ladder with no hands, or dashing into the street after a runaway ball reflects their general lack of fear. Children's spontaneity and eagerness make their actions and behaviors hard to predict. Furthermore, young children are unable to anticipate the consequences of their actions.

Safety awareness must be practiced continuously. Particular attention should be given to a child's physical environment, whether it be at home, school or a day care facility. Major sources of danger are usually not difficult to identify and correct, but other safety hazards are not always so readily apparent and require more careful identification. Special attention should be given to situations that can result in falls, fires and burns, poisonings, and drownings.

It is difficult, if not impossible, to eliminate all risks of accident and injury. A carefully planned and well-supervised play yard and classroom, however, helps to ensure the safety of both nonhandicapped and handicapped children. Important measures that should be taken by every teacher to lessen the risks of accidental injury include

- inspection of all equipment and areas occupied by children
- establishment and enforcement of rules
- adequate teacher supervision

Play areas and equipment should always be inspected before children are permitted to use them. Toys and equipment should be appropriate for the ages of the children, their abilities, their interests, and the amount of space available. Equipment should be in good repair, with large pieces firmly anchored in the ground and placed far enough away from concrete or asphalt surfaces to prevent injuries should the children fall. Surface materials under climbing equipment and swings should be relatively soft and resilient, e.g., mats, grass, sand, bark chips. Equipment and toys with broken parts or sharp edges should be removed and repaired or discarded. Play areas should be fenced in for younger children. These areas also should be inspected carefully for sharp objects, such as sticks and broken glass, and for poisonous flowers, shrubs, and trees, such as hyacinth, daffodil, iris, oak trees (acorns), black locust trees, yews, and buttercups. In order to prevent accidental drownings, fences should be placed around bodies of unattended water. These same precautions should be taken by parents when their children use public playgrounds, recreational areas, or even equipment in their own back yards.

Children's play must be carefully supervised by teachers at all times. Teachers and staff members should distribute themselves around the room or play area so that each child can be clearly seen. Activities that involve climbing, jumping, wheel toys, or water require an adult in attendance at all times. Children should not be allowed under climbing or jumping structures when other children are using them. Special attention should be given to children's clothing; long skirts, dresses, or pants that are too long, hard-soled shoes, long scarves, or ties make climbing and running activities hazardous.

Rules for safe use of play equipment and appropriate classroom behaviors should be carefully explained, even to very young children, in clear, simple terms. The explanation should include the reasons that such rules are necessary. Threats or fear should not be used to gain a child's cooperation. Compliance can best be achieved through friendly, consistent reinforcement from the teachers and staff. For example, a teacher might praise a child's good behavior by saying, "Jeffrey, you rode your bicycle so carefully around the other children." or "Katherine, you remembered how to put your scissors back in the box when you were through." When a child misuses play equipment, the teacher can gently remind the child of the rules. If the child behaves inappropriately, the teacher must remove the child from the area temporarily with the simple statement, "I cannot let you throw sand."

Safety must also be a major concern when teachers or parents plan activities for children. How safe is an activity for the preschool child? What special precautions must be taken for the handicapped child? What are the inherent risks of injury or accident? It is impossible to provide standardized lists of activities and directions for teachers to replicate in their own programs. Furthermore, such lists would destroy the creativity, ingenuity, and resourcefulness that each early childhood practitioner brings to the field. There are, however, certain guidelines for selecting and conducting various learning activities.

Careful planning and organization are key factors in ensuring the safety of any activity. Even greater precautions and more precise advanced planning are required for some activities, such as those that involve any of the following items:

- pointed or sharp objects, such as scissors, knives, and woodworking tools (e.g., hammers, nails, saws)
- pipe, boards, blocks or objects made of glass or other material that shatters
- electrical appliances (hot plates, radio, mixers)
- hot liquids (wax, syrup, oil, water)
- cosmetics, cleaning supplies, chemicals

Whenever an activity involves these items, an area separated from other classroom activities should be used. The number of children engaged in such an activity should be limited to only the small number of children that a teacher can work with and adequately supervise at one time.

The condition of all electrical appliances used in an activity should be checked carefully before use. Appliances should be kept away from any water or wet areas, including sinks and wet floors. A safe distance should be maintained from any appliances to ensure that hair, clothing, or fingers do not become entangled. Special precautions should be taken, such as turning handles to the back of the stove or hot plate, when hot liquids are involved. Safety plugs should be placed in all electrical outlets when they are not in use.

When a teacher is planning art activities for the classroom, the safety of the materials, methods, and equipment should be given careful thought. Is the paint or glue nontoxic? How many children can a teacher safely supervise at a time for activities that require the use of scissors? What collage materials could be substituted for dry peas, beans, nuts, rice, buttons or popcorn? Because objects of this small size can be easily stuffed in noses, inserted in ears, or quickly swallowed, it is far better to choose some other media that can be more safely used with young children. Can plastic bottles and jars be used in place of glass containers for most art activities? When art activities require the use of water or other liquids, or dry media (e.g., rice, beans, flour, cornmeal, or leaves), a hard-surfaced floor should be covered with newspapers or rugs to help prevent slipping and falling.

Through such careful adult supervision and encouragement, children can learn to live and play safely while they explore, investigate, experiment, and interact with their environment and other children. Safely prepared environments are also less stressful for the adults who supervise the children's activities.

PROBLEMS AND SOLUTIONS

Pinpointing Potential Problems

Four-year-old Timothy has been enrolled in a day care center for the past 18 months. He has been absent frequently because of ear infections. Timothy's parents have expressed concern about his inability to follow directions. The teacher is concerned about Timothy's problems with attending behavior, as well as his slow speech development. The teacher should take the following approaches:

- Identify and record the actual number of absences due to colds or ear infections.
- Check with the parents to see if medical attention (diagnosis and treatment) is being sought in each instance of ear infection. If help has not been sought, stress the importance of doing so.
- Reinforce the parents' efforts when they do contact the physician.
- Note whether the child's ear infections have been more frequent since being placed in a child care program.
- Question the parents to see if the child's ear infections are more frequent during any particular season of the year.
- Check over a period of several days to see whether the child appears to be adequately nourished and rested.
- Evaluate the child's language skills. If a speech clinician is available, refer the parents and the child. If the services of a speech clinician are not available, the teacher can sample and record the child's language skills.
- Observe the child closely. Is the child frequently inattentive when verbal instructions are being given or during activities that require listening? Does the child answer questions inappropriately? Does the child yell or talk loudly in the classroom, or is he quiet and withdrawn?
- Arrange for an evaluation of the child's hearing. Request special permission from the parents to have a hearing screening completed.
- Compare the results obtained from the teacher's observations with those from speech and hearing evaluations.

If the child does have a hearing loss or impairment, the teacher should

- encourage the parents to follow through with any medical advice or suggested treatment
- make sure that teachers move closer to the child and look directly at the child's face when giving directions or speaking
- encourage other children to come closer and face the child whenever they are speaking
- avoid exaggerating the pronunciation of words or speaking in an excessively loud tone of voice
- accept the child as an individual, not as a hearing-impaired child, and help other staff members and children to learn acceptance

Influencing Parents To Seek Help

When Suzanne, a child with developmental delays in social and verbal functioning, first arrived at school, her teachers thought that she was much older than her actual 3 years and 8 months. Her mother seems to take pride in the fact that Suzanne is a "big" girl and has a rather "healthy" appetite. Being overweight makes it difficult for Suzanne to run and play with the other children, however. The teacher should take the following approaches:

- Help the parents to accept the fact that the child is overweight and to understand its impact on her overall development.
- Advise the parents to have the child examined by a physician to rule out medical complications or illness.
- Explore, very gently, the child's feelings about herself.
- Have the parents maintain a log of the child's food intake for a period of one week. Meet with the parents to discuss her food habits or refer them to a nutritionist for dietary counseling.
- Serve carefully planned low-calorie meals and snacks to the child at school.
- Limit the amount of food the child is allowed to take or is served at mealtime.
- Increase the child's activity level by encouraging her participation in vigorous activities, such as walking, running games, playing ball, riding a bicycle.
- Provide the child with positive experiences that bolster her sense of achievement and self-esteem. Take a personal interest in the child's efforts and success.
- Weigh the child on a regular basis and reward any weight loss with encouraging words or other forms of positive reinforcement.
- Encourage the parents to enroll in a parenting skills class.

The Overconcerned Parent

Torri's parents are worried about his clumsiness. They think that he cannot ride his bike, climb, or play ball as well as other 4-year-olds. The teacher has tried on several occasions to reassure Torri's parents that he is not exceptionally clumsy, but they continue to question and show concern. The teacher should take the following approaches:

- Collect normative data, e.g., simple counts or anecdotal notes, or keep a running record for several weeks of incidents involving clumsiness.
- Check the fit of the child's shoes.

- Advise the child's parents to arrange for a perceptual-motor evaluation.
- Invite the child's parents to visit the classroom and observe the children functioning in a variety of activities. Point out that all children stumble about occasionally, just as their child does.
- Schedule extra parent conferences to report on the child's progress.
- Test the child's motor skills in the classroom by using a developmental screening tool, such as the Denver Developmental Screening Test.
- Encourage the parents to attend a parent training class to improve their understanding of children's normal growth and development.
- Encourage the parents to talk with parents of other children. Often, they discover that their child is not the only child who exhibits the behaviors that worry them.

Reversing Poor Habits

During health inspections, the teacher observes that Mickey's teeth are seldom brushed when she arrives at school. They are already quite discolored, packed with food particles, and have numerous cavities. When the teacher asks Mickey why she has not brushed her teeth, her reply is always the same: "I didn't have time because we got up late." The teacher should take the following approaches:

- Check with the parents to determine if the child has a toothbrush available.
- Determine how important the parents consider the practice of toothbrushing for children.
- Encourage the parents to try to get up ten minutes earlier in the morning to allow time for toothbrushing.
- Conduct a program of dental health education in the classroom. Supervise each child's toothbrushing technique.
- After obtaining parents' permission, provide children with red disclosing tablets to chew after brushing their teeth. (Any plaque that is not removed will be stained red.)
- Discuss the importance of good nutrition for dental health, e.g., limiting sweets and carbonated beverages, while including fresh fruits and vegetables, milk products, and whole grain cereals and breads. Invite the parents to attend.
- Gain the parents' cooperation. Help them to understand the need for children to brush their teeth daily.
- Involve parents in the program by having them monitor the child's toothbrushing habits. Meet with them on a regular basis to check on the child's progress.

- Continue to question the child about brushing her teeth before arriving at school. Reinforce her efforts with praise.
- Encourage the parents to take the child to a dentist for professional dental care.

Handling an Injured Child on the Playground

Several children are riding their tricycles around the play yard sidewalk pretending to be "firemen." While hurrying to put out a "fire," Betsy turns a corner too sharply, causing her tricycle to tip over. As she falls to the ground, she hits her head on the cement. Betsy appears dazed as she lies motionless on the sidewalk. The teacher should take the following approaches:

- Keep calm. Panic and fear will frighten the child. Reassure the child that everything will be all right.
- Check immediately to be sure the child is breathing and has a pulse. Follow the Red Cross instructions for mouth-to-mouth or cardiopulmonary resuscitation if breathing or pulse are absent.
- Leave the child lying down. Do not move the child until the extent of the injury has been carefully evaluated.
- Examine the child's head for profuse bleeding, bumps, or cuts. Use direct pressure to control heavy bleeding.
- Examine the ears and nose for presence of clear fluid.
- Look at the child's eyes. Check to be sure the pupils of the eyes are of equal size.
- Do not leave the child alone. Send another child or teacher for help if it is needed.
- Be prepared for the possible development of shock, which is indicated by pallor, rapid breathing, nausea, and cool, clammy skin.
- Keep the child warm; cover with a blanket if symptoms of shock develop. Elevate the child's legs 8 to 12 inches.

If the child has not suffered a serious head injury, the teacher should

- notify the child's parents of the accident.
- continue to observe the child during the next 24 hours. The parents should also watch for signs of slurred speech; convulsions; vomiting; severe headache; unequal pupils; bleeding from the nose, ears, or mouth; drowsiness; or dizziness.

- apply cold compresses or ice wrapped in a cloth to any bumps.
- encourage the child to remain quiet for a short time following the injury.
- complete an accident report that includes the date, time, type of injury, how the accident occurred, a description of all treatments administered, and the condition of the child when released to the parents.

Managing Communicable Illness in the Classroom

During the past two days, Trevor has not been able to concentrate on any activity he started. In addition to being restless, he scratches his head frequently. At first, the teacher attributed this to Trevor's restlessness. On careful examination, however, the teacher discovers that Trevor has head lice. The teacher should take the following approaches:

- Notify the child's parents. Request that the parents call their physician or the public health department at once.
- Check the scalps of all other children in the classroom daily for two or three weeks. Pay special attention to the areas at the back of the neck and behind the ears.
- Advise the parents of the other children in the classroom to examine members of their family daily for the next two or three weeks and obtain treatment from their physician if necessary.
- Maintain an atmosphere of calm and control. The subject of head lice is highly emotional and often regarded with panic.
- Alert all other teachers and staff members, including research personnel, clinicians, therapists, the cook, and the bus driver. Teachers of siblings of infected persons should be especially careful when inspecting children in their classrooms.
- Explain to all parents and staff that head lice are a common problem among young children and those who work closely with them. Reassure them that having head lice does not mean they are dirty or irresponsible and that the cure is relatively simple.
- Help to educate parents regarding control measures.

  1. Persons with an identified case of head lice should wash and shampoo their hair with a special medicated shampoo.
  2. Brushing and combing the hair after drying helps to remove the dead lice and nits.
  3. The heat from a hair dryer also helps to destroy the lice.

4. Clothing and bed linens of the infected person should be washed in hot water and detergent and dried at high temperatures (140°F) for 20 minutes. All nonwashable items (e.g., coats, hats, blankets) should be dry cleaned.
5. Items such as mattresses, chairs, and car seats should be sprayed with an approved insecticide.
6. Combs, brushes, and curlers should be soaked in very hot water (140°F).

• Utilize control measures in the classroom.

1. Vacuum carpeted areas daily.
2. Spray or wipe off lockers, coat hooks, sleeping cots, coat racks, furniture, or play equipment used by infected children.
3. Remind children to practice frequent hand-washing.
4. Discourage children from sharing personal items, e.g., hairbrushes, combs, hats, blankets, sweaters.
5. Try to limit the amount of physical contact children have with one another during an outbreak of head lice.
6. Wash all play clothes and hats shared by the children.

• Readmit infected children only after they have been treated, the nits have been combed out of their hair, and their clothing has been laundered.

CONCLUSION

The concept of preventive health care stresses the need for individuals to be actively involved in their own health care, making wise decisions and good choices that will maintain and improve their health status. Self-actualization and self-fulfillment are the ultimate goals of the preventive health care approach. This concept has significant implications for early childhood programs. First, it acknowledges the negative effects of illness or health impairments on a child's ability to learn and achieve. Second, it recognizes that there is a direct relationship between health education and well-being. It implies that children need to learn how to control the quality of their health through active participation, the development of favorable attitudes, and the ability to make positive decisions.

Early childhood practitioners must demonstrate a commitment to preventive health care. Through their skills of observation, identification of children with special health problems, and coordination of services, they can do much to improve the health of children. Teachers must accept the fact that they alone cannot promote children's health, however. Families and communities also influence children's basic beliefs and attitudes about health care.

REFERENCES

Allen, K. *Mainstreaming in early childhood education*. New York: Delmar, 1980.

Bedworth, D.A., & Bedworth, A.E. *Health education*. New York: Harper & Row, 1978.

Children's Defense Fund. A children's defense budget: An analysis of the President's FY 1984 budget and children. Washington, DC: Author, 1983.

Feinbloom, R. *Child health encyclopedia*. New York: Dell, 1975.

Freidman, J.L. Teacher awareness of hearing disorders. In R.H.A. Haslam & P.J. Valletutti (Eds.), *Medical problems in the classroom*. Baltimore: University Park Press, 1975.

Hart, T.H. (Ed.). *The parent's guide to baby and child medical care*. Deephaven, MN: Meadowbrook Press, 1982.

Marotz, L.R., Rush, J., & Cross, M.Z. *Early childhood—Health, safety and nutrition*. New York: Delmar, in press.

Oberteuffer, D., Harrelson, O.A., & Pollock, M.B. *School health education*. New York: Harper & Row, 1972.

O'Brien, S. *Child abuse*. Provo, UT: Brigham Young University Press, 1980.

Report on preschool education. Arlington, VA: Capitol Publications, Inc., December 29, 1981.

Ricciuti, H.N. Adverse environmental and nutritional influences on mental development. *Journal of American Dietetic Association*, 1981, 79(2), 115-120.

Smith, G.F., & Berg, J.M. *Down's anomaly*. New York: Churchill Livingstone, 1976.

Winick, M. Nutrition and brain development. *Natural History*, 1980, 89(12), 6-13.

Chapter 6

Working and Communicating with Parents

Joan L. Reiber and Lynne H. Embry

Even though children may spend many hours under the care and guidance of teachers, parents continue to be the primary influence in the lives of all young children. Parents are also children's major resource for their physical and psychological needs. Therefore, to be truly effective with young children, today's teachers must have experience and training in parent education in addition to their expertise in child development and curriculum planning. In order to work and communicate effectively with parents, early childhood teachers must understand the history of parent involvement in early education, past and current child care practices, nontraditional family structures, special needs of families with a handicapped child, as well as the diverse and changing roles of both teachers and parents.

THE CHANGING TIMES

Without doubt, the 1960s brought profound changes in philosophies and practices regarding early childhood education. From the results of the research efforts of Hunt (1961, 1964) and Bloom (1964), educators began to realize that the kinds of learning experiences children have during the first five years of life may be crucial to all subsequent learning. It was also during the 1960s that the employment of mothers of small children began to increase dramatically, that the emphasis in the education of the handicapped shifted to education in the least restrictive environment, that the first summer Head Start programs were established, and that the War on Poverty gradually but steadily focused on child care and education for preschoolers and kindergartners (Allen, 1980; Morrison, 1976; Nixon & Nixon, 1971). Numerous research demonstration projects for young handicapped and nonhandicapped children during this decade included both a parent involvement and an education component (Gray, Klaus, Miller, & Forrester, 1966; Weikart & Lambie, 1968).

The positive results of parent involvement in child care projects and programs emerged clearly in the 1970s when Gordon and Hess (1975) reviewed 29 intervention programs designed to serve low-income preschool children and their families. Although each program placed a different emphasis on working with parents, the critical factor appeared to be the *degree* of parent involvement in the program activities; children made the greatest intellectual gains when educators worked directly with the parents (Nedler & McAfee, 1979). From the findings of two of the projects, the summaries of some of the programs in Project Head Start, as well as from the Portage Project designed for families with young handicapped children, it has been concluded that parent involvement in child care programs is possibly the essential ingredient for sustaining developmental progress of young children (Boyd, Stauber, & Bluma, 1977; Dittmann, 1980; Gordon, 1973; Madden, Levenstein, & Levenstein, 1974; Zigler, 1978). Rarely, however, does parent involvement in child care programs occur unsolicited, nor does it occur until positive relationships have been established between teacher and parent. In order to develop such relationships, teachers will need to understand past and current influences upon families and their lives.

Child care practices have swung back and forth between authoritarian and permissive views and now seem to be focusing on more democratic and systematic approaches to child rearing (Abidin, 1980; Becker, 1971; Dinkmeyer & McKay, 1976; Fine, 1979; Gordon, 1975; Norton, 1977). Certainly for handicapped children, systematic approaches are crucial for optimal learning and development.

The traditional family familiar to previous generations—the father who works, the mother who remains in the home, and two or three children—is no longer necessarily typical (Caldwell, 1980). More prevalent are single-parent and two-parent families, consisting of a working mother (and/or father) and often only one child (Bronfenbrenner, 1976; Brooks, 1981; Fine, 1979; LeMasters, 1977). In the past 10 to 15 years, this difference in family structure has significantly altered the role of both the early childhood teacher and the parent of a young child. Understandably, these changes have influenced parent-teacher relationships.

In the past, the relatively few mothers who worked outside the home made child care arrangements with relatives, neighbors, or friends. Day care centers were rare, nonexistent for handicapped children, or used only by the economically disadvantaged. Nursery schools stressed enrichment for a few hours a week and were patronized by those families with normal or gifted children who could afford to pay tuition. Teachers in day care programs were seldom trained in child development or curriculum planning, because everyone viewed the family as the primary source of education. Paradoxically, while "warm and loving" were the only stated teacher qualifications, parents turned to these same teachers for advice regarding many aspects of child development. During this same time period, parents relied heavily on members of their extended family, such as grandparents and relatives, yet parents were expected to be the sole educators and caregivers of their preschool children. The only other major resources parents had available at that time were government pamphlets published periodically by the U.S. Department of Labor, Children's Bureau, and the U.S. Department of Interior, Office of Education, and books such as *Infant and Child in the Culture of Today* (Gesell & Ilg, 1951) and the very popular *The Common Sense Book of Baby and Child Care* (Spock, 1957).

Today, the role of the early childhood teacher is more diverse and comprehensive than ever before. More and more women are working and using child care outside the home. Handicapped children are enrolled in either special or mainstreamed preschool classrooms. The preschool and day care staff is taking the place of grandmother, aunt, or friendly babysitter down the street. The child care home or center has become, in a sense, the extended family.

Some working mothers feel confident in many areas of child care; others may feel guilty for not being at home with the children. Because mothers who work have fewer opportunities to visit and chat with other mothers, and because relatives are often hundreds of miles away, these mothers may rely heavily on teachers for advice and information. Almost all parents are expecting more and more from their children's teachers. Parents ask teachers questions regarding child development that in the past were referred to child psychologists or special education professionals. They are interested in their child's daily schedule and in what activities their child is offered throughout the day. They want teachers to help them with home discipline techniques and expect teachers to advise them on the effects of a handicapped child's special needs, an impending divorce, a new baby, or almost any change in the family routine or structure. Teachers, although they should never assume the role of therapist, need to be proficient in communication and interpersonal skills because these daily, informal chats with parents are essential to the overall development of every child.

Because of this new, diverse role of today's early childhood teacher, a trusting relationship must be established between parent and teacher. Only with the cooperation and assistance of parents can teachers have a truly positive influence on a child's life. Teachers frequently feel that they are being evaluated by parents. Parents often feel the same way—that they are being judged by teachers. Teachers should be aware that parents feel ineffective when negative statements are made about their children. ''Warm and loving'' are still vital characteristics of a good teacher, yet children and their families need and want so much more.

Today's professional teacher should provide a challenging and stimulating program for a young child by supplementing—but never supplanting—the home. Teachers move in and out of a child's life; the parent is the one, continuing influence. If parents are encouraged to become involved in their child's program, there will be more support for the teacher and the daily program, and a positive and cooperative relationship should develop between teacher and parent. The result will be a healthier, happier, better adjusted child who loves to learn and who has reason to trust adults.

THE POWER OF POSITIVE PARENTING

Good teachers spend a great deal of time preparing themselves and their materials so that children in their care will benefit academically, socially, and emotionally. Too often, teachers feel the frustrations of too little time and too few resources when attempting to achieve their goals. Many teachers do not realize that they have access to resources that, with a little preparation, can provide special, individualized learning experiences, sensitively tuned to a child's needs. Of course, these natural resources are the child's parents.

Even before the child is ready for a teacher, parents have supported the development of complex language, motor, and social skills in their child and have made a commitment to the child's growth and development that will help to sustain the child throughout the years to come. For the parent of the handicapped child, this may involve a lifetime commitment that brings special problems and needs. Because of their unique knowledge of their child, parents are often their child's best advocates.

Like any natural resource, there is a great deal of variation. Parents have differing skill levels, interest in their children's school progress, and personal circumstances. Furthermore, in order to gain the most benefit, parent participation and involvement must be developed and nurtured by the teacher, the child development specialist. Just as teachers spend time preparing themselves and their classroom materials, they must spend time preparing parents to assume active roles in the children's learning, both at school and at home. Just as each child learns and grows in a special way, each parent's involvement must be developed in a special way.

Parents are effective teachers, and their interest and approval are important to the young child. Shipman, McKee, and Bridgeman (1976) found that the factors most related to children's cognitive performance and development up to 9 years of age are the mother's use of an active teaching style; her requests for feedback; her expressions of affection, praise, and language specificity; and her positive statements about school. Other researchers also noted that parental characteristics are better predictors of children's later intellectual development than any and all types of intelligence tests or developmental checklists (Bronfenbrenner, 1974; Elardo, Bradley, & Caldwell, 1975; White & Watts, 1973).

In the early 1960s, when the importance of early intervention in the lives of "disadvantaged" or at-risk preschoolers was becoming evident, the federal government funded the landmark Head Start program (Horowitz & Paden, 1973). In Florida, however, a somewhat different early intervention program was developed and implemented under the direction of Ira Gordon (Gordon, 1973; Gordon & Guinagh, 1974). The Gordon program, entitled Home Start, also provided early childhood educational services to disadvantaged preschoolers and their families, but not through the more typical, center-based preschool Head Start program. Instead, "parent educators" made weekly home visits to each participating family, provided teaching materials, and instructed parents and other family members on how to use them. Parents were encouraged to read to their children at least once a day and to engage the child daily in brief teaching sessions using the educational materials. These parent educators also monitored the child's developmental progress by means of standardized developmental checklists and intelligence tests. The intellectual gains these children made with their parents as sole teachers were equal to, and in some cases, greater than those of children participating in the center-based Head Start programs. A similar approach was the basis for the eminently successful Portage Project (Weber, Jesien, Shearer, Bluma, Hilliard, Shearer, Schortinghuis, & Boyd, 1975), a home-based early intervention program for handicapped, preschool children and their families.

Not only has it been demonstrated that parents are effective teachers in a directive manner, but also it has been shown that such parental involvement in teaching results in stronger emotional ties. In a study of children's attachment to their mothers, children who were in day care from infancy on were compared with children who never participated in any type of out-of-home care (Farren & Ramey, 1977), and no differences were found in either children's or mothers' responses in learning, play, or high-stress situations. Children explored new settings, sought protection and soothing, and concentrated on learning new tasks no matter which type of early care they had received. Mothers were always the preferred teachers, playmates, and protectors, however. Both groups of mothers were equally skilled in teaching, entertaining, and soothing their children. Given the importance and effectiveness of parental support in mediating children's intellectual and social development, teachers would do well to invest time and energy in developing children's (and their own) most valuable resource, i.e., skilled parental involvement in children's growth and development.

Finally, early intervention with families may be instrumental in helping to prevent later learning and emotional problems. Children with early, untreated problems (physical or psychological) are more likely to have subsequent school problems (including dropping out), to engage in delinquent behavior, and to require therapeutic counseling for emotional problems later in life (Lewis, 1965; O'Neal & Robins, 1958). Parents of these children often report that these children had behavioral and learning problems at early ages (3 to 5 years).

Early problems that may seem minor can lead to severe disruptions in the parent-child relationship. In fact, families in which there are children with mildly handicapping conditions (e.g., language delay, partial hearing loss) are much more prone to experience parent-child difficulties than families with severely handicapped children or families without handicapped children (Blager & Martin, 1976; Martin, 1975; Smith & Hanson, 1974). Important precursors of disruptions later in the parent-child relationship are (1) mother-infant separations because of illness or other factors at birth and through the first year of life, (2) a highly active child with a gentle parent who prefers a less demanding interaction style, (3) a temporary or mild hearing loss at critical points in a child's social or language development, and (4) a child with atypical sleeping or eating patterns (or problems) in the first year of life.

Embry (1980) suggested that, if a child suffers a hearing loss from repeated ear infections during the toddler years,

> the child may have difficulty imitating speech sounds modelled by the parents, and if the child does not respond to a parent's vocal initiations at an early age, the parents may consider the child unresponsive and difficult to enjoy. When the child does not learn to speak normally, interactions with others will be impaired, compliance with parental requests will be limited, and responses to parental social initiations may be unsatisfying. The parents find the child difficult to manage, to care for, and to enjoy. Eventually, they are confronted with a child with a mild to moderate hearing impairment, speech and language delay, behavior management problems, and a poor self-image. (p. 30)

If the child is not responsive to the parent's social interactions and if the parent feels "punished" and unrewarded for efforts to interact with or teach the child, the parent may reduce additional attempts to stimulate the child. Such a sequence of interactions serves to reduce further the child's opportunities to learn those crucially needed social, language, and self-help skills. Thus, the support of healthy family relationships may be crucial to the normal development of the child. The lack of a supportive family relationship itself may handicap a child or worsen the effects of a mild or secondary handicapping condition.

Families with severely, multiply handicapped children experience additional difficulties that may further tax the parent-child relationship (Roos, 1978). Child care routines may be complex and time-consuming. It may be difficult to arrange for child care, particularly babysitters; the child usually requires a much longer period of time to learn even basic self-help skills, exposing both the parent and child to long-term frustrations; and, in order to learn, the child may require a lifetime parental commitment, as well as special sequencing of materials and special apparatuses not easily available to a parent. These parents and children should be made aware very early that there are available resources, such as the child development specialist, to provide information and to support successful early learning experiences for these children and their families (Roos, 1978).

All parents feel their child is special, and all parents at one time or another are faced with special problems associated with their child. The parents of a handicapped child may have to cope with more problems at an earlier age, however, and the solutions may be more complex. Thus, the impact of the handicapped child on a family may require special efforts, understanding, and skills from the child care professional if early intervention is to be successful.

If intervention and support begins at an early age, it may have a more long-lasting impact. Furthermore, it is undeniably easier to treat the learning delays or temper tantrums of a 3-year-old than those of a 14-year-old with a long history of failure in school and frustration at home. Parental interest in helping a child with problems is also greater if the child is younger, for there has not been the long history of stress. Parents of teen-agers often have long years of frustration, failure, and anger behind them which is hard to overcome.

BASIC PRINCIPLES

It is important for teachers to keep in mind that, whenever they communicate with parents on any subject, they are also laying the foundation for open communication in other areas. For example, if there is a discussion of preventive health care pertaining to the nutritional needs of young children, specific mealtime or nutritional problems a family may be experiencing are likely to be interjected into the conversation. Thus, teachers must listen "between the lines," thereby encouraging parents to bring up their concerns. The next step is to communicate to parents that their problem will be dealt with in an accepting but direct manner.

Teacher vs. Parent Perception

As teachers educate and care for children, they have opportunities that parents do not have. For instance, teachers often spend as many as six hours a day with a child, which may be more time than parents can spend with their child. Because teachers work with more than one child, they can compare the unique strengths, problems, or delays of each child with those of many other children of the same chronological or developmental age. Behaviors that parents view as problems may be quite normal for a child of a given age, especially in the areas of eating, sleeping, or toileting. All children, even those with handicaps, have strong points in which a parent can be helped to take pride. On the other hand, because teachers work with many children, they may notice a problem that has gone undetected by parents. For instance, it may be difficult for parents to recognize developmental delays in such areas as large and small motor coordination or language acquisition. Teachers can frequently be more specific about a child's behavior or development than parents, because teachers are usually more objective and less emotional about a child's problem.

There are several guidelines that teachers may find helpful for detecting potential handicaps in young children. Allen, Riecke, Dmitriev, and Hayden (1972) have developed a comprehensive checklist for teachers to use while working with preschoolers in a group setting. Through careful and systematic observations, teachers can assess the appropriateness or inappropriateness of a young child's behavior. This checklist, or commercial tests such as the McCarthy Screening Test (McCarthy, 1978), the Brigance Diagnostic Inventory on Early Development (Brigance, 1978), the Carolina Developmental Profile (Lillie & Harbin, 1975), or the Portage Project Checklist (Bluma, Shearer, Hilliard, & Frohman, 1976), not only will assist teachers in assessing each child's strengths and weaknesses, but also will provide them with many useful ideas for program planning.

Desired Teacher Qualities

In order to be effective in any child care program, teachers must possess certain qualities that will enable them to build positive relationships with both parents and children. Teachers should strive to be accepting, noncritical people who are flexible and open-minded. Both parents and children often need reassurance with regard to their self-worth, their beliefs, or their actions, and teachers should be sympathetic to their concerns and needs. In addition, teachers need to find out what parents and children want and expect from them and their program. Of course, most parents and young children like teachers to be warm and nurturing. This becomes apparent when parents participate in interviews of applicants for teaching positions; many of the questions asked by parents are intended to determine whether the applicant can respond to children in a physically tender and loving manner. Furthermore, both children and parents instinctively look for teachers who are flexible yet firm, humorous, empathetic, impartial, loving, energetic, serious, and friendly, and who do not care about getting their clothes dirty and love sitting on the floor—no small order! They also want teachers who can be trusted, who can help solve problems, and who will listen to their concerns.

Teachers must also be able to plan and implement a curriculum suitable for preschool children in all phases and areas of development. They should be knowledgeable, well-organized, and capable of providing a well-balanced program with emphasis on emotional, physical, creative, and social development, as well as on intellectual enhancement.

All of the foregoing are standard demands of knowledgeable day care consumers. Furthermore, these teacher qualities are not separate entities. They form a composite picture or description of an outstanding teacher who could meet most of the expectations of both parents and children.

Initial Parent Contacts

First contacts between parents and teachers may be brief or lengthy, planned or spontaneous, in the classroom or on the playground. Parents who are considering the possibility of enrolling their child should be encouraged to view the facilities and the daily activities while the program is in session or after hours during an open house. Unscheduled contacts may take place on field trips, on walks in the neighborhood, or when a parent brings an acquaintance along while picking up or leaving a child who is in the care of the teacher. During any of these contacts, first impressions are established, and teachers and parents evaluate each other—fairly or unfairly.

A difficult period for many children, for their parents, and for teachers as well is the first week or two of the child's enrollment. It is during this adjustment period that trust must be developed among everyone concerned. Teachers need to know a great deal about the new child before that all-important first day. Before this day, for example, parents should be asked to fill out a form regarding the family and the child's history and development. Teachers should also attempt to learn the parents' philosophy on child care and the role of teachers. For instance, do parents believe that an optimal learning environment requires a great deal of teacher preparation and direction? Through informal conversations, teachers may also be able to ascertain how mothers and fathers view themselves as parents.

The initial adjustment to a child care center experience is frequently painful for all concerned. Parents may have mixed emotions about leaving their child for so many hours, especially if the child is handicapped or under 3 years of age. The parent and the child should be invited to visit once or twice before the first scheduled day of attendance. Through careful observation, parent-child interaction patterns may be apparent to the teacher. Teachers, following the initial visit, should analyze what approach to use with the new child. Some children reject overt initiations from new adults, while others respond to a smiling, friendly person.

Parents may need guidance as to what is expected of them when they leave their child for the first time. For the first several days they may be asked to stay for 10 to 30 minutes and to return early for their child. Parents must be told that they should never suddenly disappear, because this can be most distressing for the child. Parents should tell their child that they are leaving, give assurances that they will be returning, exchange hugs and kisses, smile, and then leave *quickly*. Worried or forlorn glances and hesitations at the door suggest to children that this may not be a pleasant experience after all. If a child cries, teachers should gently reassure parents that everything will be all right and that they can leave as planned. Teachers are frequently able to entice a young child into an interesting activity or use a special toy to attract the child's attention. Parents can be encouraged to call an hour or so later to check on the child. For the child who continues to cry each day when the parents leave, yet gets along well the rest of the day, it may be necessary to use other techniques, such as ignoring the child until the crying stops; in this way, the child learns that it is noncrying behavior that gains attention from teachers. During this initial period of adjustment, the use of frequent, informal conversations helps to put parents at ease and enables the teacher to identify parental concerns.

Informal Parent Contacts

Interactions between parents and teachers must be cultivated and strengthened in order to grow and develop in a positive way. The establishment of positive, open communication through daily interactions makes teachers sensitive to each parent's needs in much the same way that teachers learn to respond to each child's individual learning style.

There are numerous avenues for encouraging parent participation and involvement in the child care programs. Even if parents work full-time, there are ways to help them feel more a part of the child's day. By being open, receptive, and chatty, teachers encourage parent interest and commitment. The ideal way to encourage parent participation is to emphasize daily parent-teacher interactions, such as in the first or last few minutes of the day. In both part- and full-day programs, however, various obstacles may interfere with or discourage daily contact between teachers and parents. In a part-day program, for example, many of the children arrive or leave at the same time, and it may be too hectic or confusing for teachers and parents to do much more than exchange pleasantries. In full-day programs, children may arrive before classroom teachers do, and teachers may leave before the children do. In these situations, aides frequently take care of the children during the early and late periods of the day and have little to share with the parents about the children's full day.

Because successful, day-to-day parent-teacher interactions are so essential to each child's well-being, teachers in full-day programs occasionally should arrange to arrive earlier or stay later than scheduled. Parents often form opinions about their child's program during arrival and departure times; unfortunately, in full-day programs, these periods are usually not indicative of the daily program. Therefore, special efforts must be made to communicate frequently and effectively with parents during a limited and often less than optimal time. If parents arrive early, it will help to gain their cooperation and interest if teachers acknowledge their presence, greet them, and in some way convey something about the child's day: "John, your father is here. I bet he'd like to see our new guinea pig!" If parents are kept abreast of small gains or simple problems, communication is more effective. A short step out of the classroom and away from the child frequently gives the needed privacy. It may be possible for teachers in part-time programs to be available outside the classroom door for a few minutes *before* the program begins or ends, when child care responsibilities are somewhat lessened. The judicious use of aides to greet and say goodbye to the children can provide the time necessary to communicate with parents.

Because brief and informal conversations with teachers are not nearly as intimidating as scheduled conferences for some parents, they are more likely to mention a difficulty or concern when a teacher is readily available and when no extra effort is necessary to communicate the concern. Brief contacts at the beginning or end of the child's session can open the door and signal the teacher's willingness to communicate. Parents need to get to know the teacher before they will share their concerns, just as the teacher must get to know the children in order to be a more effective teacher and parent counselor. Frequent, informative conversations are a sensitive and simple way to keep the lines of communication open between parent and teacher, home and school.

Other Ways To Communicate with Parents

While person-to-person contact is the most effective way to communicate, some parents rarely, if ever, have a chance to engage in even brief, informal conversations with teachers; their children may come in a carpool, work schedules may not permit such flexibility, or teachers may be too involved with children and classroom responsibilities when certain parents arrive. Other ways must be found to keep parents informed under these circumstances. In some programs, especially those for infants, toddlers, and handicapped children, daily notes may be written by parents in the morning, and teachers may send brief notes home at the end of the day. Since these children are too young or are unable to talk about their day, this personalizes the child's experiences and serves as a basis for "conversations" at home in the evenings.

For more verbally competent children, daily notes on which teachers check off a few items and describe a moment or two of the day are an excellent way to improve home-school communication. Such a communication system may be difficult to establish, but once in place, it is relatively simple to maintain. Again, aides may be needed to free the teacher for 20 to 30 minutes to complete the notes. These notes may serve not only to convey important information about the child's day, but also to remind parents about other events in the program.

A blackboard or bulletin board can also be used to communicate with parents. The teacher can write a summary of the day's events on a large blackboard for all parents to read. Such things as which children slept can be listed, for example. To report something special or different to parents who arrive after teachers have left, teachers should write a note and pin it to the bulletin board, attach it to the child's clothing with a safety pin, or tape it to the child's locker.

Cork boards glued to the wall above lockers are ideal message centers for individual parents. Each child can have a single cork square on which daily, weekly, or even bimonthly one-page messages to that child's parents can be placed. A mimeograph machine makes written communication with parents simple and easy. Teachers can write daily or weekly one-page letters to parents, describing past events and stating the plans for coming events. If a mimeograph machine is not available, a hand-written, one-page note can be posted on the classroom door. Newsletters from the center itself are usually more comprehensive than notes from a single classroom and thus require a fair amount of effort and expense. Keeping a file of interesting formats and good ideas to include in letters helps this task go more smoothly.

Finally, books should be made available for parents to read. A parent bookshelf or small book corner should include books on such topics as resources for parents of handicapped children, basic health care, child growth and development, discipline, positive family communication skills, and specific curriculums. A lending library is an informal way to bring parents in contact with the knowledge and necessary expertise to recognize and deal with their child's special problems and to seek appropriate assistance to foster their child's growth and development. A list of resources for all families, but especially families of handicapped children, is included in Appendix 6-A.

Planned Parent Contacts

Parent Conferences

Basically, there are two types of parent-teacher conferences. One is the regularly scheduled progress report type of conference that may take place two or three times a year between the teacher and each child's parents. The other is a conference scheduled in response to a parent's or teacher's request for a meeting to discuss problems occurring at home or in the child care program. Such a conference differs from the regularly scheduled one in that only specific topics are scheduled to be covered.

Teachers should be well-prepared for both kinds of conferences; otherwise, 20 to 60 minutes can pass, and important aspects of the child's development will not have been covered (Goetz, 1975). It is advantageous for teachers to write down specific information pertaining to the child's development and behavior before either kind of conference. Always, teachers should accent the positive aspects of the child's behavior between discussions of concerns or problems. Ample time must also be allowed for parents to express their concerns and for parents and teachers to seek joint solutions to problems.

In the regular, end-of-the-term meeting, progress in self-help and toileting skills, social adjustment, friendships, and the manner in which the child handles conflicts and frustrations are usually more important to the parents than such issues as the number of alphabet letters the child can label. During this conference, every effort must be made to cover briefly all aspects of the child's development. The way in which a child reacts to peers warrants as much coverage as the frequency with which the child engages in art, music, or dramatic play activities. Parent-teacher conferences are excellent times to share information not only about the skills or gains the child has made, but also about those skills and problems the child is currently developing.

For the special request conference, the discussion of the problems the child is having calls for a delicate balancing act. On the one hand, the teacher must not alarm or alienate the parents; on the other hand, the teacher must not gloss over the severity of the problem. There is no perfect way to do this. The teacher who knows the parent beforehand is in a much better position to communicate such information clearly and tactfully, as well as to ensure that the parents respond in a way that will be helpful to the child. As mentioned earlier, parents are important resources in all situations, but they are especially important when their child is having trouble. Furthermore, requests for parental ideas to supplement the teaching staff's ideas are a good way to convey to parents their own importance.

A record of the conference should be kept on a special form (Figure 6-1). Information given and obtained during conferences is confidential, however, and should be kept in each child's individual folder in a locked file. If possible, a copy of the conference report should be shared with the parents.

Parent Meetings

Some time during the first month or so of the new school year a parent-teacher meeting should be scheduled. This meeting is generally the most popular one of the year, and parents require little urging to attend. There are many reasons for having this early parent-teacher meeting. Some teachers may be newly hired, children may be placed in different classrooms, and parents enjoy an opportunity to get acquainted. Too, there may be families new to the program, and an early parent-teacher meeting is an opportunity to meet the new children's parents. Even if the teachers and parents are well acquainted, the children may have developed different interests and needs as they have grown a year older.

Special Meetings

Sometimes speakers are invited to special group meetings, or a series of group meetings are planned to impart information of particular interest to teachers or parents. Parents always seem interested in discussions pertaining to discipline, mealtime, toileting, whining, or dawdling. Parents may be asked to designate their topic interests for such special meetings (Figure 6-2).

Good planning is as crucial to the success of group meetings as it is to the success of a parent-teacher conference. There is nothing as disappointing as going to a great deal of effort to promote what seemed to be a highly desired program, to

Figure 6-1 Sample Record Form for Parent-Teacher Conference

Date of conference: _____

Child's name: _____   Parents present: _____
Age: _____   Teachers present: _____
Classroom: _____   _____
Conference was   (a) initiated by parent _____; staff _____
                   (b) special request _____; regular end-of-session _____
If special conference, what was the concern or topic? _____
_____
_____

Topics covered in conference (fill out what is appropriate):

A. Staff report
     1. Child's general adjustment to center:

     2. Child's relationship with peers:

     3. Child's relationship with adults:

     4. Behavior, e.g., how child responds to frustrations, conflicts:

     5. Self-help skills (or areas that need improvement):

     6. Mealtime, eating habits:

     7. Nap time or rest time:

     8. Toileting skills, toothbrushing, independence:

     9. Outdoor play and large muscle development:

    10. Music, art, and other creative skills:

    11. Language development, e.g., vocabulary, articulation, verbal initiation:

Figure 6-1 continued

    12. Fine motor development, e.g., puzzles, manipulatives, writing (if age-appropriate):

    13. Imagination, role playing:

    14. Intellectual development (list some cognitive skills):

    15. Child's overall disposition:

    16. Listening and participation skills in large group (circle time):

    17. Staff concerns:

B. Parent report:

C. Solutions, recommendations, and summary:

Preparer's name: _____

Parent signature: _____

                                   Date: _____

have only a handful of parents attend. Convenience must be considered. Evenings, for example, are busy times for families; a meal must be prepared and consumed, household chores completed, and family time worked in—all before a young child's bedtime. Evening meetings offered by child care programs often run a poor second to all these activities, especially when coupled with the difficulty of finding and affording babysitters. Thus, attendance at group meetings can be improved if (1) they are held immediately after the program ends or early in the evening, (2) child care is available, (3) they include a potluck supper (or a sack supper) so the family can be fed, (4) they end early so the children can go home to bed at their normal times, and (5) they invite the children's participation in a song or story time so part of the time can be considered family time. Except for special interest groups that meet on a continual basis (e.g., weekly), many of these techniques are easily adaptable to evening group programs.

Figure 6-2 Sample Survey of Parent Interests

FIRST Wednesday of Each Month, 7 P.M.

The following are possible topics you might want to discuss when we meet. Please check the things that interest you the most and hand in before or at the first meeting.
See you Wednesday!

_____ 1. What is a good routine to use to get children to bed?

_____ 2. What can I do when my child constantly gets out of bed?

_____ 3. What do I do when my child lies a lot?

_____ 4. What do I do when my child constantly leaves toys or belongings around the house?

_____ 5. What do I do when my child refuses to go to school or misses a great deal of school?

_____ 6. How can I help my child develop a positive attitude about school?

_____ 7. What do I do with a fussy eater who won't eat most foods?

_____ 8. How do I handle a sloppy or messy eater?

_____ 9. Should I spank or slap my child?

_____ 10. What rewards can I use to get my child to do what is expected?

_____ 11. What are logical consequences for "bad" behavior?

_____ 12. How should I handle my toddler's temper tantrums?

_____ 13. How and when should I explain a new separation or a pending divorce to my child?

_____ 14. What can I do when my child constantly whines?

_____ 15. How do I handle sibling fights?

_____ 16. What kinds of pre-reading and pre-math activities can I do at home with my child?

_____ 17. How can I help my child become less aggressive?

Another method of obtaining parent participation in the center is to get parents interested in forming or joining a parent group that meets on a regular basis. The *Systematic Training for Effective Parenting* (STEP) program (Dinkmeyer & McKay, 1976) is just one example of a commercial program that can be offered to parents on a weekly basis for a total of nine weeks. Groups of single parents or stepparents often meet once a month, sometimes for specific discussions and sometimes for unplanned gatherings. Very often, parents suggest that an outside speaker be obtained to discuss a topic of particular concern. For all meetings, attendance is greater if a sitter is available; the parents who use the care can share the cost.

Potpourri for Parent Involvement

Parents can become involved in their children's program in many ways. Some parents may enjoy serving on the child care center's advisory board where they can assist in establishing policies or in interviewing prospective teachers. Other parents may enjoy planning social events for children or families, helping with parties, editing the newsletter, serving as a driver on field trips, or becoming involved in fund-raising for tuition scholarships or expenses of the center.

Parents may also participate in their child's program by completing a written feedback form (Figure 6-3). When such a form is used, it should be easy to complete (no more than one page), cover the important aspects of the daily program, be sent out once or twice a year, and, of course, allow parents to be anonymous in their response. If there is more than one program, however, parents should be asked to designate which class their child attends. The feedback obtained on all forms can be collated and presented to the advisory board (if there is one) and to the staff as a whole. Individual feedback pertaining to each classroom is confidential and should be read only by the teachers who work in that room. A survey not only can convey parental satisfaction or dissatisfaction with a child care program, alerting teachers to certain aspects of a program that need strengthening, but also can reinforce capable, hard-working teachers for a job well-done. If all parents are not encouraged, even urged, to participate, only those with complaints may fill out the survey, and the results will be negatively slanted. Because parent input, support, and involvement are the keys to success of any child care program, parent feedback should not be overlooked.

PROBLEM AREAS AND SOLUTIONS

Children may have problems that are apparent at home but are not observed in the child care program, or vice versa. Even if problems occur in only one setting, they are more easily handled if parents and teachers can work cooperatively. Whether teachers are interacting with a parent on an intervention or prevention basis, they should realize that there are usually many choices for dealing with a problem, and several viewpoints are often better than one. While teachers are the professionals, parents often have more insight, for they know the child best. When it is the teacher who has the problem with the child, it is helpful to ask the parents

Figure 6-3 Sample Parent Feedback Form

PLEASE take the time to fill out the parent feedback form. Teachers want your input and appreciate your comments. In the past, only 25 to 40 percent of the parents returned parent feedback forms. Help to make it 100 percent. Please participate so we can get a true picture of parent feelings and satisfaction. If possible, return by _____. Thank you.

Classroom: _____   Teachers: _____   Date: _____

My satisfaction with	Completely satisfied	Very satisfied	Satisfied	Neither satisfied nor dissatisfied	Dissatisfied	Very dissatisfied	Not applicable
1. Overall operation of the center							
2. My child's classroom							
3. Enthusiasm of teachers							
4. Warm and loving care							
5. Creativity of program							
6. Challenging curriculum							
7. Handling of discipline							
8. Field trips, walks, outdoor play							
9. Naps and rest time							
10. Meals, snacks							
11. Teachers' response to my concerns							
12. Safety of children							
13. Classroom appearance							
14. Playground supervision							
15. Building appearance							
16. Music program by music teacher							
17. Early and late care (before and after teachers)							

18. Your positive comments:

19. Any complaints or suggestions for improvement:

If you are not satisfied, please tell us WHY!! (Use back of sheet.) THANK YOU VERY MUCH!!

for advice. Young, new teachers, often without children of their own, are especially likely to benefit from parental input.

Certainly, teachers need training and knowledge in behavioral and developmental principles in order to manage problems. They should be well-informed in normal and atypical development, and they should be aware of alternative causes and solutions to problems. In addition, teachers should learn to match solutions to the family and to the particular child. For example, teachers should not recommend books for parents who seek assistance but who do not enjoy reading or who have a marginal literacy level. Parents need the appropriate kind of recommendations and support from teachers. Also, teachers must be nonjudgmental. In suggesting to parents what course they might follow, teachers should describe what might be tried, indicate what can go wrong, and postulate what the child's responses are likely to be, with no intimation that the parent will be to blame for any failure.

Some children or families are confronted with stressful situations that are short-term, e.g., special events or traumas, such as the birth of a new baby, the death of a relative, or the separation of parents. Each of these can have an immediate effect on family members. During these times, teachers often become the one stabilizing person in a child's life. These family circumstances may be negative influences on the child's life at the moment, but children are resilient; they can almost always successfully adjust to these new events in their lives with the help of supportive, caring teachers. It is often teachers who help parents and children feel adequate and resourceful.

A child's best interest must always be foremost in a teacher's mind, especially if the parents appear to be the source of the problem. The teacher must be the child's advocate. If parents are harming or are likely to harm their child, the teacher must act. In most states, a teacher who suspects child abuse or neglect is required by law to report such suspicions to the proper authorities. In addition, it is important to document suspected abusive episodes by noting the date, exactly what happened (if known), the child's physical state, and the child's and parents' responses to inquiries about the incident. Of course, it is also important to increase careful and systematic observation of the child and parent-child interactions at the center. Since the current social-legal emphasis is on keeping the child in the home, it is the teacher's responsibility to help win cooperation from the parents and to try to work out acceptable solutions for all concerned. In all situations, but especially in cases of abuse or neglect, a strong, positive, and cooperative relationship between teacher and parents is needed to provide a better and happier life for the child.

For families with certain kinds of problems, teachers should recommend that the family seek assistance from someone with special expertise and experience in such problems. Thus, teachers should not serve as marriage counselors, financial advisors, or diagnosticians of a child's physical problems. Outside help is needed if

1. the problem is severe (e.g., the child vomits often when upset)
2. there is a history of long-standing problems for which the family may or may not have sought and received assistance in the past
3. the family appears to be disorganized and reports difficulties in many areas within their family relationship

In the first two instances, the severity and duration of the problems may require complex interventions that call for careful monitoring, either intensive or continued over a long time period; the second situation may indicate that the family is unwilling to solve their problems, no matter what they may say to the contrary. In the third circumstance, problems may be so numerous and so complex that the family may be overwhelmed; interventions, although individually clear and easy to do, may be more than the family can handle without first working out some of their more basic conflicts.

Mealtime

There are basically three types of family problems that revolve around children's consumption of food and mealtime behavior. The first, and often most difficult to remedy, involves the child who has extremely limited food preferences and refuses to eat by crying or having a tantrum when offered or "required" to eat whatever else the family is eating. The second develops when parents feel that their children must clean their plates at every meal, every day. The third consists of a variety of problem behaviors at mealtime; the child may leave the table many times, constantly spill food, not use utensils or use them inappropriately, or engage in a host of other irritating behaviors, such as whining, continuously kicking the table, or complaining incessantly about the food.

The first step in determining exactly which problem or combination of problems the family has is to have the parent note everything the child eats each day for three to five days. Dietary intake information is helpful not only in determining whether the child is eating enough, but also in detecting problems. If the child snacks on soda, fruit juices, or various carbohydrate "junk" foods just before meals, for example, the child is not hungry at the regular mealtime because of temporarily increased blood sugar levels; however, the child is hungry and clamoring for food a short while after the meal is completed. Teachers, too, should check what the child eats while in their care and observe the child's eating behavior as well. If the child is a "picky" eater, the child may eat little at school unless the food offered is one of his or her preferred foods.

Limited Food Preferences

Once teachers and parents have ascertained that the child's food preferences are truly limited, the parent should be asked when these problems began (often periods of illness trigger the onset of eating problems), whether the child has a history of allergies, and what the child's responses are to new foods. If the child and family have no histories of allergies and the child's response to offers of new foods is refusal or tears—but not vomiting—teachers (with parents' permission) may begin an intervention program designed simply to get the child to taste and swallow single, very small bites of new foods. If the child's response to new foods is to vomit the food, however, the family should be referred to *both* a physician and someone with expertise in helping children and families with such problems.

A three-part program to increase a child's tolerance for new foods that has been found effective (Embry, Schilmoeller, Kelley, & O'Malley, 1975) is based on

1. providing large amounts of positive feedback to the child for tasting and swallowing nonpreferred foods
2. restricting the child's intake of any food except at mealtimes
3. approaching the problem by reducing the child's distaste for foods slowly but systematically

A child cannot be forced to like a food, but the child's tolerance can be increased to at least a willingness to sample nonpreferred foods. Thus, a nonpreferred food, as a single bite, should be offered early in the meal and followed by a bite or sip of an especially preferred food. If the child tastes and swallows the offered food, the parents (and teachers) should express their pleasure clearly; if the food is refused, no comment should be made and the food should be offered again in a few minutes.

Negative contingencies should *not* be used for this type of problem except under special circumstances, and mealtimes should last no longer than it takes the rest of the family to finish, perhaps 20 to 25 minutes. Learning to tolerate nonpreferred foods can be difficult for some children; those 2½ years of age or older often need and will work very hard to earn a tangible signal of their success, such as a sticker or a happy face for tasting a nonpreferred food at a meal. The use of stickers also reduces the likelihood of tantrums. This sort of program should proceed slowly but can gain momentum in four to six weeks when the child's list of tolerated foods has grown.

Cleaning the Plate

Parental insistence that children must clean their plates at every meal every day is not usually a child behavior problem, but rather a parent problem. Resolving this conflict has a number of components. One is to provide parents with developmental information about children's nutritional requirements and typical variability in total consumption on a week-to-week, sometimes day-to-day, basis. For example, many parents report that, at about 2 years of age, their children suddenly appear to have poor appetites and eat much less. Parents should be informed that this is a normal developmental process; at about 2 years of age, physical growth slows dramatically. Thus, a child's necessary food intake is naturally reduced; it also becomes quite variable because of increasing variability in the child's daily activities. A second approach to solving the conflict is to ask the parent to write down everything the child eats for at least a week. It may be that over a period of several days the child actually does have a balanced and adequate diet. It is important to provide much gentle reassurance and sensitive questioning about parents' feelings. Some parents feel that, if their child does not eat, the child is rejecting them or making them appear to be inadequate parents.

Nutritional information is best provided in a group with other parents so that variability in children's consumption can be described by the other parents, rather than the teacher. Some of the other parents may be models of a more relaxed approach; the troubled parent can see that a child who does not eat everything all of the time is not a reflection of bad parenting. In this group, the parents may discuss their nutritional beliefs. Many people were raised to believe strongly in the importance of eating everything one is served (which is thought, by the way, to be related to many weight problems). If some parents are unable to override this early upbringing, other parents can encourage them to serve small first portions so the children will clean their plates, not ''waste'' food, and will ask for more if they are still hungry.

Other Problem Behaviors at Mealtime

Children who dawdle, have poor table manners, or engage in a variety of irritating behaviors, such as frequently leaving the table, whining, making negative comments about the food, playing with the food, kicking the table, or kneeling on or rocking the chair, also create mealtime difficulties. If only one or two of these is the problem, a combination of much positive feedback, a sticker chart, and planned ignoring of the mild problem behavior usually works.

If several of these behaviors are problems, a chart of the target behaviors with a space for the parent to record pluses for each positive mealtime behavior has proved effective. If the child earns 75 to 90 percent of the possible pluses, a sticker can be awarded to signal the child's success; this strengthens the impact of the program and is often necessary for long-term results. Timeout, defined as a restriction to a specific place (chair, room, locker) for a brief period (e.g., three to five minutes) during which no one interacts with the child nor may the child interact with anyone, may be necessary to reduce more severe problem behaviors, such as screaming, crying, or continuous whining.

Natural consequences may be employed for two common problems. If a child leaves the table before the meal is finished, the child may be forbidden to return to the table; that child's meal is finished. If a child dawdles excessively and is not finished when the rest of the family has finished, the meal is over for everyone, including the child; all plates are removed. Between meal snacks should, of course, be restricted to ensure that the child is hungry at mealtimes. All newly introduced procedures should be carefully explained to the child before they are implemented. If the child is ''surprised'' by the unannounced enforcement of such a family rule, the child will quite naturally be upset and, thus, quite likely to have a tantrum. Even with forewarning, the child may have a tantrum; parents should be prepared for such a response. The probability of a tantrum is greatly reduced, however, if the child knows what decision has been made. Ordinarily, these techniques work very quickly, usually within a meal or two, so the negative effects are short-lived.

Handicapped children often have histories of feeding problems that commence in infancy and increase the probability of mealtime problems later in life; always there is heightened parental concern. The most likely problems that these children and their families will encounter are those faced by nonhandicapped children and their families, and such problems may be handled similarly. Other problems that are specific to children with severe motor, anatomical, or neurological involvement may occur, however. One child may have difficulty with the transition from a soft or liquid diet to a semisoft or more regular diet; another may have difficulty learning self-feeding skills.

Resolution of these difficulties often requires the use of a combination of mechanical aids and devices; adaptation of equipment, such as special bottles, nipples, plates, chairs; and behavioral teaching and management skills, such as task analysis, sequencing, shaping, and fading. Much support must also be provided to both the parent and child in their teaching and learning efforts. (For a discussion of specific approaches to such specialized problems, see Baker, Brightman, Heifetz, & Murphy, 1976; Copeland, Ford, & Solon, 1976; Sontag, Smith, & Certo, 1977; Worthington, Pipes, & Trahms, 1978.)

Bedtime/Naptime

Parents often report bedtime difficulties. Children may refuse to go to sleep, or even to stay in their bed; children may wake in the middle of the night either crying or coming to bed with the parent(s); children may not go to sleep without crying, without asking for many different things, or without insisting that the parent lie down with them. It must be remembered, however, that waking in the middle of the night and crying or screaming out, ''night terrors'' as this is sometimes called, is quite different from waking to sleep with the parent(s).

Although there are some ways to encourage children to go to sleep quickly with a minimum of fuss, there is almost no way to avoid several evenings of crying and screaming if the problem is chronic and severe. One strategy found most effective involves the establishment of a pleasant, relaxed bedtime routine so that the child will feel confident of the parent's interest and willingness to spend time with the child. After a reasonable period, the parent firmly and gently holds to the agreed upon limit by saying "good night" and leaving the room. If the problem has been that the child gets out of bed and the child stays in bed, the door stays open; if the child leaves the bed, the door is shut. If the problem has been that the child screams and cries, the door stays open as long as the child is quiet; the door is shut, however, if the child begins to cry and scream. It can be reopened when the child is quiet for a few minutes. For children 3½ years of age and older, a positive, tangible consequence, such as a special sticker or treat in the morning, can be an effective way to reduce the crying more quickly. It has been found that a child who has been allowed to cry for periods of time in the past before the parent goes to the child will cry on the first night of the new program double the longest time the child has ever been allowed to cry in the past. Allowing a child to "cry it out" is extremely difficult; parents need a great deal of support to carry out these procedures. Thus, it is important to prepare parents for the initial negative phase in order to meet their goal of a peaceful bedtime.

Middle-of-the-night problems often involve many of the same behaviors as the going-to-bed problems. They can be treated in much the same way, with one exception. Parents should always check their child before letting their child "cry it out." The child who is ill must be cared for, of course; the child who is afraid can be reassured. If the child is not ill and has been reassured, the parent must then set the limit gently but firmly by saying "good night" and leaving the room. Occasionally, the problem is that the child creeps into the parents' bed without the parents being aware of the child's presence until the next morning. This is easily dealt with by placing some bells on a string across the door to the parents' bedroom so that the parents will be wakened when the child attempts to creep in and can return the child to bed.

Some parents, however, prefer to have their children sleep with them. If this habit persists, the parents should be encouraged to seek counseling. If one parent wishes to resolve the problem and the other does not, the family should be referred to someone with expertise in dealing with family problems.

Toileting

Toilet training is a major developmental milestone. Although the ideal age for training has yet to be determined, it is clear that the older the child is before training is begun, the easier the training will be accomplished. Currently, most developmental pediatricians, nurses, and psychologists recommend waiting until sometime after a child is 2 years of age. The average length of time required for toilet training is about six months (Azrin & Foxx, 1974). There are a number of books available on ways to toilet train, and most of them contain good suggestions. However, teachers should be prepared to discuss some important considerations with parents.

Toileting has two components: the physiological process of bladder control and the actual use of the toilet. A good toilet training program should focus as much on staying dry as on the actual use of the toilet. Thus, a program in which the parents make frequent "dry pants" checks and provide positive feedback to the child for clean, dry pants is much stronger than one in which only use of the toilet is encouraged. Toileting is the one behavior for which tangible reinforcers are highly recommended if it appears that problems may develop. Stars, stickers, surprise bags with treats, brightly colored shorts or pretty panties are well worth using to encourage correct toileting. Paired with much positive feedback through hourly dry pants checks, the combined regimen usually produces the desired outcome in a fairly short time period, i.e., two to four weeks, of intensive, positive training.

All children have toileting accidents at one time or another; this is natural and developmentally appropriate. Children should never be punished for such accidents. Preparing parents for those instances and the negative, angry feelings they may have is important. If parents are aware ahead of time of the frustration they are likely to feel, they can plan to control their anger and, thus, their desire to punish the child.

Children who are 3 years of age or older and are having toileting problems may not need the intensive training program used for younger children. However, they should have the same positive teaching program in which dry pants checks are conducted and stickers may be earned for several hours of dry pants or for correct toilet use. Preschool and primary age children should also be expected to take primary responsibility for cleaning up after their accidents.

The sudden onset of toileting problems in an older child often signals either an infection or a serious emotional upset; both possibilities should be investigated. Children with bowel problems that involve either retention or nonretention of feces should be referred to *both* a pediatrician and a professional with expertise in treating encopresis. Many children wet the bed long after they have been toilet trained. If a child is older than 6 or 7 years of age and is still wetting the bed, the family should be referred to *both* a pediatrician and a professional with expertise in treating nocturnal enuresis.

A number of effective toilet training programs have been developed for the handicapped or retarded child. Basically, these programs involve the same training techniques, but the task is divided into smaller steps to ensure success. In addition, they provide special information on toilet training children who are nonambulatory (teaching the child special cues to get parental or teacher assistance) and children who are on seizure medication and should not consume large quantities of liquids. Such programs usually take several weeks (even several months) longer than those for normally developing children and involve more intensive training efforts by parents and teachers.

Whining, Crying, and Dawdling

If there is one behavior that is guaranteed to set both a parent and a teacher on edge, it is whining. Dawdling, which children do only when someone is in a hurry (or so it appears to adults), produces a similar reaction in caregivers. Because these two behaviors are likely to occur when a parent has many other things to do, they are also likely to result in parental responses that are far more negative than the severity of the behavior may seem to warrant.

Parents seem to tolerate whining for a variety of reasons, e.g., because the child is handicapped; because the child is hungry, tired, or grumpy "today"; or perhaps because the parents feel guilty about being home so little. They know, too, that attempts to stop the whining often worsen it and result in a tantrum that the parents cannot deal with when they are tired, hungry, or in a hurry. It is important to convey to the parents that continual whining on the part of the child only increases parental feelings of tiredness, anger, and frustration. Because of these feelings, the parents spend even less time with the child in a positive fashion and, also, inadvertently teach the child to use a socially inappropriate communication technique. Of course, whining is occasionally "legitimate"—a child may be truly hungry on the way home after a long day at school. The provision of fruit or vegetables to snack on in the car is usually effective in solving this problem. Unfortunately, most whining occurs at other times, and a direct behavioral intervention program is necessary.

Children between the ages of 2 and 3½ tend to whine the most. They may whine so often, in fact, that parents appear not to notice it and often respond to it unintentionally, thus strengthening the habit even more. When this is the case, an intervention program must include an identification component for both the parent and the child ("That's whining. Ask nicely.") in addition to

1. positive feedback from the parent when the child stops whining or does not whine at all
2. planned ignoring for short bursts of whining
3. timeout for repeated or long duration whining

This is a most tenacious behavior that is susceptible to relapse even when it has been under control for awhile; however, the intervention program described above has been effective with children of all ages (Isaacs, Embry, & Baer, 1981).

Dawdling is almost always a child's response to being hurried or pushed by parents. A first step may be to encourage parents to allow more time for children's routines; a second step is to help parents reassess their own deadlines to see if all of them are truly mandatory. Some children, in spite of adult efforts to allow more time, appear to be chronic dawdlers. One effective way to handle the problem in these children is to set a timer for completion of an activity and to increase the number of positive interactions during that time period. As an alternative, a positive consequence could be planned for the time that will be saved if the child has not dawdled. For dawdling during particular routines (e.g., getting ready in the morning), a chart listing each activity to be completed, with spaces to mark pluses and a space for a sticker or happy face, can be an effective strategy. Such a chart helps both parents and children plan ahead.

Managing Fears

There are three types of problem crying: (1) crying that is actually a variant of whining and should be treated as whining, (2) crying that is part of a tantrum and should be treated as a tantrum, and (3) crying that is part of a fear. Families with children who have severe or frequent tantrums and engage in self-destructive behaviors during a tantrum, such as banging the head, vomiting, or biting themselves, should be referred to a professional clinician with expertise in such problems. Crying that is the outcome of fear should not be ignored, nor should a child *ever* be placed in timeout for responding that way.

Fears may be simply attention-getting devices, or they may appear suddenly and spontaneously, triggered by a specific incident or circumstance, such as a fear of doctors following a traumatic or painful hospitalization. Attention-getting fears may be distinguished from the second type of fear by the fact that the child has usually exhibited the fear a long time with little reason actually to be fearful (e.g., "boogie men under the bed"). With such fears, adult reassurance and explanations given over a period of days produce little improvement; instead, the child seems to be manipulating the adult to produce more and more reassurances. It may be necessary in such cases to let the child "cry it out." However, if the fear is of the second type, if it is not clear which type of fear it is, or if it is quite unusual for the child to respond in such a manner, it is important to respond to the child in a gentle, confident, and firm manner.

The parent who is also fearful of the feared objects or situation should be encouraged to let some other adult help the child overcome the fear. If a fearful parent is attempting to teach a fearful child not to be afraid, the parent's scarcely concealed nonverbal cues will probably only increase the child's fear. The child should never be ridiculed, spanked, or treated as silly for expressing real fear. A combination of information, positive reinforcement for even small improvements, and frequent but limited exposure (in the company of a protective adult) to the feared objects or situations is important. The child should not be permitted to avoid the feared situation completely, but contact should be extremely limited at first and then gradually increased as the child is able to tolerate it. The child should never be thrust into the feared situation just to prove that the child will not get hurt.

Children older than 3 years of age should be taught very specific coping techniques or actions to follow when confronted with the fear-producing situation, e.g., breathing slowly, checking to be sure an adult is present, turning on a light, saying something to themselves, such as "I'll be O.K." or "I know what to do; I can breathe slowly." The children should rehearse the steps until they can say or do them easily when not under stress. Then gradually, they should be exposed to greater and greater levels of the feared situation and encouraged to use the practiced coping techniques, even though they may still respond fearfully.

Unfortunately, there may be occasions when the exposure cannot be limited and gradually increased. Under these circumstances, practice sessions at school and at home are crucial. For example, a child had to have eye drops placed in her eyes six times a day following cataract surgery. The eye drops were extremely painful initially; the child screamed, kicked, and became hysterical whenever the parent prepared to place the eye drops in her eyes. Coping techniques that this child was taught included screaming, crying, and clutching a doll, all without kicking or twisting her head. The techniques were first practiced with and taught to the child's doll by her mother, who then had her daughter "teach" the doll how to scream and cry while holding still. The child and parent then practiced the techniques in the bathroom where the eye drops were usually placed in the child's eyes, but without the eye dropper. During the practice sessions and during the actual procedure, the parent continuously praised the child for holding still and explained that it was all right to cry and scream. Within 12 hours, the child had learned to tolerate the eye drops with less hysteria. As a result, it took much less time to place the eye drops in her eyes.

CONCLUSION

Parents of today have busier and more exacting schedules, their information needs are greater and more varied, and they bring to their child-rearing both greater awareness *and* greater confusion about the importance of the decisions they make for their children. Thus, today's early childhood education professional must be more flexible and creative in meeting those needs. Multiple communication channels to and from the parents must be established and nurtured, and greater sensitivity to parental knowledge levels and confusion is required on the part of the teacher.

Although intervention strategies for helping families over rough spots are important, prevention-oriented child management activities help both teachers and families develop healthier communication patterns. Such patterns may preclude later needs for intensive intervention and most surely will help to establish happier living and learning environments for children, both at home and at school. Meeting families' information needs today is a complex task.

Communication with parents requires as much planning and care as the planning and care that go into the direct teaching time with the children. Early childhood education is for the child and the whole family, a teaching role not to be assumed lightly by teachers. In today's changing world, children's and families' needs for information and practical assistance challenge teachers to draw on new knowledge and techniques in fulfilling their role as significant resource persons.

REFERENCES

Abidin, R.R. (Ed.). *Parent education and intervention handbook*. Springfield, IL: Charles C Thomas, 1980.

Allen, E.K. *Mainstreaming in early childhood education*. Albany, NY: Delmar, 1980.

Allen, E.K., Riecke, J., Dmitriev, V., & Hayden, A.H. Early warning: Observation as a tool for recognizing potential handicaps in young children. *Educational Horizons*, 1972, *50*(2), 43-55.

Azrin, N.H., & Foxx, R.M. *Toilet training in less than a day*. New York: Simon & Schuster, 1974.

Baker, B., Brightman, A.J., Heifetz, L.J., & Murphy, D.M. *Steps to independence: A skills training series for children with special needs*. Champaign, IL: Research Press, 1976.

Becker, W.C. *Parents are teachers: A child management program*. Champaign, IL: Research Press, 1971.

Blager, F., & Martin, H.P. Speech and language of abused children. In H.P. Martin (Ed.), *The abused child*. Cambridge: Ballinger Publishing, 1976.

Bloom, B. *Stability and change in human characteristics*. New York: Wiley, 1964.

Bluma, S., Shearer, M., Hilliard, J., & Frohman, A. *Portage guide to early education*. Portage, WI: Cooperative Educational Service Agency, 1976.

Boyd, R.D., Stauber, K.A., & Bluma, S.M. *The Portage parent program*. Portage, WI: Cooperative Education Service Agency 12, 1977.

Brigance, A.H. *Brigance diagnostic inventory of early development*. Woburn, MA: Curriculum Associates, 1978.

Bronfenbrenner, U. *Is early intervention effective? A report on longitudinal evaluations of preschool programs*. Vol. 2. Washington, DC: DHEW, 1974.

Bronfenbrenner, U. Who cares for America's children. In V. Vaughan & T.B. Brazelton (Eds.), *The family—Can it be saved?* Chicago: Year Book Medical Publishers, 1976.

Brooks, J.B. *The process of parenting*. Palo Alto, CA: Mayfield Publishing, 1981.

Caldwell, B.M. The changing family: Where is it destined? *Educational Horizons*, 1980, *59*(1).

Copeland, M., Ford, L., & Solon, N. *Occupational therapy for the mentally retarded*. Baltimore: University Park Press, 1976.

Dinkmeyer, D., & McKay, G.D. *Systematic training for effective parenting*. Circle Pines, MN: American Guidance Service, 1976.

Dittmann, L.L. Project Head Start became a long-distance runner. *Young Children*, 1980, *35*(6), 2-12.

Elardo, R., Bradley, R., & Caldwell, B. The relation of infants' home environments to mental test performance from six to thirty-six months: A longitudinal analysis. *Child Development*, 1975, *46*, 71-76.

Embry, L.H. Analysis, assessment, and development of family support for handicapped preschool children: A review. In J.A. Gallagher (Ed.), *New directions in special education*. San Francisco, CA: Jossey-Bass, 1980.

Embry, L.H., Schilmoeller, G., Kelley, M.L., & O'Malley, J. *A parent class for training parents as their children's therapists*. Paper presented at the 83rd annual convention of the American Psychological Association, Chicago, 1975.

Farran, D.C., & Ramey, C.T. Infant day care and attachment behaviors toward mothers and teachers. *Child Development*, 1977, *48*, 1112-1116.

Fine, M.J. *Parents vs. children*. Englewood Cliffs, NJ: Prentice-Hall, 1979.

Gesell, A., & Ilg, F. *Infant and child in the culture of today*. New York: Harper & Brothers, 1951.

Goetz, E.M. Parent conference can work. *Day care and early education*, April 1975, 13-15.

Gordon, I. The young child: A new look. In J.L. Frost (Ed.), *Early childhood education rediscovered*. New York: Holt, Rinehart and Winston, 1968.

Gordon, I.J. *The Florida parent education early intervention projects: A longitudinal look*. Gainesville, FL: University of Florida, College of Education, Institute for Development of Human Resources, 1973.

Gordon, I.J. Parent education and parent involvement: Retrospect and prophecy. *Childhood Education*, 1977, *54*(2), 71-79.

Gordon, I.J., & Guinagh, B.J. *A home learning approach to early stimulation: Final report*. Washington, DC: National Institute of Mental Health, 1974.

Gordon, I.J., & Hess, R. *Parents as teachers of young children: An evaluative review of some contemporary concepts and programs*. Stanford, CA: Stanford University Press, 1975.

Gordon, T. *P.E.T. Parent effectiveness training*. New York: New American Library, 1975.

Gray, S.W., Klaus, R.A., Mille, J.O., & Forreste, B.J. *Before first grade*. New York: Teachers College Press, 1966.

Horowitz, F.D., & Paden, L.Y. The effects of environmental intervention programs. In B. Caldwell & H. Ricciuti (Eds.), *Review of Child Development Research*. Vol. 3, 1973, 331-402.

Hunt, J.McV. *Intelligence and experience*. New York: Ronald Press, 1961.

Hunt, J.McV. The psychological basis for using preschool enrichment as an antidote for cultural deprivation. *Merrill-Palmer Quarterly*, 1964, *10*, 209-248.

Isaacs, C., Embry, L., & Baer, D.M. *New therapists: Preschool-age siblings in the home*. Unpublished manuscript, University of Kansas, 1981.

LeMasters, E.E. *Parents in modern America*. Homewood, IL: The Dorsey Press, 1977.

Lewis, W.W. Continuity and intervention in emotional disturbance: A review. *Exceptional Children*, 1965, *31*, 465-476.

Lillie, D.L., & Harbin, G.L. *Carolina Development Profile*. Winston-Salem, NC: Kaplan Press, 1975.

Madden, J., Levenstein, P., & Levenstein, S. *Longitudinal IQ outcomes of the mother-child home program, 1967-1973*. Freeport, NY: Verbal Interaction Project, Family Service Association of Nassau County, and State University of New York at Stony Brook, 1974.

Martin, H.P. Parental response to handicapped children. *Developmental Medicine and Child Neurology*, 1975, *17*, 25.

McCarthy, D. *McCarthy Screening Test*. New York: The Psychological Corporation, 1978.

Morrison, G. *Early childhood education today*. Columbus, OH: Charles E. Merrill, 1976.

Nedler, S.E., & McAffee, O.D. *Working with parents: Guidelines for early childhood and elementary teachers*. Belmont, CA: Wadsworth, 1979.

Nixon, R.H., & Nixon, C.L. *Introduction to early childhood education*. New York: Random House, 1971.

Norton, G.R. *Parenting*. Englewood Cliffs, NJ: Prentice-Hall, 1977.

O'Neal, P., & Robins, L.N. The relation of childhood behavior problems to adult psychiatric status. *American Journal of Psychiatry*, 1958, *114*, 961-969.

Roos, P. Parents of mentally retarded children—Misunderstood and mistreated. In A.P. Turnbull & H.R. Turnbull (Eds.), *Parents speak out: Views from the other side of the two-way mirror.* Columbus, OH: Charles E. Merrill, 1978.

Shipman, V.C., McKee, D., & Bridgeman, B. *Stability and change in family status, situational and process variables and their relationship to children's cognitive performance.* (Progress report 75-28). Princeton, NJ: Educational Testing Service, 1976.

Smith, S.M., & Hanson, R. 134 battered children: A medical and physiological study. *British Medical Journal,* 1974, *2,* 666-670.

Sontag, E., Smith, J., & Certo, N. (Eds.). *Programming for the severely and profoundly handicapped.* Reston, VA: Council for Exceptional Children, Division of Mental Retardation, 1977.

Spock, B. *The common sense book of baby and child care.* New York: Duell, Sloan and Pearce, 1957.

U.S. Dept. of Health, Education and Welfare, Office of Human Development, Office of Child Development, Children's Bureau. *Your child from 1 to 6.* Washington, DC: U.S. Govt. Printing Office, 1962.

Weber, S., Jesien, G., Shearer, D., Bluma, S., Hilliard, J., Shearer, M., Schortinghuis, N., & Boyd, R. *The Portage Guide to Home Teaching.* Portage, WI: Cooperative Educational Service Agency, 1975.

Weikart, D.P., & Lambie, D.A. Preschool intervention through a home teaching program. In J. Hellmuth (Ed.), *Disadvantaged Child* (Vol. 2). Seattle: Special Child Publication, 1968.

White, B., & Watts, J. *Experience and environment: Major influences on the development of the young child* (Vol. 1). Englewood Cliffs, NJ: Prentice-Hall, 1973.

Worthington, B.S., Pipes, P.L., & Trahms, C.M. The pediatric nutritionist. In K.E. Allen, V.A. Holm, & R.L. Schiefelbusch (Eds.), *Early intervention—A team approach.* Baltimore: University Park Press, 1978.

Zigler, E.F. America's Head Start program: An agenda for its second decade. *Young Children,* 1978, *33*(5), 4-13.

Appendix 6-A

Bookshelf for Parents

Arnold, L.E. (Ed.). *Helping parents help their children.* New York: Brunner/Mazel, 1978.

Azrin, N., & Foxx, R. *Toilet training in less than a day.* New York: Simon & Schuster, 1974.

Baldwin, V.L., & Fredericks, H.D. *Bud, isn't it time he outgrew this? Or a training program for parents of retarded children.* Springfield, IL: Charles C Thomas, 1973.

Baratta-Lorton, M. *Workjobs . . . for parents: Activity-centered learning in the home.* Menlo Park, CA: Addison-Wesley Publishing, 1975.

Blumenfeld, J., Thompson, P., & Vogel, B. *Help them grow!* Nashville, TN: Abingdon Press, 1971.

Boston Women's Health Book Collective. *Ourselves and our children.* New York: Random House, 1978.

Brazelton, T.B. *Toddlers and parents.* New York: Dell Publishing, 1974.

Brown, S.L., & Moersch, M.S. (Eds.). *Parents on the team.* Ann Arbor, MI: University of Michigan Press, 1978.

Brutten, M., Mangel, C., Richardson, S. *Something's wrong with my child.* New York: Harcourt Brace Jovanovich, 1979.

Cansler, D. (Ed.). *Programs for parents of preschoolers: Parent group activities designed to broaden the horizons of young children.* Winston-Salem, NC: Kaplan Press, 1978.

Christophersen, E. *Little people.* Lawrence, KS: H & H Enterprises, 1977.

Comer, J.P., & Poussaint, A.F. *Black child care: How to bring up a healthy black child in America.* New York: Pocket Books, 1976.

Cunningham, C., & Sloper, P. *Helping your exceptional baby: A practical and honest approach to raising a mentally handicapped child.* New York: Pantheon Books, 1980.

Cutler, B.C. *Unraveling the special education maze.* Champaign, IL: Research Press, 1981.

Disability in early childhood. *The Exceptional Parent,* 1978, (1), D1-D32.

Frazier, C.A. *Parents' guide to allergy in children.* New York: Grosset & Dunlap, 1978.

Ginott, H.G. *Between parent and child.* New York: Avon Books, 1969.

Ginsbert, G., & Harrison, C.H. *How to help your gifted child: A handbook for parents and teachers.* New York: Monarch Press, 1977.

Gordon, T. *P.E.T. Parent Effectiveness Training.* New York: New American Library, 1975.

Gould, T. *Home guide to early reading.* New York: Penguin Books, 1976.

Hannam, C. *Parents and mentally handicapped children.* Baltimore: Penguin Books.

Hart, V. *Beginning with the handicapped*. Springfield, IL: Charles C Thomas, 1974.

Hayes, M.L., *Oh dear! Somebody said "learning disability!"* Norato, CA: Academic Therapy Publications, 1975.

Ilg, F., & Ames, L. *Child behavior*. New York: Harper & Row, 1955.

Jenkins, G.G., & Shacter, H.S. *These are your children,* Glenview, IL: Scott, Foresman, 1975.

Justice, B., & Justice, R. *The abusing family*. New York: Human Sciences Press, 1976.

Knox, L. *Parents are people too*. Nashville, TN: Intersect, 1978.

Koontz, C. (Ed.). *Koontz child development program: Training activities for the first 48 months*. Los Angeles: Western Psychological Services, 1974.

Kroth, R.L. *Communicating with parents of exceptional children*. Denver, CO: Love Publishing, 1975.

Levy, J. *The baby exercise book*. New York: Random House, 1975.

Markel, G.P., & Greenbaum, J. *Parents are to be seen and heard: Assertiveness in educational planning for handicapped children*. Impact Publishers, 1979.

Moore, C.B., Morton, K.G., & Mills, J.B. *A reader's guide for parents of children with mental, physical, or emotional disabilities*. DHEW publication #(HSA) 77-5290. Rockville, MD: U.S. Dept. of Health, Education & Welfare, Public Health Service, Health Services Administration, Bureau of Community Health Services, 1976.

Murphy, A.T. *Special children, special parents: Personal issues with handicapped children*. Englewood Cliffs, NJ: Prentice-Hall, 1981.

Oksman, B.B. *Learning disabilities: A family affair*. New York: Warner Books, 1980.

Orlansky, M.D., & Howard, W.L. *Voices: Interviews with handicapped people*. Columbus, OH: Charles E. Merrill, 1981.

Spock, B. *The common sense book of baby and child care*. New York: Duell, Sloan and Pearce, 1957.

Stein, S.B. *On divorce: An open family book for parents and children together*. New York: Walker, 1979.

Stevens, L.J., & Stoner, R.B. *How to improve your child's behavior through diet*. New York: New American Library, 1979.

Turnbull, A.P., & Turnbull, H.R. (Eds.). *Parents speak out: Views from the other side of the two-way mirror*. Columbus, OH: Charles E. Merrill, 1978.

Wagonseller, B.R., & McDowell, R.L. *You and your child: A common sense approach to successful parenting*. Champaign, IL: Research Press, 1979.

White, B. *The first three years of life*. New York: Avon Books, 1975.

Wolery, M.R. *Parents as teachers of their handicapped children*. Seattle: Western States Technical Assistance Resources (WESTAR), 19.

Chapter 7

Mainstreaming: Adapting the Program to the Children

Deirdre Hickey

The mainstreaming of young handicapped children into preschools for normally developing children has been a long-time policy in many centers (Allen, 1980); however, legislative action addressing the needs of handicapped individuals did not begin until the early 1960s with the passage of P.L. 88-164, Facilities for the Mentally Retarded. Through this legislation, and several legislative acts that followed, funds were provided for training, education, and research related to handicapping conditions. During this early period, provisions also were made for the funding of educational services for preschool handicapped and nonhandicapped children, though integration of children in a mainstreaming setting was not mandated.

The Handicapped Children's Early Education Assistance Act of 1968 provided funding for the development, validation, and replication of modern early education programs. This system of innovative programs is often referred to as the First Chance Network. Through these programs, many thousands of young handicapped children have been served in every state.

In 1972 came the passage of the Head Start Economic Opportunity and Community Partnership Act, which strengthened Head Start's "open door" policy toward atypical children by requiring that 10 percent of a state's total enrollment opportunities be reserved for handicapped children. The inclusion mandate was further strengthened in 1974 by an amendment requiring that services be provided to meet the individualized needs of severely handicapped children. Speech-impaired, deaf and hearing impaired, blind and visually impaired, mentally retarded, health and orthopedically handicapped, and emotionally disturbed children were to be included and provided with appropriate services.

The editors wish to thank Sidney Roedel for giving unstintingly of her expertise and energy in producing the final revision of this chapter.

The practice of integrating handicapped children into classrooms with non-handicapped children gained momentum from the passage of P.L. 94-142, the Education for All Handicapped Children Act, which requires that all children have equal educational opportunities; a free, appropriate education was to be provided all handicapped children by September, 1978. Furthermore, this act requires that children be educated in the least restrictive and most appropriate environment, thus calling for the integration of handicapped and nonhandicapped children to the maximum extent appropriate.

By integration, the law arguably intends more than placement of handicapped and nonhandicapped children together in the classroom; it requires that schools take steps to ensure the inclusion of all children in appropriate classroom and extraclassroom activities. The law does not mean, however, that the same educational format is appropriate for all children. Instead, it means that all children have special needs and may have advanced or delayed skills that require individual programming. By placing handicapped children in regular classrooms, the law is saying simply that the special needs of these children can be met with individualized programs in the regular classroom.

Even so brief a sketch of selected legislative events makes it evident that the 1970s (and the late 1960s) brought forth several "firsts" aimed at advancing the well-being of handicapped children and youth. Certainly, where young children were concerned, there was increasing emphasis on early identification and intervention services for those considered to be handicapped or at developmental risk.

An affirmation of such legislation occurred, at least indirectly, when the long-lasting and positive effects of the 1960s early intervention and compensatory programs for disadvantaged children began to be reported (Lazar & Darlington, 1982; Schweinhart & Weikart, 1980). It seems reasonable to extrapolate from these longitudinal follow-up studies that early intervention and related measures, such as mainstreaming, will have a similarly positive effect on handicapped and developmentally impaired children. The future of such programs is not clear, however, since the 1980s have brought efforts to reduce, deregulate, and redistribute federal monies for special educational purposes. To what degree early identification and intervention programs will expand or even continue to serve handicapped children and their families cannot be foretold. Only one prediction seems safe: child and family advocates, child developmentalists, and early childhood education specialists have too many indications of benefit (Guralnick, 1981) to allow young handicapped and developmentally delayed children to be excluded from the mainstream of community life ever again.

It is known that the primary means of transmitting culture from one generation to the next is the education of the young (Garwood, 1983). The integration of handicapped and nonhandicapped children in regular classrooms exposes the children to the culture's attitudes and practices regarding individual differences, deviations, and handicaps. When handicapped children are excluded from mainstream activities, all children—handicapped children included—learn that it is not acceptable in our culture to be different. As Sarason and Doris (1969) pointed out, if mental retardation were an acceptable condition, society would not have engaged in elimination (sterilization), exclusion (institutionalization), and isolation (segregated special classes) as treatment for these people (children).

Play and interaction with peers seem to be essential to all children's normal growth and development (Appoloni & Cooke, 1978; Strain & Kerr, 1981). Peer interactions appear also to influence children's behavior and attitudes. When handicapped children are included in the daily education activities of nonhandicapped children, all children are provided with opportunities to interact with persons both alike and different from themselves and to learn to be tolerant of the differences among them. In addition, since all children in a regular preschool classroom vary in their social and family backgrounds, interests, and skills, the learning environment should be designed to provide experiences relevant to these differences. By building on the children's diversity of skills rather than concentrating on their deficits, the regular classroom can provide valuable learnings for both handicapped and nonhandicapped children.

PLACEMENT CONSIDERATIONS

Teachers, parents, and others have observed the benefits of mainstreaming that accrue to both handicapped and nonhandicapped children; they have also encountered the difficulties that arise when careful planning does not precede and accompany placement of a handicapped child in a regular classroom.

Collecting Information

When a handicapped child is placed in a mainstream setting or transferred from one setting to another, as from day care to a preschool or kindergarten setting, the child must be carefully observed before and during the transition process (Fowler, 1980). This task of making detailed observations often becomes the responsibility of the child's teachers. The role of the classroom teacher in the initial placement and successful transition of the handicapped child has many dimensions. When a new placement is being contemplated, the teacher can act as observer and information gatherer, as well as an information source, for others who may be involved in the child's placement.

It is important to observe the child systematically when gathering information. Systematic observation means critically watching the child in as many natural settings as possible—at home, in the preschool, or at the day care center. Critical watching encompasses not only the child's behavior, but also the context of the behavior, i.e., the physical aspects of the environment and the behavior of significant adults and peers as they interact with the child. Functional observations, therefore, should include an assessment of the structure of the child's environment:

- Does the physical arrangement of the room and the materials facilitate success; that is, is the classroom arranged in a consistent manner? For example, is each child's name tag at the same seat every day so that he or she can readily find the right work place? A child who experiences a small success such as this each day is likely to be more willing to try more difficult tasks.

- Are materials accessible to the child? A language-delayed child, for example, who does not have the verbal or social skills necessary for requesting materials in an appropriate way may appear to be disruptive when attempting to get materials that are out of reach. If free choice materials are at child height, however, children learn very quickly that they are permitted to play with the toys on the open shelves. Children understand consistency, learn from it, and more quickly achieve a measure of independence.

- Are materials and activities appropriate for the child's developmental level? A child with delays in fine motor skills may become frustrated if required to manipulate small, hard-to-grasp plastic pegs and so lose interest or begin to use the pegs in ways that teachers consider inappropriate or disruptive. On the other hand, that same child, provided with larger, more easily grasped pegs is often able to work appropriately for long periods of time.

- Is the classroom furniture suitably sized for the children who will be using it? Is it simple in design and placed in accessible areas? The child with a physical handicap may be unable to get in and out of poorly designed furniture and may risk injury moving across a crowded, cluttered room. In contrast, a room with appropriate furnishings, carefully arranged with clearly defined traffic paths, can facilitate greater exploration and interaction for all children.

In addition to carefully observing the child's environment, the teacher should note the behavior of significant adults and peers:

- How do adults instruct the child? Is the child instructed only as part of a group, or are instructions given directly to the child? A child who does not respond when the teacher says "Children, time to get your coats." may be able to respond easily when the teacher says "George, time to get your coat." Using the child's name at the outset of the instruction cues the child to listen.

- How do teachers and peers respond to the child's verbal and social initiations? Does the teacher, for example, turn promptly to the child when the child talks in a quiet voice appropriate for indoor use? Do other children respond when the child attempts to initiate a social interaction?

- Do other children play with the handicapped child? The handicapped child may appear isolated because other children have not yet learned to play with a child who does not play the same way they do. Does the teacher help by showing how the children are alike? For example, "Look, John, Sue likes to fly airplanes just like you do!"
- What child behaviors do adults consider disruptive or inappropriate? How do adults respond when the child exhibits one of these behaviors? Does the adult deal with the situation calmly? Does the adult scold, ignore, or redirect the child after inappropriate behavior? How does the adult redirect the child?

The observer should note, too, those people or activities that seem to be of particular interest to that child. For example, does the child

- watch the other children play? Appear interested?
- respond to peers' attempts to engage the child in play?
- attempt to initiate play activities with peers?
- respond to the teacher's praise? How? Does the child smile and continue to work, or does the teacher's attention seem to have little or no effect?
- engage in constructive activities during free time? What activities? What kinds of success does the child experience in these activities? Answers to these questions can give the teacher an idea of the activities that could be used to motivate the child.
- solicit help? How? Vocalize? Cry? Gesture?
- get a response from others when asking for help? How soon? First call, second call, or not until the child whines, nags, or behaves inappropriately? Sometimes, a child's initial effort to solicit assistance is quite appropriate; when no response is forthcoming, however, the child may engage in behaviors that are less and less appropriate, finally forcing others in the environment to respond. The result is a build-up of inappropriate behaviors.

By making such observations, the teacher can construct a well-rounded profile of the child. The profile can then be integrated with observations made by other professionals and by the child's parents. From this pool of information, an initial developmental and instructional program can be formulated for each handicapped child.

Putting the Information Together

Prior to the handicapped child's placement in the integrated classroom, the parents and other adults involved with the handicapped child should meet to exchange information and to discuss the appropriateness or possible shortcomings of the proposed placement. Such a meeting can help to establish a communication system between parents and professionals. The teacher's observations can be discussed and compared with observations made by others. Much can be learned through sharing; a child may be reported to behave quite differently in different environments with different people. It is also important to note how perceptions of the child vary. Some may describe the child in a way that reflects interest and concern for the child as a total functioning person, while others appear to focus on the handicapping condition. It should be kept in mind, however, that no observation is "wrong." As environments change, so does the behavior of the child. The exchange of observations is important because it makes it possible to enhance and perhaps replicate environments that facilitate appropriate behaviors, as well as to modify those that encourage inappropriate behaviors.

PREPARATION FOR INTEGRATION OF HANDICAPPED CHILDREN

Preparing the Staff

Once the decision has been made to place a handicapped child in an integrated classroom, the members of the teaching staff must prepare themselves to work with the handicapped child. Not only do they need information about the particular child, but also they need general information about the handicapping condition itself. Such information can be obtained from "experts," i.e., from the parents and the family and from professionals or clinicians who have had experience working with this particular handicapped child or with children similarly handicapped. The parents, for example, can tell the teachers about the child's favorite activities or toys so that school activities can be planned to use materials with which the child has previously experienced success; the nurse can instruct teachers in managing a potential insulin shock episode; the nutritionist can help teachers understand the necessity for maintaining a rigid dietary regimen throughout each day.

Teachers must be informed of the unique needs of each handicapped child and how these needs can be dealt with in the classroom. If, for example, a cerebral-palsied child is about to begin school, teachers must be told whether the child is likely to have seizures. If so, all classroom staff must be trained in appropriate methods for handling seizures. A handicapped child may have other medical conditions that require supervision by the teaching staff. Since unmet medical needs could be life-threatening, it is essential that the staff be made aware of such needs and instructed in handling each situation.

If a child must be given medication during the preschool day, close and continuous communication between the teaching staff and medical staff must be arranged. A specific staff person should be designated to administer medication, although more than one person should be trained to carry out the procedures so that a second staff member is prepared to take over, should the need arise. All medications must be clearly labeled with the child's name, the name of the medication, the dosage, and the times it should be given. All medications must be packaged in child-proof containers and stored in a locked cabinet. A record of the time that each dose was administered, the amount given, and the person who administered it should be posted in a visible location near the medication. Even with the utmost in safety precautions, accidental consumption of medication can occur; thus, all staff members should be proficient in administering the appropriate antidote.

Medical needs are just one type of special consideration that may be required by a handicapped child. The child may also have special equipment. Before the child enters the classroom, the staff should be instructed in the use and care of this equipment. A young hearing-impaired child can rarely deal independently with a malfunctioning hearing aid, for example. When the device is not functioning, the handicapped child misses important instructions, as well as many social and verbal interactions. Thus, it is a good routine policy for the teacher to check the child's amplification equipment every day when the child arrives. Replaceable parts for special equipment, such as batteries for hearing aids, should be on hand in the classroom for use when needed. During this equipment check, in addition to making certain the equipment is in working order, the teacher can be instructing the child in the equipment check procedures. In this way, the child will learn to be more responsible and independent in taking care of these needs.

Preparing the Children

All children enrolled in an integrated classroom—the children already enrolled and the handicapped child about to be enrolled—must be prepared for the placement of the handicapped child. The classroom children should receive some preparation before meeting the handicapped child; later, the nonhandicapped children and the handicapped child can interact together in preparation for the handicapped child's entrance into the classroom.

Teachers can begin simply by telling the children that a new child will be coming to the classroom. Talking with children in small groups is probably the best way to ensure that all children receive this important message. The next step is to tell the children that the new child has a handicap. The word *handicap* is not particularly enlightening, so a description of the child must follow: "A new boy will be coming to our class next week. His name is Jeff. Jeff is 5 years old, just like Christy and Jerry and Minda; but Jeff can't walk—he uses a wheelchair." The teacher can then ask if anyone knows what wheelchairs are and the reasons some people might need to use them. Discussions of this type not only give the children information about the new child and the child's handicap, but also allow the teacher to probe subtly to assess how much the children already know about handicapping conditions in general and the child's handicap in particular.

The initial discussions should also introduce the idea that certain changes in the classroom will be needed to accommodate the new child. The children should be actively involved in the problem solving that precedes classroom rearrangements so that changes do not appear to be arbitrarily imposed on the children by the teaching staff. Teachers can involve children in various ways: "Mary has a difficult time hearing voices. She wears a hearing aid. She will need to sit where she can watch the teacher. How do you think we could rearrange the tables and chairs so Mary can see my face?" As the children offer solutions to the problem, the teacher can give them feedback, thus helping them to evaluate their answers. In addition, the teacher can offer additional information to ensure a successful solution.

During the time the children in the classroom are in the initial stages of preparation, the handicapped child can be prepared for a first visit to school. A home visit by the classroom teacher—if it is possible to arrange one—helps the transition proceed more smoothly. The teacher can tell the handicapped child about the other children, classroom activities, routines, and schedules. Snapshots of the other children and the teacher engaged in classroom activities can be most helpful. In working with a verbal child, the teacher may encourage a discussion of which activities the child enjoys, as well as any other information that could be used in preparing the classroom for the child. As in preparing any child for initial entry into school, misinformation or fears about school can be addressed at this time, too.

The next step in the preparation process is to arrange a time when the handicapped child, accompanied by parent or caregiver, can visit the classroom (Allen, 1980). The first visit to school should take place when the other children are not present so that the handicapped child can explore the classroom freely. The teacher can show the child where and how to hang outdoor garments, point out the table where the child will work and the shelves where toys are stored, and tour the bathroom and the outdoor play yard. During this first visit, the child can be given an opportunity to play with some classroom materials, e.g., put a puzzle together, build with blocks, or color a picture to take home. Because the first visit to school can set the tone for the child's adjustment to the classroom, it is important to allow sufficient time for the child and the parents to get to know and feel comfortable with the teachers and the surroundings.

The next visit to the classroom should be a brief period in which the new child can meet the children already enrolled in the classroom. This meeting must be carefully planned to ensure its success. The time of the day chosen for this visit is critical. The handicapped child's skill should be kept in mind when the time is chosen; it must be a time when the visiting child can experience success by participating as fully as he or she wishes in the classroom activities. The child who wears leg braces or is confined to a wheelchair, for example, would probably feel more successful if the visit were made when a sedentary activity rather than a vigorous outdoor play period was planned.

After the handicapped child's visit, the children and teachers should reassess the integration plan. Is the easel high enough to accommodate the wheelchair? Who will assist the child at the lockers? Is the seat that was chosen for the new child an appropriate one? Will the child be able to see the teacher's face? The teachers should comment on the child and the child's handicap in a positive, helpful manner; they can talk about all the things the handicapped child can do and the ways in which the new child is like all the other children:

- "Johnny likes to paint with red paint, too, just like you, Michael."
- "Tommy, did you hear Mary say your name? She learned your name right away."
- "Did you see that Stephen remembered where John had left his mittens? I think Stephen will be a good helper in our classroom."

The teacher can also comment on the ways in which the children helped the new child adjust to the classroom:

- "Bobby, you helped Susan find her locker. That was good of you."
- "Michael showed John how to stop his paint brush from dripping. John seemed to like your help, Michael."

The children need to be actively and continuously involved in the integration process to ensure successful adjustment by all involved. The "official explanation" originally given to the children about the handicap is only the initial step in teaching about handicaps. Children continue to wonder and even to fear that the same thing may happen to them. For example, in one classroom, a teacher overheard the year-long classmates of a child with a congenitally shortened forearm and misformed hand discussing why Josh was late coming to school. The children were acutely aware of Josh's absence.

> One child told the teacher, "I bet he had to go to the doctor."
> The teacher asked, "Why do you think Josh had to go to the doctor?"
> "His arm probably got broken again. It got broke off up at the elbow some more."
> "You know his 'little' arm," one child said, looking at the teacher questioningly.

The teacher realized that the children, as fond as they were of Josh and as accepting as they were of his handicap, did not really understand that Josh's arm was not broken and that the same thing could not happen to them. Thus, the teacher and children talked about Josh once again—that his "little" arm was not broken, "that it did not hurt," that he had only three fingers on his "little" arm because he was born that way. The children seemed satisfied, but the teacher realized that the subject would probably need further discussion from time to time.

Developing an Individualized Program

Once the handicapped child has been placed in an integrated classroom, developmental and educational goals and objectives must be formulated (LeBlanc, Etzel, & Domash, 1978). Since the major reason for placing a handicapped child in the regular classroom is to involve the child in an environment that provides normal models and expectations for the child, goals and objectives must be assessed in terms of the handicapped child's functioning in the broader, natural environment of home, school, and community. It is important to ask: Do the skills learned in the classroom allow the child to interact with increasing success in the social contexts in which the child is expected to function?

Because children of the same age learn and grow at individual rates and in individual ways, the learning goals and objectives for each child vary. Nevertheless, when goals are set for the handicapped child, appropriate educational goals for comparative peers should be kept in mind (LeBlanc, 1977; Etzel, 1977) in order to ensure that the learning goals chosen for the handicapped child approximate the learnings of the immediate community of nonhandicapped children. With such planning, every skill the handicapped child acquires should result in easier, more successful functioning for that child in the classroom and in the community.

The choice of comparative peers for the purpose of formulating appropriate goals is sometimes difficult. On what dimension should the comparative peers be chosen—similar chronological age, developmental age, cultural backgrounds, or diagnostic categories? Etzel (1977) and LeBlanc (1977) suggested that comparative peers be selected from the handicapped child's regular classroom and that different comparative peers be chosen for different skill areas. For example, the language development objectives for a 5-year-old hearing-impaired child may reflect the skill of normally developing 3-year-olds, while motor development objectives may reflect the skills of chronological age mates. As the child acquires a greater number of skills in various skill areas, new comparative peers may be needed. Thus, as the hearing-impaired child acquires more language skills, a 3-year-old comparative peer is no longer appropriate; a comparative peer closer in chronological age should be chosen.

The importance of choosing appropriate comparative peers cannot be over-emphasized, since the value and impact of skills taught in the classroom must be measured by the changes in the child's behavior in the broader natural environment. Certain questions must always be kept in mind: Will the skills the child is acquiring be functional? Will they make the child appear less handicapped? Will the community's perception of the child be improved? When the answers to these questions are "yes," the chosen goals are appropriate; when the answers are "no," the goals should be reassessed and changed so that they are functional in comparison with the behavior of comparative peers in the natural environment.

ORGANIZATION OF THE CLASSROOM

A typical day in a preschool classroom includes many routines and transitions. There are times for the children to work and play in groups and times for them to work and play as individuals. Most programs include teacher-directed and child-initiated activities, indoor and outdoor activities, and vigorous as well as quiet activities. Each of these program components requires careful planning and continuous evaluation by the teaching staff to ensure successful integration of the handicapped child (Ashton-Lilo, 1981). In addition, it may be necessary to provide special services to the handicapped child during school hours. Many times, the child must leave the classroom to receive services, such as speech therapy. Thus, when scheduling a therapy session, the teacher and therapist should select a time that does not conflict with those classroom activities required to meet specific educational goals for the child. It is also important to consider the fatigue factor. A young child tires easily in instructional settings. Therapy sessions can best be sandwiched between the less demanding classroom activities. Many educators and clinicians contend that the most effective, therapeutic intervention takes place in the classroom itself, however. (For a discussion of this issue, see Allen, 1978.)

Routines and Transitions

A specific staff member should be assigned to help the handicapped child learn the classroom routines (Hart, 1982). Too often, teachers assume that children will learn class routines automatically just by being there in the classroom or by watching others. The learning of routines is seldom accomplished that easily, however, even by normally developing children. For a handicapped child, who may have great difficulty learning new skills, it is especially important that the teaching staff make specific plans in this regard.

One approach is to have a teacher and a few children, including the handicapped child, make a "dry run" of the classroom routine. The teacher and children walk through the entire daily schedule, practicing the particular skills needed in each situation: motor skills, such as putting on mittens for going outdoors; verbal amenities, such as saying "Good morning" on arrival; placing the paper towel in the trash receptacle—all the behaviors expected from the child during the routines.

As the child learns more and more steps in each routine, the teacher's assistance is gradually reduced until the child is reasonably independent. At that point, the teacher's role becomes one of prompting and preparing the child for transitions and activity changes:

- "Good, Michael, you remembered to say good-bye to your father. What do you do next? That's right—you go to your locker and hang up your coat." (prompt)
- "Sandy, soon it will be time to put the puzzles on the shelf and come to snack." (preparation)

When learning a routine, the child is actually learning a chain of behaviors (hanging up the coat, going to a table, sitting down, beginning to work on the material the teacher has set out). Therefore, these routines should be consistently carried out in prescribed order; e.g., after hanging up their coats, the children *always* go to the table, sit down, and begin to work. Of course, schedules do change; a rigid and inflexible routine can never provide an optimum learning environment for any child. When changes are introduced, teachers should prepare all the children in advance for the change in routine.

Children who know the classroom routines well can serve as models for the newer members of the class. Thus, a teacher may say to a new child, "Look how Stephanie and John are hanging their coats on their hooks. Now it's your turn to hang your coat on your hook." As the child manages to get the coat to stay on the hook, the teacher provides descriptive praise: "You hung up your coat just like John and Stephanie did. Good for you." Such descriptive praising of the child's actions seems to facilitate learning in any young child and to be especially useful in teaching and integrating a handicapped child into classroom routines.

During transitions, a peer helper can be a valuable assistant to the classroom teacher busy with groups of children. These assisting children must be chosen carefully, however, so that they are helpers, but not doers, for the handicapped child. Because a major goal in mainstreaming handicapped children is to help them learn the self-management skills needed in society, nonhandicapped children must learn how to help in ways that encourage greater self-sufficiency in the handicapped child. Assistance should be subtle. Thus, if a hearing-impaired child does not hear the teacher's instructions regarding the start of transition times, a child helper can be taught to signal unobtrusively to the nonhearing child that it is time to make the transition. The helper can touch the other child on the arm, gesture, and then repeat the teacher's instructions, "Mary, it's almost time to put the puzzle on the shelf."

In the case of a visually impaired child, subtle assistance may involve a peer who helps the handicapped child locate the appropriate locker by touching and counting the lockers until the right one is located. In a classroom that has cubbyholes or drawers, a textured piece of fabric can be glued to the blind child's cubbyhole or drawer. At first, the sighted child can guide the visually impaired child until the identifying piece of fabric is touched; soon the child will not need to be helped, and the teacher then encourages the helping child to withdraw assistance.

The teacher needs to work with both the handicapped child and the helping child to teach them effective ways to work together. These situations must be monitored continually to make certain that the handicapped child is not merely being helped, but is being helped in a way that will lead to mastery of self-help skills. When properly managed, peers-helping-peers provides a fine opportunity for handicapped and nonhandicapped children to interact and learn from one another.

A note of caution seems important at this point. Careful attention must be directed toward the peer helpers to ensure that they are enjoying and learning from the task of assisting the special classmate. Signs of weariness or discomfort should be attended to immediately so that the job does not become a burden. At all times, the child helpers should enjoy the job and be made to feel "special" for providing such assistance.

Free Play Periods

Because the ability to be self-managing in making choices is one of those skills that teachers need to help children acquire, free play periods are usually an important component of each preschool day. During these times of child-initiated activity, interest centers are set up in the classroom, and children are free to select a center. To help children decide where they will work or play, teachers should preview the activities that are available. This technique is especially useful in assisting young handicapped children, who often find it difficult to manage situations in which there are several options. Thus, the teacher might say, "Today we have fingerpainting. We also have dress-up clothes in the housekeeping corner. At the easel there is blue and yellow paint." As each child chooses an area to begin work, the teacher can review the choices so the children hear many times what the options are: "Michael has decided to fingerpaint. Linda and Carol are going to play dress-up in the housekeeping corner."

The handicapped child should be asked to choose an activity after several other children have chosen theirs, so the child hears the available options many times. It may be helpful to pair the handicapped child with one of the other children who has already chosen the same activity; in this way, the handicapped child receives individual assistance in locating the appropriate work area and has a peer to model the appropriate way to begin the activity.

Child-initiated activities must be carefully planned so that the handicapped child can engage in them successfully. For example, when a visually impaired child is participating in an art activity, the teacher should describe and locate the materials with the child: "Here is the big circle to paste the little circle on; here is the container with the little circles; on your right side is the paste cup and underneath is the sponge to wipe your fingers." The teacher can help the child locate and identify each item by guiding the child's hand. Once the visually impaired child has learned the location of the materials, it can be frustrating for that child to have the materials moved from the prescribed location. On the other hand, telling the other children not to touch the visually handicapped child's materials seems arbitrary and may even cast a subtly negative reflection on the child. Instead, children can be taught the simple courtesy (due all children) of stating what they are doing whenever they use or change another's materials: "Kelly, I need to use some of your paste. Let's move it over here so I can use it, too. Let me show you (through touch) where I'm moving it. Now we can share." For the hearing-impaired child, visual cues, such as the actual materials or pictures of children engaging in the activity, can be helpful in explaining the choices available.

With an orthopedically handicapped or cerebral-palsied child, the first need is quite simply to ensure that the activities are accessible to the child, i.e., that there is enough room between the activity centers to allow the child to move about easily without bumping into furniture or other children. Additional factors need to be considered, too. Can the child successfully manipulate the materials that are available? Can the child with cerebral palsy hold the paintbrush? Is a paintbrush with a thicker handle needed? Is the child in the wheelchair able to remove the blocks from the shelf? If the blocks are accessible, on what surface can the child build with them? Is a low table a more accessible surface for the child? Many of these questions cannot be asked or answered until teachers see the handicapped child in action. As always, when problems develop, the teacher, the handicapped child, and the other children can work together to develop options and try out possibilities.

During child-initiated activity periods, children not only learn to use a variety of materials, but also have the opportunity to play with one another, thus developing social skills. The teacher plays a vital role in facilitating social interactions during this time. More often than not, social interactions do not just happen; the teacher must make them happen (Allen, Benning, & Drummond, 1972; Peterson, 1982). As with any new child in the classroom, but especially with a handicapped child who may look different, children may hesitate to initiate play with that child. Teachers can facilitate interactions between handicapped and nonhandicapped children in a variety of ways. For example, they can arrange materials strategically to indicate that a group project is in order: a "bus" set up in the dramatic play area, a group mural or collage along one wall, or a large tub to be filled with sand. Teachers can also encourage the inclusion of the handicapped child in a play activity by giving the child raisin "pills" to dispense in hospital play, a punch for punching the "tickets" in train play, and rolling pins and cookie cutters to hand out at the dough table. Finally, and most effective, is descriptive praising when children do play together: "Mary and Marty, you're having such a good time together in the rocking boat. It's fun to watch you play together."

Group Activities

In formal group activities, the teacher is the focal person in the group, giving the instructions and directing the activity. Group sizes vary according to the type of activity. A large group get-together is often a time for music, rhythmic activities, and songs, while a small group is more conducive to preacademic activities, stories, snack, and conversation. Although the size of the group and the goals of the activities vary, there are certain techniques a teacher can use to mainstream handicapped children into group activities successfully.

The handicapped child's skills must be carefully considered when group activities are planned. How long is the child's span of attention? Can the child attend to group instruction for the entire time or only for one or two activities? In the latter case, the teacher should keep group instructions to a minimum and intersperse individual activities with group activities. When the handicapped child has successfully participated in group activities for a short while, the child should then be allowed to go to a specially prepared area for a different activity—one the handicapped child knows and enjoys. It is important that the child leave the group activities *while still successful,* a strategy often referred to as "catching the child being good." Teachers should never wait until the child's behavior disintegrates before having the child leave the group. Little by little, the child with a short attention span and an inability to comply with the teacher's directions will come to perform more successfully in the group situation.

Peer models and helpers are of great value in helping a handicapped child participate effectively in group activities. Partners can be assigned to move together as the group sings and acts out "Row, Row, Row Your Boat" or "Skip to My Lou." A peer helper can also work from behind a visually impaired or an orthopedically impaired child, physically prompting activities from the handicapped child's own body orientation. Thus, if a singing game calls for tapping head, shoulder, knees, and toes, the child's hands can be moved through the motions. Usually, however, this strategy must be demonstrated by a teacher on a nonhandicapped child first; then children can take turns practicing on each other before beginning to assist the handicapped child.

Songs should be simple and sung at a slow pace until children know them well. Since it is not easy for the young child—any young child—to sing words and figure out movements simultaneously, it is a good idea to rehearse (in a gamelike fashion) the movements: "Touch your head; touch your shoulders; touch your knees; touch your toes. Let's do it again." Large group activities can also be rehearsed and practiced during small group activities, thus enabling the teacher to give additional attention to children who may need special help.

For the deaf child attending a group music period, numerous adaptations can be made. Many body rhythms (clapping, hopping, and rolling activities) can be used, and a variety of rhythm instruments that the child can feel vibrating can be provided. Flannel boards with cutouts can be used to help the hearing-impaired child follow the words being sung. As always, the child should be placed so that he or she is not looking directly into the light while trying to follow the teacher's facial expressions and mouth movements. In fact, appropriate positioning of the teacher is important for all children; the teacher must always be in a position to assist, monitor, encourage, and praise each child in the group for his or her unique forms of participation.

Still another way to help children enjoy and elaborate their large group participation skills is to let parents know which songs their child is learning at school and which finger plays their child seems most eager to learn. Handouts can be made available for those parents (and there are many) who want to incorporate the classroom's songs and chants into family activities. Parents can also be asked which songs and rhymes the family enjoys at home, and these can be incorporated into the classroom activities, thus providing the child with a familiar activity and ensuring the child's success.

PARENTS AND TEACHERS

It is clear that teachers and parents need to work together closely to promote full learning opportunities for all children, especially for the preschool handicapped child (Winton & Turnbull, 1981). The successful mainstreaming of this child is the joint responsibility of the teaching staff, other professionals involved with the child, and the child's parents. Most importantly, teachers and parents must maintain continuous and positive communication, always a key to successful parent-teacher cooperation. These contacts can be brief and spontaneous (e.g., doorstop contacts at arrival or dismissal time), or planned (e.g., regularly scheduled parent conferences).

Doorstep contacts allow parents and teachers to exchange information regarding the child's activities in school or at home. As they arrive, parents should be encouraged to tell the teachers of brief incidents at home that may affect their child's behavior in school: "Michael has been moved out of his crib and had a difficult time sleeping last night." or "Jason had a seizure just after breakfast." The information shared by parents can help the teachers in planning or revising their plans for the child's day. If the parents report an overly tired child as a result of a restless night, perhaps that child should not participate in the strenuous field trip planned for that day. The parents' sharing of home events is especially important if their child has a communication difficulty and so is unable to report a situation. In many instances, the parent and child can tell the teacher together, thus enabling the child to succeed in a social exchange with two of the most important people in that child's life.

Teachers should encourage parents to report both large and small events each day, as this allows the teacher and the children to share events, whether pleasant or stressful, that happened when they were not together. "Linda's dog did not come home last night, and she is worried about it." "Carol left her favorite blanket at the babysitter's yesterday. It took her a long time to fall asleep last night without her blanket." Even seemingly small events, such as receiving a new toy or catching a ball independently, can be used later to facilitate communication among the children in the classroom.

When parents pick up their child at dismissal time, teachers have an opportunity to recount positive episodes about the child's day at school and to report *in the child's presence* gains the child made that day: "Linda climbed to the top of the jungle gym." "Today, George pulled the laces of his shoe into a knot all by himself." These brief, enthusiastic reports give the parents and the child information about the skills that are deemed important in the classroom, as well as about the child's progress in acquiring those skills. Teachers should recap only positive events in these brief contacts, however. Concerns or negative comments should be reserved for another time and should never be discussed in the presence of the child.

Teachers should be certain that at least one positive statement is made to the parents of each child every day. These brief, favorable reports can be helpful in a number of ways. First, as noted earlier, the teacher and the parents develop rapport by engaging in frequent, positive contacts. Such exchanges also help to build a buffer for the times when the teacher must share serious concerns or negative observations with the parents. Furthermore, short, positive reports help all parents, especially the parents of a handicapped child, to see their child as a more competent, developing individual. Too often, "experts" have told the parents of a handicapped child only what their child cannot do and how different their child is from other children. In contrast, daily positive contacts with the child's teacher tell the parents what their child *can* do, how their child is progressing, and how their child is like other children in the group.

All children learn skills in small steps; nonhandicapped children usually acquire the skills at a faster pace than do handicapped children and so they reach the major developmental milestones at the expected times. Handicapped children usually acquire these same skills; however, because they develop at a slower pace, the acquisition of a particular skill may go unnoticed or seem unimportant in view of the child's more advanced chronological age. The teachers can assist the parents in adjusting their expectations to the developmental pace of their handicapped child by noting frequently the small steps the child is taking toward the acquisition of a major skill. Parents of a handicapped child desperately need to hear positive statements about their child's very different growth patterns. Teachers must remember that sometimes they, the teachers, are the only professionals who see the child on a daily basis and are, therefore, the only ones able to note these slow but positive developmental changes.

In addition to reporting the individual accomplishments of the children, teachers should report times when handicapped and nonhandicapped children work and play together. Teachers have the opportunity not only to teach the children about handicapped individuals but to teach the parents as well. Reports to parents about the interactions of their normally developing children with handicapped children can be enlightening: "John and Michael built a sand castle higher than the walls of the sandbox. They are becoming good friends." It is good, too, to report incidents in which a handicapped child has assisted another child. A language-delayed child may have good motor skills and can, therefore, help another child in this area. Thus, reporting to the parents of handicapped Steven that he "helped Mary put on her mittens today" brings to their attention yet another of their child's strengths. By reporting the same incident to Mary's parents, one more positive aspect of mainstreaming handicapped children is highlighted for the parents of nonhandicapped children.

Whenever possible, it is important for teachers to portray the handicapped child as a competent, growing individual. Often, it is not only the children's first experience with a handicapped individual, but also the parents' first experience as well. By reporting these positive interactions, the teacher can help both parents and children learn that handicapped children are more *like* other children than they are *different*.

Regardless of the content of the doorstep contacts, they must be brief. If an incident seems to require additional discussion, arrangements should be made to speak privately at another time in a more formal conference. The teaching staff can assist parents who are coming in for a conference by offering child care for siblings. Younger siblings are often anxious to get into the classroom to play, and their older sibling likes to demonstrate and explain the ways of the classroom. These "extra" children in the classroom appear to present few problems to the teachers and other children, and this arrangement frees the parents to meet with the teachers.

Prearranged conferences should occur regularly throughout the school year. To delay parent conferences until the end of the year restricts their usefulness, since little time remains for alterations in the child's program. Many short conferences allow the parents and teachers to identify and remediate problems while the child is enrolled in the classroom. By keeping the conferences short, the teacher and parents are more likely to keep the conversation goal-directed, addressing only the needs of the child.

CONCLUSION

Teachers must remember, as Klein (1975) pointed out in the early days of mainstreaming, that young handicapped children have the same basic needs as all young children—they need love, acceptance, praise, and feelings of self-worth. Furthermore, the general considerations for promoting optimum physical, emotional, and intellectual growth in the early years are the same for all children, handicapped or not. All children should be helped to function as independently and productively as possible in a wide variety of school and community environments.

REFERENCES

Allen, K.E., Benning, P.M., & Drummond, W.T. Integration of normal and handicapped children in a behavior modification preschool: A case study. In G. Semb (Ed.), *Behavior analysis and education—1972*. Lawrence, KS: Printing Services, 1972.

Allen, K.E. The early childhood education specialist (ECES). In K.E. Allen, V.A. Holm, & R.L. Schiefelbusch (Eds.), *Early intervention—A team approach*. Baltimore: University Park Press, 1978, 278-308.

Allen, K.E. *Mainstreaming in early childhood education*. Albany, NY: Delmar Publishers, 1980.

Apolloni, T., & Cooke, T.P. Integrated programming at the infant, toddler and preschool levels. In M.J. Guralnick (Ed.), *Early intervention and the integration of handicapped and nonhandicapped children*. Baltimore: University Park Press, 1978, 147-165.

Ashton-Lilo, L.J. Pinpointing teacher goals to assist in a successful preschool classroom. *Topics in Early Childhood Special Education*, 1981, *1*(1), 37-44.

Etzel, B. What is behavioral change in stimulus control research? In *Predetermined confidence level vs. predetermined criterion behavior: One argument against the use of statistics in operant research*. Address presented to the Midwest Association of Behavior Analysis, Chicago, IL, May 1977.

Fowler, S.A. Transition to public school. In K.E. Allen, *Mainstreaming in early childhood education*. Albany, NY: Delmar Publishers, 1980, 242-254.

Garwood, S. Gray. *Educating young handicapped children: A developmental approach*. Rockville, MD: Aspen Systems Corporation, 1983.

Guralnick, M.J. The efficacy of integrating handicapped children in early education settings: Research implications. *Topics in Early Childhood Special Education*, 1981, *1*(1), 57-71.

Hart, B. So that teachers can teach: Assigning roles and responsibilities. *Topics in Early Childhood Special Education*, 1982, *2*(1), 1-8.

Klein, J.W. Mainstreaming the preschooler. *Young Children*, July 1975, XXX, 317-327.

Lazar, I., & Darlington, R. Lasting effects of early education: A report from the consortium for longitudinal studies. *Monographs of the Society for Research in Child Development*, 1982, *47*(2-3), Serial No. 195.

LeBlanc, J.M. What is behavioral change in applied research? In *Predetermined confidence level vs. predetermined criterion behavior: One argument against the use of statistics in operant research*. Address presented to Midwest Association of Behavior Analysis, Chicago, IL, May 1977.

LeBlanc, J.M., Etzel, B.C., & Domash, M.A. A functional curriculum for early intervention. In K.E. Allen, V.A. Holm, & R.L. Schiefelbusch (Eds.), *Early intervention—A team approach*. Baltimore: University Park Press, 1978, 331-381.

Peterson, N.L. Social integration of handicapped and nonhandicapped preschoolers: A study of playmate preferences. *Topics in Early Childhood Special Education*, 1982, *2*(2), 56-69.

Sarason, S.B., & Doris, J. *Psychological problems in mental deficiency*. New York: Harper & Row, 1969.

Schweinhart, L.J., & Weikart, D.P. Young children grow up. *The effects of the Perry Preschool Program on youths through age 15*. Ypsilanti, MI: High/Scope Education Research Foundation, 1980.

Strain, P.S., & Kerr, M.M. (Eds.). *Mainstreaming of children in schools: Research and programmatic issues*. New York: Academic Press, 1981.

Winton, P.J., & Turnbull, A.P. Parent involvement as viewed by parents of preschool handicapped children. *Topics in Early Childhood Special Education*, 1981, *1*(3), 11-19.

Part III

The Impact of Policy and Law on Early Childhood Education and Intervention

Interagency Collaboration: Applications in Early Intervention for the Handicapped

Nancy L. Peterson and Judy A. Mantle

The watchword of the 1980s for agencies involved in the various fields of human services is "interagency collaboration." Given our experience with established service programs for older children and adults with developmental and incurred disabilities, the importance of interagency collaboration to the future of the newer field of early intervention for the handicapped is becoming increasingly apparent. Professionals in education, health, social welfare, rehabilitation, child-family services, and related disciplines are referring more frequently today to phrases like these:

- cross disciplinary planning
- coordination of services
- interdisciplinary teamwork
- interagency collaboration
- interagency linkages or networks
- interagency collaboratives
- interagency consortiums

These phrases reflect a growing philosophy that agencies can better serve their clientele if they work cooperatively with other organizations that offer related and perhaps overlapping services to the same population. Collaborative activities among agencies are now viewed as a solution to much of the competition, confusion, and duplication of effort that occurs when more than one agency is charged with the responsibility of serving the same group of individuals (Baxter, 1982; Brewer & Kakalik, 1979; Elder & Magrab, 1980; Martinson, 1982). As the need for more orderly service delivery systems has forced everyone to look more critically at federal, state and local practices, interagency collaboration has become an imperative for program planning.

But what does interagency collaboration have to do with early intervention for handicapped infants and preschoolers? Years ago, this topic seemed far removed from what teachers, therapists, and parents were doing to help this young clientele. Agencies serving the handicapped or those operating programs for very young children were under little pressure to enter into collaborative relationships with each other. Despite the fact that professionals have long acknowledged the virtues of cooperation among their respective organizations, few real collaborative efforts materialized. Those that did were exceptions and often were part of a special project rather than an ongoing community-based service. When contacts did occur, they concerned primarily administrative, not client-related issues. As a result, interagency activities rarely extended downward from administrative staff to include direct service personnel who worked with children on a daily basis.

Today, the involvement of professionals at all levels in interagency activities is changing rapidly. As early childhood intervention for the handicapped has come of age, so has interest in the handicapped infant and preschooler proliferated across many disciplines and across many different agencies. Regular early childhood and special educators, therapists in specialty areas such as occupational or speech therapy, psychologists, social workers in child-family services, and nurses in family-community health are just a few of those now working in some capacity with these young children (Allen, Holm, & Schiefelbusch, 1978). As programs expand and services for handicapped youngsters under school age become more prevalent, professionals are facing an important reality: *They and the agencies they represent cannot continue to serve the same clientele and work in isolation of each other*. This is particularly so as communities attempt to organize comprehensive service programs, finance them, and deliver special services to the handicapped in an orderly way. Interagency networks can play an important role as communities tackle a remaining frontier in services for the handicapped. That task is to build a nationwide system of early intervention services for handicapped and at-risk children from birth to age 5.

A NEW URGENCY FOR INTERAGENCY COLLABORATION: THE RATIONALE

The challenge of the 1970s was one of creating equal services and educational opportunities for handicapped individuals. New programs were created and existing ones expanded to meet new mandates. It was an era of unprecedented growth in services for a previously underserved or unserved population. As in any period of rapid growth, expansion—not consolidation—was the theme of the times. With the press for new and more appropriate services, limited attention was given to issues of coordination or service redundancy.

Most collaborative efforts between agencies were voluntary. The impetus for cooperation usually came from dedicated individuals, from federally funded demonstration projects created specifically for this purpose, or from temporary problems for which alliances were advantageous. They generally did not produce change in the broader system of handicapped services, however. Funds were allocated in ways that allowed single programs and/or agencies to operate independently as self-contained entities, and most were able to maintain their operations with little or no attention to the functions of parallel service agencies with similar responsibilities or clientele.

Why Is Coordination Such an Issue?

The social, economic, and political climate of the 1980s has brought forth a new kind of challenge. Now that the rights and equal privileges of handicapped persons have been established by law and legislation has provided the means for implementing services, the task is to coordinate and refine those multiservice systems. Financial restraints and competition for the same funding dollars make it even more urgent for agencies to join forces and coordinate their efforts.

As Elder and Magrab (1980) point out, there are now scores of agencies and organizations providing services to the handicapped. These agencies differ significantly in their purposes, their organization, and in the clientele they serve. Some represent public, private, or semipublic concerns. Others are extensions of federal agencies, branches of state offices, or simply a local advocacy group. The competence, size, jurisdictions, and powers of each also vary. Some of these agencies view cooperation with related groups as important; others do not. Given the myriad of resources among so many agencies and the inevitable inefficiency and waste that come from an uncoordinated system of human services, the need for some form of collaboration is all too apparent.

Several authors have vividly described the urgent need for coordination among agencies. According to Audette (1980),

> The "patchwork quilt" of agencies, their eligibility criteria, intake systems, coordination mechanisms, and paperwork requirements, and the insulation of agency information under the guise of confidentiality— as well as many other factors—have made it necessary for advocates of children with handicaps to be highly skilled in order to successfully piece together a reasonable facsimile of a "program" that can be responsive to the individual needs of eligible persons. (p. 27)

Zeller (1980) described the difficulties imposed when numerous agencies become involved in services for the handicapped without concurrent mechanisms for cooperation in this way:

Parents once were faced with service agencies and schools that often closed the doors on handicapped children; they now may be faced with a myriad of fragmented services, each aiding a limited segment of the handicapped population. Faced with the overwhelming complexity of service systems, many individuals and families settle for whatever is offered or stop trying altogether to find assistance. (p. 66)

An extensive study on services for the handicapped by the Rand Corporation (Kakalik, Brewer, Dougharty, Fleischauer, Genesky, & Wallen, 1974) showed many problems that plague service systems for the handicapped because of the lack of coordination and collaboration among agencies. Their report was based on interviews with officials responsible for major federal and state programs, as well as questionnaire results from service providers working with the handicapped. The investigators concluded that, while insufficiency of resources is a major problem, more money is not the solution to some other basic problems. Rather, they pointed out that the system for delivering services to the handicapped is so complex, disorganized, and lacking in control that it defies efficient and effective operation. Not only do inequities and gaps in service delivery abound, but insufficient information is available across agencies to manage the service system effectively and to deliver the kinds of help children need most. While the investigators noted that a significant amount of funds were being expended on behalf of the handicapped and that beneficial effects were apparent, a number of serious problems persist. Some of the problems described in their report are summarized in the following:

- A great deal of inequity prevails in the service system for handicapped individuals, especially in regard to accessibility and the level of services provided. Per capita expenditures were found to vary greatly according to the state and the handicap involved. Eligibility rules differed, particularly in ways that shortchanged preschool handicapped children and youngsters in rural areas.
- Gaps in service were found where certain critical services were totally neglected or simply underdeveloped. Gaps were noted, for example, in the areas of prevention, identification of those needing services, and referral. The irony of these gaps was described by the investigators:

    It is especially tragic that prevention should be neglected, because for many types of disorders, high-quality preventative services are believed to completely forestall handicapping conditions in at least three-fourths of the cases of particular types of disorders handled and for some types of disorders, preventative services may forestall handicapping conditions in at least 99 percent of the cases. Yet of all government expenditures earmarked for handicapped children, only about 3 percent is spent on the vital services of prevention, identification and referral. Only about 1 percent is targeted for prevention, 99 percent gives service *after* the children are handicapped. (p. 16)

Gaps also appeared to result from the common institutional emphasis on a single kind of service. Many of the undeveloped services were not the prime responsibility of any single agency; thus, no one assumed responsibility. Furthermore, eligibility exclusions varied among states so that some children who were denied services in one state would not have been denied them in a neighboring state.

- Insufficient information sharing and a lack of reliable data on program benefits and effectiveness hampered attempts to improve service management. Some agencies collected management data, but it was often limited to resource inputs and did not cover service outputs. If information was available and quality evaluation data assembled, it was not always shared or simply was not used by agencies that would benefit from some kind of feedback information.
- Inadequate control was shown in the lack of national policies in regard to handicapped children and youth. The researchers found that federal and state service systems were

varied, fragmented, uncoordinated, and not particularly responsive to an individual's total needs. The sheer numbers of agencies dispensing funds and services under the authorization of different pieces of enabling legislation resulted in no one person or group acting as the responsible agent for planning, monitoring, and controlling services in any comprehensive fashion. Policy-making, funding, and operating decisions are often made by entirely different groups of people, who have little or no data about program effectiveness to guide them. (pp. 17-18)

P.L. 94-142, the Education for All Handicapped Children Act of 1975, was passed after the Rand study was conducted. Although this law undoubtedly has helped to address some of these problems, it has also compounded that which must be coordinated. Furthermore, it applies only to education agencies and does not affect agencies that manage resources and hold responsibility for other services relating to handicapped individuals.

Recognizing the problems reported in the Rand study, Magrab and Elder (1979) explained why better interagency linkages can remedy many of them. Programs for the handicapped, they noted, transgress traditional boundaries of the community and social field, the educational system, the health services system, and the vocational rehabilitation system. Not one, but all fields of service must be considered, since persons with most types of handicapping conditions require help from two, three, or all of these human service systems. At least, handicapped individuals are eligible for services from one or more of those systems. The way in which these various systems relate to and affect each other in their work with a common clientele thus becomes of major importance. Because of their conditions, however, these individuals are not necessarily in a good position to pick and choose the most appropriate services to meet their needs. Neither are they in a position to orchestrate their own service program across numerous agencies and bureaucratic systems.

What Factors Have Contributed to the Absence of Interagency Linkages?

Since interagency collaboration is believed to be so advantageous, why has it been so slow to evolve? What factors have promoted such isolationism among agencies? Magrab and Elder (1979), in an insightful analysis, cited several culprits that have perpetuated the problem and brought it to its current magnitude. According to their analysis, six factors have discouraged interagency collaboration, making it difficult even for those who are committed to the idea:

1. There is a lack of agreement across agencies regarding definitions of ''who the handicapped are'' and ''what handicapped persons are to be served by various programs.''
2. Special forms of assistance presently available to handicapped persons in the United States are actually fragmented bits and pieces of services that are spread across many independent service systems.
3. Overlapping legislation at the federal level has promoted fragmented, uncoordinated forms of service delivery. While over 165 different federal programs exist for the handicapped, they have been created without any mechanism for coordinating their delivery in ways that benefit the client.
4. There are multiple funding sources for services to the handicapped, and attempts to coordinate funding are often cumbersome administratively.
5. Multiple planning bodies, with each service system assembling its own representatives, engage in what have often been simultaneous, parallel forms of planning.
6. The existence of different models of service delivery across the various agencies contributes to the fragmentation of services and makes coordination difficult because some approaches do not mesh easily.

Given these circumstances, it is clear that the time has come to tackle some of the problems that have thwarted coordination among related agencies. Through federal leadership, interagency planning is now shifting from a voluntary action to a more mandatory one. In some cases, federal funds are being awarded contingent on evidence of interagency planning. New roads are opening to make collaboration more feasible. Martinson (1982) noted several of these. First, planning and management models are now being developed to allow more effective interagency collaboration. Second, broadened authority bases are being created to initiate and then maintain more comprehensive planning processes. Third, there is a growing cadre of persons who have expertise and experience in interagency systems; fourth, there is increased financial support for interagency planning efforts at both federal and state levels.

So What Is Interagency Collaboration?

Professionals across the various service systems use terms such as *interagency coordination* (Elder, 1979), *interagency collaboration* (Audette, 1980; Elder, 1980; Helge, 1981), and *interagency networks* (Roth, 1977) somewhat interchangeably to describe a variety of joint activities undertaken by two or more agencies to achieve some common goals. Elder (1980) provides the following definition of this concept:

> It [interagency coordination] can be broadly defined as an attempt by two or more agencies or programs to work together to integrate their separate activities for the purpose of improving services for a defined population. This coordination can include cooperative efforts in planning, budgeting, services delivered to a common clientele, or any functions common to participating agencies. These cooperative efforts are, then, usually spelled out in written interagency collaboration agreements. (pp. 195-196)

It is apparent that many different levels of interagency collaboration are possible. At one level, for example, agencies can *coordinate* activities in ways that facilitate each other's independent or interdependent activities. Coordination does not necessarily mean joint implementation of services, joint planning, or activities in which agencies work directly with one another, however. Frequently, coordination involves "paper agreements" or mere promises between agencies to cooperate. Beyond this, there may be no planning or development of systems to carry out any common or complementary activities.

The notion of *interagency collaboration* connotes a more involved, interactive process in which agencies work together directly to achieve a common goal. For true interagency collaboration, a more sophisticated system of interaction and decision making must be inherent to the interagency structure. Zeller (1980) suggested that the concept of interagency collaboration encompasses two broad goals: (1) improvement in the delivery of services to handicapped individuals, and (2) improvement in the efficiency and effectiveness of service delivery systems. To achieve such goals under an interagency collaboration requires a sincere commitment by everyone involved to plan, orchestrate, and deliver long-term programs and services for its consumers. It involves a set of common standards, procedures, and actions, which is very different from the mere gesture of friendly cooperation. Inherent to the resulting interagency collaboration is a system characterized by an open and honest exchange of information and resources, the joint definition of common goals and objectives, and the utilization of democratic procedures for decision making. In summary, program planning and implementation evolves from a true spirit of collaboration. This is far more desirable than a system where there is merely a promise of cooperation.

The group of agencies working together under a collaborative arrangement may be referred to as an interagency consortium, an interagency collaborative, or a network. The connections they form as a result of their agreements and their joint activities also may be called interagency linkages. One or two agencies typically take the lead in organizing the effort and in inviting others to participate. The participating agencies differ from state to state and even from one city or township to another.

INTERAGENCY COLLABORATION: AN OLD IDEA WITH NEW APPLICATIONS

The problems within human service systems are most prevalent in existing programs for adults and school-aged youngsters with developmental disabilities. They have not yet surfaced as serious limitations in programs for the very young, primarily because these programs are relatively new. Many communities are just beginning to develop full-service programs for preschool handicapped children. Few community-wide programs existed before 1968, when the Handicapped Children's Early Education Program was launched under P.L. 90-538 for the purpose of stimulating new planning and development in services for handicapped infants and preschoolers. As the early intervention movement has gained momentum, attention has focused on the most pressing need—the need to create new programs for the thousands of handicapped young children who remain unserved.

In the rush to get new programs under way, it is easy to neglect an equally important task that should be addressed concurrently. The mechanisms designed for service delivery should take into account the existence of several parallel agencies that hold some responsibility for serving the population of children under age 5. The working, functional relationships of these community/state agencies must be defined to ensure that their activities are mutually supportive, not competitive. In doing so, program planners and advocates must face several important issues. What will be the roles of the various agencies that have a vested interest in young children or in the handicapped? What responsibilities can and will each assume in relation to the broader plan for services? How will agencies cooperate in order to facilitate broad community goals and to ensure that the needs of their clients are met efficiently? What collaborative systems will be needed to ensure that cooperative activities are carried out by the various agencies? If questions like these are not addressed when programs are initially designed, the duplication, fragmentation of services, and confusion that plague older, established service systems are likely to recur in new programs for handicapped infants and preschoolers.

Why Is Interagency Collaboration Needed in Serving Young Handicapped Children?

There are special reasons why interagency linkages are important in early intervention programs for handicapped children. The very nature of the field of early intervention and the number of professionals involved in this area necessitate some form of interagency collaboration. Furthermore, economic and political conditions of this decade make it essential to devise economical, efficient modes of service delivery.

The Need for Multidisciplinary Expertise

One need for interagency collaboration evolves from the multidisciplinary character of early intervention programs. No one discipline has all the kinds of expertise required to create quality programs for infants and preschoolers with developmental disabilities; professionals from many disciplines must participate if services that are essential to the total social-emotional/physical/educational-intellectual well-being of young children are to be provided.

This multidisciplinary nature of the field creates a unique situation. Typically, professional disciplines are clustered under several different administrative agencies. Each agency provides certain kinds of categorical assistance in areas of educational, social, health, or family services. To expect any one agency to assemble the multidisciplinary personnel resources required for quality intervention programs is not very realistic; the cost alone can be prohibitive. It is possible, however, to arrange for the involvement of various disciplines in the planning and implementation of such programs through collaborative arrangements among related human services agencies. Each can contribute the expertise of its own staff. Each can share its unique resources in ways that contribute to a common program effort. In this way, multidisciplinary teams can be assembled.

The Need To Provide a Broad Array of Services

Given the diversity and unique characteristics of handicapped children from birth to age 5, it is a challenge to amass the special kinds of services that make it possible to meet the individual needs of each handicapped child. Because of their youth, handicapped children have special needs that extend across health, educational, social, and family service domains. It is no surprise, then, to find several agencies assuming some responsibility for the welfare of handicapped infants and preschoolers.

The diverse nature of this young population also calls for an unusually wide array of special services. What handicapped infants need is quite different from what toddlers or preschoolers require. The kinds of services, kinds of professional input, and types of agency involvement depend on the age group being served. Furthermore, this population includes children with all types of disabilities at all levels of severity. Although the actual number of children needing services in a given community may be small, they may require the full range of services for each disability category and at every severity level. The cost of establishing special full service programs for only a small number of children can be prohibitive, but needed services can possibly be organized without excessive cost or duplication of effort by capitalizing on resources across existing service systems.

The geographical distribution, i.e., in rural or urban areas, of this young population also influences how and by whom services can best be offered. Handicapped infants and preschoolers are not conveniently assembled together in a school building where services can easily be organized under one roof by a single agency. They may be clustered in a small area where they can be easily transported to a central service facility, or they may be scattered across a wide area. The more rural the area served, the more likely children's homes are the best site for intervention. Intervention can then be accomplished by the parents, assisted by one or more consultants who make periodic visitations to help plan and then demonstrate techniques for helping and teaching the child.

Because of the unique characteristics of the population to be served and their geographical dispersion, alternative services may be necessary, as well as alternative modes of service delivery (such as home-based and center-based programs, the use of parents and paraprofessionals as service providers, or the use of one agency to carry out selected services for another agency). It may be most difficult for a single agency to create all the necessary service options, but that task can be accomplished if several agencies work together.

The Need To Coordinate Activities of Multiple Service Providers

Service systems for both handicapped and nonhandicapped children under age 5 are operated under the auspices of a number of different administrative units or agencies that are authorized to serve one or more of the following target populations: young children, such as infants or preschoolers; handicapped or developmentally disabled individuals; or families with special needs, such as low-income families. The field of early intervention overlaps all three of these areas. As a result, many agencies hold some responsibility, albeit limited, to provide selected kinds of assistance to the same clientele. Agencies can attempt to fulfill their obligations in isolation, but this leads to fragmentation, duplication of services, and frustrations. Collaboration among agencies serving this young population is one means for resolving these overlapping responsibilities.

Because a large number of independent service providers currently operate preschool and day care services for young children, the point of greatest conflict and potential service redundancy lies here. Unlike programs for school-aged students, which fall under the sole jurisdiction of the local school district, early childhood education programs are not part of any standardized administrative system common to all communities or to all states. In states that do not mandate early childhood intervention services for the handicapped, no single agency is responsible for serving this young clientele. As a result, special programs for the handicapped have been developed through the efforts of many agencies, including nonprofit groups, religious organizations, community advocacy groups, state or local government agencies, school districts, or private foundations. Each manages its own operations, establishes its own funding base, recruits its own enrollees, imposes its own admission criteria and procedures, and delivers its own unique assortment of services. Usually, no one agency provides a full-service program; rather, each offers selected types of service because its clientele is limited to certain groups or because it does not hold sufficient financial resources to do otherwise.

In those few states with mandates requiring services for handicapped children under age 5, public school systems are responsible for organizing services. Even in those states, however, school districts are faced with the task of creating programs that may parallel or overlap existing community-based regular or special early childhood programs serving handicapped or nonhandicapped children.

Communities in which several independent agencies operate a variety of services for young children are fortunate in the sense that services are available where none may have existed otherwise. At the same time, predictable problems arise when a multitude of parallel, but independent programs exists. These problems reiterate the need for some form of collaboration and coordination between agencies:

- Independently operated preschools serving handicapped children may result in considerable duplication of effort when they offer similar services, but not full-service programs. Such programs actually compete for enrollees in order to protect their own security and financial resources.

- There may be gaps in services, even though numerous kinds of assistance are offered across all service providers. Certain populations, such as handicapped infants, may be neglected because of the lack of an advocacy group or because it may not be financially profitable for agencies to serve this group. Certain types of needed services, such as parent/home programs, may be unavailable, even though the need is great. Without a systematic interagency effort to organize a full continuum of services or to coordinate offerings across agencies, gaps are likely to go uncorrected, or even unidentified.
- There is usually no centralized place where parents can seek information when many independently operated programs make up the service system within a community. Under these conditions, parents may find it difficult to determine what service options are available and what is best for their child. Often, they must go through repeated intake procedures as each program imposes its unique procedures and admission criteria.
- Some handicapped children go unserved for a long time because of the time and effort required from their parents to work through a maze of agencies and service systems. When programs are full, agencies may not necessarily be helpful in making referrals to other sources. With no systematic screening and referral process across agencies and their various programs, many parents simply give up, resorting to day care or a general preschool program that is not designed to meet the special needs of their handicapped child.

The Need To Continue Expanding Services

Programs can be expensive, given the kinds of individual and comprehensive service systems required to deliver a meaningful intervention in the lives of handicapped infants and preschoolers. As professionals and community advocates attempt to expand service systems to include all children in this age group, however, the emerging economic and social climate of the 1980s brings new issues with which they must contend. Interagency collaboration presents one solution for dealing with some of these issues and provides a means for continuing the development of services so that the recent momentum in the field of early intervention for the handicapped will not be lost.

In recent years, there has been a tremendous upsurge of interest in programs for handicapped infants and preschoolers. By the end of the 1970s several states had passed legislative mandates requiring that services be offered to handicapped children under school age. Other states and communities were voluntarily developing an array of programs for this young age group. By 1980, when P.L. 94-142 went into full effect and programs were in place for handicapped youngsters of school age, the groundwork had also been laid for the early intervention movement to proceed ahead in full gear. The 1980s have become an era of financial exigency and federal conservatism, however. A new set of conditions, much different from those of the 1970s, now set the stage on which professionals must work to promote the early intervention movement. Funds are not as readily available as they once were. Agencies operating education and social-family services are being pressured to offer more with smaller budgets. Emphasis is on consolidation of services, not expansion of new service programs. Services for other client groups, viewed as important as those for handicapped infants and preschoolers, create new competition for a diminishing pool of federal and state dollars.

Given these conditions, it is an even greater challenge to gain financial support for new programs. When taxpayers are feeling the impact of spiraling inflation, they are hesitant to support new programs that may require higher taxes. Therefore, strategies to obtain financing for early intervention programs now are exceedingly important if these programs are to continue to grow in number. There is a need for cooperative planning among agencies so that they can focus their efforts on a commonly agreed set of priorities. Their collective voice is a stronger force in gaining legislative or local support than is the singular effort of just one or two agencies. Not only can a group of agencies form a more visible, powerful advocate group, but the pooling of their own financial resources provides a more viable means for supporting early intervention programs. To act as advocate, raise funds, and then operate full-service programs is a task of such magnitude that few agencies are equipped to handle it singlehandedly.

The Need for Comprehensive Services

Generally speaking, early intervention programs have three major purposes. One is to minimize the effects of a physical, sensory, or mental disability on the development and learning of a young child by providing early education and training and by deliberately teaching the child critical developmental skills that may not be readily acquired because of the disability. Teachers or parents must bring experiences to the child and provide special kinds of stimulation. A second purpose is to prevent, if at all possible, at-risk conditions or early developmental irregularities from becoming of such magnitude that they truly become handicapping to a child. The degree to which a problem interferes with a child's life and learning depends, to some extent, on what special help or intervention is given. Such intervention may take many forms, including medical, educational, nutritional, or family-oriented strategies. A final purpose of early intervention is to minimize and possibly prevent the development of secondary handicaps, which may occur when the initial disability is allowed to continue its interference with the child's ability to learn, to profit from experience, or to progress through expected developmental sequences.

The goal of early intervention is thus one of maximizing a child's early development in areas unaffected by the handicap. The early years are critical ones. The more powerful and effective the intervention, the greater the chances of preventing a child from falling so far behind age mates that it is nearly impossible ever to catch up. So what does an effective intervention entail and how do interagency relationships affect this? Experts and researchers in the field generally agree that there are several important ingredients in an effective intervention program (Allen, Holm, & Schiefelbusch, 1978; Bricker & Iacino, 1977; Bronfenbrenner, 1974; Hayden & McGinness, 1977; Karnes & Zehrbach, 1975; McDaniels, 1977; Peterson, 1982):

1. Early intervention services must be comprehensive in scope in order to promote optimal growth for the child across all developmental domains. Inasmuch as a child's development in all areas is intertwined, effective treatment cannot target just one area of development (such as speech and language) while ignoring others. To do so only invites other difficulties, since a disability can threaten a child's total well-being.

2. Early intervention programs should provide continuous and intensive kinds of education and therapeutic help if gains are to be maintained. Services are needed year-round and on a schedule in which many people work with the child as frequently as possible. For example, a speech therapist has the greatest impact by working with a handicapped preschooler daily or at least every other day with backup work by the parent or teacher. If that service is reduced to only once or twice weekly, its effect is questionable. Speech training is even more effective if, in addition to individual sessions, training activities are integrated into ongoing daily activities of the child.

3. Parents must be included as a part of the intervention. Since parents remain the most important teachers and caregivers of their child during the early years, their participation is essential. Not only is the parent taught special skills for working with the child, but a positive parent-child relationship is encouraged.

4. A variety of special services must be available to meet the diverse needs of young handicapped children and their parents. These span much beyond what is provided to older handicapped students, since the emphasis of their special education services is usually remediation, not intervention. If a timely and effective intervention is to be rendered to a handicapped infant or preschooler, an array of services, individually tailored to the needs of the child, is needed.

Given these program characteristics, and because the intent of these services is that of intervention, it follows that several agencies working in tandem are in a more powerful position to effect change than a few working in isolation. When human services agencies work together in behalf of the client's total needs, the purposes for which they operate individually and collectively are more likely to be realized. Services as extensive as these require multiple resources. The implications of this are summarized by Martin (1970), assistant secretary of Special Education and Rehabilitation Services, who pointed out that (a) effective education and habilitation programs for preschool children are expensive, (b) young handicapped children present very complex problems that require services beyond those typically encompassed within the programmatic resources or jurisdictions of a single agency, (c) effective intervention programs require the expertise and services of many professional disciplines, and (d) early childhood-handicapped services must involve education in "expanded educational settings" (i.e., settings outside traditional elementary school buildings, such as the children's own homes, neighborhood centers, nursery or preschools, or clinics). If professionals are to deal with these realities and yet continue to expand intervention programs for handicapped infants and preschoolers, it is apparent that the resources and professional personnel of several agencies must be pooled in order to assemble the ingredients needed to build effective programs.

What Benefits Are Possible through Interagency Collaboration?

Administrators, teachers, or therapists who are potential participants in interagency activities typically want to know:

- What good will it do for our own program if we spend the extra time working with representatives of other agencies?
- Why should we share our own resources when we don't have enough ourselves?
- How will an interagency approach benefit the children in our program?
- How will it benefit me as a professional if I put my time and effort into this?

It is not unusual for staff members to feel that it is easier to carry out all program functions themselves than it is to bring new people into the operation. The addition of another level of coordination and planning responsibilities on top of existing ones can appear foreboding to personnel who may already be overloaded with work. When agencies perceive themselves as sufficiently stable financially that they can continue to operate autonomously if they so wish, interagency collaboration may not appear so attractive. These agencies should seriously consider what interagency linkages can do for them, however.

Expanding Service Options through Resource Sharing

How can a continuum of services that is both economically feasible and programmatically sound be made available to meet the diverse needs of young handicapped children and their parents? All agencies do not have the resources to arrange and maintain a large variety of service options. Neither are they all equipped to operate comprehensive treatment programs. Interagency networks thus offer a means for expanding service delivery options without undue burden on any single organization. Each may assume responsibility for developing one or more components of a well-planned system of services, or two or more agencies may combine resources to develop a common service component that neither could create alone. An interagency collaboration provides the mechanism to build comprehensive service systems that distribute responsibilities in ways that circumvent undue financial and programmatic burdens on any one agency.

Coping with Funding Limitations

Because early intervention approaches must deal with children's development across all areas, the comprehensive services approach can be a potentially expensive one. An issue that typically affects state and community endorsement of early intervention programs is the source of funds to support such services. Single agencies do not always have sufficient funding to maintain the necessary multidisciplinary staff or to offer a variety of services.

The issue, then, is: Can single agencies bear the financial responsibilities for services to handicapped preschoolers, infants, or their parents? Or, can the financial resources of many be combined so costs can be shared to create higher quality and more varied service alternatives? Different agencies qualify for funds that come from different sources; funds available to one agency may be untouchable by another. Therefore, while one agency may be unable to generate sufficient financial support, an interagency collaboration may generate the larger funding bases necessary to support quality early intervention programs.

Improving Consumer Accessibility to Services

Whenever several agencies act as service providers for the same clientele, the public may find it difficult to determine who does what and how services differ from agency to agency. It is not always apparent what kinds of services are available, although the offerings of individual programs may be well advertised. Furthermore, to obtain services, parents may be required to contact each agency, work through their unique intake process, and negotiate services with personnel within that center.

Parents in these cases may find themselves in a difficult position: How do they arrange for full services programs for a handicapped child if they cannot be provided by just one agency? How do they avoid unnecessary repetition of the application/admission processes for each individual agency they contact? The task of shopping for services can be a frustrating experience for parents when there are a number of independent service providers. They are often subjected to repeated and unnecessary evaluations of their child's condition, repetitious interviews, and repeated requests to complete information forms. Under interagency collabora-tives, agencies can coordinate their intake/placement systems, even though each may continue to operate independent service systems. Unproductive competition among agencies for clients can be avoided, and parents can be more easily referred to the agencies that are best suited to serve them. Simply the clarification of communication and referral channels that can come from interagency collabora-tion can help potential consumers gain more rapid access to services.

Integrating and Coordinating Service Domains

In communities where no single, well-designed early intervention program for handicapped children is available, there may be several independent groups that offer some form of special help. One agency may offer day care for handicapped children, another may offer parent counseling, another may offer a preschool program a few days each week, and another may offer speech therapy. Further-more, as each agency applies its own unique style of working with the parent and child, procedures used by one may conflict with those used by another. When independent agencies offer only pieces and parts of the total service program needed by handicapped children, parents find themselves faced with the awesome job of orchestrating comprehensive services for their child. That is a role for which they are usually ill-prepared, however, and their attempts to play it may not be welcome. It is a difficult enough task for well-educated parents who have the self-confidence and skill to find their way through the maze of agencies and bureau-cratic regulations to find services for their child. For low-income parents with little education or experience in negotiating their way through bureaucratic red tape, the task may be too overwhelming for some even to attempt. No wonder so many parents simply give up. The end result is that services are not used by those who need them most.

The problem thus becomes one of coordination: How can services be orches-trated in a way that allows professionals to better focus their efforts and to work toward common goals that will benefit the child? How can the efforts of each group be combined in ways that capitalize upon what each can offer? Interagency collaboration makes it possible to consolidate the activities of several independent groups. As a collective group, their work and impact on the child can be powerful; as an assortment of independent agencies that provide piecemeal services, their benefit to the child may be small.

Normalizing Service Delivery Programs for Handicapped Children

As new programs are being created for handicapped infants and preschoolers in communities across the United States, a unique situation is being created. Agen-cies charged with the responsibility of developing early intervention programs for the handicapped are not those typically serving normally developing infants or preschoolers. Because there is no standardized system of regular preschool education, the involvement of regular preschool centers in services for the handicapped creates a difficult administrative management task. Regular programs with an interest in serving the handicapped often do not have the expertise or staff to deal with the special educational and treatment needs of handicapped children. Thus, there is a risk of creating two separate service systems for young children—one for the handicapped and one for normal children—even though the present philosophy is that early separation of handicapped and nonhandicapped children is only another version of institutionalization.

How can early intervention programs for the handicapped be created that avoid segregating and isolating those children from their normally developing peers yet which still afford them the very specialized, intensive forms of service they need? Interagency collaboratives offer a solution to this predicament. Agencies that serve normally developing children and those required to work with the handicapped can combine their efforts in ways that serve both purposes. A marriage of regular preschool education and early childhood special education programs, given some careful planning, can result in more normalizing environments for handicapped children. It may also help program developers avoid the task of starting programs from scratch when numerous programs are already in place for serving very young children.

Promoting Community-wide Planning and Problem Solving

Can public schools and other major agencies create effective service systems for handicapped preschoolers and infants that build upon existing program resources and promote cooperation rather than competition? As public schools or any other agency assume major responsibilities for early childhood special education programs for the first time, either voluntarily or through legislative mandates, they face an important decision. They can work with existing service delivery systems in ways that build upon them rather than compete against them, or they can initiate new programs that not only ignore the existence of parallel service systems but also function in direct competition. The outcome of the latter course may be the termination of programs that have taken years to develop. Interagency collaboration offers a means for agencies to engage in program development that takes total community needs and issues into account. Self-serving activities that focus on agency survival and give second priority to parent or community needs can be minimized. Patchwork problem solving occurs when agencies work to solve their own immediate problems and fail to address the service needs of children or of the community at large. By entering into cooperative planning activities, agencies can work together in ways that benefit both their independent organizations and the community.

DEVELOPING COLLABORATIVE SYSTEMS

There is no single formula for the best way in which agencies can work together. Every community differs. So do the scope and type of resources available within any given township, county, or state differ. Interagency collaboratives can be created at the grass-roots level across programs in a local community, or collaboratives can be formed across city agencies, state agencies, or even federal or national organizations. At whatever level cooperatives are formed, the underlying task is to improve services to the client and to streamline the processes of service delivery in ways that produce more efficient, less wasteful operations. In regard to early childhood special education services, there is an additional challenge: How can agencies combine their resources and coordinate activities so that services can be offered to handicapped infants and preschoolers where none may be available otherwise?

Who Are the Potential Participants in Interagency Activities?

No two communities are alike. Each contains different agencies that offer services to young children, and each has its own politics that influence who should be involved in interagency planning activities. Several key agencies are prime candidates for involvement because they operate under federal mandates or enabling legislation requiring them to serve the handicapped. These agencies have varying names in different communities, but basically they are the following:

1. State Education Agencies (SEAs) and their specific divisions concerned with the handicapped
2. Local Education Agencies (LEAs) or school districts
3. Local Title XIX (Medicaid/EPSDT) and Title XX Programs
4. Title V Programs (e.g., Maternal and Child Health Programs, Crippled Children's Services, Handicapped Children's Programs)
5. Department of Health and Human Services agencies serving developmentally disabled individuals
6. Head Start Programs

A number of other agencies or programs may also be helpful because they act as service providers for young handicapped or nonhandicapped children or because they represent potential future sponsors or service providers (Ackerman & Moore, 1976; Magrab, Kazuk, & Greene, no date; Mulvenon, 1980; Swan, 1980):

- mental health centers
- university-affiliated facilities, mental retardation facilities within universities, or other university-based laboratory or child services programs

- nonprofit, philanthropic, or advocacy groups, such as the National Association for Retarded Citizens and its local community organizations, National Easter Seal, and United Cerebral Palsy
- medical centers and hospitals
- local service agencies, such as church organizations, foundations, private centers
- nursery and preschool centers (private or public supported programs)

How Can Agencies Collaborate?

There are many types of interagency collaboratives. Cooperative activities or interagency linkages can be formed for any number of purposes and may involve agreements ranging from the very simple to the exceedingly complex. Elder (1979) points out that interagency coordination or collaboration can operate at the system, program, or client levels:

1. System level collaboration focuses on the system of services that is required to meet the needs of young children or any client group in a state or township. A state level planning council for early childhood intervention service made up of representatives from various state agencies or a state developmental disabilities council are examples.
2. Program level collaboration occurs when various agencies integrate their administrative functions to coordinate their separate operations. Collaboration on a common screening system to identify young handicapped children is an example.
3. Client level interagency collaboration occurs when local program/agency staffs work together to coordinate services for an individual client. Such mutual effort is designed to integrate separate service programs in a way that addresses a client's total spectrum of needs and avoids unnecessary duplication and fragmentation of services. The preschool center may collaborate with a local clinic to plan a program of intervention for a hearing-impaired preschooler, for example.

The issues or program activities on which agencies collaborate also vary. The types of interagency arrangements can include several kinds of arrangements (Audette, 1980; Baumheimer, 1979; Elder & Magrab, 1980; Gans & Horton, 1975).

Collaboration on Basic Standards

Each of the many different agencies that offer services to young handicapped children and their families usually operates according to its own unique rules, regulations, and service standards. These differences in how services are delivered can make communication and cooperation difficult between agencies. Public schools, preschool centers, or agencies offering related services therefore may agree to adopt a common set of standards and criteria for serving their young clientele. Such collaborative agreements may originate at the state level or at the local level, depending on the agencies involved. Commitments may be made concerning the types of children to be served, the kinds of services to be provided, and the standards to be maintained.

What *types of children* will be served by individual agencies and what criteria will be used by each to designate their population? If these kinds of agreements are made, agencies can make referrals to one another based on a clear understanding of what population each has agreed to serve. Duplication of effort and competition for the same children can be eliminated by such agreements, allowing various agencies to combine their efforts in ways that ensure that all children are receiving adequate services.

What *kinds of services* will be provided to children who are referred into a given program? If independent agencies come to an agreement on what services each can and will offer to young children, the basis for further collaborative effort has been established. Given such agreements, agencies are in a better position to refer children to one another for selected services.

What *standards* will be maintained regarding staff qualifications, pupil/teacher ratios, program planning procedures, and record keeping and evaluation? While most agencies adhere to some established set of standards, problems arise when different agencies enforce standards that are inconsistent and perhaps incompatible with one another. If they wish to enter into some form of collaborative activity, conflict is immediate because of each agency's concerns over violation of its own regulations. Public school districts, for example, follow standards defined by the State Education Plan and their own local Special Education Plan. District level management procedures also dictate standards on the administration of programs. Head Start centers have their own standards; so do privately operated centers. Whenever two or more agencies begin to work together, the question therefore quickly arises, "Whose rules . . . yours or mine?" Collaborative agreements, then, specify the ground rules and establish a common set of standards that each participating agency agrees to follow in joint activity.

Collaboration in the Use of Resources

Resource sharing is particularly crucial for the survival of many early childhood special education programs. Such collaboration may concern both financial and personnel resources, as well as facilities, equipment, and materials.

Sharing of financial resources provides the level of support needed to operate full-service programs. Financial support for early intervention programs is a constant problem where states do not require that early intervention programs be provided for handicapped youngsters. Because single agencies may be restricted in the financial resources to which they have access, it is not uncommon for early intervention programs to operate under the support of several "sponsoring" agencies. Each solicits funds from sources for which it qualifies and then contributes those monies to the collaborative project. Public schools, for example, have access to state education incentive monies and special education reimbursement funds, but not to monies from other state agencies supporting day care, other noneducational state agencies, or from the private sector. Private and nonprofit agencies, on the other hand, can obtain funds from state social service agencies, can engage in fund-raising activities, and can be a recipient of United Way fund-raising drives. By entering into collaborative relationships and drawing on each of their unique funding resources, it is possible for several agencies to amass the funds necessary to support sizeable early intervention programs.

Another way programs can cooperate on financial matters is for two or more agencies to join forces as they solicit funds from various sources. At times, agencies compete against one another and thus diminish the chances that either will be funded. By joining together in joint fund-raising endeavors or in joint applications for state and federal monies, programs can sometimes enhance their chances for obtaining financial support.

Sharing of personnel through interagency collaboration provides a vehicle for programs that are too small to employ full-time staff to get the specialized help they need. This is an especially useful strategy for obtaining the services of specialists such as speech therapists, psychologists, physical or occupational therapists, and audiologists. Programs serving only 12 to 15 children need specialists for only one-fourth to one-half time, and it is nearly impossible to find specialists who are available and willing to enter into such employment contracts. One form of interagency collaboration is for two or more programs to consolidate their personnel needs by hiring one or two full-time specialists who are then shared across each program. Time allocations and schedules are agreed upon, and each agency contributes its share to the total salary of the employee. One agency usually serves as the fiscal agent.

Sharing of facilities, equipment, and materials is a third means by which agencies can combine resources for their mutual benefit. Single agencies often do not have the financial resources to pay for the kinds of facilities, equipment, or materials needed to operate a quality program. Two or more programs and/or agencies may therefore join together to share a single physical facility. This may involve sharing space for only specified activities, such as for a screening clinic held intermittently during the year. On the other hand, some programs move into a common facility to share rent and to use a common playground, lunch room facility, or other space. Sharing of equipment and materials that are not necessarily in constant use by one group can also lead to considerable cost savings.

Collaboration by Use of Uniform Methods of Service Delivery

Interagency activities in regard to service delivery are the most complex. They not only require the paper agreements, but the implementation of procedures that may affect how each agency goes about its own operations. Agreements thus involve consensus on what must be done, as well as specifications on what procedures are to be used to ensure promises are kept. According to Audette (1980), if agencies engage in this type of collaboration, agreements of the previous two kinds (standards and resources) are absolute prerequisites. Collaborative agreements may involve several types of procedures, processes, or program activities.

Common Intake and Referral Systems. Instead of each agency conducting its own intake and evaluation procedures for handicapped infants and/or preschoolers who may be potential candidates for its programs, a single centralized intake system may be created to serve everyone. Agreements are made concerning what intake will involve, what information will be gathered, what screening and evaluative tests will be used, and who will conduct various parts of the intake evaluation. Agencies may establish a set of guidelines for making placement decisions, including who will participate and how the final referral will be made to the program(s) seeming to be most appropriate for a child.

Common Terminology. Agreements may be made to apply a common terminology in the evaluation of young children and in the gathering of information on a child. With definitional agreements, staff have a common system for communication for which meanings are clear and free of nebulous jargon. Thus, when information or reports are shared among agencies, it is presented in a way that is ultimately useful to each party.

Uniform Forms and Planning Formats. Agencies may agree to use the same forms for activities such as intake and evaluation processes, record keeping, and program planning. For example, a single set of child intake and family information forms may be designed to contain all basic information required by the public schools or any other participating agency. Parents then are not required to complete form after form when they move across agencies to obtain services. A single format for reporting child evaluation data facilitates the transfer of information across agencies. Forms for preparing written individualized education programs (IEPs) for each child are another point where interagency collaboration can be helpful; common procedures for planning and developing IEPs and a single form can make joint planning much easier.

Uniform Planning, Budgetary, and Program Calendars. Differences in the times when agencies plan yearly activities, set budgets, and schedule operating services can make collaboration exceedingly cumbersome. To accommodate such differences across several agencies requires a flexibility that can make cooperation a taxing, frustrating experience. While most agencies cannot automatically change their overall operational schedule, a calendar for planning activities/budgets/services for the interagency consortium efforts may be possible. An agreed upon schedule of activities around which each agency can plan and anticipate needs can help set the stage for interagency coordination.

Coordinated, Community-wide Program Planning. Agencies may agree to work together to plan services on a community-wide basis rather than engaging in independent planning for individual concerns only. The latter approach solves individual agency needs, but often results in gaps in services because no one examines needs from the broader community perspective. Agencies may join together in interagency committees or planning boards to consider issues and develop common strategies for meeting service needs in the community.

Coordinated Staff In-service Training Activities. Considerable time and effort can be saved when agencies that offer similar early childhood special education services and employ parallel staffs coordinate their training efforts. In-service training sessions can be scheduled to serve part or all staff across agencies. Common in-service training also provides a means to prepare staff to implement common procedures for service delivery and to employ common forms and planning strategies, as described earlier.

Integrated Data Base. Agencies can agree to combine their information systems in ways that ensure a child or family record continues with the client no matter what agency or in what center services are provided. Information collected by the public schools and/or other preschools that serve the child can be stored in a commonly controlled data system and be used by each agency as needed to conduct its own services. For example, IEPs can be prepared on a common set of forms and copies can be stored in the same data control center or computerized system used by the schools, the mental health agency, the preschool center, or clinics serving a child.

Levels of Sophistication in Interagency Collaboration—Do Communities Differ?

Just as the unique services activities around which collaborative agreements are made can differ, so do the complexity and sophistication of interagency collaboratives vary. The level of sophistication evidenced by cooperative agreements between two or more agencies is not just a reflection of the interests or generosity of each party. To what degree any agency becomes a participant in an early intervention collaborative network depends in part on:

- its perception of its own goals and responsibilities
- the absence of competing priorities that demand more immediate attention
- the degree to which it must compromise its own interests and autonomy to act as a participant
- the incentives for participating and the benefits that will come individually and collectively from collaboration
- what it believes it can contribute to the common effort without excessive response cost from its own staff or program stability

Levels of interagency collaboration may be described in a manner similar to that in which social and interactive exchanges among children are described. Early childhood special educators are familiar with the levels of interactive play exhibited by preschool children. The terms *solitary, parallel,* and *cooperative play* are typically used to describe increasingly gregarious forms of social interaction among children as they work and play together. Many agencies, for example, engage in solitary service delivery operations, conducting their own activities and carrying out their responsibilities independent of other agencies. Their systems for providing services to children and their parents bring little interaction with similar programs. Although such programs typically acknowledge the existence of related service systems, their relationship may be best described as one of "friendly neighbors." They express verbal support to one another, but they do not interact over any programmatic concerns. Cooperative exchanges are of little concern. It is important to note that, although not engaged in any real level of interagency collaboration, these agencies may do their own jobs very well. The lack of linkages with other agencies may or may not occur out of indifference. It may be that there is no apparent need or impetus to do otherwise or that the hassles involved in attempting any form of cooperation may appear too time-consuming or foreboding.

Like the youngsters they serve, some agencies engage in a form of parallel service delivery operations. At this level, agencies may begin to show some facilitative actions toward one another. While each operates independently of the others, they may share information, refer children to each other, provide verbal support, and give assistance when applications for grants are submitted and letters are needed to show community support. Selected activities may be coordinated so that they do not interfere with the parallel activities of the other agencies. For example, a preschool center may coordinate the scheduling of its spring preschool sessions with an early intervention program because many parents enroll their children in one program for the morning and the other for the afternoon. Cooperative relationships, however, in which agencies combine their efforts to achieve a common goal are not a part of the interactions at this level.

In cooperative interagency relationships, two or more agencies collaborate in planning and implementing activities that are aimed toward some common goals. These goals have been identified jointly by the participating agencies, and plans have been made jointly as to how the agencies will work together to achieve them. Like young children who engage in cooperative forms of play, there is a sharing of responsibility and a give-and-take form of exchange as the agencies work toward their common purpose. At this level of interagency collaboration, cooperation may be short-term or long-term, but it usually focuses on specific needs. The combined efforts of the participating agencies make it possible to achieve goals that a single agency would not have accomplished as quickly or perhaps at all. This type of interagency collaboration is seen when two agencies serve the same child and cooperate on matters of transportation between centers, coordinate the types of services each offers to the child, and share information on the child's progress. Joint meetings may be held to plan instructional programs, to discuss the child's progress with the parents, or to plan further services. Another example is the joint planning of a child find clinic by several agencies that serve handicapped young children in a given community. Directors of each program may meet to discuss how they will combine their staff to run the clinic, who will provide the materials, and what responsibilities each agency will undertake in the screening of children who are brought to the clinic.

Agencies may engage in joint activities that go beyond these general types of cooperative activity to a much more sophisticated form of collaboration. Children, once they begin to engage in cooperative play, show increasingly more complex levels of cooperative interaction. So it is with agencies that are concerned with educational and other services to young handicapped children and their families. The nature of their interactions may range from momentary gestures of cooperation to very complex systems of collaboration that resemble formal partnerships. This final level is the most complicated level of multiagency collaboration. It differs from simple cooperative interagency relationships in that formalized systems of collaboration that define ongoing responsibilities and agreements between parties are created. At this level, cooperation is no longer a matter of spontaneous teamwork, but a formally planned, contracted agreement that spans a specified period of time.

While each agency may continue as an independent body, the partnership produces a new entity with its own unique administrative structure, powers, and decision-making procedures. In some cases, agencies may dissolve their own identity as a separate service delivery system and develop a new identity as a part of the partnership. This level of interagency collaboration represents a serious, formal commitment. The new administrative/service system in which the agencies agree to collaborate belongs to no single agency, but to the newly formed partnership. Typically, at this level of interagency collaboration, some roles change, and each participating agency gives up some authority. Jurisdiction over the cooperative effort falls under the new consortium, and responsibility for the operation of these cooperative systems is held jointly by all members or by their designee (often a coordinator or special interagency administrator).

INTERAGENCY SYSTEMS IN ACTION: SOME EXAMPLES

The following descriptions exemplify some of the kinds of activities in which interagency groups engage. These examples are drawn from real communities and real people, although they are not documentaries on specific projects. Rather, these accounts show how interagency collaboratives differ in their level of sophistication, in their formality, and in their scope of services.

Meeting the New State Early Childhood-Handicapped Mandate in Middletown, U.S.A.—The Public School Dilemma

The Problem and the Need

When the state legislature passed a bill mandating special services for all handicapped children from birth to school age, the act was heralded as one of the most progressive moves the state had taken for early childhood education and family services. Only a few other states had set such a precedent. School districts were suddenly faced with the task of organizing systems to deliver a wide variety of services in what seemed to be a very short amount of time. The impact of the new legislation was particularly felt in Middletown School District, which was the largest district in the state, served the largest number of students, and covered a very large geographical area. Preliminary estimates suggested that the district would need to prepare to serve several thousand infants and preschoolers with developmental disabilities. To organize programs for such a diverse population in such a short time in an entirely new service area was a monumental task, especially since the school district had no previous experience with this population. Existing programs for school-aged children could not simply be expanded to include a larger number of children. From the beginning, school officials recognized that this new system would require a very different approach to service delivery. These programs would be unlike those traditionally operated for older handicapped students.

There were also a number of difficult issues to address. How could the district underwrite the full cost of a program that had to encompass such a broad variety of child/family and interdisciplinary services? What facilities could the district use? Existing facilities were already crowded and were not particularly appropriate for the new population they were now required to serve. How would the new system relate to a large number of early intervention programs already operating in the city, which collectively were serving just under 50 percent of the estimated preschool handicapped population? District officials recognized that, as they developed programs in the schools, their actions could put several centers out of business. A question they faced, then, was whether they should proceed in a way that would not allow this to occur.

Interagency Collaboration as a Solution for Program Development

Middletown school officials decided it would be advantageous to work with programs already serving handicapped preschoolers in their city. They created an interagency planning committee, composed of key administrators from the major programs in the city and representatives from organizations that could be potential service providers. The planning committee determined which services were already in place in Middletown, where service gaps existed, and what administrative/coordinating functions were lacking in the existing service systems. Based on this initial needs assessment and several months of planning and debate within the planning group, a formal interagency consortium was formed—The Middletown Early Childhood Interagency Cooperative.

Member agencies signed contracts in which they agreed to carry out certain roles in the consortium. Each also agreed to provide designated services for which the school district would contribute financial support. The framework for this new collaborative program included the following major components:

1. The school district and designated representatives from the major member agencies in the consortium agreed to operate a cooperative intake/screening/ referral system. All referrals of infants and preschoolers with suspected developmental disabilities or special problems are made into this central intake unit. Individual agencies no longer conduct their own evaluations of a child's condition; they accept the team evaluation made by the consortium intake unit. Placement decisions are made by staff of the intake unit in collaboration with the head administrator (or designee) of the potential placement sites.

2. School district personnel and staff hired under the interagency consortium aid the various community-based service centers in upgrading their operations to meet state education regulations. Early in the organization of the interagency consortium, it was recognized that the various member agencies had to comply with differing sets of regulations, depending on the administrative system under which they fell and their other sources of funding. Their involvement with the public schools under the new mandate added an even more stringent set of regulations. Meetings were held with the various funding agencies and offices that monitor preschools for their compliance with regulations. Standards relating to teacher qualifications and certifications, adult/child ratios, physical facilities, procedures for program planning

and child assessment, and due process procedures were therefore clarified for all participating members of the consortium. Consortium operations now include a training/preparation procedure for participating members to expand, adapt, or upgrade their programs in ways that bring them into compliance with the necessary regulations.

3. All agencies in the interagency consortium agreed to apply some common management systems in their independent sites. This includes (a) use of a common set of record-keeping forms and common IEP planning forms; (b) a common plan for reporting child progress, including year end reports that summarize assessments on an agreed upon set of performance areas and developmental domains; and (c) a common calendar for operating programs that places beginning and ending dates for a program year and holidays on the same schedule. All sites submit child records into a centralized, computer-based record-keeping system.

4. In collaboration with one another, each center and the school district clearly indicated what services and what functions each would carry out as part of the consortium. For example, several centers were designated for children with speech/language and cognitive impairments; four sites were designated for the majority of multiply handicapped children. Services that were found to overlap unnecessarily were rearranged to prevent duplication. Some centers agreed to serve a population slightly different from the one they had been serving in order to arrange a more appropriate continuum of services. The school district now contracts with the agreed upon sites to serve designated children. Payment schedules are agreed upon and specified in contracts with each agency.

5. Based on the service gaps that remained once existing community resources were organized, the school district created two new programs and contracted with several other agencies to develop other needed service components. To serve children with moderate to severe disabilities, the district established several small centers in elementary schools, consisting of two to four preschool classes in each. The second service the school district developed was a preschool specialist support unit. Several speech therapists, occupational therapists, nurses, and early childhood special education master teachers were employed to serve as consultants to the consortium members and to provide special services to children. Middletown School District then contracted with a local university to develop an infant-parent intervention program to serve children from birth to age 2½. Since the university already had such a program in operation, the contract allowed it to expand that program to meet the service requirement for the community. The district also contracted with a local private foundation to expand its home-based parent training program to serve the younger population of infants and toddlers in rural areas where it was too costly to operate a center-based

program. These individual agencies then assumed responsibility for developing their various service components to complete the full continuum of services for handicapped children in Middletown, U.S.A.

Commentary

This brief sketch does not describe the intricacies of the interagency collaborative that now operates in Middletown, U.S.A. Not all agencies involved with handicapped children in the city agreed to become participating members in the consortium, but the major agencies did agree. The result was a comprehensive system of services for which responsibility was spread across many groups and service providers in the city. Many of these service providers continue to operate their programs with a variety of funding sources, not only money from public school funds. Each group assumes responsibility for operating its segment of the total plan. The school district carries out a leadership role in spearheading the effort, but maintains a rather democratic system of operation.

Maximizing Access to Services—A Reason for Interagency Collaboration in Brownsville, U.S.A.

The Problem and the Need

Mrs. Ray lives in a state where services for preschool handicapped children are not mandated. A variety of agencies in her town, however, sponsor special programs for handicapped and at-risk preschoolers. A large number of regular nursery and preschool centers are also available. Each operates independently and offers services that differ in terms of both quantity and quality. Mrs. Ray's saga in finding special help for her son Chad is not unlike that of other parents who have children with developmental problems. When she first realized Chad needed help, no one seemed to know where she should go, not the doctor who suggested Chad had a problem or the pastor in her church. Eventually, a neighbor told her about a preschool for delayed children on the north side of town. Contact with that program and several others yielded only negative responses—they did not work with children like Chad. Finally, one center invited her to bring Chad in for an initial evaluation. After a long evaluation process spread over several weeks and what seemed to be an endless stream of forms on her son's early developmental history, the outcome was only another referral to two ''possibly more appropriate programs.'' This process was repeated twice before an appropriate program was found for Chad.

Even though Mrs. Ray had indicated to each new program that an evaluation had already been done, each preferred to conduct its own evaluations. Mrs. Ray patiently waded through more testing, more forms to complete, and more long hours of waiting. In her moments of impatience, she resented the repeated referrals and lost time. The cost for the time she had taken from work (unpaid) and for the transportation from center to center was alarming. She could barely afford the cost now. Fortunately, her church had helped her with baby-sitting and transportation costs. If she had been a parent with even less income, finances alone would have stopped her from looking further to find help for Chad. She found herself thinking in disgust, "If only people in this town could get organized!!" She wondered if staff from the various programs ever talked to each other. Some five months later from the day she contacted the first preschool center about Chad, her son was finally placed in a special program for preschoolers.

A Cooperative Interagency Referral System

Because no single agency is responsible for providing services to children under age 5 in Mrs. Ray's state, no one accepted the responsibility for the problem Mrs. Ray experienced. It was the local Association for Retarded Citizens (ARC) that finally took action. Acting as the facilitator and organizer, the ARC president arranged for directors of local preschool programs to meet and discuss the problem. The outcome was a common plan and agreement among the various agency representatives to follow certain procedures across programs:

1. The group would jointly prepare an information booklet describing each of their programs, including admission criteria, fees, services offered, program schedule, and the contact person. Each center would distribute the information booklet to its own contacts around the community. The ARC would assume responsibility for distributing the booklet to local doctors, churches, social service agencies, and the Chamber of Commerce for Brownsville.
2. The Rainbow Center (the largest preschool center in town) agreed to act as the central referral agent for all programs. The ARC agreed to provide support to the Rainbow Center to employ a part-time admissions/referral secretary who would receive referrals, gather preliminary intake information, and explain community resources to parents who might inquire about services. The various agencies agreed that, once a referral was taken by the admissions secretary, agencies that were potential sites for a child would individually examine the intake information to determine what program might be most appropriate. That site would then conduct the initial evaluation or screening. When two or more potential placement sites were to be considered, both sites would participate in an initial observation/screening of the child and a joint placement decision would be made.
3. The agency representatives decided to meet with one another on a regular basis every other month to discuss common programs and to deal with

referral issues. Those centers serving handicapped children agreed also to work together to conduct joint in-service training sessions for their staff members. It was agreed that each center would take a turn organizing and presenting the in-service sessions. A joint schedule for in-service training was planned so that interagency staff would meet together one day every other month.

Commentary

The interagency collaborative activities in Brownsville are much less formal than those that occurred in Middletown. A memorandum describing the agreements between sites in Brownsville was written by the ARC president and distributed among the individuals who attended the planning meeting. The ARC president continued to take the major leadership role to promote the collaborative efforts and to see that plans were carried out as agreed.

Combining Resources across Agencies—A Strategy for Building Preschool Intervention Programs in College Town, U.S.A.

The Problem and the Need

College Town has what some people consider an abundance of resources for serving handicapped children and those at risk for developmental disabilities. In a state with permissive rather than mandatory legislation for early childhood intervention services, many groups seem to be dabbling in some small way in special services for handicapped populations. Services are fragmented, however, and no one agency has enough money to create comprehensive, well-rounded programs. As a result, parents find themselves piecing together services across several agencies in order to assemble some facsimile of a full-service program. Denelle, for example, goes to a preschool program four mornings a week and then transfers to a day care center in the afternoon. Her mother takes her to the University Speech Clinic for three speech therapy sessions each week and to the University Occupational Therapy Department two days each week for motor training. It is frustrating to deal with such a schedule, but her mother has no other choice to get Denelle the help she needs. Denelle's services simply cannot be obtained under the roof of just one program.

While programs in College Town operate independently of one another, relationships are friendly. They often work out schedules that allow a child to participate in several programs and plan ways for transporting a child from center to center. Nonetheless individual programs continue to hobble along with inadequate funding and only narrowly defined, highly specialized service offerings. Many of the programs are operated on what the staff refer to as "a shoestring budget"—minimal cash resources, many volunteers, a number of university student trainees, and much dedication. Because university student participants provide much of the personnel for operating these programs and since they change constantly, the programs suffer from lack of continuity. In addition, the financial instability of the programs keeps them in a constant state of flux. Even regular staff are transient because funding from federal sources changes continuously and staff are not secure in their jobs for very long periods of time.

Multiagency Sponsorship

The interagency system that evolved in College Town resulted from the cooperative efforts of four key people and their work with each of their respective organizations. These people included (1) the director of a university-based early intervention program, (2) the director of a private school for crippled children that operated in the old university laboratory school adjacent to the campus, (3) the local school district special education director, and (4) a parent of a handicapped preschooler who served as president of the board for the local ARC. As personal friends, the group talked frequently about funding problems that plagued early childhood special education services. But for many years, they had offered only a listening ear and sympathy to one another. It was when the lack of funding threatened the continuation of the existing programs that they began to think seriously about some kind of collaborative effort among their individual operations. Actually, the community settings and the existing relationships between the four colleagues was ideal for some kind of cooperative program, as the group came to realize. The result was a consolidation of their separate interests and resources into a single early intervention program for College Town residents. Actual development of the consortium took several years, since each agency had to arrange for and then organize its own organization to fit the new cooperative system. It gradually evolved, however, into a comprehensive early childhood intervention program that worked as follows:

1. The University Special Preschool, the Public School Special Services Programs, the Crippled Children's School, and the local ARC agreed to join together as sponsors for the joint Early Childhood Intervention Cooperative Program. They also agreed to combine the unique resources to which each had access in support of the common venture. Representatives of each agency indicated the goals they considered essential to their agency's involvement. The group agreed to facilitate these individual purposes, as well as those of the collective enterprise. Individuals obtained permission from their respective agencies and supervisors to participate in the collaborative effort.

2. The two service programs for handicapped preschoolers operated by the university and the Crippled Children's School were combined into one and

expanded from one classroom in each separate site to three classes at one site. Since the Crippled Children's School had space and was conveniently located on the edge of campus where university staff could have quick access to the program, it was agreed to house the new collaborative program there.

3. The university preschool director and the director of the Crippled Children's School agreed to continue their involvement in the direct services operations of the cooperative early intervention program. As for the district special education director and ARC president, their involvement would continue in more indirect advisory and supportive roles. Specific responsibilities and role definitions were worked out between the first two consortium members. The university preschool director would oversee the program/curriculum/ interdisciplinary operations that were conducted on a daily basis. A part-time program coordinator was hired to work under her supervision to manage the day-to-day activities among teaching and therapeutic staff. The Crippled Children's School director was to handle the management of facilities, the lunch program, broad public relations with parties unrelated to the staff or children (such as visitors and other community groups), and a parent training/involvement program that was offered as a special service under the existing program in the school. That program was expanded to include all parents requesting services from the new cooperative early intervention program.

4. Funding for the consortium was achieved by the pooling of financial resources to which each individual agency had access. For example, the school district could access state ESEA funds and special education reimbursement monies that the other three parties could not obtain. The ARC was a United Fund agency and received a part of the donations made in that yearly fund-raising drive. The Crippled Children's School and the ARC could solicit private donations from businesses, foundations, and other donors that the others could not approach. The university had been successful in getting research and demonstration grants for exemplary kinds of programs. Each agency did its part to maintain its original financial resources and to create new ones in collaboration with the new consortium. The university contributed personnel whose roles in training student teachers were compatible with direct service delivery activities with children. The school district applied for state grants and also arranged to get special education funds for teaching staff. The ARC contributed its portion of funds for transportation, instructional materials and supplies, administrative costs, and a part-time parent-home trainer to add to the existing staff in the Crippled Children's School training staff. A master budget was created for the operation of the total program. Individual budgets were negotiated with each participating agency to define their financial, personnel, or service contributions to the total operation.

5. An interdisciplinary team of specialists was formed to conduct child assessments, provide specialized kinds of training to children, and to consult with parents. It included specialists in regular special early childhood education, speech therapy, occupational and physical therapy, music therapy, school psychology, and social work. Such an extensive team was possible because of the joint training/service functions that had been arranged with various university departments that needed training sites for their students. The core interdisciplinary team was paid partially from the consortium budget and partially from university training monies. Through their training roles with the university, they brought in additional personnel who helped provide services to children and thus expanded the personnel resources needed to operate a comprehensive program.

6. An executive board was formed to review program operations, make plans, evaluate the effectiveness of the consortium approach, and project future funding needs. It included key representatives from each participating agency. These representatives reported back to their respective organizations as needed to gain necessary authorizations and to coordinate all activities through the administrative ladder in each system.

Commentary

This interagency collaborative may appear to be a rather simple one on the surface, but a complex network of agreements and collaborative arrangements involving several agencies underlies the whole operation. The basis for this cooperative effort is support both for the common interests in a quality early intervention program and for the independent interests of each separate agency. Instead of competing for resources, the four groups combined their resources in ways that facilitated all of their interests. Their cooperative system capitalized on the unique contributions each could make to a comprehensive, impressive system of services. It should be noted, however, that this system involved a great deal of coordination. Because so many people were involved and so many linkages were formed, i.e., at three and four levels within the administrative system of each contributing agency, coordination and communication were particularly critical to the function of the collaborative system. As a result, there were an abundance of coordinative functions, several levels of coordinators, and an emphasis on tight adherence to agreed upon channels of communication.

CONSIDERATIONS IN COLLABORATIVE PLANNING

Because of the unique set of variables that come into play in each community, tactics that work with one group may not work for another. No doubt, the collection of agencies, programs, and individuals who take part create a unique set of social dynamics. Interagency groups seem to have their own personality—an outcome of the individual styles of the members and their interactions with each other. Even the problems and issues a group addresses are colored by the local conditions surrounding their mutual effort:

- the particular social-political atmosphere among agencies in the community (i.e., if it is a friendly, hostile, or highly competitive one)
- the scope of services for young children that the interagency group intends to address
- the availability of resources and the degree of competition for these same resources by other agencies
- the expectations and motives each participant brings to the collaborative effort
- the group dynamics that evolve among individual "players" in the group and the tactics each employs to pursue group or individual goals

Because each community or township is different, Elder and Magrab (1980) maintain that collaborative activities among agencies that affect direct services to children are best conducted at the local level. Collaborative efforts at state and federal levels can best address broader issues, such as funding, policy, and agency regulations that affect operations at the local scene.

Processes in Planning and Implementing Collaborative Systems

The notion of interagency collaboration may appear to be a simple one, but the task of applying this notion to create functional service systems for young children can be a challenge for even the most skillful, seasoned practitioners in the educational and human service fields. The task of designing and then implementing an interagency system falls roughly into three broad phases: (1) planning; (2) implementation, which encompasses transitional activities and then full-scale operation; and (3) evaluation and refinement. Each phase involves a variety of tasks or activities. Some of the key tasks in each phase, important to any group undertaking such an endeavor, are summarized in Figure 8-1.

The Planning Phase: Building the Foundation

The initial planning phase is a crucial one, simply because its end product is the blueprint for the collaborative system and the foundation for all subsequent activities. A well-developed plan clearly indicates to everyone what is to come. Although minutes of meetings in which general agreements are made can be used as records at first, the later implementation becomes more dependent on the preparation of a formally written document as the plan becomes more sophisti-

Figure 8-1 Process Schema for Interagency Collaboration

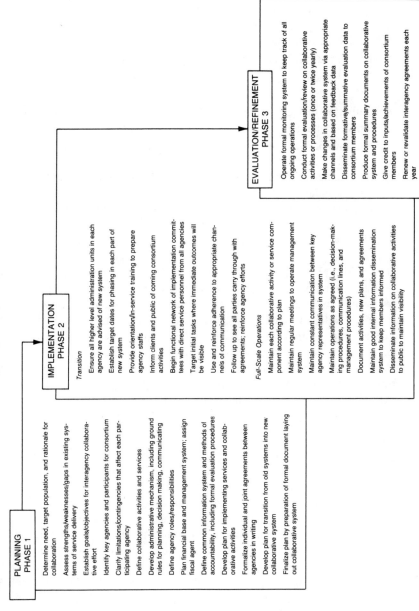

cated. The document should outline collaborative agreements, as well as the evolving plan for implementing them. A well-developed plan lays out all of the ground rules. For example, it includes agreements as to

- how decisions are made and by whom
- what the purposes and goals of the consortium are
- what roles and responsibilities member agencies and their representatives hold
- a definition of the parameters of the consortium, including where member agencies remain autonomous and where they collaborate
- what powers and rights the agencies hold individually and collectively

Differences among members on the purposes of the consortium or any other point of contention should be resolved in this first planning phase. A blueprint that is hazy and poorly developed leads only to confusion. If agencies' understanding of what the consortium entails, what responsibilities it places on them, and what returns they will get from participation is unclear, their commitment is likely to be just as unclear.

This initial phase is a period of time when the most critical interpersonal processes occur among agencies and the individuals representing them. Working relationships are established during this time and the group's style of problem solving is developed. Interaction patterns and the atmosphere created during this initial planning period will influence all subsequent activities. The attitudes formed among consortium members toward each other and toward the consortium as a whole are likely to make or break the overall success of the collaborative effort. The degree to which participants become trusting and supportive of each other will be a major factor in the sincerity of their commitment to the project.

The Implementation Phase: Putting the Plan into Action

It is easy to regard implementation of any program or service simply as one big step, but it is not that simple. The establishment of interagency systems involves two steps—transitional activities and then full-scale implementation. Each is equally important. The transition phase is the real bridge between a good plan and effective implementation. Moving from one to the other is not automatic, especially when several independently operating agencies must coordinate their efforts and when the collaborative system must be superimposed on existing operations within each agency. Inasmuch as the administrative structures and program activities of the agencies involved are likely to be quite different, the impact of the new collaborative activities on each agency will be very different. It requires change, and constructive change requires time. Bombarding agency staffs too fast with new policies and procedures or with new or modified roles and responsibilities can produce frustration and turmoil, disrupting and destroying the internal stability of their individual operations. Few administrators voluntarily throw their agency into a state of turmoil for the sake of an interagency consortium. Given such circumstances, it is understandable why some agencies withdraw support if change at an unrealistic rate is required.

The transitional phase can be an exciting, productive time, or it can be a sensitive time for staff within each agency, for its administration, and for its public image. Since each must maintain its ongoing operations with clients concurrent with its participation in the evolving interagency system, the continuity of client services can be a concern. Abrupt change may be perceived by staff as an interruption in the quality and efficiency of service delivery to clients. It can be unsettling to staff at the direct service level who must straddle the operational procedures for both the old and the new systems. Change itself can produce uncertainty when the outcomes of the old system are clear, but the potential effectiveness of the new system is yet to be seen. In fact, during this transition time, when the interagency system is new and only partially in place, it can be easily viewed as less efficient and more troublesome than "the way we used to do things." For these reasons, preparations and activities during this transition phase are especially important.

Like the initial blueprint for the overall collaborative system, the plan for the transition phase should be made with great attention to detail. The plan should delineate the steps for systematically phasing in each component of the new system and phasing out old agency procedures that will be replaced. The transition may involve budgetary changes, adjustments in staffing patterns or in staff roles, or changes in well-established practices with clients. It may involve a transfer of administrative authority from one party to another and may even result in the termination of some staff roles. Target dates should be set for the implementation of each new component or activity. Each participating agency must be given sufficient lead time so that its staff can prepare for full implementation. In-service training to orient staff for the upcoming changes and to prepare them for their roles in the new system is likely to be required. Depending on the scope and the complexity of the new interagency system, the transition may take from a few weeks to several years.

When all policies and procedures are working, the collaborative is in full-scale operation. In this part of the implementation phase, routines are set. Channels of communications are clearly defined and are being used. Services or activities that form the collaborative effort are being conducted according to the plan agreed upon initially. A system of regular meetings maintains ongoing coordination and keeps members working toward the goals of the consortium. It is most important during this phase to ensure that the plan is being followed and that participating members are reinforced for carrying out their tasks. In practice, a plan can sometimes become very different from the original to which agencies "thought" they were agreeing. Because interagency collaboratives involve so many different parties, it is essential that procedures are followed as they were agreed upon earlier. An interagency system is a delicately balanced, synchronized system. If an agency disregards procedures or fails to carry out its part, the entire system may be thrown into turmoil. Thus, in this phase it is essential that members keep in step with one another by following the plan. If changes are needed, they should be discussed by everyone and then integrated formally into the overall consortium plan. The initiation of changes, even if they are needed, by a single member without working through appropriate channels is the quickest way to produce distrust and undermine the system.

Strong leadership is essential. This requires someone who can keep the collaborative system on target and working toward its goals. It requires a person who can recognize problems and initiate appropriate action. It requires tactfulness and assertiveness to orchestrate the activities of what sometimes seems to be an unwieldy collection of individuals.

The Evaluation and Refinement Phase: Maintaining a Dynamic Functional Organization

Once the interagency collaborative activities are in place and operating, the system must be fine-tuned. Procedures that work well can be refined and further developed; procedures that do not work well must be revised. Gaps in the system can be filled in as needed. This phase is a maturing time for the consortium.

Because so much attention is given to earlier stages of planning and implementation, it is easy to neglect this phase. This is the phase that gives longevity and permanence to a collaborative system, however. When evaluation and refinement are continuous, it is more likely that the consortium will continue to benefit both its member agencies and the children being served. Keeping an interagency collaborative alive and dynamic requires unanimous commitment and constant change so that the system continues to serve its purposes. Otherwise, the consortium will fall by the wayside or will become institutionalized to the extent that it takes on the character of just one more parallel, independent agency and not the collaborative system that was originally designed.

Strategies for Enhancing Interagency Collaboration

General Guidelines

Although literature on the topic of interagency collaboration is still limited, there have been many suggestions on ways to make interagency systems work and work well. Few authors have dealt specifically with interagency activities in regard to early intervention programs, but their suggestions are generally applicable to any collaborative effort between agencies. Hall (1980), for example, offers several principles for successful interagency collaboration:

- Effective interagency collaboration requires that every participant have a basic understanding of and appreciation for the purposes and functions of every member agency.
- Participation of staff or administrators from each agency should have the support of top level administrators. Ideally, the individuals representing each agency are its key figures. They must be able to act in their agency's behalf in planning what inputs it will have and what roles it will play in the collaborative effort.
- It is advisable for each agency to be represented by someone who has a clear understanding of line level activities within the agency. Interagency negotiations can easily falter if an interagency plan is incompatible with the ongoing daily operations of an agency involved.
- Evolving administrative agreements should be based on realistic assessments of the operational constraints and regulations under which each agency operates.

Mulvenon (1980) also provides some helpful hints for communities undertaking interagency cooperatives and some guidelines for facilitating the operation of interagency planning teams:

- As a group, participating agencies should discuss and clarify their mutual goals and establish objectives for their team effort from the beginning. Since each agency is capable of providing only certain services and performing only certain tasks, those tasks or roles should be defined and clearly assigned.
- An interagency team should give itself a generous amount of lead time to iron out difficulties and establish group processes for working together. For example, it may take a week to reach an agreement on forms or procedures, but it may take a year to initiate a cooperative preschool. An interagency group should recognize from the beginning that their involvement is going to be a long-term one and that progress may take time.
- One agency or person should assume responsibility for spearheading the effort until the interagency system is strong enough to maintain and propel itself.
- An interagency team should not be an extension of any single agency. It should be an independent committee, but should have no independent powers from the agencies that comprise it. Care should be taken to ensure that the interagency collaborative system does not become simply another level of bureaucracy.

- There must be a chairman or liaison officer who, ideally, has excellent public relations and is an assertive, energetic leader. Other members of an interagency planning group should be key decision makers and leaders in major service agencies and influential organizations in the community.
- In the early development of an interagency consortium, members may need to develop special interpersonal and communication skills in order to work effectively as team members.

Facilitators to Interagency Collaboration

Several authors have described what they call "facilitators" in the collaborative process. Elder (1980), for example, describes three such facilitators: a common base of knowledge among agency staffs, effective communication, and the presence of a mediator. Elder maintains that the degree to which the staffs are informed about the scope and type of services offered by other participating agencies will largely determine how well various agencies work and plan together. Previous research suggests that staff members fail to refer tasks to other agencies and to acknowledge the contributions of other agencies because they do not understand or agree on the other agencies' responsibilities.

The second facilitator is an obvious yet forever critical one—effective communication among individuals within and across the various agencies. As Wiener (1963) described it, "Communication is the cement that makes organizations. Communication alone enables a group to think together, see together, and to act together" (p. 77). Elder suggests that good communication is a cornerstone to effective collaboration and cannot be overstressed. It is when communication is poor or lacking entirely that conflict is most likely to occur.

The presence of someone who can act in a somewhat neutral role to mediate and encourage collaborative interactions also facilitates interagency processes. This can often be accomplished by deliberately involving some person who can assume a formal position of facilitator during the initial planning and perhaps transitional phases of collaboration among various agencies. Elder (1979) described this useful role in this way:

> In order to develop the necessary working relationships between agencies at the local level, a facilitator must be available to work with program and administrative staff to develop the best possible collaborative for the benefit of the handicapped individual. A facilitator is an essential element in developing any interagency collaborative agreement, and ideally is assigned to that job function. If that is not feasible, it should be at least a major function of an individual's responsibility. It does little good to add this responsibility to someone in an agency who

already has a full time job without taking other responsibilities away so this person can devote the proper amount of time and effort to acting as a facilitator. . . . The person filling the role of facilitator should be sensitive to the needs of the clients of each agency and of the agency staff themselves. The subject of interagency agreements must be approached lightly on the basis of a "soft sell," not a "hard come on." The attitudes of many bureaucrats in agencies will have to be changed because one of the biggest obstacles to overcome is that of bureaucrats' protection of their own "turf." The facilitator must also be knowledgeable about the total service delivery system. (p. 198)

The presence of a facilitator, who has nothing to gain or to lose and is respected by all participants, can be a tremendous boon to the development of an interagency collaboration effort. This person can serve as a buffer between agencies in sensitive situations since he or she is in a position to mediate between parties.

Potential Barriers to Interagency Collaboration

Everyone who participates in collaborative activities does not necessarily become a staunch believer in their utility. The task of orchestrating activities within a single agency is difficult, but the task of orchestrating selected activities across several independent agencies that operate under entirely different management systems can be extraordinarily difficult. It takes time, patience, skillful planning, and very good management. The more complex and comprehensive the scope of collaborative agreements, the more difficult the task of implementation.

Numerous authors have given vivid descriptions of the barriers or deterrents to successful interagency teamwork. Elder (1979, 1980) described several reasons for failures among interagency collaboratives and itemized some of the roadblocks that contributed to these failures. Kazuk (1980) described some specific problems that occur in interagency efforts and offered solutions for each of them. Martinson (1982) suggested that the variables affecting interagency negotiations generally deal with technical or administrative issues, or with political, fiscal, or human concerns. He described a number of "syndromes" that exemplify obstacles to successful interagency activities. The major problems can be consolidated into three broad areas of concern: (1) personality and staff barriers, (2) governance and administrative barriers, and (3) barriers related to the mechanics of collaboration. Drawn from the sources mentioned earlier, as well as from other writers (Eskridge, 1973; Hall, 1980; Johnson, McLaughlin, & Christensen, 1982; McLaughlin & Christensen, 1980; Mulvenon, 1980), a variety of specific barriers are listed under each of the three broad areas:

1. barriers arising from personality and staff variables
   - poor attitudes toward collaborative effort and toward other members of the group
   - poor interpersonal rapport and trust among individuals and/or agencies
   - fear of risk and disruption of the status quo and, hence, passive or active resistance to change
   - lack of real commitment by key figures to collaborative effort, possibly including actions on their part that undermine interagency teamwork
   - resentment among certain agencies toward involvement of "outsiders"
   - participation by individuals to protect interest but who believe the interagency effort is unnecessary and a waste of taxpayers' money

2. barriers arising from the governance and administrative structure of the collaborative effort
   - imprecise definition of agency responsibilities and authority
   - failure to define objectives clearly so that they are understood and agreed upon by everyone
   - lack of involvement of key people from participating agencies
   - lack of organizational structure to bring agencies together around mutual interests or to allow collaborative activities to proceed
   - lack of ground rules for decision making and unclear delineation of who holds what authority
   - failure of participants to recognize and respect the needs and operations of each agency and unrealistic expectations that the consortium should supersede all other individual agency concerns
   - competition over "turf" and inability to deal with real issues, such as fear, underlying such territorialism among various agencies
   - elitist attitudes by certain agencies
   - failure to communicate at the appropriate level in the organizational structures of a participating agency so that key individuals are not involved at critical times

3. barriers arising from the mechanics of collaboration
   - lack of experience among participants in processes and techniques of interagency collaboration
   - impatience of staff members in working through issues and an unwillingness to work through processes that help the group learn to work as a team
   - lack of a centralized base of information with which everyone is familiar and failure to disseminate information on a continuous basis

- breakdown of communication systems so that not everyone has essential information or so that the necessary problem-solving/planning processes do not occur
- overfixation of consortium designers on the system design without adequate attention to the realities that define what procedures will be functional
- failure of agencies to follow through with responsibilities or excessive assignments of responsibilities on certain members
- lack of resources to carry out what has been planned and failure to take into account realistic estimates of available resources when plans are made
- inconsistent involvement or excessive absenteeism by key administrative or staff representatives
- insufficient inclusion of agency staffs in planning activities or failure to prepare them for their role in implementing the interagency system

This extensive list of barriers reflects the various issues and pressures that come into play when service providers join in collaborative activities. The fact that such problems or barriers arise is not the point; they undoubtedly evolve from legitimate concerns, real fears, or administrative realities for the agencies and individuals involved. The manner in which these barriers are discussed and resolved is more important. Individuals within interagency groups must learn to communicate effectively with one another, to be open, and to be accepting of another's position. During this initial phase, members learn to trust each other, to work as a team, and to engage in problem-solving processes rather than to barter for resources or positions of power. If these goals are achieved, individuals and the agencies they represent are in a better position to overcome any barriers. Cooperation is a goal that is not achieved without effort.

SOME REALITIES: A SUMMARY

As programs for handicapped infants and preschoolers continue to multiply in communities across the United States, interagency collaboration offers one means in which some of the difficulties that have plagued service systems for older children and adults may be circumvented. As "necessity is the mother of invention," the economic, political, and programmatic realities of the 1980s have made it necessary for agencies to cooperate and to consolidate many of their services. Because it is necessary to minimize duplication, to reduce costs, and to distribute a diminishing pool of resources across agencies with overlapping responsibilities, interagency collaboration is no longer a mere option; it is an imperative for the survival of many human services programs. Given these conditions, cooperation across agencies is critical if comprehensive, interdisciplinary services are to be made available to young handicapped children and their families. Few agencies are equipped with sufficient resources, financial or otherwise, to meet this challenge alone.

At the same time, interagency networks cannot be considered a cure-all for every limitation in human services programs. Although collaboration offers many benefits, it is not necessarily the best alternative under all circumstances (Elder, 1980; Elder & Magrab, 1980). Neither can it be assumed that the mere act of agencies joining together in some common venture can totally resolve the problems or issues described earlier in this chapter. Under the proper circumstances, however, many of the problems that seem insurmountable can be resolved if several agencies coordinate their efforts to create more powerful, far-reaching solutions.

While interagency collaboratives offer useful solutions to some pressing problems, their creation introduces new issues that continue to test the skill and commitment of administrators and direct service providers. Professionals in roles of service provider to handicapped young children are limited in their experience with the processes and techniques of interagency collaboration. It is thus a "learn-as-you-go" proposition. Given this inexperience, it takes patience, creativity, stamina, and a sincere commitment to the collaborative concept for such individuals to establish a smoothly operating, functional system. There is a tremendous need for research and for the development of effective models for operating collaborative interagency networks.

As collaborative activities among agencies become more prevalent, many professionals and the agencies they represent find themselves asking these questions: Do I (or we) want to become involved in collaborative activities with other agencies? What are the risks? Are the benefits worth the price? Am I (or is our agency) willing to make some changes and to participate in the give-and-take relationships that are necessary to make collaborative arrangements work? The answers to these questions are not simple ones. They can only be answered individually by each person and their respective agencies. In any collaborative enterprise, several realities impose themselves.

> Successful interagency systems that are functional for the agencies who create them and for the children and families who are to be served, require considerable time and effort on the part of all direct service and administrative staff.

The time required for interagency planning is typically imposed on already full schedules, since participants from each agency are usually key people who are already very busy. This creates several difficult conditions with which participating members must contend. First, a great deal of business and collaborative work must be done in limited time periods. This places pressure not only on the interagency group to make and then implement decisions efficiently, but also on consortium members to work quickly through group and interpersonal processes that ordinarily require time. Frustrations may result because limitations on everyone's time make it difficult to deal with interpersonal problems or issues adequately and still move ahead with business matters. Administrators typically must make decisions quickly, and they expect to see steady progress toward program goals; consequently, administrators may become frustrated by what seems to be a lack of progress because of the time required to work through group processes. Furthermore, the unavailability of key people, yet the need for them to work together, is likely to slow down the speed with which a collaborative system can be planned and put into operation. From the beginning, participants must understand that the development of an interagency system that is functional as well as acceptable to all parties will take time (Humm-Delgado, 1980).

> Agencies that join together into collaborative networks because of common service delivery responsibilities and interests do not necessarily represent common philosophical, administrative, or fiscal structures.

Each agency probably practices very different planning, decision-making, and management procedures. If collaboration among agencies is to be effective, these differences must be recognized and respected from the outset. No agency should assume that its administrative system is the standard to which all others should conform. Collaboration will mean negotiation, compromise, and possible change for everyone. If group plans are made by consensus rather than by authoritarian means, the task of developing procedures that are compatible with each agency's unique system of administrative management is likely to require some additional planning and adjustments within each individual agency. Under these circumstances, decision making can become tedious at times. Intermittently, it may appear that program objectives for the consortium are taking second place to the task of working through group collaborative plans and issues. This process is a necessary one, however. Democratic decision making is a must, since no agency is likely to subject itself to arbitrary decisions that affect its practices, but for which it is allowed little input (Kazuk, 1980; Humm-Delgado, 1980).

> Collaboration must provide continual benefits for participating agencies, as well as for clients, if investments of each are to be consistently maintained. Otherwise, there is no reason for any agency to participate in a collaborative relationship with other agencies.

Many motivating forces bring agencies into collaboration with each other. Broadly speaking, agencies enter collaboratives with two main concerns: (a) the quality of community services to young handicapped children and (b) their own needs and their own survival. Thus, as members negotiate collaborative activities and plan the system for managing the joint effort, the evolving structure must continue to sustain the basis for each agency's individual reasons for entering into the agreement. Hage (1975) maintained that something must be added or created to benefit each agency. The system must maximize organizational benefits and minimize organizational costs.

> Individuals and the agencies they represent may change, making it necessary for continual renewal of collaborative agreements, continual building and verification of trust among participants, and continual development of working relationships so that the cooperative system can maintain its ongoing operations.

Cooperation between agencies often evolves from the efforts of dedicated people who hold the trust and confidence of their colleagues. Formalized collaborative arrangements require carefully defined agreements and endorsement of those agreements by the administrative hierarchy within each agency. Informal collaborative arrangements are frequently built on good will previously established between individuals and may not necessarily involve formal administrative commitments on the part of the agencies these individuals represent. Such a collaboration usually derives its power from the leadership and personalities of those individuals who initiate it. Their cooperative enterprise works because of their commitment and willingness to work hard toward their own goals. The limitations of this kind of collaborative arrangement are apparent, however, if such individuals terminate their involvement. The system is not institutionalized as a standard part of the administrative system within which they work. Thus, should these key figures leave, the cooperative system must be reestablished as new people take their place, establish their own liaisons, and renegotiate the relationships among their respective agencies. Clearly, professionals must be sure that their involvement reflects not only their own personal commitment, but also that of their agency and its higher administration. As the individuals acting in behalf of their respective agencies change, it will be necessary to maintain a strong representation and a continuing commitment from the agency administrations. Commitment to the interagency system and to the plans that have been developed by the consortium may not be automatic when a new professional joins the group. New members will need information, an orientation to the collaborative system, and a welcome from present members. They may also need time to learn how to be effective team members and may have to work through the same learning processes that the original members worked through earlier. This will require time and patience on the part of other agency representatives.

The human element is a major variable in the success of a collaborative effort. It is typically the investment of individuals, although they ultimately act only as representatives of the agencies they serve, and their skill in working together that determines the success of a cooperative effort.

Although it is the agency that enters into a collaborative agreement, and not an individual, it must be remembered that the individuals who represent the agency will be responsible for establishing rapport with the other agencies. As described earlier, the interpersonal dynamics are of primary importance. Interagency activities require a willingness in each representative to communicate, to listen, and to respect other agencies' systems. Collaborative activities also demand a willingness to compromise. As Elder (1980) describes it, interagency arrangements represent a difficult process that requires great political skill. Collaboration must be approached in incremental steps; it cannot be hurried. The human element determines the success or failure of any collaborative effort.

REFERENCES

Ackerman, P.R., & Moore, M.G. Delivery of educational services to preschool handicapped children. In T.D. Tjossem (Ed.), *Intervention strategies for high risk infants and young children*. Baltimore: University Park Press, 1976.

Allen, K.E., Holm, V.A., & Schiefelbusch, R.L. (Eds.). *Early intervention—A team approach*. Baltimore: University Park Press, 1978.

Audette, R.H. Interagency collaboration—The bottom line. In J.O. Elder & P.R. Magrab (Eds.), *Coordinating services to handicapped children: A handbook for interagency collaboration*. Baltimore: Paul H. Brookes, 1980.

Baumheimer, E. *Interagency linkages in the field of developmental disabilities*. Paper presented at the Interagency Evaluation Conference, Miami Beach, Florida, May 1979.

Baxter, J.M. Solving problems through cooperation. *Exceptional Children*, 1982, *48*(5), 400-407.

Brewer, G.D., & Kakalik, J.S. *Handicapped children: Strategies for improving services*. New York: McGraw-Hill, 1979.

Bricker, D.D., & Iacino, R. Early intervention with severely/profoundly handicapped children. In E. Sontag (Ed.), *Educational programming for the severely/profoundly handicapped*. Reston, VA: Council for Exceptional Children, 1977.

Bronfenbrenner, U. *A report on longitudinal evaluations of preschool programs: Is early intervention effective?* (DHEW Publication No. (OHD) 76-30025). Washington, DC: U.S. Government Printing Office, 1974.

Elder, J.O. Essential components in development of interagency collaboration. In J.O. Elder & P.R. Magrab (Eds.), *Coordinating services to handicapped children: A handbook for interagency collaboration*. Baltimore: Paul H. Brookes, 1980.

Elder, J.O. Coordination of service delivery systems. In P.R. Magrab & J.O. Elder (Eds.), *Planning services to handicapped persons*. Baltimore: Paul H. Brookes, 1979.

Elder, J.O., & Magrab, P.R. (Eds.) *Coordinating services to handicapped children: A handbook for interagency collaboration*. Baltimore: Paul H. Brookes, 1980.

Eskridge, C.S. Problems inherent in interagency cooperation: Possible solutions. Paper presented at a multiagency conference sponsored by Rehabilitation Services Administration, Kansas City, Missouri, July 1973.

Gans, S., & Horton, G. *Integration of human services: The state and municipal levels*. New York: Praeger, 1975.

Hage, J. A strategy for creating independent delivery systems to meet complex needs. In A. Negandhi (Ed.), *Interorganization theory*. Kent, OH: Kent State University Press, 1975.

Hall, H.B. The intangible human factor. In J.O. Elder & P.R. Magrab (Eds.), *Coordinating services to handicapped children: A handbook for interagency collaboration*. Baltimore: Paul H. Brookes, 1980.

Hayden, A.H., & McGinness, G.D. Bases for early intervention. In E. Sontag (Ed.), *Educational programming for the severely and profoundly handicapped*. Reston, VA: Council for Exceptional Children, 1977.

Helge, D. *A report regarding interagency collaboration to facilitate services for rural handicapped students*. Project Report from National Rural Research of Personnel Preparation Project, Center for Innovation and Development, Murray State University. Murray, Kentucky. Prepared for Office of Special Education, Washington, DC, 1981.

Humm-Delgado, D. Planning issues in local interagency collaboration. In J.O. Elder & P.R. Magrab (Eds.), *Coordinating services to handicapped children: A handbook for interagency collaboration*. Baltimore: Paul H. Brookes, 1980.

Kakalik, J., Brewer, G., Dougharty, L., Fleischauer, P., Genesky, S., & Wallen, L. *Improving services to handicapped children*. Santa Monica, CA: The Rand Corporation, 1974.

Karnes, M., & Zehrbach, R. Matching families to services. *Exceptional Children*, 1975, *42*(8), 545-549.

Kazuk, E. Development of a community-based interagency model. In J.O. Elder & P.R. Magrab (Eds.), *Coordinating services to handicapped children: A handbook for interagency collaboration*. Baltimore: Paul H. Brookes, 1980.

Johnson, H.W., McLaughlin, J.A., & Christensen, M. Interagency collaboration: Driving and restraining forces. *Exceptional Children*, 1982, *48*(5), 395-399.

Magrab, P.R., & Elder, J.O. (Eds.). *Planning for services to handicapped persons: Community, education, health*. Baltimore: Paul H. Brookes, 1979.

Magrab, P., Kazuk, E., & Greene, L. *Interagency workbook for serving preschool handicapped children*. Prepared by the American Association of University Affiliated Facilities for the HEW Interagency Task Force pursuant Grant No. 54-P-71476/3-02, Washington, DC: (no date).

Martin, E.W. A new outlook for education of handicapped children. *American Education*, 1970, *6*(3), 7-10.

Martinson, M.C. Interagency services: A new era for an old idea. *Exceptional Children*, 1982, *84*(5), 389-394.

McDaniels, G. Successful programs for young handicapped children. *Educational Horizons*, 1977, *56*(1), 26-33.

McLaughlin, J.D., & Christensen, M. *A study of interagency collaborative agreements to discover training needs for special education administrators. Final Report, Year 1*. Blacksburg, VA: Virginia Polytechnic Institute and State University, 1980.

Mulvenon, J. Development of preschool interagency teams. In J.O. Elder & P.R. Magrab (Eds.), *Coordinating services to handicapped children: A handbook for interagency collaboration.* Baltimore: Paul H. Brookes, 1980.

Peterson, N.L. Early intervention with the handicapped. In E.L. Meyen (Ed.), *Exceptional children and youth: An introduction* (2nd ed.). Denver: Love Publishing, 1982.

Pollard, A., Hall, H., & Keeran, C. Community service planning. In P.R. Magrab & J.O. Elder (Eds.), *Planning for services to handicapped persons: Community, education, health.* Baltimore: Paul H. Brookes, 1979.

Roth, H. Networking among information providers. Presentation at Seminar in Information Resources, White House Conference on Handicapped Individuals. Arlington, VA: Office for Handicapped Individuals/Clearing House, 1977.

Swan, W.W. The handicapped children's early education program. *Exceptional Children,* 1980, 47(1), 12-16.

Weiner, N. As quoted in K. Deutsch, *The nerves of government.* New York: The Free Press, 1977.

Zeller, R.W. Direction service, one case at a time. In J.O. Elder & P.R. Magrab (Eds.), *Coordinating services to handicapped children: A handbook for interagency collaboration.* Baltimore: Paul H. Brookes, 1980.

Chapter 9

The Impact of Changing Federal Policy on Day Care and Early Intervention

Jean Ann Summers

The events of 1981 in Washington were unusual in American politics. Acting on Reagan's campaign promises, the Reagan Administration moved quickly—and surprisingly effectively—to make massive cuts in the federal budget and at the same time to "get the government off the backs of the people." The rhetoric of "supply-side economics," the "trickle-down effect," "block grants," "deregulation," and "defederalization" was heard everywhere. Assumptions about the role of the federal government that had been unquestioned since the New Deal were brought back for a rehearing.

The immediate effect of all these changes on human services professionals was disbelief and confusion. Services that two years ago stood on the solid bedrock of long-standing federal programs were quaking as the Administration methodically chipped away at that bedrock. Massive uncertainty swept through the ranks of service providers, who were simultaneously worried about their clients' plight and unsure about their very choice of a social services career. Morale was low, and speculation was rampant. There were as many opinions as there were people willing to venture them. As one program administrator put it at the time, "Anybody who claims he knows what's going on in Washington, doesn't know what's going on in Washington."

Day care and early intervention programs entered 1982 with one program—Head Start—still intact, but with rumblings from the White House about the need for still more cuts. Other funding sources for day care were reduced and lumped into various "no-strings" block grants to be passed on to the states. Thus, the fate of day care and early intervention is highly idiosyncratic for every state, as each

Partial support for completion of this study was provided by the Edward Arthur Mellinger Foundation, Inc., Monmouth, Illinois.

261

governor and state legislature sort out state priorities and distribute the reduced funds.

Problems and concerns related to handicapped and culturally deprived children are inextricably intertwined with day care in the minds of policy makers and, more importantly, in the budgets of day care programs. Thus, any consideration of the impact of change on early intervention must be considered within the context of its impact on day care in general. The impact of the new federalism of the 1980s on day care cannot be easily analyzed, however. Unlike Medicare or Social Security, there is no cohesive national policy or program for day care and early intervention, largely because of a number of unresolved problems. Furthermore, the major preoccupation of the Administration is not day care—or any other social policy, for that matter—but economic recovery. The question is whether shifts in federal budget practices reflect changes in social policy or the lack of policy. The budget authorizations of the Reagan Administration represent a significant contrast to the previous years of public support of day care services, but the events of the 1980s result from fiscal practices, not new policies. Yet fiscal policy sets social policy for many programs, including day care and early intervention.

All this has occurred at a time when educators of young handicapped children have growing evidence of the effectiveness of their work. An accumulation of studies since the 1960s has left little doubt about the importance of intervention with handicapped children as early as possible in order to mitigate the effects of the handicapping condition. Further evidence has pointed to the cost effectiveness of early intervention (see Salkind's chapter in this volume). Since the majority of support for early intervention in the past had come from federal initiatives, early interventionists are now faced with, at best, a policy vacuum and, at worst, a dismantling of long-standing programs.

From the perspective of early intervention providers, planners, and advocates who are interested in the survival of day care and early intervention programs in some form, the answers to two major questions must be explored:

1. What was the status of national day care and early intervention policy in 1980?
2. What are the expected effects of subsequent fiscal policies on day care and early intervention?

Armed with the answers to these questions, it should be possible to address the most vital question of all:

3. What are some strategies for ensuring the survival of early intervention in the 1980s?

EARLY INTERVENTION: 1980

Supporters of a national day care policy were at the apogee of their strength in 1971, when a variety of bills were introduced into the Congress. Chief among these were the Mondale-Brademas bills, which provided a comprehensive system of day care for welfare families, for the working poor, and for middle-income families, who would pay fees on a graduated scale. These bills emphasized "developmental" day care (early intervention) rather than a custodial program (Steinfels, 1973). Congress passed these bills with much fanfare as the Comprehensive Child Development Act, but the act met with an immediate veto from President Nixon. Although there have been some triumphs since that time, advocates were never able to regain the momentum lost by that veto. Therefore, the issues that led to the passage of the act—and to the veto—are still unresolved ten years later. Essentially, the controversies center around three major issues: (1) association of day care with strong symbolic images, (2) confusion over the purpose of day care, and (3) concern over costs.

Symbolic Issues

Day care and early intervention are tied to a number of symbolic red flags that inevitably touch off volleys of emotion-laden debate. Symbolic issues, according to Edelman (1967), are usually rooted in complex problems that arouse collective public anxiety. Because of their complexity, these problems cannot be readily grasped and, therefore, may be oversimplified by fixing blame for the cause or placing faith for resolution in symbol. Such a symbol might be a visible leader, e.g., the President, or an intangible value or entity, e.g., patriotism or the family. The effect of symbols on politics is pervasive, and, because these symbols arouse strong emotions, their effects are relatively impervious to empirical evidence or cool rationality.

One of the strongest symbolic issues plaguing national day care and early intervention policy has been its public image as an antithesis to family, home, and motherhood. Especially in the early 1970s predictions concerning the demise of the nuclear family and its replacement by group or other family forms were ubiquitous (Binstock, 1974; Davids, 1974; Otto, 1970). Day care was to be one of the instruments of this transformation of the family. In fact, opponents of day care have maintained since the mid-19th century that out-of-home care would violate the traditional conceptions of the family and the maternal role (Greenblatt, 1977). This worry was one of the chief reasons cited by Nixon in his 1971 veto message (Steinfels, 1973). Day care advocates have countered that (1) the availability of day care can in fact strengthen the family by allowing both parents to work, thus providing a stable means of support, and (2) maternal employment is here to stay at any rate, day care or no day care. As expressed by the then chief of the U.S. Children's Bureau in 1961, "the provision of day care services no more causes mothers to work than carrying an umbrella causes rain" (Katherine B. Oetinger, cited in Greenblatt, 1977, p. 140). The truth of the matter is that there are very few data on day care's effects on the family one way or another. As with any emotional issue, however, the association of day care with family instability cannot be broken by mere reason. If anything, concern about the strength of traditional family values and about "threats" to that stability in the form of day care programs is even more vehemently expressed today than it was ten years ago.

The mirror image of family, home, and motherhood is welfare statism, Big Government, and Big Brother. For early intervention, the vision is one of a *1984* style, state-run, clinically sterile nursery in which mother love is programmed like the morning snack. (See Kittrie, 1971, for a general discussion of the evils of the "therapeutic state" and the potential elimination of all individuality through what was then perceived as completely effective behavioral technology.) This image was in the forefront during the debate over the Comprehensive Child Development Act in 1971. For example, Senator James Buckley remarked in Congressional debate that "I cannot escape the haunting fear that if this measure is enacted we shall be taking a final, fatal step down the road which leads to a completely controlled existence . . ." (Buckley, cited in Steinfels, 1973, p. 204). This fear, which was strong in the early 1970s, was partially assuaged as the decade wore on and behavioral regimentation did not materialize, and as policy makers and professionals increasingly emphasized community control and parental involvement. Parental involvement and community control of day care may in many cases be illusory (Steinfels, 1973), but the concept of parental control is a symbolic counterimage that can help to alleviate fears of state child-raising, in spite of the resurrection of the Big Government fear that came with the Reagan Administration. A national day care policy would in many ways contradict this counterimage, but a national early intervention program with emphasis on local control might be more palatable.

Confusion over Purpose

The issue of a national early intervention policy is clouded by the question of who should benefit from a day care program: the mother? the society? or the child? Day care supporters who want to "free mothers to work" and thus allow women to enter the workforce have a different vision of day care than do supporters who see day care as one component of a "workfare" package, in which mothers *must* go to work. Advocates of child development programs have a still different vision (Nelson & Krashinsky, 1973). All three views imply a different clientele— middle-class women, welfare women, or handicapped or culturally disadvantaged children—and a substantively different program design as a consequence.

While there is no theoretical reason that a day care policy cannot be designed to accommodate all three purposes, the reality of limited resources forces a "quantity versus quality" decision on policy makers. If day care for working mothers and workfare are seen as the primary purposes of day care, then inexpensive care is a foremost consideration. It will be essential to provide care to the largest number possible to meet the heavy demand and to effect a savings over welfare costs. Indeed, this was the conclusion reached by Bernstein and Giacchino (1971) in a study of New York City day care programs. In their opinion,

> without abandoning the long-range goal of enriched preschool programs universally available for all, the public interest would best be served in the short range by reaching more children with good day care, rather than fewer with a highly enriched program. (p. 19)

Day Care for Working Women

If the primary emphasis is on providing day care for mothers who want or need to work, the question is not so much public subsidization of programs but recognition of day care as a legitimate work-related expense. This has, in fact, been recognized through tax deductions for dependent care expenses.

Day care for this purpose becomes a consumer commodity, and the character and quality of a day care program should be governed by the market. Day care cannot quite fit this traditional model, however, in that it is in many ways protected from the normal market controls. Parents may shop around for a day care center that best serves their needs, but they often have little choice or control over what happens to their child after the child is in the program. Furthermore, the child is usually unable to make an adequate evaluation of the quality of care provided in the program. Therefore, most day care advocates are agreed that some form of public quality control is required (Nelson & Krashinsky, 1973). The implication is that day care cannot (or should not) be a purely private, for-profit enterprise.

The working parent day care program must have flexibility in order to match day care with work hours. For example, there is evidence that the real concern of working mothers is not preschool care, but after-school and summer supervision of school-aged children (Hawkins, Curran, & Jordan, 1970). This requires a day care policy that is flexible, capable of handling a late afternoon influx of older children, and convenient to schools.

Day Care as Welfare

If the primary purpose of day care is to reduce welfare expenditures by allowing (or forcing) mothers to go to work, the cost-benefit orientation of day care must be considered. Is it less expensive to pay support to a mother with three children so that she can stay at home with them or to pay day care expenses for those children so that she may go to work? In a study of the Washington, D.C. welfare program, Steiner (1971) found that a working mother with two children in day care and one in elementary school would save the Washington Department of Welfare about $56 per month. If more than two children in the family were in day care, the department would save money by supporting the mother at home. Steiner also found that, in a four-person family, the net gain for a working mother graduating from the Work Incentive (WIN) program over her welfare counterpart would be approximately $22 per month. Therefore, it is reasonable to say that, from the point of view of both the recipient and the disburser, the financial trade-off is almost negligible.

One argument that might tip the scale in favor of day care and workfare is found in a study of American attitudes toward the poor (Tropman, 1981). Tropman found that the sole difference between poor who were disesteemed and those who were respected was the perception (right or wrong) of "making an effort." If people seem to be making an effort to contribute to their own support, the level of respect for them and the tolerance of public assistance "to help them over the rough times" rise markedly. Taken with the cost-benefit analysis, the main value of a policy in favor of day care and workfare, then, is that it serves as an image enhancer to make public assistance more acceptable.

Early Intervention

Many professionals and educators see early childhood education as the primary justification for day care. Early childhood education has as its goal the sharpening of children's cognitive, social, and emotional abilities to function in school and, presumably, in adult life. The child is the central concern, and the administrative responsibility for this type of day care may even be transferred from social services to education, as in Europe (Kamerman, 1980). Early intervention programs, theoretically, should be available without consideration of the parents' need (or desire) to work or of public welfare costs. This is the dominant philosophy in many European countries, where free preschools are typically available for children from age 3 to 6 and 75 to 95 percent of all children in this age group attend (Kamerman, 1980). In the United States, the clientele of early intervention programs are children who, because of some social, physical, or mental deviation from the norm, are at risk for failure in the schools. The cost-benefit formula for early intervention is greatly complicated. What is the dollar value of the future social savings gained by preventing a child from needing special education services, dropping out of school, or coming to the attention of the juvenile courts?

That early intervention is more expensive than custodial day care can be inferred from a survey of day care programs by Coelen, Glantz, and Calore, 1979. In 1977, the average annual expenditure per child in nonprofit, private centers was $1,430, as opposed to $2,190 per child for nonprofit publicly subsidized centers. The main differences in expenditures could be attributed to personnel salaries and supplementary services. To illustrate, Table 9-1 shows average operating expenditures across the four categories of centers analyzed in the study; not only were total expenses higher for the public nonprofit centers, but also personnel costs took a larger percentage of their budget, leaving a slightly smaller share for programs and materials. Table 9-2 shows services offered to families by the various centers, and Table 9-3 lists the types of professional staff available. These special services, e.g., social work and speech therapy, distinguish custodial day care from early intervention. All these data suggest that there is far less emphasis in private centers on employing skilled professionals and on offering services commonly associated with early intervention activities. The implications for reductions in federal funds, then, are arguably qualitative as well as quantitative.

Table 9-1 Annual Operating Expenditures of Early Intervention Centers

	Private Centers		Public Centers		All Centers
	Profit	Nonprofit	Profit	Nonprofit	
Total expenditures (millions of $)	258.7	297.2	114.4	616.1	1,286.3
Center averages					
Personnel	27,200	47,000	36,200	72,000	48,400
Supplies	8,600	10,100	9,800	12,800	10,600
Occupancy	7,700	4,200	9,000	6,700	6,600
Other	2,800	3,100	6,600	7,200	4,700
Total[a]	46,300	64,400	61,600	98,700	70,300
Percent allocation Center averages[b]					
Personnel	63	73	61	73	69
Supplies	18	17	16	14	16
Occupancy	15	7	15	7	10
Other	5	4	8	6	5
Total	100	100	100	100	100

[a] Totals may not equal sum of components owing to rounding
[b] These percentages have been calculated by averaging percentages across centers (e.g., average of percent of expenditures allocated to personnel). They will differ slightly from percentages calculated by dividing average expenditures in a category by average total expenditures.

Source: Adapted from *Day Care Centers in the U.S.: A National Profile 1976-1977* by C. Coelen, F. Glantz, and D. Calore, by permission of Abt Books, © 1979.

Table 9-2 Services Provided to Children and Families by Type of Center

| | (Percentage of Centers) | | | | |
| | Private Centers | | Public Centers | | |
Services[a]	Profit	Nonprofit	Profit	Nonprofit	All Centers
Services to children					
Physical exams	13	28	23	55	32
Dental exams	11	28	20	57	32
Hearing, speech, or vision exams	47	62	60	82	64
Psychological or developmental testing	32	45	43	72	50
Services to families					
Counseling on child's development	79	84	83	94	86
Counseling on family problems	36	53	46	77	55
Assistance in obtaining food stamps or financial aid	19	36	45	74	45
Assistance in obtaining community services	30	44	45	79	52

[a] The data reflect the percent of centers reporting provision of a service; they do not indicate the level or frequency with which a service is provided.

Source: Adapted from *Day Care Centers in the U.S.: A National Profile 1976-1977* by C. Coelen, F. Glantz, and D. Calore, by permission of Abt Books, © 1979.

Table 9-3 Types of Professional Staff Available

| | (Percentage of Centers) | | | | |
| | Private Centers | | Public Centers | | |
Type of Professional[a]	Profit	Nonprofit	Profit	Nonprofit	All Centers
Hearing, speech, or vision specialist	4	8	6	11	8
Social worker	6	20	9	39	21
Nurse	14	23	19	32	23
Psychologist	4	9	4	11	8
Child development specialist	23	31	39	48	35

[a] Data indicate only the presence of a staff specialist, not the intensity or frequency of services they provide to children.

Source: Adapted from *Day Care Centers in the U.S.: A National Profile 1976-1977* by C. Coelen, F. Glantz, and D. Calore, by permission of Abt Books, © 1979.

Concern over Costs

The costs of any social program are always a paramount consideration, but cost issues have been especially prominent in the day care policy debate. Although Head Start appeared in the mid-1960s as a major armament of the War on Poverty, the question of a comprehensive day care and early intervention policy did not arise on the public agenda until the early 1970s, when enthusiasm for the Great Society was on the wane. Even before that time, however, there was concern that day care could become a runaway cost (Greenblatt, 1977).

Day care, as it was proposed in the Comprehensive Child Development Act of 1971, was an entitlement program; that is, it authorized expenditures for all day care recipients on the basis of certain eligibility requirements. Budget ceilings or limitations were meaningless, since the total expenditure ultimately depended on the number of families who used the service, which could be predicted only roughly. This effectively removed day care from the fiscal control of either the Congress or the Administration, hence, the worry about runaway costs. The Child Development Act was brought up for consideration at a time when Congress was beginning to view budget deficits, and its own apparent inability to control them, with alarm—in fact, only three years later, a new, tough Congressional Budget Act was passed to help remedy the problem (Schick, 1980).

As the decade of the 1970s wore on, concern about costs deepened. Day care was only a component of more limited programs enacted for a variety of purposes. Principal among these was Title XX of the Social Security Act, passed in 1974. An omnibus social services program that reflected the growing concern over the size of the federal debt, Title XX was not an entitlement program, but a program with a definite spending lid. Under Title XX, funds were allocated to the states on a formula basis. Day care was one of the services a state could elect to provide, but it had to compete for fiscal attention with other social services, such as protective services for children, foster care, and residential care for handicapped individuals. The percentage allocated to day care in state plans for Fiscal Year 1979 varied from less than 5 percent of the Title XX formula in Idaho, Montana, North Dakota, and Wisconsin to nearly 50 percent in Delaware and New York (HDS, 1980). Nationwide, however, day care services were the single largest Title XX expenditure, amounting in Fiscal Year 1978 to $731,347,000, or roughly 22 percent of the total Title XX allocation (HDS, 1980).

Title XX was not the only source of public revenue for day care or early intervention programs. In 1980, day care centers were eligible for the Department of Agriculture's school lunch program; Medicaid provided some special services, such as medical and dental checkups, prosthetic devices, and physical therapy. The Community Services Act administered by the Department of Housing and Urban Development (HUD) provided day care facilities and some staff as one of its community support activities. Comprehensive Employment and Training Act

(CETA) participants served as staff in many centers, while Project WIN provided day care support to mothers in training for jobs. Human Development Services in the Department of Health and Human Services (HHS) administered the Head Start program, while the Department of Education was responsible for its companion, Follow Through. Elsewhere in the Department of Education, funds were available through the Education for All Handicapped Children Act for preschool services for handicapped children, and Titles I and IV-B of the Elementary and Secondary Education Act could also be used in a limited way to support preschools.

All in all, state and federal government funds of one sort or another provided 29 percent of total revenues for day care, with parent fees accounting for the remainder (Coelen et al., 1979). This overall statistic, however, disguises the fact that centers vary a great deal in the degree of their dependence on public funds. Nationwide, 31 percent of day care centers are private, for-profit programs that receive *no* public subsidies for any of the children enrolled, but 34 percent are nonprofit, public programs that receive an average of 71 percent of their funds from the government (Coelen et al., 1979). Given the current rate of unemployment coupled with reductions in federal funds, a change in the public/parent ratio on fees for day care will have an uneven—but severe—impact on families.

Because so many programs touch on day care and early intervention, the ecological balance of support for day care is very delicate. For instance, elimination of the CETA program by the Reagan Administration will have a direct effect on Head Start by eliminating one commonly used source of staff. Thus, Head Start will be adversely affected, even though the Administration specifically singled it out as a valuable program that should not be cut. Because day care is involved in a variety of social programs (e.g., workfare, early intervention) and because many day care providers have ingeniously built a "package" of support from a multitude of public sources, almost *any* cuts in *any* social service program will reverberate throughout the day care system and will, thus, have implications for early intervention for handicapped children.

Meanwhile, the pressure for appropriate child care programs continues to rise, as more and more mothers enter the workforce. In 1978, there were 12.5 million mothers with children under 18 in the labor force, an increase of 2.1 million from 1970 (Waldman, Grossman, Hayghe, & Johnson, 1979). The same economic and social problems that led the Administration to institute its economic recovery policies has left 30 million children with a need for day care as their mothers have sought work (Waldman et al., 1979). The simple fact is that a lack of government funds will not make these children go away.

EFFECT OF CHANGING FEDERAL POLICIES

Federal government policy reflects the general mood of the country, and that mood is currently one of concern over the state of the economy. Accordingly, the attention of the Reagan Administration is focused almost exclusively on the problem of economic recovery. Economic concern, however, is coupled with a noninterventionist, neoconservative view of the role of the federal government. As expressed in an HHS program announcement:

> The philosophy of this Administration in the formulation of social service legislation and programs is based on the principle that the well-being of the public is primarily a responsibility of individuals, families, and the communities in which they live. (HDS, 1981, p. 56365)

In line with this philosophy, the Administration is pursuing economic recovery and social services through the strategies of (1) massively reducing the size and influence of the federal government and (2) stimulating private investment. The reduction of federal influence involves not only cuts in the federal budget, but also a loosening of federal constraints on both states and private enterprises.

These strategies have permeated the provision of social services at all levels. First, there are the much publicized attempts to legislate changes in funding programs. For example, the block grant proposals that Congress passed in 1981 lumped together (reduced) funds authorized through several enabling laws and gave states broad discretion as to their disbursement. The enactment of the block grants has been followed by proposals for even more shifts of responsibility to the states for welfare programs. Second, and less publicized, are the consistent "hands-off" policies of federal officials, who echo the Administration's stance of minimal regulation and interpret regulations wherever possible to give more discretion to states. For early intervention, this means that the focus shifts from Washington to the various state capitals and that the future of early intervention and day care will depend on the political climate and fiscal priorities of each state.

The major strategy used to stimulate investment is the tax cut. Particular provisions and incentives have been added to encourage employers to support social programs. Specific to day care, the Metzenbaum-Hawkins amendment to the 1981 tax bill provides (1) increased personal income tax deductions for dependent care expenses, and (2) employer tax credits for development of child care assistance programs or for reimbursement of employee day care expenses. This provision is designed to encourage employers to provide day care.

State Responses

Title XX was one of the programs folded into a social services block grant. Since this program was also one of the major sources of funds for day care, it seemed that this program would be a good barometer of the various states' interest in preserving day care. Accordingly, Title XX planners in 12 states were interviewed informally by telephone to determine their assessment of the impact of the block grant and funding cuts on day care services. At first glance, their responses seemed highly idiosyncratic; no two states were taking the same actions. Some states, e.g., Arizona and Connecticut, had anticipated the shifts in federal policy and had already made preparations for the changes. Other states were still wondering what to do at the time of these interviews (October 1981). In some states, day care was facing no cuts at all; in others, it was under consideration for elimination. A broad pattern began to thread its way through the survey, however, and several generalizations are possible.

While a few states were coping with reduced funds by relaxing licensing requirements, most states where day care funds had been cut proposed to maintain the quality of care, but to reduce either the number receiving services or the size of the reimbursement per child. To reduce the number being served, eligibility requirements were usually tightened by lowering the maximum income allowed or by eliminating subsidized day care for certain purposes. For instance, many states (e.g., Colorado, Kansas, Delaware) will no longer support day care to allow low-income mothers to attend college. To reduce the reimbursement per child, the costs were to be passed on to parents by asking them to pay part of the costs. For example, Missouri plans to spend only $8 per day for day care, and the client will be asked to pay the remainder. Delaware has added a minimum fee of $10 per week per family as the bottom rung of its sliding scale. Thus, overall, fewer families will be eligible for subsidized day care, and those who remain eligible will be required to pay a larger share of the costs.

Informants in those states where no cuts in day care were anticipated invariably reported a strong parent lobby group. Often, state funds had been appropriated for day care in addition to or instead of the Title XX allotment. California, for example, paid for all day care from state revenues, and these programs were untouched by the federal cuts. The Illinois Title XX planner remarked that, in response to the governor's announced intention to cut day care (as part of an across the board reduction of all services by 25 percent), the matter had become a strong media issue, and 400 parents were converging on Springfield "this very day" (of the interview) to lobby for restoration of the day care funds.

In contrast, states like Kansas were cutting day care by 50 percent or more, making this service bear more than its percentage share of the total reduction. Other states, e.g., Idaho, were considering elimination of the service entirely. It is notable that these states did not mention a strong parent lobby group.

States where day care took the heaviest blows were inevitably rural, sparsely populated areas with day care programs that were not large in the first place. Strong support for day care was shown mostly in states with urban, industrialized centers. Even within states, the changing eligibility criteria seemed to produce the same bias toward the urban centers. For example, Alabama's respondent explained that, although Alabama had previously funded day care for five pur-poses (working parent, child abuse, parent-in-training, handicapping condition, and enrichment), one—enrichment—was being eliminated. This policy change was expected to reduce the number of eligible children by about 2,500; significantly, most of these children were concentrated in the rural, economically depressed regions of Alabama where there were few industries and correspondingly few jobs for working mothers.

Corporate Responses

The other prong of the Reagan Administration's approach, tax incentives, was based on the assumption that private employers would enter the breach created by the reduction in public programs and would establish day care centers for their employees. This is a large assumption. Considering the relative lack of fanfare with which the Metzenbaum-Hawkins Amendment has been heralded, employers may not even be generally aware of this option in the first or second year of its operation. Furthermore, as Goodman (1981) pointed out, there is some sensitivity about offering a fringe benefit that will be of interest only to a portion of a company's employees.

Nevertheless, day care does have attractions to industries other than the tax incentive, and there has been a recent quickening of interest in the topic (Friedman, 1981). It can increase an employer's ability to attract employees, reduce absenteeism and turnover rates, improve employee attitudes, provide favorable publicity, and improve community relations (Zippo, 1980). One southern shirt manufacturer, for example, reduced its turnover rate from 90 to 5 percent among eligible employees. The company found that its annual costs per child for day care were less than the estimated costs of hiring and retraining new workers (Stein, 1973). Furthermore, the increasing number of women at all levels of the corporate plant and employers' growing recognition of job satisfaction as an element of productivity leads in a logical fashion to day care as one facet of the need to bring company goals into congruence with workers' personal and family goals (Kanter, 1977; Schram, 1981).

Actual experience with company-operated centers, however, has had mixed results. Company day care centers have been plagued with underenrollment, which inflates the per child costs beyond tolerable levels and indicates a lack of enthusiasm in the employees. Some companies have opened their enrollment to nonemployees who live near the plant in order to make ends meet (Stein, 1973; Zippo, 1980). The reasons for this apparent reluctance of employees to utilize the company's facility seem to include the employees' desire for their children to make friends in their own neighborhood and their concern for after-school care. In one survey of a corporate workforce undertaken in 1967,

> approximately 57% of the mothers with children 6-15 expressed concern
> and worry about child care arrangements for their children. The time

> period from end of the school day until the time mother arrives home
> was an unsupervised time for most of the children and was a source of
> concern most frequently mentioned by this group of mothers. (Hawkins
> et al., 1970, p. 10)

The data further suggest that working mothers are less concerned about preschool care, provided most frequently by family day care or babysitting services and available for the whole working day, than the problem of "latchkey" children who are not supervised after school hours (Hawkins et al., 1970). Certainly, a company day care center, often located miles from the children's schools, is an inadequate answer to this problem.

These experiences suggest that neighborhood day care centers, near home and school, might be more practical for the needs of employees than company centers. This approach does not preclude company-sponsored centers, as they could be located in the community near employees' homes, but it does increase the costs; company day care centers have typically been able to reduce expenses by using existing space, cafeteria, and janitorial services (Baden & Friedman, 1981). These facts might explain the recent growth of other options in employer-sponsored day care, such as parent training seminars, child care information and referral, and reimbursement of employees for their child care expenses (Baden & Friedman, 1981; Schram, 1981). None of these options create new day care space, however; nor do they typically provide early intervention.

A realist must conclude that, at present, there is no way to predict whether employer-sponsored day care will be able to make a larger dent in the current demand. Assuming that it does come into wider use, certain of its effects on the patterns of day care and early intervention can be predicted, however. For example, the purpose of day care would shift from a welfare to a worker benefit, away from the poor and toward middle-class employees. Employer-sponsored day care cannot be expected to replace the child care benefits that people have lost through reductions in federal funds. One of the oft-cited benefits of employer-sponsored day care is the employer's increased ability to recruit employees (Baden & Friedman, 1981), but recruitment is hardly a problem among employers looking for blue collar workers. This shift toward the middle-class employee can be seen in the results of a survey of employer-sponsored centers cited by Zippo (1980). The survey found that 30 percent of parents of enrolled children had supervisory or professional jobs, 35 percent had white collar jobs, 18 percent had skilled blue collar jobs, and only 8 percent of the participants were unskilled workers. The effect of excluding the "working poor" from these private sector programs may be intensified by the expected state responses of reducing some forms of training as legitimate reasons for subsidized day care and of requiring parents to pay a portion of the cost.

An emphasis on corporate day care could also be expected to shift the day care orientation away from early intervention and toward custodial care. This hypothesis is based on two considerations. First, as noted earlier, the purpose will dictate the type of day care offered. Indeed, given the predominantly middle-class demographic configuration of parents who use employer-sponsored day care, handicapped and culturally disadvantaged children are conspicuously absent. Second, the higher cost of early intervention could mitigate against its implementation in company programs. After all, why should the company pay for social workers and early intervention specialists on top of its commitment to child care?

It seems reasonable to assume that large corporations are more likely to offer day care benefits to their employees than are small businesses. Since large companies are generally located in urban centers, it is also reasonable to assume that any large-scale development of corporate day care will be concentrated in the cities. Far from balancing the expected state responses that will produce a similar shift away from rural areas, therefore, corporate day care could exacerbate this tendency.

Long-Term Impacts

No doubt, the current policies will leave a permanent mark on American social services in some way or another, but the advocates of federal support for social services can be expected to regain at least some of their previous strength. In order to predict the probable long-term impact of these current policies, it is necessary to turn to the political scientists.

Sundquist (1967) developed a cyclical model of political power to explain the periodically successful passage of one or another party's agenda. Sundquist analyzed the time frame from 1952 to 1966 and documented the fate of selected national social policies (e.g., Medicare, federal aid to education, civil rights) as political power shifted from peak Republican to peak Democratic influence. The scenario, as Sundquist painted it, is that the party out of power (both its Congressional and presidential "wings") gradually builds up an agenda based on public opinion and unmet need, regains power in first one and then the other wing, and—once it has gained control of both the executive and legislative branches—sets about the task of implementing its agenda with little or no opposition. The only difference between the events of the 1950s and 1960s, as described by Sundquist, and events in the 1960s and 1970s is that in the first case a Democratic/progressive coalition regained power, first through control of the Congress and then of the presidency, while in the latter case a Republican/conservative coalition regained power, first through control of the presidency and then of Congress.

If Sundquist's model is as applicable to the 1970s and 1980s as it was to the 1950s and 1960s, it should be possible to document that the Republican/conservative triumph of 1981 was a result of a slow buildup of momentum over the decade.

Indeed, there is evidence that this may be the case. For example, Schick's (1980) narrative of the budget battles of 1969 through 1974 showed a growth of concern for fiscal reform in the federal government. At that time, the Democratic/progressive group still controlled the Congress, but there was a running battle between Congress and President Nixon, resulting in Nixon's vetoes of social programs and his impoundment of funds. The Budget Act of 1974 was seen as a way for Congress to regain a balance of power with the president in fiscal matters because it outlawed the impoundment of funds. It was also seen as a way to impose greater fiscal responsibility on spending-prone members of Congress, through the process of budget reconciliation, among other provisions of the act (Schick, 1980). This emergent concern for economic recovery through control of federal spending continued to build slowly over the remainder of the decade and produced a concerted attempt to curb spending in the last years of the Carter Administration (Schick, 1980).

These parallels make it tempting to follow Sundquist's implied trend line, in which the sheer lack of opposition to the Great Society made it collapse of its own weight (people thought events were moving "too fast"), and predict that current federal fiscal policies may collapse similarly (if people decide that government is being dismantled "too fast" or if too many people are being hurt by the sudden reduction in social programs); that is presumption, however. The lesson of Sundquist's model is that, while support may crumble rather quickly for the current Republican/conservative policies, it may take 10 to 15 years to rebuild an agenda and an atmosphere in which social programs—including early intervention—can be implemented or expanded.

Another relevant model of political analysis can be found in Schulman's (1975) dichotomy of incremental/nonincremental programs. Most analysts characterize programs as incremental in nature, i.e., they grow by small increases over the years as new tasks and more money are gradually added to their base (Wildavsky, 1979). Such programs are highly stable; it is very difficult to invade the base of a program, and controversy usually settles from year to year only on the proposed increments.

Schulman (1975) also postulated that some programs are nonincremental in nature. These programs have some large, visible objectives (e.g., going to the moon, conquering cancer), as well as an equally visible threshold level at which effort and resources must be invested to achieve those objectives. By these criteria, the current federal programs can be defined as nonincremental. First, they embody several grand objectives: balancing the federal budget through spending reductions, reducing inflation, and stimulating the economy through tax cuts. Second, the plan has strong elements of a threshold necessary for success: spending must be cut *enough* to reduce the deficit substantially (thus federal borrowing, thus interest rates); taxes must be cut *enough* to stimulate private investment.

Schulman pointed out that support for nonincremental programs tends to "boom and bust"; that is, such a program requires massive support for passage, but, because of the visible nature of the objective, its achievement (or unmistakable, highly visible failure) eliminates public interest almost overnight. Thus, like Sundquist's, this model also predicts a rapid erosion of support for the Reagan Administration's fiscal policy, whether it is successful or not. Prediction of a quick death for the Reagan Administration's economic recovery programs is strengthened by the fact that one of its objectives is an invasion of the base of other, longstanding incremental programs. The prospect for ultimate success of such an endeavor is gloomy. In fact, Greider's (1981) documentation of the rather speedy disillusionment of David Stockman, one of the Reagan Administration's key implementers of policy, seems to confirm that chances for successful accomplishment of the Administration's goals grow dimmer as time goes on and effective implementation requires cuts into successively more sensitive—and politically sacred—programs. Even if the Reagan Administration's economic recovery programs are followed rather quickly by disillusionment and stalemate, alternative policies to fill the vacuum may not be immediately available, since they require in their turn a gradual buildup of support.

In the meantime, the effects of the Administration's policies on social services have already begun to emerge. As the federal government disengages, responsibility is being taken up by states, communities, and private philanthropies. Because the characteristics of the resulting programs will vary widely from community to community and because it is necessary to piece together patchwork programs based on a diverse funding base, there are likely to be problems of coordination, conflicting goals, and a "feast or famine" spottiness in communities where one program is highly successful in getting funds while another is not.

The idea that the laws of social Darwinism may come into play and only "truly needed" programs offering high-quality services will survive ignores the reality that provision of high-quality services and adeptness in fund-raising are not the same thing. The two skills, although not incompatible, do not always exist in the same agency. Furthermore, the patterns of giving displayed in the past by private philanthropies do not include a systematic effort to determine the areas of greatest need or to identify the programs of highest quality. A foundation's priorities are typically determined by the interests of its board of directors, and its awards are made on the basis of personal contact and negotiation. While the overwhelming need produced by the simultaneous disengagement of the government and deterioration of economic conditions may force many foundations to change their modus operandi, there is as yet no indication that they will do so. In short, a greater involvement by private philanthropy is likely to shift the emphasis in social services from needs of clients to fundability of programs.

All this may be very interesting from an academic standpoint, but it is not at all reassuring to the early intervention provider who is faced with long waiting lists and short budgets. The prospect that an agenda for social services will be rebuilt and ready for implementation in 15 years is irrelevant to the 3-year-old in need of early intervention now. Practical strategies, both for the long and short term, are needed to ensure that (1) day care and early intervention programs can meet immediate demands for services, and (2) day care is included on the national agenda for long-term eventual support.

EARLY INTERVENTION: 1990

There is little doubt that day care, the context of early intervention, will survive. In 1978, there were 6,874,000 children under age 6 whose mothers were in the labor force and nearly 23 million more between 6 and 17 (Waldman et al., 1979). There is no sign that trends will be reversed and that all these women will either want to or be able to return home in the near future. The sheer size of the demand ensures the continued survival and growth of day care.

The form in which day care will survive is not so clear. The foregoing analysis has revealed three major dangers: (1) day care may become increasingly inaccessible to the working poor, many of whose children are in need of early intervention; (2) the emphasis may shift away from early intervention and toward custodial day care; and (3) day care and early intervention may become unavailable in rural areas of the United States. Each of these potential dangers requires a different strategy for action by early intervention advocates.

Day Care for the Working Poor

Moroney (1981) noted that there are two broad theoretical justifications for public assistance. First, according to the "worthy poor" theory, the government should provide assistance to those who could not survive on their own. Second, under the "human investment" argument, public assistance is justified for those who, with just a little help—e.g., training, rehabilitation, day care—can become productive and contributing members of society. The beneficiaries of these two points of view overlap to some degree; on the whole, however, they are distinct groups: the former are the "helpless" cases, such as elderly or handicapped individuals, and the latter are the "borderline" poor. Moroney also pointed out that, in times of limited resources, these groups may compete for fiscal attention.

Apparently, the current federal stance is in favor of the worthy poor theory. Numerous commitments have been made to the "truly needy" who require assistance "through no fault of their own," but direct action has been taken to eliminate such programs as CETA. This leaves early intervention, with its human investment justification, definitely outside the federal pale.

This federal stance does not preclude state governments from taking a human investment perspective of assistance, however. In fact, it encourages such a complementary posture. With the federal government serving the urgent needs of the poor, there is no theoretical reason why state governments could not and should not turn to rehabilitative type programs to assist poor people in attaining or regaining independence. A companion argument can be found in Tropman's (1981) observation that poor people who are seen as "making an effort" are given more esteem in American society. Together, these arguments provide a justification with which day care advocates can approach state legislatures.

Strategies for advocating programs at the state level are slightly different from those used at the federal level. Human service advocates who are accustomed to forming dues-paid associations and hiring professional lobbyists to pursue their interests in Washington must change tactics. As noted earlier, states where day care has been funded by state monies invariably have strong, articulate parent groups that actively campaigned for day care. As one Title XX planner noted, "the most effective lobbyist for a state legislator is his neighbor." Parents committed to strong day care programs should be located in every corner of the state and armed with information and fortitude. They should be prepared to contact state legislators, by letter and in person, both at home and in the state capital, again and again. They should have ready answers to numerous questions: Why public support? What is wrong with babysitters? What will day care do to the family?

In the private sector, an expansion of employer-sponsored day care may also help to serve the needs of the working poor. As noted earlier, most of the employees who take advantage of employer-based day care programs are professionals, supervisors, and white collar workers. Greater use of this employer benefit across a broader spectrum of the labor force must be encouraged if private enterprise is to fill the breach in this area.

Early Intervention

In some respects, the outlook for maintaining an early intervention system within the day care program framework is bright. For example, Head Start is still to be sheltered from budget cuts. In addition, in the survey of sample states, Title XX planners typically responded that they were determined not to relax licensure requirements as a cost-cutting measure.

Juxtaposed with these optimistic omens, however, is the sobering problem of expense. As noted earlier, annual costs per child in public day care programs averaged $760 more than the costs per child in private nonprofit centers. Further analysis reveals that the "fat" in public day care budgets lies in higher wages (presumably, to hire more qualified teachers) and supplementary services, such as social work and speech therapy. If it is concluded that this $760 per child is the average net difference between early intervention and custodial day care, the question becomes one of priorities: For every $10,000 invested in day care, is it more important to provide an education and intervention program for four and one-half children or a custodial service for seven? Considering the pressure on the child care market exerted by growing numbers of women entering the labor force, advocates of early intervention could easily be overwhelmed by this arithmetic. In fact, the quantity/quality trade-off has long been an issue in the design of day care policy and is yet to be resolved (Nelson & Young, 1973).

The strategy to combat such threats to early intervention is research and hard work. The evidence suggesting that early intervention is more expensive is only circumstantial. To prove the question one way or another, programs must be analyzed to determine just what components distinguish an early intervention program from custodial day care, and the costs of each component must be isolated. Only then can the relative expense of early intervention be confirmed. If early intervention is indeed found to be more expensive, there is yet another research question: must it be more expensive? Which components of early intervention contribute to its efficacy, and which do not? In an era of concern about limited resources, such research is essential.

Hard work is needed to educate parents and legislators about the importance of early intervention. Empirical evidence that children with preschool experience gain long-term benefits is useless until it is translated into an active campaign for public education. At the same time, this public education should countermand or modify the negative symbolic images of early childhood education as antimotherhood or antifamily. Parents are the consumers of day care and ultimately control the nature of the "product." If early intervention is to survive as an integral part of day care, the need for it must be demonstrated.

Day Care in Rural Areas

In many ways, the provision of day care in rural areas is the most difficult problem to solve without federal assistance. States with predominantly rural populations typically have the fewest available resources and hold the most traditional values concerning the need for human services in general and the role of women in the workforce in particular. Corporations in sparsely populated areas are often smaller businesses with neither the resources nor the inclination to provide an employee benefits package that might include child care. Nevertheless, all the strategies suggested for day care for the working poor should be applied in rural, economically depressed areas. Parent organizations might be established through the consolidated school districts. At the very least, these organizations could provide early stimulation training programs for women who babysit for their neighbors' children.

Day care service providers and parent organizations could also work in communities to form small business employer day care cooperatives. Parent-run day care cooperatives have not generally been successful because of the formidable logistics involved (Nelson & Krashinsky, 1973), but employer cooperatives, financed by modest contributions from a number of companies, could prove highly stable. Such an effort might involve creative combinations of public aid and volunteer groups as well. Again, the key to successful organization of day care cooperatives lies in a solid public education campaign. In this case, however, the information provided should include not only the educational benefits to children, but also the economic benefits to communities and individual companies through an expansion of the local labor market, improvement in employees' stability, and tax benefits.

In the long run, however, the problem of irregular availability of day care programs across states and regions—and across sectors of the population—is likely to remain as long as federal participation is restricted. There is no substitute for federal coordination; ideally, it should be the federal role to transfer resources, not from person to person, but from wealthy regions to poorer regions. It should further be the federal role to encourage research into the broad issues of day care in general and early intervention in particular.

Realistically, as noted earlier, reestablishment of a federal role in day care and other human services requires a long and careful process of agenda building and agitation for public support. Day care advocates must not sanguinely assume that their "time will come" as the proverbial pendulum moves back in a direction more favorable to human services. Therefore, not a *shift* of attention from Washington to the state capitals, but a *division* of attention is required. There must be no let-up in the effort to maintain and expand federal involvement while state, local, and private avenues of support are being initiated. No national policy has ever been implemented without national support.

Early intervention services are likely to survive the Reagan Administration's policies. These services have long struggled along without a coherent national policy, faced with limited resources and diverse funding sources; advocates have responded to this situation with creativity and hard work. While reductions in federal support will undoubtedly have negative consequences for day care, these problems can simply be viewed as More of the Same. If early childhood educators are prepared to roll up their sleeves and meet the challenge, there is no reason why a national analysis in 1990 could not reveal that day care and early intervention programs are alive and well, and, in fact, stronger than ever.

REFERENCES

Baden, C., & Friedman, D.E. *New management initiatives for working parents.* Boston: Wheelock College Office of Continuing Education, 1981.

Bernstein, B., & Giacchino, P. Costs of day care: Implications for public policy. *City Almanac,* 1971 (August), 6(2), 6-20.

Binstock, J. Motherhood: An occupation facing decline. In R.T. Francoeur & A.K. Francoeur (Eds.), *The future of sexual relations.* Englewood Cliffs, NJ: Prentice-Hall, 1974.

Coelen, C., Glantz, F., & Calore, D. *Day care centers in the U.S.: A national profile 1976-1977.* Cambridge, MA: Abt Books, 1979.

Davids, L. New family norms. In R.T. Francoeur & A.K. Francoeur (Eds.), *The future of sexual relations.* Englewood Cliffs, NJ: Prentice-Hall, 1974.

Edelman, M. *The symbolic uses of politics.* Urbana, IL: University of Illinois Press, 1967.

Friedman, D. *On the fringe of benefits: Child care and corporations.* Keynote address presented at the Conference on Child Care and Corporations: Options for the 80's, Madison, Wisconsin, November 19, 1981.

Goodman, E. The transfer-and-pray theory. *Young Children,* 1981, *37*(1), 72.

Greenblatt, B. *Responsibility for child care: The changing role of family and state in child development.* San Francisco: Jossey-Bass, 1977.

Greider, W. The education of David Stockman. *The Atlantic Monthly,* 1981, *248*(6), 27-54.

Hawkins, D.F., Curran, J.R., & Jordan, J.W. *Industry-related day care: The KLH Child Development Center* (Part I). Cambridge, MA: KLH Child Development Center, 1970.

Human Development Services. *Annual report to the Congress on Title XX of the Social Security Act, Fiscal Year 1979.* Washington, DC: U.S. Department of Health, Education and Welfare, 1980.

Human Development Services. Program announcement. *Federal Register,* November 16, 1981, *46*(220), 56365.

Kamerman, S.B. Child care and family benefits: Policies of six industrialized countries. U.S. Labor Statistics Bureau, *Monthly Labor Review,* 1980, *100*(11), 23-28.

Kanter, R.M. *Work and family in the United States: A critical review and agenda for research and policy.* New York: Russell Sage Foundation, 1977.

Kittrie, N.N. *The right to be different: Deviance and enforced therapy.* Baltimore: The Johns Hopkins University Press, 1971.

Moroney, R.M. Public social policy: Impact on families with handicapped children. In J.L Paul (Ed.), *Understanding and working with parents of children with special needs.* New York: Holt, Rinehart, & Winston, 1981.

Nelson, R., & Krashinsky, M. The demand and supply of extra-family day care. In D.R. Young & R.R. Nelson (Eds.), *Public policy for day care of young children.* Toronto: Lexington Books, 1973.

Nelson, R., & Young, D. National day care policy. In D.R. Young & R.R. Nelson (Eds.), *Public policy for day care of young children.* Toronto: Lexington Books, 1973.

Otto, H.A. (Ed.). *The family in search of a future.* New York: Appleton-Century-Crofts, 1970.

Schick, A. *Congress and money: Budgeting, spending, and taxing.* Washington, DC: The Urban Institute, 1980.

Schram, R.W. Parents, kids, and companies: New rules for business. *Personnel Journal,* 1981, *60*, 436-437.

Schulman, P.R. Nonincremental policy making: Notes toward an alternative paradigm. *The American Political Science Review,* 1975, *69*, 1354-1370.

Stein, S. The company cares for children. In P.A. Roby (Ed.), *Child care: Who cares?* New York: Basic Books, 1973.

Steiner, G.Y. *The state of welfare.* Washington, DC: The Brookings Institution, 1971.

Steinfels, M.O. *Who's minding the children? The history and politics of day care in America.* New York: Simon and Schuster, 1973.

Sundquist, J.L. *Politics and policy.* Washington, DC: The Brookings Institution, 1968.

Tropman, J.E. Copping out or chipping in (image of the poor). *Humanist,* 1981, *41*, 43-46.

Waldman, E., Grossman, A.S., Hayghe, H., & Johnson, B.L. Working mothers in the 1970's: A look at the statistics. U.S. Labor Statistics Bureau, *Monthly Labor Review*, 1979, *99*(10), 39-49.

Wildavsky, A. *The politics of the budgetary process*. Boston: Little, Brown & Co., 1979.

Zippo, M. Employer-sponsored child care comes of age. *Personnel*, 1980, *57*, 45-48.

Chapter 10

The Long-Term Effectiveness of Early Intervention

Neil J. Salkind

Now, more than ever, the political and social climates in the United States demand that those concerned with the health and well-being of all children respond to those people who would eliminate many early intervention programs simply because their value has not been clearly demonstrated. There is an increasing emphasis on accountability to public funding agencies and foundations to ensure continued support (even if it be at reduced levels), as well as on effective communication with elected and nonelected officials in *their* language and often on *their* terms to explain why a particular program should or should not be supported. A critical topic in this communication is whether early intervention programs are achieving or have achieved some "worthwhile" goal. A major problem, however, has been that the achievement of goals is often unclear, since the very nature of experimentation in settings as complex as early intervention programs often precludes the identification of which dimensions of behavior are receiving attention. Often levels of attainment, be they measures of change in a child's intelligence quotient (IQ), achievement test scores, or degree of parental involvement, must be judged and evaluated on a post hoc basis. Indeed, the less controlled influential factors are in early intervention programs (by design or necessity), the more skeptical we must be, and others will be, as to the validity of the results.

During the past 20 years, the literature in developmental psychology and special education, especially concerning severely handicapped children, has described a host of different intervention models that have been tested. All of this work has also, as one might expect, generated a number of important questions about early intervention that have yet to be addressed:

- What groups of children are most responsive to early intervention programs?
- Which of the many available early intervention models is most effective?
- What measures are the most important indicators of change?

285

- What kinds of long-term gains, if any, are shown by children who participate in such programs?
- At what age should participation in early intervention programs begin?
- When should it end?
- How might participation in an early intervention program affect other members of the family?
- What policy implications might the implementation of early intervention programs have for the educational system in the United States?

These questions are very difficult to answer. First, the data presently available on the effects of early intervention programs do not permit comparisons of different models or of similar models initiated at different stages of development. The longitudinal corsortium organized by Lazar (*Lasting Effects after Preschool,* 1979; Lazar & Darlington, 1982) is an important first attempt to take advantage of a wealth of data from several studies, but such comparisons are sorely lacking in number. Second, the times seem to demand that we do the best we can with what we have, since additional public funds are unlikely to be forthcoming in the near future. Continuation of research will be hindered not only by changes in funding patterns, but also by increased hostility toward this type of work from more conservative political groups who see it as interfering with one of the basic functions of the family, child-rearing.

TWO APPROACHES TO EFFICACY

For many years, arguments in support of early intervention programs for certain populations have been published in the academic journals of developmental psychologists and early childhood educators. Those with this substantive perspective have amassed the body of literature now available. Yet, it is becoming clear that this perspective alone is not sufficient. Its complement, the policy perspective, must be included as an integral part of any evaluative effort.

The substantive perspective deals with those issues that are child- or family-centered and are directly related to the basic questions asked by researchers and educators in fields such as developmental psychology, special education, and pediatrics. Professionals are most concerned with the substantive changes and the implications of these changes for the child's growth and development, with less regard for policy implications that are related to the child's well-being only indirectly. Only those indicators of change that reflect change in the child or the family are used for evaluation.

On the other hand, there is a more general, more indirect, and less often employed approach to evaluating the effectiveness of early intervention programs: the policy perspective. Within this framework, a variety of different factors enter the picture as "valuative criteria" (MacRae & Wilde, 1979) for determining the efficacy of early intervention programs. Such criteria as cost-benefit ratios are becoming more and more important, since legislators are most likely to understand and use this type of information in making decisions about funding priorities. These data are indirect measures of the results from early intervention programs.

In the overall evaluation of the efficacy of intervention programs, both substantive and policy perspectives must be considered. Without the substantive information on the effect of such programs, any type of policy implications becomes conjecture. In a comprehensive evaluation addressed to a variety of different audiences, substantive information is necessary, but certainly not sufficient.

A HISTORICAL PERSPECTIVE

In 1969, when Jensen reflected on the results of some of the first evaluations of Head Start and other early intervention programs, he concluded that "compensatory education has been tried and it apparently has failed" (p. 1). His extensive commentary, which appeared in the *Harvard Educational Review*, is an important historical marker in the development and evaluation of early intervention programs. Jensen's premature proclamation occurred at a point when the initial thrust of President Lyndon Johnson's Great Society programs was beginning to ebb, when both the political and scientific shortcomings of such programs were being brought to center stage for a more thorough examination. This closer scrutiny may have been a blessing in disguise, since it probably provided more clearly defined objectives and laid the foundation for what we know today about the long-term effects of such programs.

The notion that early experiences might affect later development had its primary theoretical roots in the psychoanalytic tradition of Sigmund Freud. In fact, the first theory regarding the long-range effects of "infantile stimulation" was developed by Freud. While animal studies (Dennenberg, 1964; Levine, 1957) provided some support for this hypothesis, there are inconsistencies in the findings regarding human behavior, as discussed by Caldwell (1964). The historical antecedents for today's efforts at intervening early in life include the work of Skeels and his colleagues (Skeels & Dye, 1939; Skeels, Updegraff, Wellman, & Williams, 1938), who first demonstrated the dramatic effect that early experiences can have. Unquestionably, it was their work that provided the impetus for more highly controlled studies on the effects of deprivation on young children.

Skeels and Dye (1939) confirmed the serendipitous findings of a staff member at a state mental institution that the social attention given to institutionalized infants (transferred into a ward occupied by "feeble-minded" women) resulted in significant and meaningful gains of relatively long-lasting duration. Skeels and Dye took 13 children (younger than 3 years of age and living in an orphanage) who had an average IQ of 64 and placed them with mentally retarded adults in a state institution where adults and staff interacted with them. At the same time a control group of children remained in what Skeels and Dye called an "unstimulating" environment. After one and one-half years, the IQ scores of the children in the experimental group had increased an average of 27.5 points, while the control group's average IQ score had decreased by 26.2 points. They concluded that deprivation may be reversible to a substantial degree if it does not last too long. This work was done some 40 years ago, when the leaders in the psychological community were convinced that intelligence is a fixed entity and not subject to any degree of significant change.

Most impressive, however, was the follow-up that Skeels conducted a quarter century later (1966) when he studied the same children as adults. He found that all 13 who had been in the stimulation group were self-supporting and that none was institutionalized. On the other hand, 4 of the 6 adults who had been in the no stimulation group as children were institutionalized as mentally retarded.

Kirk's work (1958, 1965) also highlights the importance of early intervention in the young mentally retarded. He investigated 27 children enrolled in a preschool education project (15 experimental and 12 control) and found that, by 6 to 7 years of age, 6 children from the experimental group had been paroled from institutions, while none from the control group had been released. In addition, children in the experimental group showed significant gains on measures of social maturity and intellectual functioning.

These findings, and the findings of students at the University of Iowa Child Welfare Station that a stimulating setting had a beneficial effect on measured intelligence, were met with a good deal of skepticism and dismay by educators and psychologists whose beliefs about intelligence were still rooted in the philosophical tradition of preformationism. In addition, the political mood of the times was that general intellectual abilities were fixed at birth and unalterable throughout the life cycle. Socially, such statements (endorsed by "scientists") proved to be a convenient way to keep certain groups of people "in their place." These types of prejudices severely limited any progress that might have been made in the direction of applied enrichment or intervention programs.

Rhinegold's (1956) classic study provided the first adequate experimental test of the effects of intervention. She selected eight 6-month-old institutionalized infants and assigned four of them at random to an experimental group and the remaining four to a control group. For seven and one-half hours per day, five days a week, the experimental group was provided with mothering attention over an eight-week period, while the control group received routine care. At the end of the eight-week period, the experimentally mothered infants were more socially responsive and had higher levels of vocalization than did the infants in the control group. A replication of the study yielded the same results. For the first time, it had been documented that systematic intervention could change the course of events in a child's life. There is no public record of a follow-up of the experimental or the control groups, although this is an empirical question well worth considering.

Social and political events also affected the general attitude toward intervention as a strategy. The passage of the Civil Rights Act and the historic decision of the Supreme Court in *Topeka v. Brown*[1] in 1954 helped to alleviate some of the burdens that less economically fortunate people in the United States had been forced to bear. Clearly, one of these wrongs was the lack of equity in the treatment that blacks and other minorities received as far as education, health care, and social service delivery were concerned.

Perhaps by coincidence, but certainly none the less timely, was the publication by Hunt in 1961 of *Intelligence and Experience,* which aggregated evidence that intelligence is not fixed by nature, but rather depends on the experiences that an individual has had. Hunt believed that "it might be feasible to discuss ways to govern the encounters that children have with their environments, especially during the early years of their development, to achieve a substantially faster rate of intellectual capacity" (p. 182). While Hunt's emphasis was clearly on intellectual development (perhaps at the expense of other important indicators of success), he provided an impetus to investigate, on a broad scale, the possibility of changing the nature of "children's encounters." As important, he gave credibility to the idea that major components of human behavior, such as intelligence, are malleable.

At approximately the same time, Bloom published *Stability and Change in Human Characteristics* (1964), in which he examined a host of longitudinal studies conducted throughout the world. Bloom's primary findings were that intellectual growth occurs most rapidly during the first five years of life and that perhaps as much as 50 percent of one's intellectual capacities are determined during that time. He reasoned, therefore, that otherwise minor perturbations in the child's life would have their greatest effect during the first five years. Hence, the importance of the "critical period notion" was established.

There were both positive and negative consequences to the Hunt and Bloom publications. On the one hand, the fact that intelligence was no longer considered "fixed" in nature, coupled with the finding that early experiences have a profound effect on later development, helped create an atmosphere conducive to serious consideration of large-scale programs. On the other hand, a somewhat illogical conclusion made popular by the press and some too eager social scientists was that, if IQ is not fixed, perhaps intellectual functioning should be the primary criterion by which the adequacy of programs for environment enrichment or remediation should be judged.

In the early 1960s, efforts were made to contrast group differences on other selected variables (such as language) between children labeled as "culturally deprived" and children who theoretically did not experience any type of identifiable social or cultural deprivation. These new studies, coupled with enormous political and social pressure to ameliorate wrongs, precipitated Head Start as "an idea whose time had come" (Zigler & Anderson, 1979).

Head Start was designed to provide the kinds of experiences for young children that would encourage certain types of intellectual achievement and would increase readiness for performance in typical school-related tasks, such as auditory discrimination and attention. This movement was the most ambitious and expensive program of its type yet to be attempted. Because of the enormous amount of money invested in the program and because of some of the unrealistic expectations of both proponents and opponents, the original design (of a summer's experience) may not have been given an adequate chance to succeed or fail. (An extensive discussion of Head Start can be found in Zigler & Valentine, 1979.)

Although there have been other programs to aid the disadvantaged child, no program involved more children, attracted more attention from the public or the politicians, and has been more controversial than Head Start. It offered the social science community a host of opportunities for practical experience in systematizing and understanding the enrichment and intervention paradigm. In retrospect, it also provided a more precise view of what efficacy means within an early intervention framework.

Trends in Evaluation: A Look at Head Start

Both politically and scientifically, the evaluation of Head Start became the litmus test for the success of early intervention programs. The most popularized of these evaluations, known as the Westinghouse report (1969), was the first large-scale study to examine the impact of Head Start on later school achievement. Perhaps the two biggest shortcomings of this national evaluation were its reliance on evaluation criteria that did not reflect the fundamental goals of Head Start programs and an unjustified emphasis on IQ as a measure of success. Although there was an attempt to measure variables other than IQ, e.g., personal and social variables, almost none of the instrumentation developed for this purpose received the attention and time necessary to ensure the development of reliable and valid measures. Poor evaluative design is becoming a less frequent occurrence in social service and social science programs, owing to a stronger movement toward accountability and the use of formative and summative evaluation models. The problem of emphasis on IQ, however, is much more complex.

The children who were evaluated in the Westinghouse report were enrolled in summer Head Start programs during 1965, 1966, 1967, and 1968. These children were tested one, two, and three years later in the fall of 1968. The results of these initial evaluations were by no means encouraging to advocates of early intervention. On both the Metropolitan Readiness and Achievement Tests and the Illinois Tests of Psycholinguistic Abilities, there were no differences between the children who participated in Head Start and those who did not.

Since the Westinghouse report, there has accumulated an extensive amount of literature discussing, and in some cases refuting, its findings (Campbell & Erlebacher, 1970; Ryan, 1974). Interestingly, the results of the Westinghouse study provided ammunition for those people who wished either to eliminate or to decrease the number of early intervention programs such as Head Start. So strong was this movement, that additional evidence of Head Start's positive outcomes seldom came to light. For example, Kirschner Associates (1970) examined the impact of Head Start programs on parent involvement in the public schools and in the use of health services. Parents of children who were enrolled in Head Start programs were found to make more use of local health facilities and to play a greater role in activities sponsored by the public schools. There is substantial evidence that such parent involvement significantly affects the health and educational status of children from low-income families. (See Salkind & Haskins, 1982, for a review of related public assistance programs and their effects.)

The most important lesson learned from the Westinghouse study was not that Head Start had failed, but that certain concerns must be addressed in evaluating the adequacy of any early intervention program. Datta (1979) identified five such concerns:

1. the potential selection bias in the choice of children who participate in the programs. For example, in the Westinghouse study, additional analysis showed that, if the neediest children are enrolled, effects on the later school achievement of the participants are reliable and positive.
2. the role of the family in early intervention programs. Bronfenbrenner on several occasions (1975a, 1979) emphasized the importance of the family in an ecological approach to understanding the impact of early intervention. In a discussion of this influence, Shipman (1976) noted that participation in programs such as Head Start might help to disrupt "the dismal cycle of determinism" that affects many children raised in very low income families. Bricker and Casuso (1979) presented similar arguments.
3. the continuity of programs. It may be necessary to maintain the intense attention present during the program before any lasting effects occur. It was somewhat naive and presumptuous of Head Start critics to expect an intervention effort lasting one summer to have a significant impact on long-range outcomes. Datta cited the work done in the various Follow Through programs around the United States as evidence that such continued participation is effective.
4. the type and quality of curriculums offered by the various Head Start programs. These were not taken into account by the Westinghouse study.
5. the selection of outcome variables. The current trend seems to be away from measures of intellectual functioning, such as IQ, cognitive styles, and information-processing strategies, toward more "applied" and certainly

more socially significant indicators, such as social competence (Zigler & Trickett, 1978) and retention in grade or placement in special education classes (Shipman, 1976). These last two indicators are especially important because they lend themselves to the types of analysis that are familar to policy makers, e.g., benefit costs and cost effectiveness.

In another analysis of issues that are important in planning and evaluating early intervention programs, Strain (1981), and Gray and Wandersman (1980), identified the following: (1) the precision of the treatment and the subsequent measurement of its effects, (2) sample selection and retention, (3) the concordance between what was taught and what outcome measures are used, (4) the reliability of the outcome measures and the adequacy of the sampling plan, and (5) the effectiveness with which the social validity of the expected long-term outcomes has been demonstrated.

The recommendations of these authors present some general classes of evaluative criteria that might be used to build a model to determine the efficacy of early intervention programs.

Away from IQ: Toward Other Measures of Efficacy

The familiar tune that was sung about the immediate effects of participation in an early intervention program was well summarized by Bronfenbrenner: at the "initial stages of intervention, children from disadvantaged backgrounds showed substantial gains in IQ and other cognitive measures, excelling their matched controls and attaining or even exceeding the average for their age" (1974, p. 167). It was, of course, the lack of permanence of these changes that proved to be problematic.

Measures of IQ usually provide a reliable measure of change, and, at a time when "intelligence" was believed to be the key to later social and economic success, it is in some ways understandable that such a strong emphasis was initially placed on this outcome alone. For example, Bronfenbrenner (1975b) focused on changes in IQ in a review of 12 early intervention programs. While substantial gains in IQ occurred during the first year of the Head Start program, they disappeared after the program was completed. In addition, this decline in previous gains appeared to be most severe following entry into public school. Children enrolled in programs in which the curriculums were "cognitively structured" showed greater gains than those enrolled in play-oriented programs. Age of entry into the program was not related to degree of gain. Most striking about Bronfenbrenner's summary of these IQ outcomes is that it indicates what was important in judging the efficacy of early intervention programs at that time. It should be noted, however, that there is substantial disagreement with the evidence of temporary gains and subsequent declines in performance—documented most notably by Lazar and associates (1977) and Darlington (1981) in their reviews of the longitudinal consortium.

Zigler and Anderson (1979) traced the influence of three factors that they believe contributed to an overdependence on cognitive outcomes as indicators of success or failure in such programs as Head Start. The initial efforts behind Head Start were based on the changing perceptions that IQ was not fixed or governed by hereditary influences. Zigler and Anderson postulated that an overreaction to this notion created an "environmental mystique" and a disproportionate investment in the impact that compensatory programs might possibly have. This overdependence was conveyed to a large extent by the media, but it came at a time when the United States was desperate to find a solution to the problems of poverty and racism. Clearly, the call for justice and the attempts to live up to the spirit of the *Brown* decision and the relatively new Civil Rights legislation played an important role as well.

Along with this changed perception of the basic nature of IQ came an increased sense of urgency heralded by the launch of the first satellite by the Soviet Union. This post-Sputnik reaction led to curriculums that focused on academic skills, at the expense of personal and social development, and clearly carried over into the evaluations of early intervention programs. Finally, the "discovery" of cognitive development during the early 1950s, and the recognition of such theorists as Piaget and Werner, not only further strengthened the bond between cognitive and intellectual functioning and success in school, but also decreased the concern with personal, social, and motivational development.

THE SUBSTANTIVE AND POLICY APPROACHES TO EFFICACY

As noted earlier, the evaluation of any social service program can take a substantive approach, focusing on outcomes related to changes in the child (or the family) as a result of some program, or a policy approach, focusing more on the requirements and needs of the public official or policy maker who often has a good deal of influence regarding the future of a program. These two approaches are strongly interrelated. In fact, one mandate that social scientists have failed to meet is making the substance of a particular area relevant to those involved in policy decisions. Regardless of the perspective from which the efficacy of early intervention is discussed, a set of criteria that are clearly articulated and easily used is needed. For those interested in extending the established research base, such a data base allows for increased confidence in replication; for the policy maker or analyst, it allows for a better understanding of the process and the associated outcomes.

The Substantive Perspective

It can be said that two outcome measures best represent the substantive criteria to judge the efficacy of early intervention programs. The first deals with school-related variables, such as placement in special education and retention in grade, while the second focuses on long-range outcomes, such as social competence, employment, and general adjustment. Because the children who were the original participants in many of the early intervention programs are just beginning to reach late adolescence and early adulthood, perhaps the most crucial test of long-range outcomes is still to come.

The Perry Preschool Project

Perhaps the best documented of all the early intervention programs is the Perry Preschool Project initiated in 1962. In this project, children assigned to the experimental group attended the program for 12½ hours per week for one year with home visits of 1½ hours per week. The children have been followed from age 3 to age 19.

The Perry Project has many impressive dimensions, but perhaps most interesting is the construction and empirical test of a chain of causal relationships such that "the most far-reaching effect is logically connected all the way back to its presumed source" (Schweinhart & Weikart, 1981, p. 30). The authors believe that this causal chain is important because it encourages systematic scientific programming.

The follow-up component of the Perry project revealed some interesting findings. By the end of high school, 39 percent of the control group had received some kind of special education services, compared with 19 percent of the experimental group. In addition, there were significant and socially "meaningful" differences in school conduct and delinquent behavior. For example, not only did children who participated in the preschool program behave better in the classroom (based on teacher ratings), but also they were kept after class less often. Most impressive, however, was the finding that 36 percent of the members of the experimental group fell into the category of chronic offenders (with five or more offenses), while 52 percent of the control group did.

The Yale Follow-Up

The Yale Child Welfare Research Program (Provence, Naylor, & Patterson, 1977) was conducted at the Yale Child Study Center between 1967 and 1972; its primary purpose was to test a small sample comprehensive intervention project with a strong clinical orientation. The program involved children from birth to 30 months of age and consisted of four components: home visits, health care, developmental examinations using standardized schedules, and full-time child care.

Although the program involved only 18 children, some of the results are impressive. A five-year follow-up of intervention families "indicated that the Yale Child Welfare Research Program has a sustained, long term impact on the children's intellectual and academic development" (Rescorla & Zigler, 1981, p. 10). Not only did the experimental children outperform the control children in the development of language skills, but also there were other, more profound differences related to the general status and upward mobility of the family. In the experimental families, for example, there was more employment for the mothers as well as a trend toward further education for them. The number of families receiving public assistance decreased from nine to five; the birth rate decreased, increasing the available resources per family member. The general improvement in quality of life points strongly toward the importance of less than "traditional" outcomes of early intervention programs. These changes in family structure and functioning become even more important when the close relationship that has been established between school achievement and socioeconomic status of the family is considered (Jencks, 1972). Perhaps most important is the fact that the results of the Yale study illustrate how outcome measures other than IQ are relevant for any comprehensive and socially relevant evaluation plan.

The Longitudinal Consortium

The Consortium for Longitudinal Studies (Darlington, 1981; Lazar et al., 1977) is "a cooperative effort of over a dozen investigators endeavoring to assess the long-term effects of early education on the lives of children from low income families" (Darlington, 1981, p. 37). It is unquestionably unique for at least two reasons. First, it is a compilation of 14 longitudinal research and demonstration studies conducted over an extended period of time. It is truly remarkable that outcome measures from so many different settings could be combined at all, let alone combined in such a way that the end product is not only understandable, but also yields significant results. Second, it was a truly collaborative effort, headed by Lazar of Cornell University who took responsibility for obtaining funding, arranging the aggregation of data from all 14 projects, and overseeing the analysis of the data and subsequent dissemination. In these times of fiscal constraints, such a framework for organizing different data bases should be publicized far beyond the audience of professionals interested in child development. Such a strategy can make it possible to use already established data bases to answer new questions.

Because the 14 projects had different objectives, the data available before the consortium was formed were diverse. After 1976, however, data collection was standardized and focused on IQ scores, school record information, achievement test scores, and the results of interviews with parents and teachers. The criteria used to evaluate the efficacy of this project (and of early intervention in general) were the number or percent of children assigned to special education and the number or percent of children retained in grade.

In an earlier analysis of consortium data in 1977, it was found that children from low-income families who had taken part in the early intervention programs were less likely to be retained in grade, as well as less likely to be placed in a special education or remedial setting. A subsequent reanalysis of the data (*Lasting Effects after Preschool,* 1979) confirmed these results. Children who had participated in at least three of the preschool programs were assigned to special education classes at a much lower rate than were children who did not participate. In the Gordon study, for example, 23.2 percent of children participating in the program were later assigned to special education classes, while 53.8 percent of the control children were so assigned. Similar findings were revealed for Gray (2.8 percent experimental vs. 29.4 percent control) and Weikart (13.8 percent experimental vs. 27.7 percent control). The other studies that were part of the consortium either did not have this information available or were not designed so that comparisons were appropriate.

The outcomes as determined by retention in grade were in the same direction as those determined by placement in special education, but only in one study were they significant. When data from the projects were pooled, however, the difference between the experimental and control children was significant at the 0.02 level. The authors believe that the weaker findings reported for retention versus special education placement are the result of different promotion policies throughout the various school districts.

It is important to remember about both of these measures of efficacy, that the significant differences between the control and the experimental groups were maintained even when factors such as initial IQ, sex, and ethnic and family background were controlled.

Other Studies

Recent movements in the direction of early intervention have focused on more "extreme" groups, such as handicapped children. Interestingly, some of the same measures of efficacy, i.e., retention in grade and placement in special education have been examined as well. For example, Karnes, Schwedel, Lewis, Ratts, and Esry (1981) conducted the Joint Early Educational Program for the Handicapped and found in a six-year follow-up that 80 percent of the children enrolled in the program were enrolled in regular education classes. In addition, 82 percent of the children did not require any remedial services. There was no control group in this study, but, in view of the results of other intervention studies, it is difficult to believe that such large advances in areas as retention and placement would be due to statistical artifacts.

Although not as systematic in its design or evaluation as some of the later intervention efforts, the very early pilot program conducted by Martin and Cynthia Deutsch (Maeroff, 1981) was, in effect, the real precursor to Head Start, Follow Through, and Title I programs. It provided the initial data base for the most extended follow-up to date. The program operated from 1961 to 1969 and involved some 1,200 children. The results of recent follow-ups of these children, now adults, again emphasize the importance of measures other than cognitive functioning.

In sum, participation in these very early programs has led to higher educational achievement and increased ability to cope with life. These children also had a better self-image and feelings of greater control; this is especially important, given the poverty in which many of these children grow up, and is highly significant in light of the work done in the area of "anomie" (or a sense of limbo), often reported as a characteristic of being poor and not in control of one's own destiny.

Interestingly, although boys and girls showed equal benefits of the program at initial testings, girls in the experimental group did not outperform girls in the control group at later testing. One possible explanation for this difference is that girls in later grades might have been punished for behavior that was encouraged during the early years of the program, such as asking questions.

The arguments in support of early intervention programs are most persuasive as the length of time increases between the onset of the treatment and the demonstration of positive results. The Harlem experiment provides an opportunity to examine long-term outcomes, especially as they relate to what might be called indicators of success, such as attending college, employment, and "meeting the expectations of society." After some 15 years, 32 percent of the children who participated in the program were attending college, while 20 percent of the control group were attending college. Fifty-seven percent of the program's children were working full- or part-time, while 44 percent of the control group's children were. Finally, 86 percent of the children who participated in the experiment were meeting the expectations of society, while 73 percent of the controls were.

There are several important, although tentative, conclusions that might be put forth from this brief overview of several early intervention studies. Early intervention programs decrease placement in special education settings, as well as grade retention, resulting in significant savings to the taxpayer. Furthermore, such indicators of success as the completion of school have been shown to be critical milestones linked to later social and economic success (Salkind & Haskins, 1982).

It can also be concluded that there is substantial evidence in the form of consistent findings and that an important criterion of scientific credibility, replicability, is present. In spite of the current political climate, few arguments can be made against the desirability of the results described and the need for future efforts in this direction.

The Policy Perspective

Gallagher, Haskins, and Farran make the point that "good" public policy rests on the three basic points: knowing what to do, knowing how to do it, and having the societal will to do it. It is fair to say that the first two of these are primarily the province of the academic community, while the third is the basic concern of policy developers, analysts, and implementers. The evidence for the efficacy of early intervention programs from a substantive view is more than adequate. In the world of funding priorities and budget considerations, however, the evaluation of early intervention programs must be approached from a policy perspective.

Of all the reasons that the process of policy analysis might be useful in the evaluation of early intervention programs, the most important is that it forces consideration of the accountability of actions. Several different criteria are incorporated into what is called a decision matrix. This matrix facilitates the comparison of several different policies (such as home-based or center-based intervention) across a set of criteria (such as cost benefit analysis). If a specific policy is clearly articulated (including goals and objectives), accountability can be increased and the entire evaluative process becomes less threatening and volatile as an issue. The application of policy analysis as an evaluative tool also encourages consideration of the implications of the actions that are about to be taken.

As defined by MacRae and Wilde (1979), policy analysis is "the use of reason and evidence to choose the best policy among a number of alternatives" (p. 4). Although different approaches can be taken in the analysis of various policies, each tends to incorporate four steps:

1. defining the general nature of the problem
2. selecting those criteria across which the different policies will be compared
3. discussing the nature of the various policies
4. analyzing the political feasibility of the various policies

The outcome measures of a policy analysis include efficiency (cost benefit and cost effectiveness), horizontal and vertical equity, stigma, and preference satisfaction.

Efficiency

The criterion most often referred to in these times of fiscal constraint is efficiency, which includes both cost benefit analysis and cost effectiveness analysis. In both cases, the criterion of efficiency is premised on the maximum return on any policy, given a certain commitment of resources. In essence, the funds allocated for early intervention programs must be spent in the most efficient way, i.e., to get the "biggest bang for the bucks."

Both cost benefit analysis and cost effectiveness analysis deal with dollars input, but their functions begin to differ after that point. Cost benefit analysis is appropriate when both costs and benefits can be expressed in fiscal terms, that is, when both input and output can be assessed on the same scale, usually expressed as the amount of money "invested" and the amount of money "returned."

On the other hand, cost effectiveness is appropriate when the outcomes of a policy cannot be assigned a fiscal value, such as the changes in parents' ratings of their child's school performance as a function of an early intervention program, as reported by Karnes and associates (1981). Effectiveness then is measured in whatever units are appropriate. In a more general sense, cost effectiveness is appropriate whenever costs and the value of outcomes are measured in different units.

Cost Benefit Analysis

Given the increasingly convincing evidence, it is not difficult to see the intrinsic value of early intervention's benefits, such as improved quality of life, access to health care, and perhaps increased family cohesion. Expressing the value of these benefits in quantitative terms, however, is an entirely different matter, since the value of these effects to the public (as a "public good") must be calculated; however, such estimates are frequently done. For example, Salkind and Haskins (in press) reported that the use of a negative income tax as an income maintenance strategy can increase the number of children from low-income families who will complete their last year of high school. In turn, the completion of the last year increases salary earnings, which increases lifetime earning, finally resulting in an increased tax base as a public good.

The Deutsch finding that 57 percent of the children who participated in the program were working as adults, as compared with 44 percent of the children who had not been part of the program lends itself to a similar analysis. The costs associated with *not* working (e.g., costs of public assistance, increased health problems and their associated costs, or the costs of the well-established relationship between unemployment and crime) could be calculated. Likewise, dollar values could be attached to the benefits, such as an increased tax base. Then, the two could be compared.

The traditional way to determine whether a certain policy is cost-beneficial is to compare its benefits to its costs in the form of a ratio. In general, if the ratio is larger than 1, the program can be considered cost-beneficial. In some cases, however, this ratio may not have to be greater than 1 for the program to be efficient. For example, other criteria may be more important than the criterion of cost benefits.

While the benefit-cost ratio can be an important indicator of efficiency, the absolute difference between the costs and the benefits may be even a better indicator. The relationship between costs and benefits is most efficient when the total benefits exceed the total costs by the largest amount and the net benefit is the largest possible.

As far as early intervention programs are concerned, it must be assumed that values can be assigned to the costs and the benefits and the two can be compared. Figure 10-1 illustrates a model for comparing the costs and benefits of a given intervention project. Here, the hypothetical value of costs and benefits is known for a variety of alternative approaches to early intervention.

Assume that F, G, and H in Figure 10-1 represent various intervention projects that differ in size, focus, or along any number of other dimensions. The efficiency of project A can be estimated as a ratio of AF/BF, as can be done for G (CG/DG) and H (EH/EH). It can be seen that benefits equal costs for project H, and there is no purpose in continuing the cost benefit analysis of this policy.

Even though the ratio of AF/BF might be larger than that of CG/DG, it is not necessarily the most cost-beneficial. An early intervention project is judged most beneficial if the total benefits of any one program exceed the total costs by the greatest possible amount. In this example, although the ratio of AF/BF (2.5) is greater than the ratio of CG/DG (2.0), the total benefits exceeding the total costs is greater for project G (50 − 25 = 25) than it is for F (30 − 10 = 20).

Figure 10-1 Costs and Benefits of Intervention Projects F, G, and H

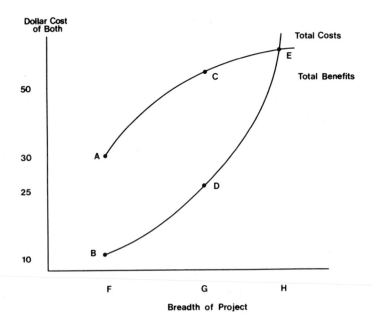

One other factor that is routinely ignored in the use of cost benefit analysis is the notion of time and its effect on benefits. The value of a benefit varies over time; the inflation rate suggests that this value will be less. When future benefits are worth less and costs increase, then discounting has to be taken into account.

There are some objections to cost benefit analysis as it applies to early intervention programs. One of the primary concerns revolves around who receives the benefits and who pays the costs. This is by no means a simple question. For example, it has long been argued that people who do not have children must contribute to the school tax base, since education is a public good. Such an argument can be made for early intervention programs as well, but it certainly is a sensitive issue open to political and fiscal discussions.

Zigler and Trickett (1978) are concerned about the application of cost benefit analysis since it is so difficult to determine which variables should be included or excluded and to assign a dollar value to certain outcomes, such as a gain in IQ scores. While these are worthwhile and important considerations, they do not negate the importance of cost benefit analysis. They only strengthen the argument that criteria such as efficiency should be part of the evaluative package.

An Example of Cost Benefit Analysis

There are valid concerns that must be taken into account when any kind of cost benefit analysis is undertaken. Some of these may be policy-specific and must be dealt with as the issues arise. However, cost benefit analysis can be very helpful in evaluating the efficacy of early intervention programs. One reason for this is the objective nature of this kind of analysis. Furthermore, only cost benefit analysis can allow cross policy comparisons, at least as far as outcomes (when expressed in dollars) are concerned.

One well-documented cost benefit analysis of an early intervention program (Weber, Foster, & Weikart, 1978) was completed on longitudinal data from the Perry Preschool Project. As a result of this analysis, three different types of benefits were found. The first was the reduced number of children (and the associated reduction in costs) who required some form of special education and/or institutionalized care. Interestingly, this is a direct application of one of the substantive criteria. The second was that those students who participated in the Perry Project had higher projected lifetime earnings, as measured by factors such as IQ scores, family background, and additional information about the students' school performance. Finally, the amount of time that parents had for possible employment was increased as a result of their child's participation in preschool. In their evaluation of the costs and benefits of the Perry Project, Weber and associates used the concept of marginal costs, rather than total costs. Where total costs reflect the cost of the program, marginal costs represent the total difference in costs between educating the experimental and the control groups.

A summary of the analysis reveals (Schweinhart & Weikart, 1981) that the total cost per child of two years of operation of the Perry Project was $5,984. The total benefits accrued, including the three factors, was $14,819 per child for an estimated return of 248 percent on the original investment (based on a sample of 28 children). These estimates do not take into account the discounting of benefits and the increased costs associated with inflation. The analysis of Weber and associates (1978) does such and shows that the rate of return for one year (9.5 percent) of preschool is greater than that for two years (3.7 percent).

Several lessons can be learned from this analysis. For example, cost benefit analysis as a measure of efficacy is only one criterion in a set that should be considered simultaneously. One may be weighed more heavily than another, but all should at least be considered. Given some of the positive benefits (beyond economic ones) that might accrue from participation in such a program (e.g. increased employment and decreased crime) a rate of return of 0 percent or even a marginally negative return might be a sufficiently positive indicator of success to continue such programs.

It is interesting to note that this specific cost benefit analysis appears to be the only systematic one offered regarding the general efficacy of early intervention programs. Garland, Stone, Swanson, and Woodruff (1981) pointed out that the later a child begins, the higher the cost of special education, but did not include any data on the associated benefits. For example, the cost of an intervention program beginning at birth through age 18 is some $37,273, while the cost for a child beginning an intervention program at age 6 is $53,340. Other data also indicate that early intervention programs are more effective if they are begun earlier (Horowitz & Paden, 1973); therefore, the benefits could be expected to increase the earlier the child starts.

THE FUTURE

In spite of the documented success of early intervention programs, the philosophy and practice of compensatory and enrichment programs have not been universally received with open arms. This lack of acceptance can be remedied, however.

Substantive Concerns

The high return on the investment made in compensatory education programs and early intervention efforts illustrates that these programs actually return more money than it costs to fund them. Interestingly, this outcome seems to be true for all the studies that applied a cost benefit or cost effectiveness criterion. In other words, all studies were found to be cost-beneficial.

The movement away from cognitive measures as the sole indicators of effectiveness is increasing, to be replaced by an emphasis on other indicators of social and economic success, such as placement in school, involvement with the courts, and quality of life. Given the somewhat myopic range of outcomes that IQ alone can predict, this movement will enlarge the opportunities for effectiveness of these programs, since they are likely to be more broadly based.

Especially now, since most of the children who were participants in the first early intervention programs are now coming of age, serious efforts must be made to continue long-term monitoring across the wide range of variables available.

Efforts to employ cost benefit analysis must be continued, since this is one standard whose validity is widely understood by lawmakers. In addition, sufficient documentation must be presented as to how the costs were calculated and what variables are assigned costs.

Policy Concerns

In the future, early childhood educators will be asked to accomplish more with less. Given the sharp cuts in funding that have occurred and are likely to continue, more efficient and creative ways of using what is already available (such as the longitudinal consortium efforts) must be encouraged and explored.

Because of the funding cuts at the federal level and the displacement of responsibility for many social programs from the federal government to the state government, active policy work and lobbying must begin to focus on the state level. Although the state bureaucracy may be no less cumbersome than the federal maze (Nocera, 1982), it may very well be more responsive to citizens' needs and mandates.

There is a strong need to educate lawyers as to the fundamentals and purposes of science and scientific endeavors. This can occur not only within the framework of their legal education, but also as an integral part of their legislative activities.

Since most of the people who allocate funds for various projects are in office for a relatively short period of time and are interested in "quick" fixes that reflect well on them, programs and lobbying efforts should be organized and implemented to satisfy this political need. While the overall importance of long-range changes is emphasized, short-range measures of effectiveness, such as nutritional benefits and opportunities for education, are more immediate outcomes that are related to the types of programmatic outcomes needed.

The political, social, economic, and educational climates must be considered forces that operate separately in shaping social science policy. Therefore, advocates of early intervention programs must be aware of especially receptive people and times, when the introduction of a certain policy might be more appropriate than others. For example, while Head Start flourished with an almost religious fervor, day care as a general philosophy never had the social imperative that it needed to be accepted and made available to families who might desire it (Peters, 1980).

If states do indeed take the leadership role in the implementation of major policy programs (as seems might be the case), programs for the handicapped and other intervention programs might become a part of regular school offerings and not stigmatizing "special" programs.

REFERENCES

Bloom, B.S. *Stability and change in human characteristics.* New York: Wiley, 1964.

Bricker, D., & Casuso, V. Family involvement: A critical component of early intervention. *Exceptional Children,* 1979, *46,* 108-116.

Bronfenbrenner, U. *Is early intervention effective? A report on longitudinal evaluations of preschool programs* (Vol. 2). Washington, DC: Department of Health, Education and Welfare, Office of Child Development, 1974.

Bronfenbrenner, U. Is early intervention effective? Facts and principles of early intervention: A summary. In A.M. Clarke & A.D.B. Clarke (Eds.), *Early experience: Myth and evidence.* New York: The Free Press, 1975. (a)

Bronfenbrenner, U. Is early intervention effective? In M. Gultenlag & E.L. Struening (Eds.), *Handbook of evaluation research* (Vol. 2). Beverly Hills, CA: Sage Publications, 1975. (b)

Bronfenbrenner, U. *The ecology of human development.* Cambridge: Harvard University Press, 1979.

Caldwell, B.M. The effects of infant care. In M. Hoffman & L. Hoffman (Eds.), *Review of child development and research* (Vol. 1). New York: Russell Sage Foundation, 1964.

Campbell, D.T., & Erlebacher, A. How regression artifacts in quasi-experimental evaluations can mistakably make compensatory education look harmful. In J. Hellmuter (Ed.), *The disadvantaged child* (Vol. 3). New York: Brunner/Mazel, 1970.

Darlington, R.B. The consortium for longitudinal studies. *Educational Evaluation and Policy Analysis,* 1981, *3,* 37-45.

Datta, L. Another spring and other hopes: Some findings from National Education of Project Head Start. In E. Zigler & J. Valentine (Eds.), *Project Head Start.* New York: Free Press, 1979.

Dennenberg, V.H. Critical periods, stimulus input and emotional reactivity: A theory of infantile stimulation. *Psychological Review,* 1964, *71,* 335-351.

Gallagher, J., Haskins, R., & Farran, D. Poverty and public policy. In T.B. Brazelton & M. Vaughn (Eds.), *The family: Setting priorities.* New York: Science and Medicine Publishing Company, in press.

Garland, C., Stone, N.W., Swanson, J., & Woodruff, G. *Early intervention for children with special needs and their families.* Monmouth, OR: Western States Technical Assistance Resource, 1981.

Gray, S.W., & Wandersman, C.P. The methodology of home-based intervention studies: Problems and promising strategies. *Child Development,* 1980, *51,* 993-1009.

Horowitz, F., & Paden, L. The effectiveness of environmental progress. In B. Caldwell & H.N. Riccuiti (Eds.), *Review of child development research* (Vol. 3). Chicago: University of Chicago Press, 1973.

Hunt, J. McV. *Intelligence and experience.* New York: Ronald Press, 1961.

Jencks, C. *Inequality.* New York: Basic Books, 1972.

Jensen, A.R. How much can we boost IQ and scholastic achievement? *Harvard Educational Review,* 1969, *39,* 1-123.

Karnes, M.B., Schwedel, A.M., Lewis, G.F., Ratts, D.A., & Esry, D.R. Impact of early programming for the handicapped: A follow up study into the elementary school. *Early Childhood*, 1981, *4*, 62-79.

Kirk, S.A. *Early education of the mentally retarded.* Urbana, IL: University of Illinois Press, 1958.

Kirk, S.A. Diagnostic, cultural, and remedial factors in mental retardation. In S.F.Osler & R.E.Cooke (Eds.), *The biosocial basis of mental retardation.* Baltimore: The Johns Hopkins Press, 1965.

Kirschner Associates, Inc. *A national survey of the parent child center program.* Prepared for Project Head Start, Office of Child Development. Washington, DC: Government Printing Office, 1970.

Lasting effects after preschool (Final report of HEW Grant 90C-1311). Denver: Education Commission of the States, 1979.

Lazar, I., & Darlington, R. Lasting effects of early education: A report from the consortium for longitudinal studies. Monographs of the Society for Research in Child Development, 1982, No. 195.

Lazar, I., Hubbell, R., Murray, H., Rosche, M., & Royce, J. *Preliminary findings of the developmental continuity longitudinal study.* Paper presented at the office of Child Development's Parents, Children, and Continuity conference, El Paso, 1977.

Levine, S. Infantile experience and resistance to physiological stress. *Science,* 1957, *126,* 405.

MacRae, D., Jr., & Wilde, J. *Policy analysis for public decisions.* North Scituate, MA: Duxbury Press, 1979.

Maeroff, G.I. After 15 years, a Harlem experiment is reappraised. *New York Times,* 1981, pp. 15/17.

Nocera, J. Learning from Lourdes. *The Washington Monthly,* 1982, *12,* 32-36.

Peters, D.L. Social science and social policy and the care of young children: Head Start and after. *Journal of Applied Developmental Psychology,* 1980, *1,* 7-27.

Provence, S., Naylor, A., & Patterson, J. *The challenge of day care.* New Haven, CT: Yale University Press, 1977.

Rescorla, L.A., & Zigler, E. The Yale Welfare Research Program: Implications for social policy. *Educational Evaluation and Policy Analysis,* 1981, *3,* 5-14.

Rhinegold, H.L. The modification of social responsiveness in motivational babies. *Monographs of the Society for Research in Child Development,* 1956, (*2,* Serial No. 63).

Ryan, S. (Ed.). *Longitudinal evaluations: Vol. 1: A report on longitudinal evaluations of preschool programs.* DHEW pub. no. (DHD) 74-24. Office of Child Development, 1974 (ED093500).

Salkind, N.J., & Haskins, R.T. The impact of the negative income tax on the family. *Journal of Family Issues,* in press.

Schweinhart, L.J., & Weikart, D.P. Effects of the Perry preschool program on youths through age 15. *Early Childhood,* 1981, *4,* 29-39.

Shipman, V.C. *Notable early characteristics of high and low achieving black low-SES children.* Princeton, NJ: Educational Testing Service, 1976.

Skeels, H.M. Status of children with contrasting early life experiences. *Monographs of the Society for Research in Child Development,* 1966, *31* (No. 105).

Skeels, H.M., & Dye, H.B. A study of the effects of differential stimulation on mentally retarded children. *Proceedings and Addresses of the American Association on Mental Deficiency,* 1939, *4,* 114-130.

Skeels, H.M., Updegraff, R., Wellman, B.L., & Williams, H.M. A study of environmental stimulation: An orphanage preschool project. *University of Iowa Studies in Child Welfare,* 1938, *15,* 7-191.

Strain, P.S. Conceptual and methodological issues in efficacy research with behaviorally disordered children. *Early Childhood,* 1981, *4,* 111-124.

Weber, C.V., Foster, P.W., & Weikart, D.P. An economic analysis of the Ypsilanti Perry Preschool project. *Monographs of the High/Scope Educational Research Foundation*, 1978, No. 4.

Westinghouse Learning Corporation. *The impact of Head Start: An evaluation of the affects of Head Start on children's cognitive and affective development*. Executive Summary, Ohio University, Athens, Ohio, 1969.

Zigler, E., & Anderson, K. An idea whose time had come: The intellectual and political climate. In E. Zigler & J. Valentine (Eds.), *Project Head Start*. New York: Free Press, 1979.

Zigler, E., & Trickett, P.K. IQ, social competence, and evaluation of early childhood intervention programs. *American Psychologist*, 1978, *33*, 789-798.

Zigler, E., & Valentine, J. *Project Head Start*. New York: Free Press, 1979.

Chapter 11

Protecting the Preschooler and the Practitioner: Legal Issues in Early Childhood Programs

Jan B. Sheldon

Ted Anderson, who has been the director of a preschool for 18 months, just had a talk with 4-year-old Kerry's parents. Because Kerry is so withdrawn, the staff at the preschool had decided to make a concentrated effort to involve Kerry in social activities with other children. Consequently, they had not emphasized his pre-academic skills. Kerry's parents, however, informed Ted that they are not at all worried about Kerry's ability to get along with others—"that will come *naturally* with time." They have instructed Ted and his staff to concentrate on Kerry's preacademic skills so that he will excel when he starts school. Ted knows that he and the other staff members have the ability to do this, but he is afraid of what might happen to Kerry if they put all their efforts into his preacademic skills. To whom is the staff responsible? What do they ethically "owe" Kerry, and what do they "owe" his parents?

Four-year-old Jenny was climbing on a jungle gym one spring afternoon at Sunny Acres Preschool. Two of the bolts holding a crossbar were loose. As Jenny swung from the crossbar, the bolts fell out and the bar dropped. Jenny fell several feet to the hard earth below, dislocating her collarbone. As she lay there screaming in pain, the teachers looked accusingly at one another. Several had known the bolts were loose; none had taken the responsibility for having them tightened. Would this accident have been prevented if the teachers had had the jungle gym repaired? Do teachers have a legal responsibility to detect unsafe conditions and repair dangerous equipment and to ensure that children are not allowed near the equipment until it is in proper condition?

Another accident had occurred days earlier when several children had been playing on the playground. Most of the teachers were on one side of the play-

---

This chapter offers general legal guidance for early education professionals. For specific legal problems, a lawyer should be consulted.

ground, attending to Kevin, who was crying because he had not been allowed to join in a game of hide-and-seek. Just at that time, Leslie, who was with a group of children on the other side of the playground, threw a rock. Unfortunately, the rock hit 3-year-old John and made a large cut over his eye. Hearing his screams, the teachers hurried over, each feeling that it was the other's responsibility to have been supervising the children. Why had all the teachers been in one area, together, leaving a large group of children unsupervised? If a teacher had been in the vicinity, could the accident have been prevented?

Mary Johnson, the director of ABC Preschool, believes that a good swat on the bottom at appropriate times can keep most children in line. One day, Mary observed 4-year-old James taking 3-year-old Jean's toy. When Jean would not voluntarily give it up, James knocked her down and ran off with the toy. Mary immediately went over to James and gave him a couple of swats and a lecture about taking other children's toys. She asked if James understood why he was spanked, and he nodded that he did. Mary was surprised when she received a call that night from James' parents, who were quite upset that Mary had ''beat on'' James that afternoon. James' father, an attorney, let Mary know that he thought her behavior might constitute an act of battery and essentially told her that, if she ever did that again, he would ''slap her with a lawsuit.'' Mary hung up the telephone in disbelief. In her 15 years of teaching, no one had challenged her disciplinary techniques. Could it really be true that someone could sue her for engaging in what she felt was a time-tested practice?

Carrie was 3 years old, small for her age, diagnosed as developmentally disabled, and very shy and withdrawn, although quite likeable. Her mother had enrolled her in a day care facility three months earlier when Carrie and her family had moved into town. The teachers had made great progress in ''bringing Carrie out of her shell'' and in teaching her some basic self-help skills, but one big problem remained. From the first day Carrie had arrived at the day care center, the teachers had noticed large bruises, welts, and cuts on her back, legs, stomach, and arms. Once Carrie had appeared with a black eye. Carrie's mother always brought up the matter of Carrie's bruises, stating that Carrie was accident-prone, but many of the teachers suspected that one of Carrie's parents was abusing her. They were reluctant to report it, however, for fear that Carrie would be removed from the center. Furthermore, if their guesses were wrong, how could they face Carrie's mother again—what would they say to her? One day Carrie did not come to the center. That night, the teachers were shocked, saddened, and guilt-ridden to read in the newspaper that Carrie had been found dead—beaten to death. Carrie's stepfather was being held on charges of voluntary manslaughter. What legal and ethical responsibilities did these teachers have? Should they have reported the suspected abuse to the authorities? Are they legally liable for not having done so? More importantly, could they have saved Carrie's life by reporting the suspected abuse?

These examples illustrate only a few of the problems that preschool and child care teachers may face. Some are more unusual than others, but none are uncommon; they have occurred in child care and preschool settings in the past. With the current emphasis on accountability, however, the potential for lawsuits is much greater than it has ever been. Consumers are demanding quality goods and services; courts and legislatures are mandating them. With the emphasis on providing effective programs and safeguarding individual rights, it is not surprising that the field of human services is coming under both public and judicial scrutiny. No one is exempt. Professionals in early education programs, who have assumed that they enjoyed immunity from lawsuits, must now be aware of the legal issues that arise daily in the operation of their activities. Administrators and teachers in the early education field must be well-informed of their potential liability and educated in ways to avoid ... ming, expensive, and damaging

... al and day care experiences.

... al pitfalls and offers practical

... ication programs.

... ation of an early education

... ed in determining what type

... t-for-profit, sole proprietor-

... ure contract, tax, licensing,

... Administrators should also

... aspects involved in ensur-

... pics (e.g., Aikman, 1977;

... ld seek professional legal

... es on the issue of legal

... to another person; legal

... legal liability in an early

... m of careless or heedless

... 1971). Generally, negli-

... nd careful person would

... The concept of legal

... behaved negligently to

... nce. A legal cause of

... ur elements be proved

... , that requires a person

... able risks or harm.

2. There must be a failure on the part of the person to conform his or her conduct to the standard required.
3. A close causal connection must exist between the conduct and the resulting injury.
4. There must be actual loss or damage to another person.

All four elements must be proved before one person can recover compensation from another. Such a claim would be called a tort claim, which essentially means that a civil, rather than a criminal, wrong has taken place.

In a professional child care setting, it is not difficult to determine that a duty exists. Those who represent themselves as able to care for young children have a duty to do so properly. Adams and Taylor (1981) have identified three origins of this duty. There is the voluntary assumption of a duty; people working in early education programs assume certain legal responsibilities to care for the children properly that would not be imposed on the average person. Thus, certain types of screening and training may be needed to ensure that preschool or day care personnel can provide proper care for the children. There are also duties that are required by statute. For example, certain laws or regulations may require a minimum number of teachers for a certain number of children, or they may require compliance with certain health and safety rules. The third origin of a duty is that which is inherent in the situation. Adams and Taylor (1981) specified that there are two types in this category: "those arising from interpersonal relationships between the child care leader and the child, and those which are administrative in nature" (p. 16). In interpersonal relationships, the child care leader functions much like a parent (*in loco parentis*) and is, therefore, responsible for protecting the child. Unlike the parent, however, the child care leader must respond as a reasonable and prudent professional trained in this field would respond. Finally, the administrative duty requires that the child care leader provide a setting and facilities that are safe and relatively danger-free.

As mentioned previously, because child care leaders are professionals, they will be held to a standard of care that is higher than that the average person must meet. A child care professional is not required to ensure safety, however, but only to act as a reasonable and prudent child care professional would act in similar situations. When working with mentally or physically handicapped children, an even greater degree of care is required because of the children's mental and physical limitations. The teacher-student relationship has been found to be a special one, with teachers owing students adequate supervision, proper instruction, and the exercise of good judgment (*Buttorf v. Waltz*[1]). If harm is foreseeable, the child care professional will generally be held liable if an accident occurs; if an injury that is

---

1. 369 A.2d 332 (Pa. Super. 1976).

unforeseeable occurs, liability generally will not be imposed. It must be kept in mind that acts of omission as well as commission can result in liability. Thus, for example, failure to use the best professional judgment in supervising activities or children, maintaining equipment, selecting activities, or caring for injuries can be considered a failure to conform to the proper standard of care.

A causal relationship between the failure to conform to the required standard of care and the injury that has occurred must be demonstrated. When accidents occur because the equipment is defective or because the facility is dangerous, it is normally not difficult to prove that there is a causal connection between the defect and the resulting injury. In other situations, the causal relationship may be more difficult to demonstrate. If, for example, an accident occurs when a teacher is not present or is not supervising an activity, it may be difficult to prove that the accident would not have occurred had the teacher been present and supervising the activity. This would be a question of fact for a jury to determine.

The final element is often the easiest to prove: resulting loss or damage to a person. Usually, it can be readily determined whether a child has been injured or hurt. The question that arises is the amount of damage that has occurred.

CRIMINAL LIABILITY

In some instances, there is a possibility of criminal charges being brought against a child care professional. For example, a teacher who spanked a child, using "too much force," might be charged with the crime of battery. In addition, some statutes require child care professionals to behave in certain ways. The professional's failure to comply with the requirements of the statute may constitute a criminal offense. For example, most states have child abuse reporting laws that require those professionals who work with children to report any suspected child abuse. Failure to do so may constitute, for example, a misdemeanor.

VIOLATION OF A STATUTORY REQUIREMENT

Violation of some state or federal laws pertaining to child care programs is not a criminal offense, but prohibits the center from receiving state or federal funds. For example, if a child care facility is providing education to handicapped children and is receiving funds under the federal Education for All Handicapped Children Act, the facility is required to have an individualized education program for all the children. Failure to comply with this requirement does not constitute a criminal violation, but means that the center cannot receive government funds under this act.

DETERMINATION OF RESPONSIBILITY

The issue of liability raises the concurrent issue of responsibility. Obviously, each individual teacher or child care professional is responsible for his or her own acts. Thus, a teacher can be held liable when an injury results from that teacher's negligent behavior. Administrators can be held liable for any negligent administrative acts, e.g., inadequate supervision, inadequate maintenance of equipment or of the playground, the establishment of rules or regulations that are inappropriate, or the failure to maintain safe conditions.

Administrators can also be held liable, under the doctrine of *respondeat superior,* for the negligent acts of an employee if the employee was acting within the scope of employment. Under this doctrine, an employer can be held vicariously liable for the negligent acts of an employee, since the law assumes that the employee is acting under the direction and control of the employer. The phrase *within the scope of employment* refers to those acts that are connected with what the employee was hired to do. As Prosser (1971) stated, an employee's conduct is within the scope of his or her employment if "it is of the kind which he [or she] is employed to perform, occurs substantially within the authorized limits of time and space, and is activated, at least in part, by a purpose to serve the [employer]" (p. 461). Thus, if a cook injured a child while preparing hot soup, the director of the child care facility might be held liable, since the cook was performing that duty within the scope of his or her employment. If, however, the cook attempted to care for a child's broken arm and in the process further injured the child, the administrator would most likely not be held liable, since the cook was acting outside the scope of employment (i.e., not on the advice of the administrator).

Adams and Taylor (1981) pointed out a third level of responsibility—the board of directors or owners of the child care facility who set policy. Their liability would extend to negligent policies, rules, or regulations that are set by the board or owner. In addition, the board of directors or owners may be liable for an employee's actions if the employee is acting as an agent of the board or owner at the time of the tortious conduct.

Defenses can be raised in response to liability actions (Adams & Taylor, 1981; Aikman, 1977; Prosser, 1971). It should be noted, however, that privately owned and for-profit child care facilities are often exposed to greater liability than are city-, county-, or state-operated not-for-profit facilities because of the doctrine of sovereign immunity. In the past, this common law doctrine provided that the government could not be sued (since the government was comprised of the people, the people could not sue themselves), thus protecting government-operated services. This doctrine has been eroded, however, and several states have done away with the doctrine (by statute). Thus, all child care facilities would do well to investigate the possibility of obtaining liability insurance and to contact an attorney if a question or problem arises.

Potential Problem Areas in Operating a Child Care Facility

Legal liability can arise in almost any situation, especially one that involves young children. Unlike adults, children do not have the reasoning ability to comprehend dangerous situations and cannot assume part of the risk that may be inherent, yet obvious, in certain situations. Furthermore, they are not as physically capable of protecting themselves from injury. Consequently, those professionals who work with small children must protect them. Although most of the cases cited here arose in elementary or secondary schools, the principles involved are applicable to early education programs as well. If the preschoolers are handicapped, an even higher standard of care will be required because these children are even more dependent on adult caregivers.

Failure To Supervise Children Prudently

Negligence is found in early educational programs most commonly as a result of failing to supervise the children properly. Although child care teachers and administrators are not required to ensure that all children will be safe at all times, they must act prudently in order to protect children from foreseeable harm (VanBiervliet & Sheldon-Wildgen, 1981).

There are many situations in which a court might find that there was a lack of proper supervision. If children are involved in an activity that is potentially dangerous and the teacher does not intervene to stop the activity, the court may impose liability on both the teacher and child care facility. In a California case, a teacher and school district were held liable for failure to supervise the students properly (*Lilienthal v. San Leandro Unified School District*[2]). In this case, while the students who were enrolled in a metal class were outdoors, one student started throwing a knife into the ground. Although the teacher was present and observed the knife throwing, the teacher did nothing to stop it. On one throw, the knife struck a drawing board and was deflected into another student's eye. An appellate court found both the teacher and the school district guilty of negligence. Thus, if children are engaged in a dangerous activity, such as throwing rocks, jumping off high places, or running into the street (even if it is against the commands of the teacher), the child care professional has an affirmative duty to stop the activity and, therefore, prevent an injury. Teachers must do more than merely warn preschool children about a dangerous activity; they must actively intervene to stop it.

Other problems may arise if no teacher is present to supervise children. The courts have developed various tests to determine liability when a teacher is not present. For example, the more dangerous the activity, the more careful the

---

2. 293 P.2d 889 (Cal. Ct. App. 1956).

supervision must be (*Christofides v. Hellenic Eastern Orthodox Christian Church*[3]). Other considerations include determining whether the injury would have occurred if a teacher had been present (*Albers v. Independent School District No. 302*[4]; see VanBiervliet & Sheldon-Wildgen, 1981) or whether the possibility of injury without a teacher's presence was reasonably foreseeable (*Sheehan v. St. Peter's Catholic School*[5]). Although it is important to consider the foreseeability of danger as well as the degree of danger, it seems unlikely that there would be many instances in which injury would not be foreseeable if preschoolers were left alone. Thus, child care professionals would be well-advised to have at least one teacher present with preschool children at all times.

This, obviously, raises the issue of staffing; the presence of too few staff for too many children may result in injury and liability. Child care facilities should definitely abide by state statutes or regulations that require a certain number of teachers for a certain number of children. There may be some situations, however, in which the number of teachers should be increased. If, for example, the children are going on a field trip and could get lost, wander off, or be exposed to harm, more teachers should accompany them to provide the appropriate amount of supervision. In addition, if the child care facility is for handicapped children, the administrator may want to increase the number of staff.

Courts have been quick to impose liability when teachers or supervisors had previous knowledge of a child's tendency to engage in a dangerous activity if left unsupervised, even if it was against the teachers' orders. In one case, a mentally retarded youth who was known to have a tendency to pull his wagon in the street when going anywhere was hit and killed by a car as he pulled his wagon, full of records, home after a dance one night. The court held that, since the staff knew of the youth's tendency to walk in the street, the staff had breached its obligation to supervise him properly; the court felt that someone should have accompanied him home (*Daniels v. Connecticut*[6]). Thus, if a teacher knows that a child is likely to run into the street rather than to wait at the curb, the teacher has an affirmative duty to restrain the child.

Likewise, if it is foreseeable that a child could harm another child, the court will impose strict standards of supervision on the staff. A child who hits other children or who throws objects at others, for example, may have to be more carefully supervised than a child who does not regularly engage in such behavior. Once again, the foreseeability of the harm is a critical issue in determining the amount of teacher supervision required (see, e.g., *Abille v. United States*,[7] *Becton v. United*

---

3. 227 N.Y.S. 2d 946 (1962).
4. 487 P.2d 936 (Idaho Sup. Ct. 1971).
5. 188 N.W. 2d 868 (Minn. Sup. Ct. 1971).
6. 378 So. 2d 451 (La. Ct. App. 1979).
7. 482 F. Supp. 703 (N.D. Cal. 1980).

States,[8] *Bohrer v. County of San Diego,*[9] *Castello v. United States,*[10] *Frank v. Utah,*[11] *Smith v. United States*[12]).

Failure To Maintain Facilities and Equipment Properly

Administrators and teachers have an affirmative duty to inspect the facility (e.g., classroom and playground) and the equipment, and to keep them in repair and in safe working order (VanBiervliet & Sheldon-Wildgen, 1981). The question of how frequently these inspections should be made has not been answered. In most child care facilities, the classroom and playground are used daily; therefore, teachers have an opportunity to observe frequently the condition of the facility and the equipment. Thus, general inspections might be made daily, with more careful inspections made less frequently. If the staff has an idea of the approximate frequency with which certain items need repair, that length of time can be used as an indicator of how often inspections should be made. In any event, when a staff member sees that some part of the facility or some item of equipment is dangerous, the staff member should notify the proper persons and steps should be taken to remedy the situation.

Several court cases in this area have involved situations in which the school knew, or should have known, that a potentially hazardous condition existed (see, e.g., *Kidwell v. School District No. 300, Whitman County,*[13] *Nicholson v. Board of Education of the City of New York*[14]). Examples are numerous, but common ones include storage of materials or equipment in such a manner that a child might be harmed if the child went to use the items, improper fencing of a playground, use of equipment that is not properly secured to the wall or ground, or entrances, exits, and stairs that are not properly lighted or are dangerous to young children.

Any staff member who observes a dangerous or defective situation should be required to notify a supervisor formally. Often, staff are asked to make this notification both verbally and in writing to ensure that no question will subsequently arise about the notification. One staff supervisor should be made responsible for regularly inspecting the premises and the equipment and for ensuring that all repairs are made within a reasonable time. This supervisor should have a checklist of items that need to be regularly inspected: all electrical appliances,

8. 489 F. Supp. 134 (D. Mass. 1980).

9. 163 Cal. Rptr 419 (Cal. Ct. App. 1980).

10. 552 F.2d 1385 (10th Cir. 1977).

11. 613 P.2d 517 (Utah Sup. Ct. 1980).

12. 437 F. Supp. 1004 (E.D.Pa. 1977).

13. 335 P.2d 805 (Wash. Sup. Ct. 1959).

14. 330 N.E. 2d 651 (N.Y. App. Ct. 1975).

equipment, and outlets; all outdoor equipment; all fire safety equipment; and all areas or equipment that might be potentially dangerous.

If an area is found to be dangerous or if some equipment is in disrepair, the situation should be remedied as quickly as possible. Since many conditions cannot be changed overnight, staff should be made aware of the danger so that they can keep children out of the dangerous area or away from the dangerous equipment. The dangerous situation should be remedied as quickly as possible, however, since failure to do so may constitute negligence on the part of the child care facility. Dangerous pieces of equipment or dangerous areas are regarded, legally, as attractive nuisances. For example, a jungle gym that has some loose bolts or a swimming pool with a slippery floor may present dangers to preschool children. When a person or facility maintains such an attractive nuisance, especially for long periods of time, courts have imposed liability for any injuries that occur. Therefore, although repairs need not be made immediately, they should be made fairly quickly or the defective item should be completely removed.

Failure To Care for Injuries Properly

In any situation, accidents and injuries can occur. In the event of an accident, child care staff must ensure that they provide the proper medical treatment to an injured child and, in nonemergency situations, that they refer the child to or summon the proper medical authority. Although most people are under no legal obligation to help an injured person, the relationship between the child care worker and the child is such a special one (because the child is dependent on the adult) that an implied duty is often held to exist (VanBiervliet & Sheldon-Wildgen, 1981). It is presumed that a teacher will act in a prudent manner to help an injured child. Failure to do so might constitute negligence on the part of the teacher. Thus, for example, failure to take an injured preschooler from the playground and to provide proper care might easily constitute negligence, as the court decided in *Ogando v. Carquinez Grammar School District*.[15] In that case, a child who was playing on the playground ran her arm through a glass pane in a door, severing an artery. The girl, being confused, ran around the playground screaming until another student took her to the nurse's office. The nurse stopped the bleeding and called a doctor; the girl was taken to the hospital, where she died from a loss of blood. The teachers and school district were held liable for failing to supervise the playground properly and, therefore, for failing to care for the girl's injury properly.

Teachers should be trained in proper nonemergency first aid procedures and should be instructed to help any child who is sick or injured *immediately*. Teachers, however, should not attempt to treat those injuries that require the

---

15. 75 P.2d 641 (Cal. App. Ct. 1964).

expertise of a medical professional. Although a teacher may not be liable for the accident that produced an injury, once the teacher intervenes and attempts to help, failure to do so in a prudent and reasonable manner can result in liability being imposed. Therefore, it appears that teachers have a professional duty to aid injured or sick children promptly, but they must do so with some caution. If it appears that the child should not be moved, the teacher should summon professional medical help immediately. For those cases that do not require professional medical treatment, prompt attention should be given. In any event, if the help given causes further harm, the teacher and child care center can be held liable.

Staff should be aware that trained medical professionals should be called in for any care required beyond first aid. Teachers have been found liable for attempting to dispense medical treatment when they were not qualified to do so. Furthermore, teachers who provide unnecessary treatment in a nonemergency situation run the risk that the treatment itself will cause an injury. In *Guerrier v. Tyson,*[16] for example, two teachers attempted to treat a boy's infected finger. Although the finger did not require emergency treatment, the teachers insisted on immersing the finger into scalding water for ten minutes, despite the boy's protests. Subsequently, the boy had to be hospitalized for severe burns. The court found the teachers guilty of negligence for administering a treatment that was likely to produce further injury, especially in a nonemergency situation that did not call for immediate action on the part of the teachers.

If an early educational program has a nurse in its employ, that nurse must behave in a reasonable and prudent manner to provide the best type of treatment possible. Thus, all judgment decisions and all treatment administered by this nurse must conform to the normal standard of treatment expected of other nurses in the community, especially nurses practicing in school settings.

Each child care center should establish set procedures to follow in case of accidents and emergencies. First, the center should have an emergency medical treatment authorization form signed by each parent that allows the center staff to obtain emergency treatment for the child in the event it is necessary and the parent cannot be reached. The child's physician should be listed on this form. If the parents are unwilling to consent to emergency medical treatment (perhaps for religious reasons), they should be required to sign a form stating that (1) they are unwilling to have their child receive emergency medical treatment and (2) they agree to release the center from any liability for damages that might be incurred from a failure to receive proper medical treatment. (This does not relieve the center from liability that might be imposed for an accident that occurred as a result of a teacher's negligence.) Parents should also be required to fill out a form specifying the address and telephone number of the place where they can be contacted in the event of an emergency, in addition to a list of the names and telephone numbers of

---

16. 24 A.2d 468 (Pa. 1942).

other persons who should be notified if the parents or guardians cannot be contacted.

Finally, in the emergency procedures, the center should specify the steps to be taken in different types of emergencies. For example, if the injury is serious and it is felt that the child should not be moved, an ambulance should be called immediately and parents or guardians notified at once. If the injury is serious but it is felt that the child can be transported, the parents should be called, informed of the situation, and asked to meet the center's personnel at the hospital or doctor's office. If the injury does not need *immediate* attention, the parents should be called and informed of the nature of the injury, and asked to take responsibility for obtaining appropriate medical treatment (Treadwell, 1980). For minor scrapes or cuts, the necessary first aid should be provided and the parents informed of exactly what happened when they pick up the child. Each child care center should keep a precise log of all accidents and the center's responses to those accidents.

Failure To Care for Sick Children Properly

Child care facilities, especially those that provide full-day care, are often faced with children who are ill. Since many working parents depend on the day care centers for daily care, most centers attempt to be as flexible as possible without unnecessarily exposing other children to illnesses and aggravating the sick child's condition. Preschools, on the other hand, may be less willing to accept a child on days when the child is sick. In any event, the child care facility should develop a written statement explicitly detailing the center's policy on sick children, and this statement should be given to parents when they enroll their child so that future problems can be avoided and parents can make the necessary arrangements for their child on days when the child is ill.

Treadwell (1980) has listed some questions that should be considered in deciding what type of policy is best for a particular facility. First, Treadwell suggested that the facility administrator consider whether the facility is capable of caring for mildly sick children: Is there a safe, comfortable area that is somewhat isolated so that other children will not be exposed to infectious diseases? How many sick children can be cared for at one time? What is the relationship between the facility and the families that it serves? For example, if the facility is a small one (perhaps operating in someone's home) with an informal, flexible policy, day care providers may feel a stronger obligation to care for sick children than if they operated a large day care center with relatively formal relations with the families. In any event, the obligation to care for sick children must always be weighed against the obligation to protect the other children from exposure to illnesses, especially serious ones. If a child has the mumps, measles, or chickenpox, for example, it is probably unwise to attempt to care for the child at the center. The potential risk of liability is much greater than the benefits to that one family.

All child care personnel should review their state regulations to determine what their state licensing board requires with respect to sick children. Many states mandate that early education facilities perform daily health checks of the children. Often, the regulations state that, if a child shows signs of an illness, the staff should attempt to determine the nature of the illness, isolate the child from other children, and contact the parents or guardian. If the illness appears to be serious, parents and medical personnel designated by the parents should be contacted immediately.

The center definitely needs an established written policy regarding the administration of medication to children. If the center staff are to administer medication, they must have legal authority to do so; this legal authority can be obtained by having the parents give their *written* permission, which is signed and dated, for the staff to administer medication to their child. Treadwell (1980) has provided a medication authorization form that she suggested parents should be required to fill out before any medication is administered.

If the center staff are to administer medication, they should be given the original container with the medication in it. The container should have the name of the medication on it, the child's name, the dosage to be given, and the times of administration. In addition, the parents should fill out a form specifying the same information, the date, the manner in which the medication should be administered, and the length of time it should be given. All medications should be kept out of the reach of children, and a specific record should be kept noting any medication that was administered, the time it was administered, and the amount (Treadwell, 1980).

Finally, child care administrators may require that the parents agree to abide by certain written rules regarding illness and medication before they will accept a child into the program. For example, the parents may be asked to agree to inform the child care personnel if the child has been ill during the last 24 hours or if any member of the child's family has had a contagious or communicable disease.

Failure To Supervise Field Trips and School Outings Properly

Children normally love to go on field trips. These outings, however, can expose an early education center to a great deal of liability because of the varied risks. For example, transportation accidents can occur, and children can get lost.

Here again, the center should have a written policy on the procedures to be followed on field trips. If field trips are to be part of the child care center's curriculum, parents should be notified of this in writing before they enroll their child. Parents should then be asked to read and sign a field trip permission form (Treadwell, 1980), indicating that they have been notified in advance that field trips are part of the program and that they allow their child to go. The center should use discretion with parents who refuse to allow their children to go on field trips. Some centers do not accept children whose parents will not allow them to participate in school outings, because they feel that these school outings are an important part of the early education program, because the children would feel left out, and because there is no one to care for these children while the rest of the staff is on the outing. Other centers are willing to make exceptions on a case-by-case basis.

Even if parents sign a general consent form allowing their children to go on supervised field trips, they should be notified immediately prior to each field trip. The parents should be told where the field trip is to be taken, what the purpose of the trip is, who will be accompanying the children, and approximately how long they will be gone. It is best to have parents sign another consent form for each trip. Although some authors (e.g., Treadwell, 1980) suggest that parents be asked to sign a waiver of liability form, these forms are not always upheld in court, since center staff cannot protect themselves from liability for their own negligence by having parents waive liability. These forms are useful, however, when an accident occurs that is unforeseeable and does not result from negligence, and the center does not have accident insurance. The court may uphold the waiver of liability, since no negligence was involved.

Once on the field trip, teachers must use extreme care to protect the children from any foreseeable injuries and should be constantly on guard against any unforeseeable injuries. These teachers have a duty to safeguard the children, and this duty may be even greater on a field trip where children are in strange and unknown places.

When child care facilities transport children, especially to and from field trips, they can be held liable for any injury that occurs during the transportation. Clearly, therefore, child care facilities should carry automobile liability insurance that protects all staff when they are transporting children. Even with this insurance, VanBiervliet and Sheldon-Wildgen (1981) have identified some procedures that should be followed and issues to be considered when planning transportation for children. All drivers must be licensed, have a good driving record, and be known as safe and cautious motorists; they must be insured. Courts have often held that school bus drivers must exhibit and exercise an extraordinarily high degree of care when the safety of the children being transported is involved (see, e.g., *Davidson v. Horne,*[17] *Van Cleave v. Illini Coach Co.*[18]). The automobiles that are used must be in safe running order with no known dangerous defects. They should be regularly inspected so that hazardous defects can be discovered and repaired. The center must take all reasonable precautions to protect the children from foreseeable harm caused by automobile defects (Prosser, 1971).

---

17. 71 S.E. 2d 464 (Ga. Ct. App. 1952).

18. 100 N.E. 2d 398 (Ill. App. Ct. 1951).

An employee using one of the child care center's cars is protected under the center's liability insurance only when the employee is using the car for the center's business. Thus, if an employee takes several children on a field trip and, in returning, decides to stop at a food market for that night's dinner, any accident that occurs on the side trip would most likely not be covered under the center's insurance policy. If the employee were found to be acting outside the scope of employment, the employee would be solely liable for any injuries that may occur.

Many accidents occur while children are boarding or disembarking from school vehicles, and most school transportation accidents that result in lawsuits happen during this time (National Education Association Research Division, 1963). Thus, child care administrators must develop strict procedures for getting in and out of school vehicles (or vehicles used for school purposes) as well as for governing the conduct of the children while riding in the car, van, or bus. These procedures must be consistently and strictly enforced. In addition, most states have requirements specifying the number of children who can be allowed to ride in each vehicle and the number of adults who must accompany them in the vehicle. These rules, as well as any rules regarding the use of seat belts or child restraints, *must be followed*.

Finally, child care facility administrators should never allow a child to ride in a staff member's or parent's personal car for a school outing unless the administrators know that (1) the person has an excellent driving record and is a safe and cautious driver, (2) the car is in good repair, and (3) the driver is fully covered by a comprehensive automobile insurance policy. A staff member or parent who has an accident while transporting a child on a school function can be held liable for any damages that may be incurred. Furthermore, the child care center may also be held liable if it is determined that the center was negligent in allowing the child to ride with someone who did not have the necessary qualifications.

DISCIPLINARY MEASURES

All children, at one time or another, misbehave. There are a number of reasons for misbehavior: for example, the child may be immature and want his or her own way; the child may enjoy the attention that misbehavior produces; the child may not feel well on a particular day and is, therefore, grumpy or grouchy; or the child may have been unconsciously reinforced in the past for misbehavior. Although it is important to attempt to determine the cause of these inappropriate behaviors, it is equally, if not more so, important to attempt to eliminate them. The key here is to find an effective, yet ethically humane way to handle inappropriate behaviors. (See Chapter 2 in Allen and Goetz, 1982, for additional information about these procedures.)

Positive Reinforcement of Alternative or Incompatible Behaviors

One of the most benign techniques for eliminating undesirable behaviors is the use of positive reinforcement (both social praise and tangible reinforcement). Several studies (e.g., Lovaas, Freitag, Gold, & Kassoria, 1965; Watson & Tharp, 1972) have demonstrated that inappropriate behaviors can be decreased by differentially responding to alternative, appropriate behaviors, especially those that are incompatible with the undesirable behaviors. Two legal and ethical considerations must be addressed in regard to this technique, however. First, the behavior to be decreased should not be life-threatening or extremely harmful to either the child or others in the child care setting, since it may take a long time to eliminate the problem behavior by means of this technique. Second, the alternative or substitute behavior to be reinforced should be one that most parents, teachers, and community members agree is an appropriate behavior. For example, a problem was presented when Rekers and Lovaas (1974) sought to "normalize" a young boy's sex role behavior. Although both reinforcement and punishment (response cost) techniques were used, the main ethical problem that was subsequently raised by Nordyke, Baer, Etzel, and LeBlanc (1977) concerned not the procedures used, but rather the target behaviors. Thus, early education teachers must look beyond their own social and moral values and determine what is best for a particular individual. One method of obtaining that information is by consulting other parents and professionals in the community.

Extinction (Ignoring the Behavior)

Another popular technique used to eliminate inappropriate behavior is a procedure called extinction, i.e., the discontinuation of reinforcement (usually social reinforcement) for a specific inappropriate behavior. Once again, this appears to be a fairly benign type of procedure to use in a child care setting. If the behavior that is to be eliminated with extinction can cause severe harm to the child exhibiting the behavior or to other children in the area, this may not be the procedure of choice, however. Like positive reinforcement of alternative behaviors, extinction often requires a long time before the frequency of the inappropriate behavior is decreased. For example, Lovaas and Simmons (1969) found that, although extinction appeared to eliminate self-destructive behavior in retarded children, the extinction procedure required so much time to produce beneficial results that the children were exposed to a considerable amount of pain and discomfort. In fact, it appeared that one child would have mutilated herself and died before the extinction procedure would have proved successful.

Extinction is a difficult procedure for an entire child care staff to follow. It is easy for one staff member periodically to forget that a certain behavior should be ignored, and intermittent reinforcement of an inappropriate behavior has proved to be a powerful technique in maintaining the inappropriate behavior. In addition, child care staff are not the only ones who reinforce inappropriate behaviors. Other children and even parents may attend to an inappropriate behavior that the staff has worked hard to eliminate—only to see it increase in frequency. Finally, even when extinction is used consistently, there may be an increase in the undesirable behavior before it is eliminated. Staff must be prepared for this so that they do not become discouraged and give up on the extinction program.

Although many problems are associated with the use of extinction, it remains an ethically sound and legally justified procedure for use in an early education program. Staff should ensure, however, that they provide a great deal of positive reinforcement for appropriate behavior whenever they are using extinction procedures for inappropriate behaviors. Otherwise, the center will take on a very negative atmosphere that is not conducive to learning.

Timeout Procedures

In the timeout procedure, the child is physically withdrawn from the situation in which the inappropriate behavior has occurred in an attempt to eliminate any reinforcement that may be offered by that situation (Fischer & Gochros, 1975). The normal timeout procedure in classrooms has been to place the child being disciplined off to one side of the room where the child cannot observe the other children or activities; the child definitely is not allowed to interact with others in activities or to speak with them. Other timeout procedures have involved actually removing the child from the classroom to an isolated booth or room. To be effective in either case, timeout must be applied immediately and consistently. Several researchers have reported success in using timeout procedures to eliminate behaviors such as yelling, screaming, fighting, swearing, disobedience, defiance, dangerous climbing, self-destructive behavior, and tantrums (Blackham & Silberman, 1971; Kanfer & Phillips, 1970; Patterson, 1965).

Although timeout appears to be an extremely effective procedure, it has received considerable criticism recently, primarily because of its susceptibility to abuse. For example, in the 1970s, many institutions caring for the mentally ill, the developmentally disabled, or juvenile offenders misused the concept of timeout by confining residents for long periods of time (e.g., 90 days); allowing them no visitors; stripping them of their own clothing; and making them exist in cells with inadequate ventilation, heating, cooling, or lighting, with no access to reading or writing materials, and with only limited access to bathroom or shower facilities (see, e.g., *Inmates of Boys' Training School v. Affleck*,[19] *Morales v. Turman*,[20]

---

19. 346 F. Supp. 1354 (D.R.I. 1972).
20. 364 F. Supp. 166 (E.D. Tex. 1973), vac. 535 F.2d 864 (5th Cir. 1976), rev'd 430 U.S. 322 (1977); remanded for evidentiary hearing 562 F.2d 933 (5th Cir. 1977).

Wyatt v. Stickney[21]). Placement in these "timeout" facilities was often a substitute for treatment, done for the convenience of the staff or for retribution. Courts, after being made aware of these conditions, forbade the use of timeout in institutions.

Recent community regulations have also forbidden what is termed seclusion and allow only therapeutic timeout (e.g., placing a child off to the side of a room contingent only on an inappropriate behavior, with constant monitoring of the child, and granting of bathroom privileges, for no more than perhaps 30 minutes). Often, the regulations also state that therapeutic timeout should be used only after less restrictive procedures have proved to be ineffective and never for retribution, for the convenience of the staff, or as a substitute for treatment (Massachusetts Department of Mental Health, 1980). Some organizations feel that timeout should never be used since, by its very nature, it does not allow for any positive teaching to occur (National Teaching Family Association, 1979). In any event, when deciding whether to use timeout in a child care facility, the staff should consider the parental and community response and whether that response could jeopardize the program.

Response Cost

As stated by Fischer and Gochros (1975), "response cost refers to the removal of a positive reinforcer contingent on the occurrence of an undesired behavior" (p. 210). In the child care setting, the child loses a reward or privilege, such as the right to go outside to recess, the right to engage in a special activity, or a tangible object (e.g., a token) that the child has earned, contingent on an inappropriate behavior. Response cost has been shown to be quite effective with children who engage in inappropriate behaviors such as fighting, swearing, thumb-sucking, tantrums, or self-destructive behavior (Bandura, 1969; Blackham & Silberman, 1971; Sherman & Baer, 1969).

Response cost can be an effective technique for reducing undesirable behavior, especially when used in the context of a token economy. Child care providers should be aware, however, that courts have carefully scrutinized residential programs that have, in any way, attempted to place contingencies on what the courts and Congress consider "basic rights" (e.g., food, clothing, bedding, privacy, interaction with the opposite sex, religious worship, outdoor exercise, or visits or communication with others). The courts have stated that, unless proper procedures have been followed (e.g., demonstrating that less restrictive procedures have failed and having the procedures in question approved by a Human Rights Committee), these items cannot be withheld (see VanBiervliet & Sheldon-Wildgen, 1981, for a more in-depth discussion of this issue). Although the

21. 344 F. Supp. 387 (M.D. Ala. 1972).

restrictions would not appear to be as stringent in a community-based child care facility, administrators and staff should not deprive children of any of the "basic rights."

Physical Punishment

Normally, physical punishment involves the immediate application of an aversive stimulus contingent on an inappropriate behavior in an attempt to decrease the probability of such a behavior's occurrence in the future. It is generally reserved for extremely dangerous behaviors, such as self-mutilation and aggressive attacks on others (Baer, 1971; Lovaas & Simmons, 1969). These procedures vary from the application of electric shock to air blasts or squirts of lemon juice to physical swats or spanks. Because this is another area that is open to misuse, it has been strictly scrutinized by the courts (e.g., *Morales v. Turman* [see Footnote 20] and *Nelson v. Heyne*[22]). The end result has been that many procedures, such as electric shock and physical and mechanical restraints, have been prohibited.

The area of most concern to personnel working in early childhood programs centers around the use of verbal reprimands and spankings. Although there is little case law directly addressing the use of verbal reprimands, many state and federal statutes and regulations specifically prohibit the use of verbal language that would degrade or humiliate clients (e.g., Massachusetts Department of Mental Health, 1980). These statutes apply primarily to mentally ill and retarded individuals, but the theory on which they are based is applicable to children (especially preschoolers).

The use of physical punishment (e.g., slapping or hitting) with residents in institutions and community-based facilities has been strictly prohibited (e.g., *Morales v. Turman* [see Footnote 20] and *Nelson v. Heyne* [see Footnote 22]). Interestingly enough, that prohibition has not been extended to the public school system. In a landmark case, *Ingraham v. Wright*,[23] children in Florida sought both an injunction against and damages for the excessive use of corporal punishment that they were receiving for trivial offenses. One of their primary arguments was that such severe physical punishment constituted cruel and unusual punishment, which is prohibited by the Eighth Amendment. In addition, the plaintiffs felt that they should have due process safeguards (e.g., a hearing) before receiving corporal punishment. The Supreme Court rejected the plaintiffs' arguments, stating that the Eighth Amendment applied only to criminal defendants and that due process requirements would place too great a burden on the school system. The Court did state, however, that there were remedies at civil law to handle

---

22. 355 F. Supp. 451 (N.D. Ind. 1972).

23. 525 F. 2d 909 (5th Cir. 1976), aff'd 97 S. Ct. 1401 (1977).

inappropriate corporal punishment (e.g., a lawsuit for monetary damages for excessive and/or unwarranted corporal punishment).

The critical point of the *Ingraham* decision for professionals in the early education field is that the Supreme Court has opened the door for, if not encouraged, parents to bring private civil lawsuits against teachers and school administrators. Thus, parents who believe that a teacher has inappropriately hit their child or has done so with too much force, can bring a civil suit for assault and battery in a state district court. Even if the case is subsequently dismissed or decided in favor of the teacher or school, the teacher must, nonetheless, hire an attorney and defend the action.

In view of the problems that can arise in regard to disciplinary procedures, each center should develop policies that specify exactly what disciplinary procedures are to be used, under what circumstances, and with what safeguards in effect. In addition, every disciplinary action should be recorded in writing; the record should include

1. a description of the inappropriate behavior
2. what had been done in the past to handle that problem (and when it was done), along with the results of those procedures
3. *exactly* what was done in the present disciplinary procedure
4. what witnesses were present
5. the behavioral effect of the procedure

Finally, it is extremely important for the facility and the staff to carry liability insurance to protect them from lawsuits brought by upset or disturbed parents. Most policies also provide for legal representation, which can save the center an enormous amount of money.

FAMILY ISSUES

Because of their intimate involvement with the children in their facility, child care personnel are often exposed to a variety of family problems. In order to be supportive of both the children and the parents, staff in early education programs must be understanding and, often, willing "to go the extra mile." The children's feelings and emotional security are of the utmost importance, and staff should do everything possible to encourage positive experiences for the children. This may require that child care personnel attempt to keep abreast of any family happenings—both positive and negative (e.g., the birth of a sibling, the death of a family pet, or perhaps a separation or divorce)—and they should be willing, if asked, to talk with the parents or the children about any issue. On the other hand, child care staff can be placed in numerous awkward and potentially liability-producing situations in regard to family problems. For example, staff may find that parents more and more frequently neglect to pick up their child on time, or they may be caught between parents in custody matters, not knowing to whom the child should be released. Even worse, problems relating to suspected child abuse may arise. In all of these examples, personnel in early education programs have legal respon-sibilities and can be exposed to legal liability.

Properly Caring for Children after Closing Hours

All child care centers should have set hours, and parents should be informed of these hours when enrolling their children. In most instances, parents will pick up their children by the closing hour, especially since children can become upset when all the other children have left; they begin to worry that their parents may have forgotten them. Undoubtedly, however, there will be situations in which parents are late. Child care personnel are often willing to accommodate an occasional lateness, although many programs attempt to discourage parents from being late by imposing additional fees or, if the problem continues, by suspending the child from the program.

Several problems arise when parents are late, but legal issues develop primarily when the parents are extremely late (e.g., more than one hour) and have failed to contact the center. If all persons (e.g., the child's relatives or close friends of the family) who are to be notified in case of an emergency have been contacted and none is able to pick up the child, the child care personnel must decide what to do with the child. There are a variety of options available to the staff, all of which should be considered; the child care center staff may then want to develop a written policy delineating the procedures that should be followed.

The most prudent procedure in caring for a child after hours is to have the child remain at the child care facility with a regular teacher to supervise the child (Training for Child Care Project, 1979b). The negligence of the parents in not picking up the child on time does not relieve the child care staff of their duty to care for the child properly. Thus, the same procedures that are followed during the regular hours of operation should be followed after hours. Furthermore, since the facility has been examined and licensed as meeting all the necessary fire, life, and sanitation requirements, liability is less likely to arise if the child is kept at the center than if the child is taken to a staff member's home (Training for Child Care Project, 1979b).

The normal standard of care used for supervising children must be maintained after hours, which raises the question of whether temporary staff or aides should be allowed to stay with the children after hours. Many centers institute a policy allowing aides or temporary staff to care for the children in these circumstances, even though this arrangement increases the risk of liability. First, aides or temporary staff may not be able to provide the supervision that is normally given.

Second, they may not have the requisite knowledge or experience to make the necessary decisions (e.g., how long to wait before contacting the child protection agency or reporting the incidence as suspected child neglect). Thus, the most prudent policy requires a regular teacher or administrator to remain at the child care facility with the child. This may not always be possible, however.

There are other alternatives, but their risks should be noted. Some centers allow aides to stay at the facility to supervise the child, but have a regular teacher or administrator on call to answer any questions or to provide assistance, if necessary. This teacher or administrator also makes any necessary decisions. Although this procedure does not provide the direct supervision that there would be if a regular teacher or administrator were at the facility, that person is available if needed. In addition, centers could have written policies that specifically outline what an aide or teacher should do when supervising children after hours, thus approximating the standard of care given during regular hours.

Probably the least desirable alternative is to take the child to a teacher's or administrator's home. Whenever a staff member transports the child in a vehicle, there is the risk of an accident. If the staff member is using his or her own vehicle, the center's insurance may not cover any accidents that occur. Thus, the staff member should ensure that he or she has adequate liability insurance. A teacher who is asked to drive a child home should follow all state laws and regulations (e.g., having the child wear a seat belt), should drive in an extremely careful and prudent manner, and should ensure that the child enters and exits the vehicle properly. After they have arrived at the teacher's home, the teacher must be extremely careful in supervising the child.

Occasionally, parents or guardians may request that the teacher drive the child to the child's home. Although this eliminates the problem of remaining with the child, there are still the liability risks associated with transporting the child. Thus, staff may be reluctant to do this and may not want to make a practice of it.

If parents are consistently very late and do not make alternative arrangements for their child or call the center to notify them, the staff may consider reporting the parents to the juvenile court authorities for possible child neglect. If the staff have discussed the issue and feel it is a reasonable course of action, they should notify the parents that, if the child is left late again, the staff will contact the juvenile court or a social service agency. The staff should explain to the parents why they feel this is necessary. Thus, the parents will have been warned and cannot legitimately question the staff's future actions. The staff should be prepared for the parents to withdraw their child if this type of action is taken. If the staff feels the problem of lateness is serious enough to contact the juvenile court, however, the child may be neglected in other ways and may benefit from the court's intervention.

Late parents can present a major problem for child care programs, but the seriousness of the problem can be reduced by developing a standard procedure for handling children whose parents are late, having it explicitly written, and giving it to all parents and staff. The written policy should include all rules, such as how long the staff will keep a child before calling the child protection agency, the police, or the juvenile court. For example, the center may have a rule that, if the parents are two hours late and have not contacted the center or sent someone to pick up the child, the staff will notify the proper authorities to pick up the child and keep the child in their custody. If parents understand the consequences of being late, some of the late problems may be avoided.

Releasing Children to Authorized Persons

When a child is placed in a child care program, the center has physical custody of the child and is responsible for that child while the child is in the center's care. At the time of enrollment, the staff should obtain in writing, signed by the parent or guardian, a list of persons to whom the child can be released. The child should be released only to someone listed, with the exception of a child protection agency worker or a law enforcement officer (any of whom must show proper identification). If the parents or guardians desire to have someone who is not listed pick up the child, they must give written, signed, and dated authorization to the child care staff in advance. Staff normally should not release a child to a person who comes with a written note from the parents, since the note may be forged. If the staff feels that the request is legitimate, however, they should contact the parent and verify it. Although the center cannot guarantee that a child will never be released to an unauthorized person, the center must develop a prudent policy that is written and that all staff follow. Failure to act in a prudent and reasonable manner in releasing a child could result in liability being imposed on a teacher, administrator, or the center, especially if harm comes to the child as a result.

In custody disputes, one parent may want to forbid the other parent from visiting or taking the child from the center (Training for Child Care Project, 1979b), and child care personnel can be placed in an awkward and difficult position if the parent in question arrives at the center and requests to see or take the child. In order to protect the child, the custodial parent's rights, and the program, the staff should know the law, and the center should have a written policy specifically delineating the actions to be taken in a custody dispute.

If one parent is not on the list of persons authorized to pick up the child, the staff should ask if there is a custody problem. If there is a problem, the staff must inquire about the legal status of the marriage and what legal decisions have been made regarding the child's custody. Since *both* parents are presumed to have legal custody of the child, the staff would be required to release the child to either parent unless one parent produces a legal document stating that the other parent either is not allowed to see the child or can see the child only at specified times (Treadwell, 1980). The staff should explain to the parent with custody of the child that it is necessary to see a court order specifying custody before the other parent can be prevented from visiting or removing the child.

Often, parents separate without legally determining that one parent does not have the right to see the child. Even in divorces in which custody is awarded to one parent, rarely does the court forbid the other parent to visit the child or to take the child for visits. Although court orders may allow "reasonable visitation" or may specify the times of visitation, they generally do not specifically address the issue of visiting a child at or taking the child from a child care center. If one parent asks that the other parent not be allowed to visit or remove the child from the center, the child care staff should explain that the parent will need to obtain an additional order from the court specifically stating that the other parent is not to be allowed to visit or remove the child from the center. Without that written order, child care staff cannot legally prevent the other parent from visiting or taking the child.

It is not unusual for the child care staff to become intimately involved with the family problems. They may know, for example, that the parents are going through a spiteful or revengeful divorce and that the noncustodial parent has threatened to kidnap the child. The staff may want to help the custodial parent, but all they can do is notify him or her if the noncustodial parent comes to the center, and attempt to delay the removal of the child (Treadwell, 1980). In any event, the staff have a duty to protect not only the child in question but all the children in the center; if it appears that any of them are placed in danger, the staff must take the necessary steps to protect them.

If an unauthorized person comes to the center and attempts to take the child, the staff must do all that they can to prevent the person from doing so. The Training for Child Care Project (1979b) offered some good advice on handling an unauthorized parent who attempts to take the child, and the advice would apply to any unauthorized person. It was recommended that the staff deal with the person in a calm manner, recognizing that the person is likely to be under a great amount of stress and, therefore, may act irrationally. Staff can attempt to avoid aggressive behavior "by letting the person know that they understand [the person's] feelings and suggesting some form of compromise, such as visiting on the premises rather than leaving with the child" (Training for Child Care Project, 1979b, p. 7). If the parent accepts that solution, a staff member should remain with (or nearby) the parent and child to ensure that the child is not harmed or taken from the center. Talking with the parent in a calm and understanding manner, as well as showing empathy and consideration for the parent's feelings, may avoid a potentially unfortunate situation.

Above all, child care staff should make every effort to protect the physical and emotional well-being of the children in the program. It is undesirable to have them observe confrontations and emotionally upset parents. Staff, therefore, should attempt to talk with *both* parents in advance and work out an amicable solution. If a solution cannot be reached and an unauthorized parent arrives at the center, an administrator should attempt to talk with the parent in private. If possible, the child should be hidden from the unauthorized parent. The center's legal duty is to notify the custodial parent of the situation, take reasonable and prudent steps to keep the unauthorized person from removing the child, protect the children to the greatest extent possible, and call the police, if necessary. If an unauthorized person succeeds in removing the child, the staff should call the parent and the police, and provide them with a description of the person, the car, and the license tag number (Training for Child Care Project, 1979b).

Reporting Suspected Child Abuse or Neglect

Since the passage of the federal Child Abuse Prevention and Treatment Act of 1974, all states have passed child abuse and neglect reporting statutes (Rose, 1978). These statutes ordinarily require certain persons (usually those who, in their professional capacity, come into contact with children, e.g., teachers, child care employees, doctors, nurses) to report any suspected case of child abuse or neglect. The terms *abuse* and *neglect* have been variously defined, but they usually include any form of physical, emotional, sexual, or mental abuse. Some states require that a report be made within a certain length of time (e.g., 36 hours) after the suspected abuse is discovered. Failure to report suspected abuse or neglect is usually a criminal offense (e.g., a misdemeanor). Courts have also held that failure to report suspected abuse may be the basis for imposing civil liability for damages, especially if the child receives further injuries (*Landeros v. Flood* [24]).

Most statutes provide certain forms of protection for those persons who, in good faith, report suspected abuse or neglect. These statutes commonly grant immunity from any liability, civil or criminal, that might otherwise be imposed—provided the report was made without malice. Thus, for example, a child care provider who reports a suspected case of abuse that subsequently turns out to be the result of a bona fide accident cannot be held liable for slander, libel, or defamation of character by the parents, *if* the report was made without malice. Finally, most statutes prohibit an employer from firing or imposing any other type of sanction on any employee who makes a report of suspected child abuse in good faith.

Child care staff should be aware that child abuse is much more prevalent than once believed. Therefore, they should be extremely watchful of any unusual injury, illness, or condition in the children. Staff should be especially watchful with handicapped children, who, because of their disabilities and the problems associated with their disabilities, are more often the target of abuse.

The law is specific in requiring child care employees to report any suspected cases of child abuse or neglect, but most child care personnel are reluctant to do so. Many child care staff members feel that they cannot professionally determine

---

24. 17 Cal. 2d 399, 131 Cal. Rptr 69 (1976).

whether a condition or injury is the result of abuse, neglect, or an accident or illness. In addition, they have normally worked hard to develop a relationship with each child's family. Reporting suspected abuse to the authorities could jeopardize, if not destroy, that relationship; could be extremely embarrassing to all concerned; and could result in some type of action against the person who made the report. Finally, child care staff worry that, if they report a suspected abuse, the parent(s) will withdraw the child from the program and perhaps further abuse the child. They often feel that it is better not to report the suspected abuse and to have the child remain in the program where they can keep a watchful eye on the child and, in their opinion, provide better protection for the child.

Although these reasons often seem convincing, especially to someone who must decide whether to report a suspected abuse, the law does not accept them, which is justifiable. Failure to report suspected abuse generally results in a continuation of harm to the child, rather than a cessation of abuse. For each of these reasons not to report suspected abuse or neglect, a counterapproach can be suggested. For example, no one expects child care providers to have the requisite medical knowledge to determine if a child has been abused or neglected. Nonetheless, child care providers should examine a child daily and should be able to recognize any unusual injuries or conditions. Many child protection agencies, as well as pediatricians, have brochures that describe what to look for in cases of child abuse. Treadwell (1980) provided a list developed by the Oakland Children's Hospital's Trauma Center in California that advises those people working with children to ask for professional medical consultation when any of the following are present:

> When the child (1) has an unexplained injury; (2) shows signs of dehydration and/or malnutrition without obvious cause; (3) has been given inappropriate food, drink, and/or drugs; (4) shows signs of overall poor care; (5) is unusually watchful or fearful; (6) is unusually passive; (7) is seen by the parents as "different" or "bad"; (8) is (in fact) different in physical and emotional makeup; (9) shows signs of sexual abuse; (10) shows signs of repeated skin injuries; and/or (11) shows signs of repeated broken bones. (Oakland Children's Hospital Trauma Center as cited in Treadwell, 1980, p. 88)

Child care staff should perform daily health checks and should record the findings of those health checks. If abuse or neglect is suspected, the staff should discuss the issue and decide how to proceed. Many child care personnel feel that they should discuss their suspicions with the parents before reporting the suspected abuse to the proper authorities. If the staff has developed any type of rapport with the parents, it is probably best to give them the opportunity to explain what may have caused the injury, illness, or condition. Discussions with the parents not only can protect the relationship between the child care center and the parents, but also can avoid potential embarrassment if the injury or condition is, in fact, the result of a bona fide accident or illness. At least, the parents will know that the staff thought enough of them to speak with them first. If the parents become belligerent or refuse to talk about the incident, child care personnel should gently explain that they are required by law to report the suspected abuse and that there undoubtedly will be some type of investigation. The staff may want to offer their help and support, and they may want to explain that most child protection agencies are more than willing to help the family work out their problems if the parents are willing to do so.

If the explanation given by the parents does not seem plausible, the child care staff should contact the appropriate authorities. All child care personnel should know the appropriate procedure for reporting suspected child abuse. In some states, suspected abuse or neglect must be reported to a child protection agency; in others, to the district or county attorney; and in still others, to the juvenile court. If the report is made by telephone, the person making the report will be asked to give his or her name and position; usually, a written report will be requested later. Following the initial report, the authorities will investigate the home, the parents, and the child. The child care staff may be contacted by the police, the district attorney, or a child protection worker, who may ask detailed questions about the suspected abuse. If the case ends up in court, the child care staff may be asked to testify at the hearing. There, a daily health check record that can be referred to is very useful. The more detailed the description of the injury, illness, or condition, the more useful it will be.

Child care staff have not only a legal obligation to report suspected child abuse or neglect, but also a moral and ethical obligation. These personnel, as child care providers, often spend more time with the child than anyone other than the parents. If the child care staff fail to report the abuse, it may well be that no one else will report it. The longer they delay in reporting the suspected abuse, the longer it will be before the child and family can receive the needed help. The end result may be irreparable injury or even death to the child.

EDUCATIONAL EXPERIENCE

Over the last decade, there has been an increasing effort in early education programs to develop a comprehensive, yet individualized curriculum to prepare children physically, socially, intellectually, and emotionally for public schools, as well as to help them in their everyday lives. Few child care centers today consider themselves only structured play facilities. Advertisements for early education programs indicate that children can be provided with activities designed to develop and improve their cognitive abilities, their motor coordination, their creative capacity, their ability to interact socially with peers and adults, and their performance in large and small group activities, to name only a few. Thus, it has become more important for programs to develop appropriate educational experiences for the children they serve.

Providing Appropriate Education for the Handicapped Child

The importance of providing appropriate educational experiences for handicapped children has been recognized and emphasized repeatedly in legislation and court decisions (e.g., Education for All Handicapped Children Act, *Maryland Association for Retarded Children v. Maryland,*[25] *Mills v. Board of Education of the District of Columbia,*[26] *Pennsylvania Association for Retarded Children v. Commonwealth of Pennsylvania*[27]). In addition, educators have demonstrated that early intervention with handicapped children can help these children make greater progress when they enter the public school system. Although early educational programs undoubtedly help all children, they appear to be critical for handicapped children.

The federal legislation that has probably provided the impetus to develop early educational programs for handicapped children is the Education for All Handicapped Children Act, which provides federal funds to be used for education programs for handicapped children. All states receiving federal funds under this act must comply with the statutory regulations, which require, in part, that the states provide a free appropriate public educational opportunity to all handicapped children between the ages of 3 and 21 by September 1, 1980. The states are *not* required, however, to provide a public education to handicapped children aged 3 to 5 and aged 18 to 21 if to do so would be inconsistent with state law or practice. Thus, for example, if a state has a law prohibiting the use of state funds for preschool education, that state would be exempted from the requirement to provide preschool education for handicapped children aged 3 to 5, since the federal requirement is inconsistent with state law. Many states that have inconsistent state laws are reexamining and changing them. Thus, it is wise for early education programs to know the legal requirements of the Education for All Handicapped Children Act and be prepared to meet them, if they are not already required to do so. Interested readers should see other sources that delineate the specific requirements and implications of this act (Martin, 1979; Turnbull & Turnbull, 1979).

The Act imposes several requirements on schools (and school districts) in order to ensure that each handicapped child is provided with a free appropriate public education. There are requirements providing for a child census in an attempt to

---

25. Equity No. 100/182/77676 (Cir. Ct., Baltimore Cty., April 9, 1974).

26. 348 F. Supp. 866 (D.D.C. 1972).

27. 334 F. Supp. (E.D. Pa. 1971) and 343 F. Supp. 279 (E.D.Pa. 1972).

identify all the children who may need special help. There are also requirements concerning screening techniques and comprehensive evaluations of children. One of the most important requirements that early education staff should be aware of is the mandate that an individualized education program (IEP) must be designed for each handicapped child.

The IEP is a written statement developed during a meeting of education professionals, the parents, and the child, if appropriate. An IEP can be developed without parental involvement if the parents are unwilling to participate, but the cooperation of parents is extremely valuable, since they can provide necessary information about the child and the child's skill levels. Furthermore, early education programs for the handicapped child can be even more successful if parents are willing to work on target goals with the child at home.

The IEP must contain a number of elements. First, there must be a statement of the child's present levels of educational performance. This should address performance levels in such areas as self-help skills, social development, motor skills, speech, language, communication skills, and academic achievement. Second, there must be a statement of the annual goals (i.e., the anticipated educational performance of the child by the end of the school year). Along with the annual goals, there should be short-term (e.g., 9 to 12 weeks) instructional objectives that provide measurable intermediate steps between the present level of performance and the annual goals. Third, there must be a statement of the specific special education and related services to be provided to the child. In most early education programs, handicapped children are served with nonhandicapped children, but the federal law requires a statement specifying the extent to which the child will be able to participate in regular education programs. It should be noted that the law emphasizes educating the child in the least restrictive environment possible. Fourth, the IEP must include the projected dates for initiation of services and the anticipated duration of the services. Finally, as an accountability measure, the IEP must contain appropriate objective criteria and evaluation procedures and schedules for determining whether the short-term instructional objectives and the annual goals are being achieved. Along with the criteria, it may be useful to list the names and positions of the individuals who are responsible for the implementation of the child's IEP. Each IEP must be reviewed and revised at least annually.

The Education for All Handicapped Children Act also guarantees to the child and the child's parents or guardians procedural due process in an attempt to ensure that a child is not excluded or misplaced in school and that the education received is appropriate to the child's needs. The procedures are designed specifically to inform the parents or guardians when any changes are to be made in the child's education; other procedures are outlined in the event that there are irreconcilable differences between the education professionals and the parents. Basically, the due process procedures provide for a series of hearings (at the school district's expense) where the parents can challenge their child's educational placement, the type of services being provided, or the goals and objectives of the IEP. At these hearings, the education professionals must justify their placement procedures, services, goals, and objectives. Both sides are allowed to present evidence and to have legal counsel. Although the procedural safeguards provided by the act are quite extensive, parents and teachers are urged to attempt to work out their differences without recourse to hearings. Most early education teachers find that, by initially working cooperatively with the parents, effective education can be provided and confrontations avoided.

Although the Act was designed for handicapped children, the procedures appear reasonable for all children. Thus, once the child care staff have developed their procedures for implementing and carrying out the Act's requirements for handicapped children, they may want to extend them to the nonhandicapped.

Providing Appropriate Education for All Children

When designing any education (or treatment) program for young children, early education personnel must attempt to ensure that all the goals benefit the children rather than the teachers or parents. For example, many teachers and behavior analysts teach children certain skills, such as sitting in their seat, refraining from talking without permission, or raising their hand before speaking. Winett and Winkler (1972) argued that these children are essentially being taught to "be still, be quiet, and be docile" and that this type of training can, in fact, destroy not only a child's desire to learn, but also a child's creativity. O'Leary (1972) pointed out that these types of behavior may be crucial to effective learning, but he cautioned teachers and behavior analysts to question their own motives and values when seeking to change certain annoying or bothersome behaviors. Teachers should always ask whether the behavior change benefits the child or whether it is being done for the convenience of the staff or the child's parents.

The personal morals or values of either the parents or the teachers must not be allowed to influence the selection of goals unduly. Obviously, no one exists in a value-free society, and certain behaviors will not be tolerated, especially those that injure or harm the child or others. The more difficult issue centers around behaviors that are not harmful, but may be distasteful to either the parents or teachers. For example, some have argued that the modification of a young male's preference for a "female" sex role is not only stereotyping the boy, but also may produce more harmful than beneficial results (Nordyke, Baer, Etzel, & LeBlanc, 1977). Thus, teachers must look beyond the responses generally considered normal for children and attempt to determine whether certain behaviors will benefit the child or whether they will be detrimental. Usually, the answer is not clear-cut, and teachers must seriously weigh all sides.

Teachers may sometimes find that they are in conflict with parents about what the child is to be taught. Parents may want to emphasize one aspect of development (e.g., intellectual) to the detriment of other important aspects (e.g., social). Teachers generally should attempt to select goals and teach behaviors that make the child a well-integrated individual, rather than emphasizing any one area. Teachers need to explain this to parents and provide good rationales for its importance.

Finally, it must be emphasized that it is the *child* who is being shaped, molded, and changed in early education programs. Yet the child has very little control over this process. Teachers must remember that, although they are hired by parents or other agencies, the child is their primary client and the child's best interests must be their primary consideration.

The fact that teachers have a multiplicity of clients and, therefore, goals, may lead to conflicts. Katz and Ward (1978) suggested that early childhood practitioners develop a code of ethics to help resolve such issues. This code of ethics can help to clarify each client group's position and to resolve questions of which goals to teach. Ayllon and Azrin (1968) suggested that, when selecting behaviors to be taught, teachers should always consider the relevance of behavior rule, i.e., only behaviors that will continue to be reinforced after training should be taught. There are, however, situations in which a variety of behaviors satisfy this rule.

Teachers should ensure that they consider all possibilities in selecting behaviors to be taught and that they include the parents and the child, if possible. They should determine their own values, the parents' values, and society's values. After considering several possible alternatives, they need to develop explicit, realistic, and positive goals. They need to give these goals priorities in terms of their importance to the social, physical, intellectual, and emotional development of the child. Finally, teachers must ensure that the goals chosen will benefit the child without doing harm in any area.

Controlling Records

The Family Educational Rights and Privacy Act of 1974 (commonly referred to as the Buckley Amendment) provides that parents must be given access to their child's records in education programs that are funded by the federal government. In addition, parents have a right to request that inaccurate or misleading information be amended or deleted from the child's records. If the education agency refuses to amend, correct, or delete the information, the parents must be notified of that decision and advised of their right to a hearing to determine whether the challenged information is inaccurate, misleading, or in violation of the child's legal rights.

Parental consent must be obtained before any personally identifiable information can be disclosed to anyone other than certain authorized persons or agencies (e.g., teachers with a legitimate educational interest in the material). As Rose (1978) pointed out, "the requirements of the act apply not only to traditional educational institutions, but to a wide range of agencies carrying out such federal education programs as . . . education for the . . . handicapped'' (p. 54). Early education programs receiving federal funds should determine if this act applies to them. If it does, they must ensure that personally identifiable information about each child in their program is protected and not illegally disclosed. Failure to comply with this law can result in the withholding of federal funds.

RECOMMENDATIONS

Early education programs should provide appropriate and pleasurable educational experiences for the children while ensuring their safety. Although teachers should not be so concerned with the legal and ethical aspects of an early education program that they neglect to provide appropriate experiences for the children, they do need to be aware of the legal issues involved in operating such a program and must address these issues adequately in order to have the best program possible. The following recommendations are provided to help teachers, administrators, and staff protect the children, themselves, and the program.

The administrators and staff should discuss and establish the goals and objectives of the program. A statement should be written that specifically delineates what the program will attempt to accomplish. For example, the purposes of the early educational program may be to teach children, to train teachers, and to provide a research setting to investigate the development of young children. Parents, at the time of enrollment or before, should be given this statement so that they are adequately informed about the type of program in which their child will be participating before they enroll their child.

The administrators and staff should have other written policies and procedures manuals that describe how the program is to operate. The Training for Child Care Project (1979a) specified in their book on day care management that four written documents be developed in addition to a statement of the goals and objectives of the program:

1. The parent policy handbook is to be used by parents and should include the goals and organization of the program, as well as the policies of operation, e.g., hours and admissions, custody of the child, daily program and routines (including a description of field trips), health procedures, children's personal items, and a discussion of the respective responsibilities of the parent and the child care center.
2. The operations manual is to be used by employees and should give extensive information about the standards of the organization and the operations of the facilities. The Training for Child Care Project recommended including (a) information about the conduct of major tasks of program operation, for example, admission policies, education philosophy and daily plans, group-

ing, materials, use of space, special child arrangements, health and safety, parents and community, record keeping, business practices, and transportation; (b) instructions on appropriate attitudes and behavior to promote the development of children; and (c) detailed instructions to staff concerning how they should carry out their jobs.

3. A personnel policies and procedures manual should provide a description of the rights and duties of both the employer and the employee. Thus, such things as working conditions, employee status, salary structure, attendance procedures, vacation and sick leave, evaluation standards, and types of disciplinary actions should be specified.

4. Detailed job descriptions delineating the specific qualifications needed and job duties required should be available.

It is critical that each program develop written policies and procedures, because such written statements demonstrate that the staff and administrators have seriously considered the issues and have decided on certain procedures to be followed. As VanBiervliet and Sheldon-Wildgen (1981) pointed out, these policies and procedures establish an explicit standard of care for the program and can potentially reduce the risk of liability. If a lawsuit were brought against the child care program, the court would determine at least two things: ''was the standard of care established by these policies and procedures an appropriate standard and were the staff members following these policies and procedures when the claim, leading to the lawsuit, arose'' (VanBiervliet & Sheldon-Wildgen, 1981, p. 186).

The more the policies and procedures reflect and follow a standard that is normally used in child care facilities, the greater the probability that a court would find the standard of care appropriate. If the staff members were not following the policies and procedures, the employees may be held solely liable for any damages that may have been incurred. In such a case, the court might find that the employees were acting outside the scope of employment by not following the required policies and procedures and, thus, liable in an individual capacity. On the other hand, the court may find that the policies and procedures allow employees some flexibility (as most do) and that, had adequate supervision been given, the injury would not have occurred. If this is the finding of the court, liability may be imposed on the administrators, board of directors, or owners of the center. It is, therefore, extremely important that employees know the policies and procedures, are adequately trained, and are consistently supervised to ensure that they comply with the standards set by the written policies and procedures.

Finally, early education centers are well-advised to have accident/liability insurance to cover any injuries that may occur. Usually, policies can be purchased to cover each child who is enrolled in the program. Also, staff may wish to purchase professional liability insurance to cover any malpractice action that might be brought against them. Individual staff members can purchase these policies, which generally cover attorneys' fees for representing the staff member or center if a lawsuit is brought, as well as any monetary judgments (up to the limit of the policy).

Although these recommendations undoubtedly require much thought, once written procedures have been developed, they can be used indefinitely with only minor revisions. Ensuring staff compliance is a daily task, but the program should run quite smoothly once staff are trained and understand the appropriate standard of care that they must provide. Providing a legally safe and ethically sound program can produce satisfied parents, happy children, and a secure and comfortable staff—a pleasant environment for all involved.

REFERENCES

Adams, P.K., & Taylor, M.K. Liability: How much do you really know? *Day Care and Early Education*, Spring, 1981, 15-18.

Aikman, W.F. *Day care legal handbook: Legal aspects of organizing and operating day care programs*. Urbana, IL: ERIC Clearinghouse on Early Childhood Education, 1977.

Allen, K.E., & Goetz, E.M. Early childhood education: Special problems, special solutions. Rockville, MD: Aspen Systems Corporation, 1982.

Ayllon, T., & Azrin, N.H. *The token economy*. New York: Appleton-Century-Crofts, 1968.

Baer, D.M. Let's take another look at punishment. *Psychology Today*, October 1981, 31.

Bandura, A. *Principles of behavior modification*. New York: Holt, Rinehart, and Winston, 1969.

Blackham, G.A., & Silberman, A. *Modification of child behavior*. Belmont, CA: Wadsworth, 1971.

Fischer, J., & Gochros, H.L. *Planned behavior change: Behavior modification in social work*. New York: The Free Press, 1975.

Gifis, S.H. *Law dictionary*. Woodbury, NY: Barron's Educational Series, 1975.

Kanfer, F.H., & Phillips, J.S. *Learning foundations of behavior therapy*. New York: John Wiley, 1970.

Katz, L.G., & Ward, E.H. *Ethical behavior in early childhood education*. Washington, DC: National Association for the Education of Young Children, 1978.

Lovaas, O.I., & Simmons, J.Q. Manipulation of self-destruction in three mentally retarded children. *Journal of Applied Behavior Analysis*, 1969, *2*, 143-157.

Lovaas, O.I., Freitag, G., Gold, V.J., & Kassoria, I.C. Experimental studies in childhood schizophrenia: Analysis of self-destructive behavior. *Journal of Experimental Child Psychology*, 1965, *2*, 67-84.

Martin, R. *Behavior modification: Human rights and legal responsibilities*. Champaign, IL: Research Press, 1974.

Martin, R. *Educating handicapped children: The legal mandate*. Champaign, IL: Research Press, 1979.

Massachusetts Department of Mental Health. Mental health community residential alternatives, 104 C.M.R. 1403 et seq. as reported in 4 *Mental Disability Law Reporter* 126 (1980).

National Education Association Research Division. Who is liable for pupil negligence? Washington, DC: National Education Association, 1963.

National Teaching Family Association. *NATFA ethical standards*. Omaha: Author, 1979.

Nordyke, N.S., Baer, D.M., Etzel, B.C., & LeBlanc, J.M. Implications of the stereotyping and modification of sex role. *Journal of Applied Behavior Analysis, 1977, 10,* 553-558.

O'Leary, K.D. Behavior modification in the classroom: A rejoinder to Winett and Winkler. *Journal of Applied Behavior Analysis,* 1972, *5,* 505-511.

Patterson, G.R. An application of conditioning techniques to the control of a hyperactive child. In L.P. Ullmann & L. Krasner (Eds.), *Case studies in behavior modification.* New York: Holt, Rinehart, and Winston, 1965.

Prosser, W.L. *Handbook of the law of torts* (4th ed.). St. Paul, MN: West Publishing, 1971.

Rekers, G.A., & Lovaas, O.I. Behavioral treatment of deviant sex role behavior in a male child. *Journal of Applied Behavior Analysis,* 1974, *1,* 173-190.

Rose, C.M. *Some emerging issues in legal liability of children's agencies.* New York: Child Welfare League of America, 1978.

Sherman, J.A., & Baer, D.M. Appraisal of operant therapy techniques with children and adults. In C.M. Franks (Ed.), *Behavior therapy: Appraisal and status.* New York: McGraw-Hill, 1969.

Training for Child Care Project. *Day care personnel management.* Atlanta, GA: Southern Regional Education Board, 1979.(a)

Training for Child Care Project. *Legal and program issues related to child custody and late parents.* Atlanta, GA: Southern Regional Education Board, 1979.(b)

Treadwell, L.W. *The family day care providers' legal handbook.* Oakland, CA: BANANAS, 1980.

Turnbull, H.R., & Turnbull, A.P. *Free appropriate public education: Law and implementation.* Denver: Love Publishing, 1979.

VanBiervliet, A., & Sheldon-Wildgen, J. *Liability issues in community-based programs.* Baltimore: Brookes Publishing, 1981.

Watson, D.L., & Tharp, R.G. *Self-directed behavior: Self-modification for personal adjustment.* Belmont, CA: Brooks/Cole Publishing, 1972.

Winett, R.A., & Winkler, R.C. Current behavior modification in the classroom: Be still, be quiet, be docile. *Journal of Applied Behavior Analysis,* 1972, *5,* 499-504.

Index

About the Editors

ELIZABETH M. GOETZ is director of the Edna A. Hill Child Development Laboratory Preschools at the University of Kansas. She has published many research articles on the application of behavioral principles in understanding and resolving a variety of problems in early childhood. The resulting approach is behavior analysis for the whole child. Creativity and developmentally appropriate early reading are her two main areas of expertise. She is an associate professor in the Department of Human Development and Family Life at the University of Kansas.

K. EILEEN ALLEN is a pioneer in the field of behavioral research with young children in the naturalistic environment of the preschool. She is the author of several texts and many published articles related to early intervention with young children. She is a professor in the Department of Human Development and Family Life at the University of Kansas and has spent the last year in Washington, D.C. as a Congressional Science Fellow of the Society for Research in Child Development and the American Association for the Advancement of Science.